38/- NET

D1346813

Studies in Child Development

Street Club Work
in Tel Aviv and New York

Studies in Child Development

The National Bureau for Co-operation in Child Care

Street Club Work
in Tel Aviv and New York

ARYEH LEISSNER, B.A., M.S.W.
Senior Research Officer
The National Bureau for Co-operation in Child Care

LONGMANS
in association with
THE NATIONAL BUREAU FOR CO-OPERATION IN CHILD CARE

LONGMANS, GREEN AND CO LTD
London and Harlow
Associated companies, branches and representatives throughout the world

THE NATIONAL BUREAU FOR CO-OPERATION IN CHILD CARE
Adam House, 1 Fitzroy Square, London W1

SBN 582 32444 0

Printed in Great Britain by
Western Printing Services Ltd, Bristol

Contents

Foreword

The prevention of many types of maladjustment in children and youth has been a major concern of the National Bureau for Co-operation in Child Care since its inception. Also the relationship between prevention and rehabilitation has been an implicit issue in most of the Bureau's work and research. This book offers a wide range of thought and experience regarding the prevention of delinquency and the rehabilitation of delinquent youth.

The vivid description of the daily practice of street club work, a specialised group work approach, offers insights into the problems facing street corner youths and 'detached' youth workers. The detailed discussions of the relationship between theory and practice may serve to stimulate further thinking and discussion of the important issues raised.

The book should prove valuable to the theoretician as well as to the practitioner. It offers guidelines for the training of youth-workers, as well as making it possible for the interested and concerned layman to gain deeper understanding of our wayward youngsters and of a difficult, but also challenging and rewarding, method of helping them.

Street Club Work, the approach described in this book, offers no panaceas and it is not the only method of delinquency prevention and rehabilitation. It is, however, a method which has shown promising results in the two countries discussed in this book and elsewhere. Some youth work along the same lines is being attempted in Britain at the present time. The material offered in the following pages may well make an important contribution to the further development of this service to youth in trouble in this country.

SIR GEORGE HAYNES

Introduction

A man whose opinions and experience I respect, and who doesn't suffer fools gladly, told me recently that he was tired of listening for the ninety-ninth time to lengthy explanation of the surmise that delinquency is one or another aspect of behaviour. I hope he will not regard this book as another such exercise.

The book claims neither to be 'scientific' nor 'objective'. It does try to relate some of the theories which have been put forward and which seem to make sense, to the practical experience of working with youngsters in trouble. What is said and described relates to certain types of such youngsters and to a specific approach of helping them and working with them. It is clearly a biased book because, in whatever I say or speculate upon, I am on the side of the youngsters. The book offers no 'cure' for delinquency. That will have to wait until someone comes forward with a workable theory for a 'cure' of the vast syndrome of ailments and malfunctions which we call our 'society' or 'social system'.

If this book has any 'theses' to put forward, these can be summed up in three brief statements:

Things being what they are, 'juvenile delinquency' will be with us for a long time to come. We shall have to accept it as a challenge and obligation, just as we accept the tasks of feeding, clothing, educating and loving all our children.

Allowing for some cultural, economic or politically imposed differences, 'delinquent behaviour' is expressed the same way and causes the same reactions in all countries where the lives of people are ruled by the values and techniques of modern industrial society.

There are no 'un-reachable' youngsters, but there are all too many adults in all walks of life and in all professions who are incapable of communicating with boys and girls who don't fit the slots and niches into which they would like to fit them.

The book is partly based upon the records of my work as a street club worker in New York and upon the material gathered during my work in Tel Aviv, partly published in Volumes I and II, *Research Project on Forces Acting in Street Corner Groups*, Leissner, Rubin and Bors, Jerusalem 1967 (mimeographed).

I cannot hope to thank all those whose help has made this book possible. Dr M. L. Kellmer Pringle and the National Bureau for Co-operation in Child Care, of which she is Director, have enabled me to write and publish the book. The staff of Longmans, Green and Company, London, have accepted my manuscript with encouragement and understanding. Above all I owe a debt of gratitude to Richard E. Cloward of the Columbia University School of Social Work who, more than anyone, has been my teacher. I hope he will forgive me if I have applied what he has taught me inadequately.

I am indebted to my friends and colleagues in New York and Tel Aviv, especially Bernie Clyne, Laurel Bolgiano, Nissan Rubin, Sally Bors, Avram Saad, David Moses, Ofer Yisraeli, Yuda Amorai, Sylvia Farstendiger, Aya Weissman, Gad Kaufman and Aboul Latif Tilawy. I want to express my gratitude for their support and encouragement to Professor Carl Frankenstein of the Hebrew University, Batya Mintal, Deputy Director, Tel Aviv Social Service Department, and to Yona Cohen, Chief Probation Officer at the Israel Ministry of Social Welfare.

Above all I am grateful to the boys and girls of New York's Yorkville, the Lower East Side and East Harlem and of Tel Aviv's street corners in Kfar Shalem, Shkhounath Ezra, Ramath Yisrael, Sheikh Mounis and Jaffa. I hope they have learned half as much from us as we have learned from them.

ARYEH LEISSNER

London, 1968

An evening with a Tel Aviv street corner group

A few weeks after my arrival in Israel, I spent an evening with one of the Project's field workers and his group of youngsters in one of Tel Aviv's poor neighbourhoods. I was introduced by the worker, met some of the distrustful stares and curious questions of the youngsters and settled down in the familiar position of the street club worker, my back comfortably supported by a wall near a small coffee shop, puffing my pipe and observing the teenagers milling about noisily, restlessly.

Half an hour passed and, a bit drowsy after a long day's work, I found myself transplanted back to a street corner in New York, surrounded by the youngsters of one of 'my' gangs. Around me there was the familiar 'sounding' and teasing highlighted by the bursts of laughter when one of the boys 'scored' with a smart remark. There was the boasting about the boys' exploits, the casual use of obscenities interspersed with 'your mother . . .' profanities. Two boys had a heated argument about the pros and cons of various makes of cars, two others were engaged in a 'cool', sophisticated conversation about making an 'easy buck', and at the entrance to the coffee shop, a boy jostled an elderly, disreputable-looking man and called him a 'bum'.

I could have been standing at a street corner on New York's Lower East Side, keeping a weary eye on the 'Commanders', a group of Puerto Rican youngsters with whom I worked two years ago. That little group of slim, quick-moving youngsters making derisive remarks about the 'cops' looked very familiar in their somewhat shabby elegance of tight black pants and colourful silk shirts, with their brown, lively faces and brilliantine-glistening dovetail haircuts. I felt quite at home with the nervous gesturing of the hands, the cigarettes glued to the corner of the mouths, the incessant shuffle-and-bop of the feet.

There was the small group of pretty, dark-haired girls across the street, keeping their distance, but very much aware of the boys, who ignored them pointedly. The short, flowery dresses, the clinging toreador pants would not have looked out-of-place at any Manhattan street corner. The high-piled, puffy 'bee-hive' hair-do had just become the latest fashion when I left New York.

The skinny youngster making a teasing lunge and a mildly insulting remark at one of the girls who had come over to get a soda at the coffee shop, could have been Pepito of the 'Commanders' or Bobo of the 'Mirages' in East Harlem.

If I ignored the dark complexions and the 'Spanish' look of the kids around me for a moment, I could be standing at a street corner in York-ville with the 'Emperors', a group of German and Irish boys. That stocky youngster, who was just now taking a couple of quick jabs at another boy, his shirt sleeves rolled up tightly to the shoulders to display the bulging biceps, could be Cooch, showing off as usual. The boy over there, relating the story of the latest movie with great dramatic pathos and wild gestures of his hands—'then this guy, you know, the bad guy, the one that plugged the cop, that guy grabs that bitch and starts slap-ping her around . . .'—could be Italian Joey, the 'talk-man' of the 'Emperors'. And here was a new arrival who quickly became the centre of attention, everybody clustering around to hear what he had to say. This one was a tall blond boy with clear blue eyes, dressed 'sharp but conservative' in a natty suit and polished, pointed shoes. He was talking about a party with girls and a band. Standing at the corner of 82nd Street and York Avenue, he would fit right in with the rest of the crowd.

The Lower East Side, Yorkville, East Harlem, Upper Broadway, Harlem, or any other street corner in a gang neighbourhood in New York: here was the familiar atmosphere of noisy banter, interspersed with periods of uneasy quiet. There seemed to be nothing strange and new about the surface bustle of friendly activity and the constant aware-ness of the tension underneath the tension that was discernible in the huddle of three boys nearby who were discussing a 'job' they had pulled the night before. Lowering their voices with a quick, distrustful glance in my direction, they were saying something about 'police' and 'getting rid of the stuff'. There was nothing new and strange about the 'trouble' that was in the air in the midst of the joking and the jostling, the trouble that lay in the worried look of the street club worker sitting at a table inside the coffee shop, talking earnestly, intensely, to a nervous, fidgeting boy, the trouble that could at any moment rise to the surface with a quick outburst of anger, the thud of a fist, the trouble the Project worker recognised when the three boys who had been whispering in a corner suddenly walked off with set, purposeful faces and disappeared in the dark of a small, unpaved side street.

As had been my custom when first making contact with a street corner group in New York, I tried to identify the leader. Was it the broad-shouldered, muscular youngster whose deep, resonant voice rose above the din made by the group of youngsters surrounding him—'I'm telling you guys: *no good*. A lot of talk, but when it comes to action you punk out . . .' Or was it the quiet, tall boy standing at a little distance from the others, leaning against a lamp post, smoking, a thin gold chain glittering in the open V-neck of his black silk shirt. Almost every one of the two dozen youngsters present had gone over to exchange a few words with him since I had arrived.

I shook off my comfortable drowsiness and took a closer look at my surroundings. As things came into sharper focus the feeling of familiarity, the many parallels to the New York street corner, remained. But these were not the dilapidated five-floor walk-ups that faced air-conditioned luxury apartments across the street in Yorkville. Nor was my back leaning against one of the walls of the dingy, grimy tenement houses of Harlem, nor did I have to crane my neck to look at the twelfth floor windows of a New York housing project towering around me in all its uniformity and drabness.

I was standing near the entrance of a small coffee shop where thick, sweet Turkish coffee was prepared in long-handled copper pots over a kerosene stove. On a bench opposite me, in the dim light of a street lamp, two youngsters were playing cards with the same concentration with which the kids played cards on the stoops of New York tenements. But inside the coffee shop the boys played Shesh-Besh, a traditional oriental game of chance. Over there some boys were discussing the latest soccer scores with excited, high-pitched voices. Depending on the season, they would have been discussing baseball or football in New York.

The coffee shop was located in the centre of a sprawling conglomeration of small, squat, poorly constructed one- or two-room houses, many of them with a walled-off courtyard in front. The houses were divided by narrow, winding, badly lit streets, all of them unpaved. A jeep and a little Renault stood nearby, and there was a motor-scooter leaning against a wall, but further up the street a cart-horse was tethered to a door post and somewhere in the distance a donkey brayed. Some of the crumbling houses had television antennae on their flat roofs and some had refrigerators in their kitchens, but only a few of them had modern plumbing.

The conversation of the youngsters around me resembled in tone and content the talk I used to hear on many a street corner in New York. But the language spoken here was Hebrew, spiced with colourful and unprintable expressions in Arabic. The 'sharp' clothes, the gestures and mannerisms of the boys would look familiar to anyone who had worked with gang youth in New York's lower-class neighbourhoods. But these were Israeli youngsters of 'Oriental' descent, and if one looked closely one saw that some of them had sandals on their bare feet, and a few wore khaki shorts. The blond boy, who would not have aroused comment entering the 'Emperors', favourite Irish bar in Yorkville, was the son of Polish Jews who had survived the Nazi holocaust. He had come over from an adjoining neighbourhood with a mixed population of Oriental and European Jews. In his neighbourhood the houses were newer and higher, some of the streets were paved, and some of the more colourful cursing done in Yiddish instead of Arabic. As a Yorkville boy 'Blondie' would have thought twice before visiting the hang-out of a Puerto Rican gang. It is doubtful whether he would ever have been standing with a group of 'spics', discussing a party his group was throwing. I knew that, here too, smooth relations between youngsters of Oriental and European origin were not taken for granted.

Blondie's neighbourhood was a new housing area that existed only about ten years. The youngsters who were clustered around him here lived in a former Arab village, left by its original inhabitants during the 1948 war, and now inhabited by immigrants from Syria, Persia and Iraq. Most of the boys had been born and had spent their childhood and adolescence in this slum. There were other areas, where one could find similar street corner groups, which had been slums since the days of the British Mandate. Some of them were inhabited by second and third generation Israelis of Sefardic and Yemenite descent. There were still other such areas which were forgotten remnants of the refugee shackvilles of the early days of the State. There an admixture of hard-core families of European and Oriental slum dwellers eked out a bare existence 'on the dole'. There were neighbourhoods where North African or East European communities had been hastily settled in utilitarian housing units that had soon deteriorated.

All these neighbourhoods had been engulfed by the big, sprawling, dynamic city of Tel Aviv, with its comfortable residential areas, its industrial quarters and shopping districts, its clusters of one-family houses and its wide, modern streets, lined with fashionable stores and sidewalk cafes. These islands of poverty and neglect exist among the ultra-modern office buildings, the parks and theatres, the high-rental apartment houses and the luxury hotels. The slums had already appeared, like poisonous weeds in a well kept garden, in the brand new, rapidly spreading suburban areas that surround the city of Tel Aviv.

As in New York, and as in big cities all over the world, there exist here islands of poverty and frustration in a sea of bustling ambition and prosperity. I was not unduly surprised to find that the youngsters in the underprivileged areas of this city seemed in many ways similar in their appearance and behaviour to those found in slum areas in New York.

1 Concepts and definitions: A discussion of theory

1 What is 'delinquency' and who is 'delinquent'?

There are a wide variety of such [delinquent] acts. Some are clear-cut violations of the law—murder, theft, breaking and entering. Some are acts of constant and sizeable community disturbance such as gang fighting or drunken brawls. Some are disapproved in primarily moral terms, such as casual sex activity; some are acts of omission, such as not going to school. Others are incidents of hostility towards adults in positions of authority, such as insolence to a teacher, and still others are activities allowed or tolerated on the part of adults but disapproved of or forbidden to children—the use of liquor, private gambling parties, being out extremely late at night. Some are acts of racial hostility reflecting adult attitudes and even adult acts in their own community. Within a typical street-corner group all these types of actions may occur; in fact a single individual may be involved in this total variety of acts. These acts cannot be viewed as single and unrelated incidents. They are the reflection of a set of attitudes, of a code of values which brings a group and its individual members again and again into formal conflict with the law or with the formal moral code of the community. The adult community fears this group behaviour more than just the occurrence of a single act of theft or vandalism. . . . It is the unpredictableness of individual acts, the feeling of violence behind the simplest incidents, such as a scuffle on a bus, the overwhelming of group acts of violence, the sense of hostility toward all adults and all institutions that have brought on much of the public outcry. The feeling that this behaviour has a widespread influence on adolescents in general and may even effect one's own child creates almost a sense of panic in many parents.

D. M. AUSTIN, 1957, p. 46

We all want to 'tell them' but few of us take the time to stop and listen, to see what juvenile delinquency is telling us about youth, and about out times. . . .

ERIK H. ERIKSON
in Witmer and Kotinsky, 1955

The term 'juvenile delinquent' (in Hebrew called more poetically *Avaryan Tza'eer*, meaning young sinner or trespasser) has become a source of confusion to the public and an object of controversy and discomfort among professionals. It is a term or label which, like so many others of its ilk which have become common usage, raises more questions than it answers. Nevertheless, all the many well-reasoned protests notwithstanding, the terms 'delinquent' and 'delinquency', usually in association with the word 'juvenile' seem to be here to stay and we shall have to make use of them in this study.

Robert K. Merton warned that 'the concept "juvenile delinquency" belongs to the family of blanket concepts which obscure rather than clarify our understanding of human behaviour'.[1] Professor Kvaraceus

---

[1] Witmer and Kotinsky, 1955, p. 27.

(1965) stated his objection by saying that: 'The term "juvenile delinquent" represents a nontechnical and pejorative label; it does not stand for a meaningful diagnostic category, but includes a pot pourri of many kinds of youthful offenders.' The reader is advised to keep these verdicts in mind when the term 'juvenile delinquent' is used for the sake of convenience and lack of a better word, in describing youngsters involved in a wide range and variety of conflict and problem situations.

We are compelled to make do with the term 'juvenile delinquent' mainly because it has become fully accepted in legal terminology, in the language of law enforcement agencies and the judiciary, in Israel as well as in most other countries. In Israel the term 'juvenile' is applied to boys between the ages of fourteen and sixteen, and to girls up to the age of eighteen. Youngsters below the age of fourteen are regarded as children, while boys above sixteen and girls above eighteen are legally responsible as adults (Reifen, 1965). In practice, however, children as well as juveniles are apt to be treated as 'juvenile delinquents' by the police and the courts,[1] while treatment agencies find it difficult and impractical to exclude seventeen- and eighteen-year-old offenders from the 'juvenile delinquency' category.

Israeli law distinguishes between 'juvenile delinquents' and 'children in need of care and protection'. Judge Reifen (1965, p. 84) of the Tel Aviv Children's Court explains:

Juvenile delinquents are those who commit an offence which is regarded as an infringement of established law in a given society, and therefore proceedings are taken against them. On the other hand, in the case of children who are in need of care and protection proceedings are taken on their behalf, because they live under conditions which are detrimental to their upbringing.

This distinction, while highly desirable and beneficial in many instances, obviously raises some further questions. In the case of a delinquent youngster who has come to the attention of the courts, it is often a debatable point whether he (or she) should be the object of proceedings taken against him because he has broken the law, or whether he is 'in need of care and protection'. The official definition of the delinquent seems to be in danger of equating cause and effect. The result is that whether a youngster is to be cared for and protected, or whether he is to be punished, depends frequently upon whether he has already had time and opportunity to engage in unlawful behaviour precipitated by

[1] Israeli courts assign approximately 12 per cent of arraigned offenders under sixteen to the Youth Probation Service for treatment and supervision. Other youngsters are sent to institutions for wayward youth or given suspended prison sentences. In some cases, however, youngsters as young as fourteen are sent to jail. The last such case occurred in December 1965, when a fourteen-year-old recidivist who has repeatedly escaped from an institution was sent to jail for eighteen months.

the detrimental conditions in which he lives, or whether he has been lucky enough to come to the attention of the authorities before that. In most cases the difference between the 'juvenile delinquent' and the youngster 'in need of care and protection', is one of age, namely the difference between the 'juvenile' and the 'child'.[1]

In street club work practice it is difficult to separate the 'juvenile delinquent' from the youngster 'in need of care and protection' mainly because so many of the youngsters of our client groups live 'under conditions which are detrimental to their upbringing'. I prefer, therefore, to include the assumption of the need for care and protection in a definition of the 'juvenile delinquent'.

Sophia M. Robison has emphasised the fact that any definition of the phenomenon we call 'juvenile delinquency' must be related to the contemporary system of social values and expectations, and that such definition is subject to modification and change.

Professor Robison (1960, p. 3) writes:

The legal term 'delinquency' is an umbrella for a wide variety of socially disapproved behaviour that varies with the time, the place, and the attitudes of those assigned to administer the law. Moreover, there exist many extralegal definitions, put forth by a variety of 'experts'—parents, teachers, psychiatrists, social workers, preachers, sociologists, judges—that are often inconsistent and mutually exclusive.

Faced, however, with the necessity to establish some axiom which will permit exploration and discussion of the phenomena involved, the author decided to define delinquent behaviour 'as any behaviour which a given community at a given time considers in conflict with its best interests, whether or not the offender has been brought to court' (ibid, p. 11). This definition can be accepted exchanging, however, the word 'community' for that of 'society' because it is important to distinguish between societal attitudes and the values and norms of certain communities within a society. The dominant values of society may regard as 'delinquent' or 'deviant' attitudes and behaviour which are regarded as permissible or even desirable by a certain population group within that same society, a state of affairs which makes the life of a youngster all the more confusing, and the tasks of educators and youth workers all the more difficult.

The Hebrew term for 'delinquent', *Avaryan*, has its roots in the Mishnah concept of sin. Without exceeding my competence by engaging in theological speculation, I may say here that the concept of the sinner has always been closely associated with that of the sinned-against. The

[1] Over 70 per cent of the youngsters brought to court as 'in need of care and protection' are under 10 years old (Reifen, 1965, p. 85).

word 'delinquent' comes to us from legal usages of Ancient Rome and denoted a person remiss in his duties, one who did not fulfil his obligations to society. We certainly can define the young delinquent as one who has not fulfilled his duties nor met his obligations in the legal and moral sense, on the condition that we immediately inquire whether society has fulfilled *its* duties and met *its* obligations toward the youngster.

Professor Robison (1960, p. 11) wrote that, in the face of the present state of confusion regarding a universally accepted definition of delinquency, and in order to permit the study of the problem, it is necessary 'to examine delinquency in as many as possible of its aspects in order to determine what it is and equally important what it is not'. The street club worker faces this complex task every night at the street corner.

It may safely be assumed that the great majority of today's youngsters get into some mischief at one time or another during the years of adolescence, mischief which may include truancy, vandalism, fighting, sexual offences and theft. These youngsters would, in fact, be classified as 'delinquents' if they were apprehended. Street club work, as defined in this discussion, is not concerned with the whole range of these youngsters, but regards as its target population a relatively small segment of society's youth. I shall attempt to illustrate this with the following, albeit oversimplified, diagram:[1]

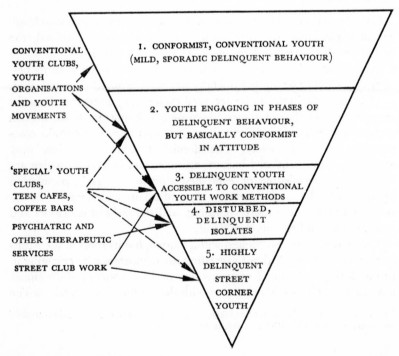

[1] The arrows with dotted lines indicate areas of overlap.

The 'detached' or street club worker may be assigned to a cluster of Class 3 youngsters (see diagram), with the goal of getting them to make use of a youth club or coffee bar in the area, preferably one which is specifically geared to their needs. However, the street club worker's actual target population for long-term service is the class 5 youth.

Who, then, are the 'delinquents', what, in very broad terms are the main characteristics by which we recognise them? A British investigator has summed up the answer as follows:

Three major themes have emerged from the variety of classic accounts of delinquent behaviour and values, although consensus is limited to substance and not interpretation: (i) delinquents are typically immersed in a restless search for excitement, thrills or 'kicks'; (ii) delinquents commonly exhibit a disdain for 'getting on' in the realm of work; (iii) delinquents characteristically accept aggressive toughness as a proof of masculinity.

(i) is not accommodated by legitimate outlets such as organised recreation, for the very fact that an activity involves breaking the law is precisely the source of excitement. In courting danger, provoking authority, etc., 'the delinquent is not simply enduring hazards: he is also creating hazards in a deliberate attempt to manufacture excitement'. The excitement that stems from danger and law-violation, e.g. especially in 'chicken runs' and 'rumbles', is not a by-product, but a—possibly the—motivating force.

(ii) places the delinquent firmly in the category of the unemployed, the casual worker, or the boy in the 'dead-end' job. Even where 'occupational goals involving the steady job or cautious advancement' are available, 'it takes deep faith—and naiveté—to believe that hard work at the lower end of the occupational hierarchy is a sure path to worldly success'. . . .

(iii) is commonly interpreted as an index of the delinquent's alienation from the larger society, his aggression—whether verbal or physical, seen as an outlet for basic hostility, hatred, and the urge to injure and destroy. This may be so for a typical big-city 'structured' gang. More typically, it expresses the delinquent's familiarity with the ethic that manhood is reached via an ability to 'take it' and 'hand it out' (Downes, 1966, pp. 243–4).[1]

[1] The author draws attention to the interesting conclusion of Matza and Sykes (1961), who regard 'adolescents in general and delinquents in particular as the last leisure class', and who emphasise the affinities of delinquent behaviour with that of Veblen's 'gentleman of leisure'.

2 Group or near-group, street corner group or gang?

The term 'group' serves as a convenient sociological designation for any number of people, larger or smaller, between whom such relations are discovered that they must be thought of together . . . a number of persons whose relations to each other are sufficiently impressive to demand attention.

ALBION W. SMALL (1905), p. 495

The gang boy's conception of his role is more vivid with reference to his gang than to other social groups. Since he lives largely in the present, he conceives of the part that he is playing in life as being in the gang; his status in other groups is unimportant to him, for the gang is his social world. In striving to realise the role he hopes to take he may assume a tough pose, commit feats of daring or vandalism, or become a criminal. Thus, his conception of his essential role as being in the gang helps to explain why the larger community finds difficulty in controlling him. If acquiring a court record, or being 'put away' in an institution gives him prestige in the gang, society is simply promoting his rise to power, rather than punishing or 'reforming' him. Agencies which would attempt to redirect the boy delinquent must reach him through his vital social groups where an appeal can be made to his essential conception of himself.

FREDERIC M. THRASHER (1927)

The word 'group' itself has a good, solid common sense ring to it, and it can be assumed that most people will know what is meant by the term. It is, however, so fundamentally important to our approach to working with young delinquents, that we must be more specific. For our purposes, the concept of the 'dynamic group' as defined by Hubert Bonner seems the most useful. Professor Bonner (1959, p. 45) tells us:

A dynamic group . . . is not a collection of interdependent individuals, merely, but a group of persons who are psychologically aware of their interindividual relationships and who are moving toward a goal that they have agreed upon collectively. The interaction of one person with others forms a web of relationships in which the action of each takes place more or less spontaneously. Their interactions are integrated in such a way that their psychological tensions are shared. The 'togetherness' of the group as a dynamic structure is due to a 'circular' reaction in which there is a high degree of self-intensification in each member of his own 'excitement' as he finds it reflected in others. In this process shared feelings and tensions, which in each member separately had no adequate outlet, are freely expressed. When a person's responses to others is shared by them, when these experiences become reciprocal or interactive, there exist the basic conditions of group behaviour.

This definitive description offers a set of criteria which enables us to determine whether our observations and our experience in working with street corner youth permit us to conclude that the congregations of these youngsters do indeed constitute groups, dynamic groups which contain in their structure a potential for change. However, the definition offered here applies to a whole range of groups, which could include the members of a Chassidic sect as well as a wife-swapping club in a fashionable New York suburb, a chapter of the Ku Klux Klan or the Bnei Brith, a football team or a sewing circle. Street club work is not concerned with either of these, but focuses upon groups of adolescent youngsters all, or the majority of whom, are known or presumed to engage in delinquent behaviour. There has been considerable controversy in the professional literature as to what such groups should be called.

One investigator of delinquent street corner youth has denied that they form groups at all, and prefers to call whatever it is that they do form, a 'near-group', which he describes as 'characterised by some of the following factors: (1) diffuse role definition; (2) limited cohesion; (3) impermanence; (4) minimal consensus of norms; (5) shifting membership; (6) disturbed leadership; and (7) limited definition of membership expectations' (Yablonsky 1962b, p. 303).[1]

This description appears to be the result of mistaking a certain phase in the fluctuating picture of some street corner groups for the dynamic process of such groups in its entirety. It implies a rigid, one-dimensional conception of the group by failing to conceive of such factors as impermanence, diffusions in certain areas, changes in membership composition etc., as inherent in most 'natural', spontaneously formed groups at some stages in their history. Each of this author's seven 'characteristics' are evident at street corners in New York, Tel Aviv and elsewhere. As such they do not offer a characteristic picture of the delinquent street corner group in an underprivileged neighbourhood.

Difficulties in identifying precise delineations of group membership in areas of high concentration of street corner youth led another research team to coin the term 'gang-clusters'.[2] The need for such a term is, at least in part, due to the misconception that 'natural' groups of teenagers are (except in times of extreme crisis), highly organised and clearly restricted to a limited membership. Experienced street club workers know that this is rarely the case, that street corner groups 'hanging out' in close geographic proximity, are often so intermeshed as to be nearly undistinguishable from each other, and that it takes long and intimate acquaintance to sort them out.

Searching for a suitable descriptive term I would prefer to avoid the

[1] There is a useful critical review of Yablonsky's theory in Downes (1966), pp. 15–16. Downes states that the 'near-group' is 'a mere neologism for what is more familiarly termed the unstructured gang'.
[2] Los Angeles County Probation Department and Youth Studies Center (1964), p. 19.

word 'gang' because of its 'invidious coloration' (Bloch and Niederhoffer, 1958). In English as well as in Hebrew, the term implies an exclusive preoccupation with violence and crime. The label 'gang' applied to a group of youngsters seems in the public mind to preclude change, and in fact constitutes a serious obstacle to it.

Most writers on the subject stress the criminogene and destructive factors of the 'gang'. An Austrian investigator, for instance, described the gang as a group which is not adjusted to its environment and which activates tension and aggression towards its surroundings, while the environment reacts with tension and aggression towards the group. The result of this process is described as an increasing narrowing-down or hemming-in of the group. The voluntariness of membership becomes more and more a fatalistic necessity, the individual loses his individual traits and characteristics and, in the end, becomes the normative representative of a group ideology which through its suggestive influence fosters strong commitment, but releases tendencies towards extreme behaviour (Wilfert, 1962).

A leading American criminologist (Taft, 1950) has been cited as stating that:

The gang influences individuals toward delinquency and crime in a number of ways: by promoting attitudes of hostility toward community agencies of social control, by teaching techniques of crime and general patterns of destructiveness, by enforcing its system of assigning highest prestige to the most daring or skilled criminals, and by serving as a medium of contact between beginners, more experienced juvenile delinquents, and older professional criminals.[1]

All this is no doubt true of the most severely delinquent groups, and partially true of all groups of delinquent youngsters. However, the term 'gang', widely applied, assigns these extreme characteristics by inference to all groups of youngsters who, to varying degrees of severity, engage in delinquent behaviour. Street club work experience shows that this is misleading.

Despite its semantic clumsiness, the term 'street corner group' seems to be most suitable because this term avoids the implication of exclusive preoccupation with violence and crime, and because the term leaves room for a range of characteristics found in many other kinds of 'dynamic groups' of adolescents which have none of the attributes of the sinister image which is conjured up by the term 'gang'.

A street corner group can be defined as a conglomeration of youngsters who gather habitually at a certain street corner, in a park, in the vicinity of a local cafe, candy store or bar, etc. Ranging in numbers from five to fifty, and in age from early to late adolescence and young adult-

[1] Cited in Broom and Selznik (1957), p. 622.

hood, they exhibit group behaviour to varying degrees of intensity. Depending upon a variety of local conditions and circumstances, these youngsters may hang about loosely or in small cliques, drift apart and even disperse temporarily under police pressure or other threats. In times of crisis, such as an attack by another group, or under a unifying influence, for example an upsurge of hostility against an influx of strangers in the neighbourhood or the emergence of a new, powerful and glamorous leader, the group may draw together and become 'tight' and cohesive for a while.

Usually the street corner group presents the picture of a diffuse, rambling, loose-knit clustering of youngsters. In New York as in Tel Aviv, however, street club workers who maintained relationships with such groups over a period of time, soon became aware of a discernible structure: a fluctuating, but always present hierarchical 'pecking order' divides the group into leaders and led. This hierarchy can also be seen as a grouping in concentric circles, in which the leaders are at the centre of a 'core group' of the most active and influential youngsters, the core group is surrounded by the rank and file (the regulars), and a number of 'fringe' members hang around on the periphery. In drawing this oversimplified picture, it must be emphasised that it is never a static one, but in constant flux. This structure is usually not apparent at first glance, and it takes time, skill and a high degree of mutual trust and acceptance before an outsider gains insight into its dynamics.[1]

The sociographic sketches on the following pages are recommended as examples of a method of gaining a clear picture of the situation and the dynamics of a street corner group. As the situation is one of constant flux, the worker should draw up sketches of this type at least once every six months. This 'tool' may serve to give the worker some perspective on what is happening in the group over a period of time. A 'six-months-later' version of the sketches provided here may, for instance, show how the composition of friendship cliques has changed, that members of the fringe have penetrated the core, or that interaction between certain group members which seem to be centred on drug use or homosexual relations have increased or decreased. The quantity of interaction lines leading to a particular youngster may indicate changes in the group's leadership. Note, for instance, the number of frequent interaction arrows

[1] Structure and dynamics of street corner youth in a London lower class neighbourhood are described in Willmott (1966), ch. 2, 'Fraternities of the Street', pp. 22–36. A delinquent 'gang' in the same area is discussed on pp. 158–61 of the same work in relation to the theories of Cloward and Ohlin, W. B. Miller, and D. Matza (p. 160 nn). Another description of delinquent gangs can be found in a report by Spencer (1964) on the Bristol Social Project, ch. 9: 'Toffs, Bums, and Espressos', esp. p. 161. An earlier account of street corner youth is given by Peter Scott (1956).

leading to Aron of Group 1, or, in diagram D, the intensive contacts between Groups 1 and 3, and Group 4's apparent lack of contact, with Group 2. The coinciding of contacts between drug users and youngsters who engage in homosexual behaviour may give the worker food for thought, as may the relative isolation of one or another boy. When the worker sits down to draw his sociographic sketches of the group, he may recognise patterns and discover phenomena of which he had been only dimly aware in the (usually quite hectic) day-by-day involvement with the youngsters A thoughtful weighing of the picture provided by the graphs may be useful in evaluating past and in planning future action.

The sketches have been taken from the records of the Tel Aviv Street Club Project. Group 1 consisted of twenty-one members in the fourteen to eighteen age range. This group was deeply involved in delinquent activities, such as vandalism, brawling, petty and vehicle theft and, occasionally, burglaries. Group 2, five boys, of fourteen to sixteen years could be regarded as a low-status 'satellite' group of Group 1. Their involvement in delinquent behaviour was relatively mild. Group 3, seventeen youngsters in the sixteen to nineteen age range, came closest to being an organised gang, and had adopted the name of a detective sergeant who had become their special nemesis. These boys engaged in vehicle theft and burglaries, and procuring and selling of hashish. This group was the most severely and consistently delinquent of the cluster of four groups. Group 4, eight young men ranging in age from eighteen to twenty-eight, were the undisputed leaders of the local delinquent subculture. They engaged in a variety of criminal activites, including burglary and procuring, and all of them were hashish users.

Diagram A: Groups 1 and 2

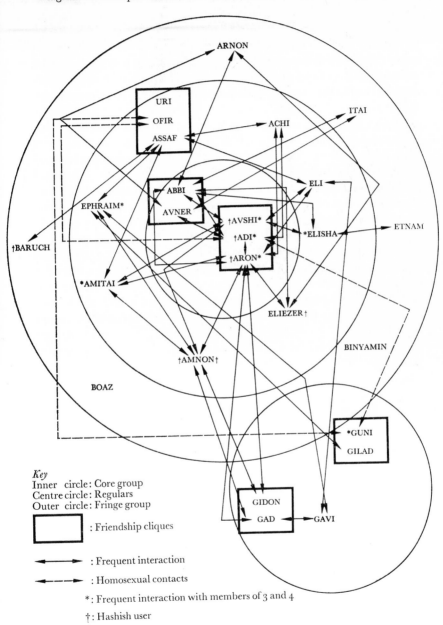

ARNON

URI
OFIR
ASSAF

ACHI

ITAI

ELI

ABBI

EPHRAIM*

AVNER

†AVSHI*

†ADI*

*ELISHA

ETNAM

†BARUCH

†ARON*

*AMITAI

ELIEZER†

BINYAMIN

†AMNON†

BOAZ

*GUNI

GILAD

Key
Inner circle: Core group
Centre circle: Regulars
Outer circle: Fringe group

⬛ : Friendship cliques

◀━━━▶ : Frequent interaction

◀━ ─ ─▶ : Homosexual contacts

* : Frequent interaction with members of 3 and 4

† : Hashish user

GIDON
GAD ◀━ ━▶GAVI

Diagram B: Group 3

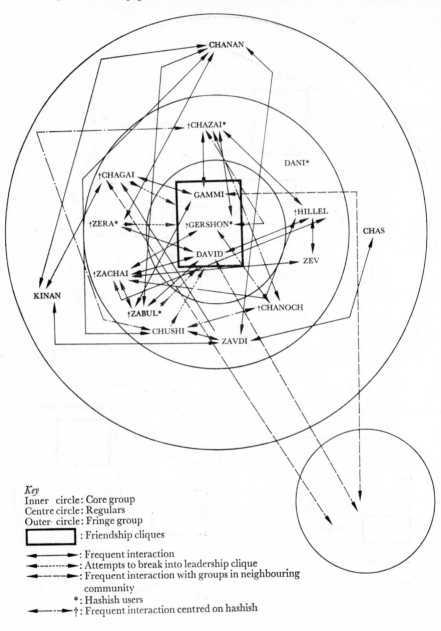

Key
Inner circle: Core group
Centre circle: Regulars
Outer circle: Fringe group
▭ : Friendship cliques

◄——————► : Frequent interaction
◄------------► : Attempts to break into leadership clique
◄— — —► : Frequent interaction with groups in neighbouring
community
* : Hashish users
◄—·—† : Frequent interaction centred on hashish

Diagram C: Group 4

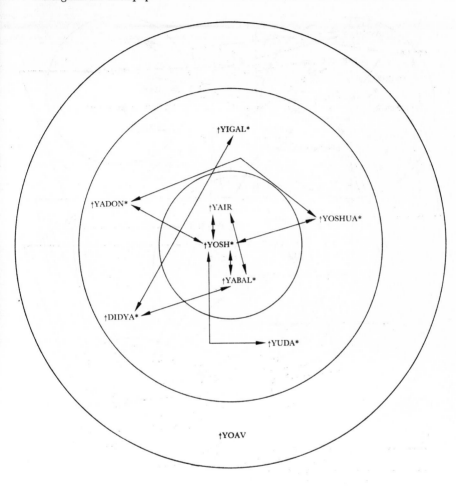

Key
Inner   circle: Core group
Centre circle: Regulars
Outer   circle: Fringe group
⟶ : Frequent interaction
*: Frequent interaction with members of groups 1, 2, 3
†: Hashish users

Diagram D: Interactions between members of the four street-corner groups[1]

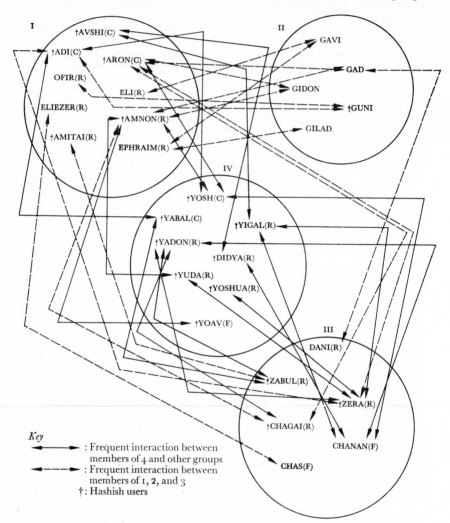

Key

⟵———⟶ : Frequent interaction between members of 4 and other groups

◀- - - -▶ : Frequent interaction between members of 1, 2, and 3

† : Hashish users

[1] The sketch does *not* list the names of those boys who have *no*, or only infrequent, interaction with members of other groups.

3 Delinquent subcultures

Each society has a distinctive culture. Variations which amount to subcultures, if they modify a great deal of behaviour, distinguish the subgroups which compose large societies. The relationship is like that between a language and dialects. Regional subgroups speak dialects; occupational, age, and other subgroups and social 'sets' develop their own 'lingo'—modifications of the language and additions to it usually indicative of subgroup behaviour. Language is used sometimes spontaneously, sometimes willfully to circumscribe subgroups. Thus, linguistic peculiarities often suggest regional origin, occupation, education and social class. And children, as well as people who feel the need to belong to a distinct group, may deliberately invent linguistic peculiarities intelligible only to insiders, thereby distinguished from outsiders ('squares' or 'cornballs').

ROSS AND VAN DEN HAAG (1957), p. 92

It has become fashionable in the behavioural sciences recently to speak of subcultures: the ways of behaving peculiar to a particular group within a larger one. Thus there are subcultures for longshoremen, professional baseball players, university professors, members of the beat generation, inmates of a prison, Texas oilmen, a boy's gang, the world of fashion, jazz musicians, behavioural scientists, and any other group of some size. . . .

BERELSON AND STEINER, (1964), p. 645

In another of those 'circular' phenomena which haunt the investigator as well as the practitioner, the delinquent street corner group is both a generator and a product of the 'delinquent subculture'.

This concept of the delinquent subculture has become widely accepted in recent years and constitutes an important breakthrough in the quest for understanding of delinquency, by veering away from the over emphasis on intrapsychic explanations, by offering a dynamic view of the intermeshing of psychological and social factors, by relating the overall structure to the social milieu in which the delinquent is located, and, last but not least, by pointing out characteristic differences between different kinds of delinquent behaviour patterns.

Cloward and Ohlin (1960, p. 7) distinguish between the 'deviant' and the 'delinquent' subculture:

The delinquent subculture is a special category of deviant subculture. The latter term is generic, encompassing all sub-culturally supported behaviour that violates some conventionally sanctioned set of social expectations or rules of conduct. Such behaviours as truancy, profanity, property destruction, petty theft, illicit sexual experiences, disorderly conduct, and drunkenness, for example, are deviant; indeed, when they occur among adolescents they are often dealt with as delinquent acts by criminal-justice authorities.

The distinction is useful, in that it points at the fact that a wide range of deviant behaviour may be tolerated (though possibly frowned upon) by society when it occurs among certain groups of the population, while the same behaviour may result in legal procedures and punitive measures when it occurs in other population groups. For our immediate purposes, however, we can dispense with quibbling over what is deviant and what is delinquent. Almost all behaviour which is in conflict with conventional mores and expectations is, in practice, regarded as delinquent behaviour when it occurs among those with whom we are concerned here, namely lower-class adolescent street corner groups.

Cloward and Ohlin (1960, p. 7) define the 'delinquent subculture' as 'one in which certain forms of delinquent activity are essential requirements for the performance of the dominant roles supported by the subculture'.

Another author (who is also an experienced street club worker), defines the delinquent subculture as 'the organised set of shared values, beliefs, and norms governing the behaviour of youths in interaction with each other which is determined to be in serious violation of desirable modes of conduct and consequently is identified as delinquent by the official culture' (Spergel, 1961, p. 35).

In discussing the behaviour of individuals and groups who adhere to delinquent subculture values and norms, the term 'antisocial' is frequently used as synonymous with 'deviant'. Thorston Sellin (1962, p. 7) writes:

All conduct has been socially conditioned, since personality is a social product. Therefore, it is unwise from a scientific point of view to speak of anti-social as opposed to social conduct. These terms belong to the language of social reform. It would seem best, in order to avoid misunderstanding, to speak of normal and abnormal conduct, i.e. conduct in accord with or deviating from a conduct norm.

Behaviour which deviates from official norms is 'behaviour which violates institutionalized expectations—that is, expectations which are shared and recognized as legitimate within a social system' (A. K. Cohen, 1959, p. 462).

Based upon the American experience, Cloward and Ohlin (1960) differentiate between three main categories of delinquent subcultures:

. . . There appear to be three major types of delinquent sub-culture typically encountered among adolescent males in lower-class areas of large urban centers. One is based principally upon criminal values; its members are organized primarily for the pursuit of material gain by such illegal means as extortion, fraud, and theft. In the second, violence is the keynote; its members pursue status ('rep') through the manipulation of force or threat of force. These are the 'warrior' groups that attract so much attention in the press. Finally, there are subcultures which emphasize the consumption of drugs. The participants in these drug sub-cultures have become alienated from conventional roles, such as those required in the family or the occupational world. They have withdrawn into a restricted world in which the ultimate value consists in the 'kick'. We call these three sub-cultural forms 'criminal', 'conflict', and 'retreatist' respectively (p. 20).

. . . Members of the criminal sub-culture, for example, believe that the world is populated by 'smart guys' and 'suckers'; members of the conflict gang see their 'turf' as surrounded by enemies; retreatists regard the world about them as populated by 'squares'. Similarly, each culture is characterized by distinctive evaluations: criminals value stealth, dexterity, wit, 'front', and the capacity to evade detection; street-warriors value 'heart'; retreatists place a premium on esoteric 'kicks' (p. 14).

When we leave the books for a moment and join the worker at the street corner, we find that what we have so far been told about the delinquent subcultures is helpful, but not enough. The street club worker has to look further and dig deeper in order to gain a thorough understanding of what he sees and hears and feels.

D. M. Downes (1966, p. 9), taking a critical look at Albert K. Cohen's 'General theory of subcultures' (1955) classifies subcultures as follows:

(a) Those which precede, or which are formed *outside* the context of the 'dominant culture': for example, the 'culture' of immigrant groups which become 'sub-cultures' in the context of the host culture: also regional sub-cultures which precede, but come to co-exist, merge with or differentially respond to the enveloping 'dominant' culture.

(b) Those which originate *within* the context of the dominant culture: these fall into two sub-categories:

   (i) Those which emerge in *positive* response to the demands of the social and cultural structures; for example, occupational sub-cultures, age-group sub-cultures, and

   (ii) Those emerging in *negative* response to the social and cultural structures' demands; e.g. delinquent sub-cultures; religious messianic-revivalist sub-cultures; political extremist sub-cultures.

If we look, for instance, at a group of young thieves in one of the 'Oriental' poverty areas of Tel Aviv and at a group of similar delinquent adaptation in a Puerto Rican slum in New York we find the following picture:

Both groups are part of a subculture which has been formed outside the dominant culture and their way of life is, at least to some extent, regarded as 'deviant' and undesirable by the host society.

Both groups are part of a lower-class subculture which is, at least to some degree, at variance with the middle-class values of the dominant culture.

Both groups are part of the adolescent age group subculture which transcends the boundaries of the ethnic/immigrant and of the delinquent/ thieves subculture. As part of this age subculture, these youngsters share some of the attitudes, behaviour patterns and stresses of most non-delinquent adolescents.

Moreover, the norms and behaviour patterns of either group may find support or, at least, toleration from the subcultural values of their own community, or else may be regarded as deviant by this community. While the Puerto Rican community in which our New York group of young thieves lives may tolerate, or even encourage fighting, they may have no use whatever for boys who steal. The Tel Aviv group's criminal activities may be ignored by some, connived at by other members of their community, but harsh punishment may be meted out to them for their rebellious attitudes toward orthodox religious observance, an attitude which, on the other hand, is tolerated, even encouraged by the host society. In both cases these groups find themselves in the ambiguous position of being part of their neighbourhood subculture, though regarded as deviant by the dominant culture, in some of their attitudes and activities, while in other areas of their lives they exist as a deviant fringe group within their own subcultural environment.

Cloward and Ohlin (1960, p. 11) write:

> . . . the delinquent sub-culture imparts to the conduct of its members a high degree of stability and resistance to control or change. Delinquent activity is an essential feature of the social role which a member must perform in order to maintain his acceptance by other members of the group. As long as he finds satisfaction in these associations, the delinquent behaviour can be expected to continue. His actions are integrated with the actions of other members who rely on him to carry out his role. . . . Because of this network of expectations and obligations, it is difficult to change or control one member's behaviour without first changing the character of the entire group. Furthermore, efforts to induce a member to feel shame or guilt are blocked by the rationalizations and reassurances which the group provides.

It has been my impression that in New York, as in Tel Aviv, delinquent street corner groups vary considerably in the degree to which they adhere to, and are integrated in, a delinquent subculture. Usually the degree of subcultural integration appears to be indicated by the level of structure and cohesion found in any given group. In New York as well as in Tel Aviv I have observed that, the more 'loose' the group, the less clearly defined are its delinquent values and norms. On the other hand, the more 'tight' and 'close' the group, the more deeply its members are likely to be committed to the norms and values of a delinquent subculture. This does not necessarily determine the severity and frequency of delinquent behaviour at any given time, but it does seem to influence decisively the consistency and persistence of such behaviour and its resistance or accessibility to change.

The enmeshment of a group of youngsters in a delinquent subculture cannot, however, be estimated solely on the basis of its cohesiveness and close-knit appearance. There is no more close-knit group than a football team, at least upon surface observation, but such a group is not necessarily delinquent. In order to indicate the degree of integration in a delinquent subculture, the observed 'closeness' of a group cannot be based on functional, common interest or friendship ties alone. It must be measured by the degree to which common delinquent norms, values and beliefs 'bind' the membership of the group. There are many ways in which the street club worker may encounter evidence of such norm-cohesion. For example:

At a gathering of fighting gang youngsters in a basement in East Harlem I once discussed the various members of one of the gangs with their leader. Pointing at one boy who seemed to belong to the group, I asked about his standing. I was told: 'He's all right. He hangs around with us, but he's not with the gang. He's never been in a fight. He don't know how to fight, so he ain't in with us.'

One of the street club workers observed that the boys of a Tel Aviv thieves group were exerting considerable pressure upon a youngster to participate in delinquent activites. This youngster was fairly well liked, but remained something of an outsider, because he objected to stealing. After several months the worker heard that the boy had finally gone along with members of the group who broke into a store. The boy was arrested and spent a few weeks in jail, after which he was put on probation. When the boy returned from jail, he was welcomed warmly by the group. The leader of the group expressed the feelings of the boys by saying: 'Now you're one of us, man. You made it.' The same leader, incidentally, was on one occasion told by the worker (who, ill-advisedly, attempted to 'get him on his side' in this manner) that he was smarter, less inclined to do 'bad' things, than the other boys of the group. The boy, who usually had a very good relationship with the worker, turned angrily on him, shouting: 'Don't give me that stuff, man, I'm no different from anybody here. I've done everything anybody here has done and more. I'm a thief, that's all.'

In the summer of 1967 I visited a 'Cafe Project' in one of London's lower-class areas with one of the former workers of the Tel Aviv Street Club Project who visited me here. We struck up a conversation with a group of the young clients of the Cafe and, within the hour, each one of about a dozen youngsters assured us that he was a 'juvenile delinquent'. All boasted that they were frequently involved in fights, several of the boys volunteered the information that they had done some 'thieving' and stole cars, and three youngsters told us with obvious pride that they had been in jail. All the youngsters seemed eager to impress us with their adherence to the delinquent norms of the group, although the youth worker in charge of the project later assured us that some of the claims of 'being bad' were exaggerated.

Most of the street corner groups we observed in Tel Aviv tend to be of the less cohesive, more 'loose' and fluctuating variety. Their adherence to delinquent norms and values is undoubtedly a strong factor in their lives, but in many cases it is not as complete and deeply ingrained as in the majority of such groups in New York.

Some more tightly structured and cohesive groups have also been identified in Tel Aviv. These groups are usually either more skilful and 'professional' in their criminal activities, or else exhibit more violent, aggressive behaviour.

I am under the impression that street club workers will have to apply different techniques and modes of approach according to whether the group served is still loose and unstable in its normative structure, or whether it has already become rigid and deeply committed to the norms and values of a delinquent subculture.

In his work with the loose group, the street club worker may have to move in more quickly with techniques of challenging behaviour patterns, intervening in and preventing delinquent activities, educating and setting limits. This approach may serve to prevent the still fluid delinquent adaptation from 'jelling' and becoming deeply rooted in the delinquent subculture.

With the rigid group, the worker may have to prepare himself for a much longer period of passive observation and non-intervention. He may have to invest a considerable length of time in establishing an unshakeable relationship with the group, while he accepts and tolerates delinquent activities without intervening or objecting.[1] His focus will have to be the enrichment of the group's social life, by providing non-delinquent activities that are acceptable and satisfying to the boys. These may serve gradually to dilute the group's concentration upon delinquent activities, and thereby eventually loosen the hold of delinquent values and norms. However, the worker may have to wait for a considerable period of time before delinquent behaviour actually decreases in severity and quantity; during that time he will have to seek to prevent the consequences of such behaviour from becoming factors which will destroy all chances of the youngsters' emergence from the delinquent subculture. In all but the most severe cases the worker will therefore have to attempt

---

[1] The great Russian pioneer in re-educating young criminals wrote: 'From my first collective I did not demand that they should not steal. I knew that here I could not convince them at all. But I did demand that they should get up when necessary. They stole and for a time I ignored this' (R. S. Cohen, 1955, p. 209).

to help the youngsters to obtain probation or other forms of rehabilitative measures instead of incarceration in penitentiaries or commitment to state training schools.

Certain characteristic attitudes, values and beliefs of lower-class youth described by Walter B. Miller (1958) are as strongly in evidence in Tel Aviv as in New York. The most obvious of these are: a constant concern with the anticipation and avoidance of 'trouble'; toughness as a value in itself and as proof of masculinity; value put upon 'smartness', the ability to outwit others; excitement and thrills as a necessity of life serving to relieve boredom and counteract the monotony of work; a certain fatalism that accredits the events of one's own life to 'the slings and arrows of outrageous fortune'; ambiguity with regard to one's personal autonomy, expressed in vacillations between resentment of all authority, readiness to become overdependent, and preference for strong limits and forceful restrictions. These typical manifestations of lower-class psychology are much in evidence among street corner boys in urban poverty areas. We must, however, beware of equating characteristic lower-class attitudes with delinquent ones. The street club worker must be aware of the significance of the former, but he should also understand that most lower-class communities prohibit such delinquent activities as vandalism, stealing, use of narcotics, etc.

To repeat Cloward and Ohlin's (1960, p. 14) summary of the characteristic beliefs and values of the three delinquent subcultures:

. . . Members of the criminal sub-culture, for example, believe that the world is populated by 'smart guys' and 'suckers'; members of the conflict gang see their 'turf' as surrounded by enemies; retreatists regard the world about them as populated by 'squares'. Similarly, each culture is characterized by distinctive evaluations: criminals value stealth, dexterity, wit, 'front' and the capacity to evade detection; street-warriors value 'heart'; retreatists place a premium on esoteric 'kicks'.

In New York, one or the other of these sets of values and beliefs can be discerned as being dominant in certain street corner groups. These values and beliefs determine the norms that rule the behaviour of thieves' groups, fighting gangs and groups of retreatists (among whom I count drug addicts as well as groups of homosexual youngsters).

The situation observed in Tel Aviv shows similarities and differences with New York. In the street corner groups we have encountered, the beliefs and values of the 'criminal' subculture are usually dominant.

Like their counterparts in New York, the Tel Aviv youngsters believe that there is an abundance of 'suckers' and 'rich guys' who are easily victimised, conned and exploited. Moreover, the youngsters feel justified in victimising such persons. As they see it, 'everybody (even in conventional society) is doing it', and the 'suckers' (the slang word used here is 'fryer') are 'asking for it'.

Here, as in New York, guilt feelings are neutralised and antisocial values are reinforced by justifying delinquent behaviour through emphasising the youngsters' own underprivileged, deprived socio-economic status, real or imagined ethnic discrimination, and the prevalence of unfair practices, corruption and injustice in 'respectable' society.

Here, and in similar groups in New York, I have heard delinquent street corner boys express their feelings in the very same words: 'Everybody cheats and steals, man. Only the big guys get away with it. Look at the way we live here' (pointing at their surroundings), 'what else can we do, except be "bad". . . ?' 'We ain't got a chance to make it "going straight". The only way we can get our kicks is by "robbing" and "hustling".'—'The cops are after us all the time anyway, man. They got us down as "bad" guys so we might as well be "bad" and have some fun while it lasts.'

As in thieves' groups in New York, the status of the Tel Aviv street corner delinquent depends upon his smartness and skill in planning and carrying out confidence tricks and thefts.

A member of a Tel Aviv street corner group told me with great pride how cleverly he and his friends conned a middle-class boy who sought their company, out of a sum of money, by pretending to collect contributions for a party among all members of the group. Every boy pretended to pay his share, while actually only the sucker handed over the requested cash. He was then told to wait, and was left standing while the boys used his money to go to the movies.

In another Tel Aviv group a boy, who was previously held in low esteem, gained considerable status by inventing a new tool that proved useful in prying open the shutters of kiosks (small candy stores) in order to steal cigarettes and candy.

Here, as in New York, the youngsters gain status by out-smarting the police, 'snowing' (deceiving) the authorities, or through the value of the objects they steal. There is, for instance, a decided difference in the prestige accorded to the boy who steals an old jalopy, and the youngster who shows off in a new and expensive stolen car. (The girls of the group show a marked preference for taking rides in the more expensive models of stolen cars.)

As in similar groups in New York, the youngsters' routine interests and behaviour rarely centre exclusively on delinquent activities. (A fact which is often not realised by persons whose dealings with delinquents focus primarily upon the youngsters' law-breaking.)

Membership of a street corner group usually involves participation in a range of activities that include general socialising 'fooling around', 'shooting the breeze' (telling stories and gossiping), attending movie shows and parties together, dancing, athletic activities, picking up girls, etc. The content and quality of these sociable activities are strongly influenced and flavoured by the group norms that prevail. The failure to realise this is often the cause of lack of success in drawing street corner groups into community centres and youth organisations.

In New York I saw it happen that a Puerto Rican fighting gang, which was willing and ready to join a community centre, withdrew resentfully when the boys were told that a house rule obliged them to remove their 'bopping hats' upon entering the building.

In Tel Aviv the no-smoking rule of most youth clubs is unacceptable to street corner boys.

In New York, members of an East Harlem group stopped using the facilities of a youth centre when staff members objected to the close, sexually stimulating, dancing of the boys and girls.

In Tel Aviv the youngsters keep away from youth centres which permit folk-dancing, but prohibit such dances as the twist.

The personal status of the individual member of the delinquent street corner group depends often as much upon his successes in the general social life of the group, as it depends upon his delinquent involvements. Here his personal appearance and mode of dressing (in accordance with the group's fashion standards) count for much, his physical prowess, his wit and agility in verbal repartee, his successes with girls, generosity with money, his loyalty and reliability, his knack of entertaining the group, etc.

The awareness and understanding of the social aspects of the life of a delinquent group is of considerable importance to the street club worker. It offers him a range of opportunities to help members of the group to find sources of satisfaction and prestige which are provided within the normative structure of the group, but do not solely depend upon destructive, delinquent behaviour. The worker has a reasonably good chance of reducing the more serious delinquent activities by supporting the more positive and acceptable satisfactions the group offers its members, that is, provided the worker is ready to accept the limitations imposed by the subcultural norms, at least until he senses that the group is ready for attitudinal change.

In working with the 'Emperors', a highly delinquent and aggressive thieves' group in New York, I encouraged and frequently participated in parties 'thrown' in one of the boys', or even my own apartment. At these parties the atmosphere was usually one of harmony and fun, and at least in my presence, no disorderly behaviour (such as the usual brawling,

drunkenness and sexual molesting of girls etc.) occurred. As these youngsters were used to having alcoholic drinks at all their get-togethers, I
permitted a limited amount of drinking. This moderate permissiveness
made the parties acceptable to the boys, and led them to prefer this kind
of activity to the usual rowdy and destructive ways of spending their
evenings.

In organising a trip with a group of street corner girls in Tel Aviv,
one of the Project's field workers tolerated a certain amount of bawdy
talk, noisy behaviour and running about, despite the disapproving
glances of passers-by. Although the worker firmly set limits to aggressive
behaviour on the train, and to an attempt at pilfering of coins from the
fountain of the Hebrew University, the girls told her after the trip that
they had enjoyed themselves especially, because the worker 'understood
that we're not angels'. The girls later repeatedly asked for trips and other
organised activities, saying that they preferred them to hanging around
and 'getting in trouble' at the street corner.

While in New York the fighting gangs and the groups of retreatist
youngsters seem to match or outnumber the thieves' groups, we have so
far not found any evidence for the existence of street corner groups that
could be classified as representative of the 'conflict' or the 'retreatist'
subcultures in Tel Aviv.

This does not mean that some of the values and behavioural expressions of conflict and retreatist adaptations do not exist among the street
corner boys of Tel Aviv lower-class areas. As in thieves' groups which I
have observed in New York, some of the attributes of the street fighter
and the addict play a role in the attitudinal and behavioural patterns of
such groups here.

The concept of the clearly demarcated and often bitterly contested
'turf', which plays a decisive role in the behaviour patterns and the life
style of the New York fighting gang, seems to be unknown in Tel Aviv.
However, the attitudes that underly that concept, namely defensiveness
and distrust of outsiders, are as much in evidence in certain Tel Aviv
slums as in such areas in New York.

It is possible, though at present only a matter of speculation, that the
turf mentality and other attributes of the conflict subculture, may be
rooted in the ghetto atmosphere that pervades certain lower-class communities, and that the aggressive possessiveness of the turf mentality may
become the major preoccupation of street corner groups in Tel Aviv
where a threat to the clannishness and exclusiveness of the community
develops.

In New York I observed an Italian Lower East Side community,
'threatened' by the incursion of Puerto Ricans. Here the adult population

fostered, encouraged and actively supported the bellicose stance of local street corner groups. These groups had previously been classified as belonging to the 'racket' variety of the 'criminal' delinquent subculture, but now began to exhibit all the characteristics of fighting gangs.

I have no knowledge of similar occurrences in Tel Aviv. However, a certain amount of tension between different ethnic groups exists and may, in some cases, lead to conflict adaptations.

Tel Aviv street club workers observed several instances of physical attacks upon intruders by members of street corner groups. For example, the youngsters of a thieves' group in a slum area administered a severe beating to a boy who was trying to pass them unobserved. Three boys did the beating while the rest of the group, including several girls, watched. The boy was warned not to show his face any more and permitted to run off. The explanation given to the street club worker was, that this boy 'had no business here', and had been previously warned 'to keep out of our neighbourhood'.

An example from my New York experience may serve to show that sudden outbursts of turf mentality in street corner groups which cannot be termed fighting gangs, are not unknown elsewhere: Boys of the 'Emperors' cornered a small group of Puerto Rican youngsters and challenged these youngsters' right to pass through their neighbourhood. A knife fight ensued in which two youngsters on each side were stabbed, before the 'intruders' got away.

The rep (reputation) and status-enhancing manifestations of fighting prowess and reckless courage (known as 'heart' among New York fighting gangs and called 'Dumm', the Hebrew word for blood, by our youngsters) is highly valued among the members of Tel Aviv delinquent street corner groups. A distinctive mode of dress, perhaps the most visible characteristic of the New York fighting gangs, has also appeared among Tel Aviv youngsters in the form of tight black chino pants, T-shirts sporting painted symbols (such as a clenched fist), or black leather jackets. The influence of American gang-lore movies is unmistakable here.

In all the described instances of apparent conflict behaviour, the dominant adaptation of the groups observed in Tel Aviv appears to be that of the 'criminal' subculture. Whether conflict patterns may become dominant in one or the other of Tel Aviv's lower-class street corner groups, remains to be seen. There are some indications that such a development is not outside the realm of possibilities.[1]

[1] As my contacts with 'detached' and other youth workers in England led me to believe that the 'conflict adaptation' and the fighting gang are regarded as a distinctly American phenomenon, unknown in English cities, I find the following quote of some interest: '. . . More recently, in Islington and Shoreditch, for example, youth workers and police have been worried by the increase in "tooling up" with guns instead of knives,

There is, at this time, no evidence for the existence of a distinct retreat-ist subculture among lower-class youngsters in Tel Aviv. Occasional smoking of hashish (marijuana) among street corner groups is fairly widespread, and may be related to the fact that hashish use is not the subject of strict cultural prohibitions among certain oriental population groups. (A significant number of the youngsters claim that they learned to smoke hashish from adults in their community, in some instances from their own fathers.) Excessive and habitual use of hashish is restricted to a relatively small number, but these few do exist in several of the groups we observed. Heroin, cocaine and other more esoteric drugs, have appeared only in rare and isolated instances and have apparently not taken hold among the youngsters.

The group norms of thieves' groups, while not prescribing the use of hashish, seem to tolerate it. In some instances certain subgroups or cliques of a street corner group have been observed to withdraw to an isolated spot and have hashish-smoking sessions, comparable to the 'tea' or 'pot' parties held by such cliques of New York thieves' groups and fighting gangs.

Individual boys who use hashish excessively and habitually, to the point where this activity becomes the focus of their interest, usually have low status in the group and are regarded with a mixture of pity and con-tempt, but are not excluded from the group's activities. In some cases leading members of street corner groups have asked the worker to 'help' these boys. In one case a habitual user who pleaded for a 'smoke' was teased and subjected to a number of humiliating activities before one of the boys 'fixed him up' with a hashish cigarette.

One of the street club workers found great concern over the heavy hashish use of one of the youngsters in his group. During a group meeting the matter was discussed heatedly, and some youngsters advocated am-bushing and beating the person who was the main supplier, while others agreed that it would be preferable to inform the police. In a comparable case in New York the youngsters of a street corner group agreed with me that it would be 'right' to inform the parole officer of a youngster who had begun to supply heroin to one of the younger boys.

It has been my impression that excessive consumption of alcohol (in distinction from occasional drinking), observed among a few of our youngsters, must also be regarded as expressive of retreatist tendencies.

etc. The case for "detached work" in such areas, and in Soho,—a focal point for buying and selling weapons—is particularly strong. The "detached worker" would serve as much to give an unbiased picture of what is happening in an area, as for any possible "preventive" role. At present it only needs one "near-group" mobilised by the seriously disturbed youngster with a gun to spark off claims that "gang warfare" has broken out' (Downes, 1966, p. 213 n).

Frequent 'heavy' drinking among the members of a Yorkville Street corner group can be regarded as symptomatic of the cultural emphasis of drinking as showing 'manliness' and as an accepted social activity among the Irish, German, Czechoslovakian and Hungarian lower-class population of that area. However, excessive drinking in a predominantly Oriental lower-class community in Israel, where consumption of alcohol is not the custom, may be a form of escape and isolation which is characteristic of the retreatist adaptation.

The Tel Aviv youngsters who drink excessively are often found to become habitual hashish users. Here one may perhaps draw a parallel to the phenomenon of excessive drinking among Puerto Rican youngsters in New York which, in my experience, is often closely followed by the first experimentations with narcotics. In a few cases Tel Aviv street club workers have observed that youngsters try to obtain more esoteric 'kicks' by drinking cognac or arrak and smoking hashish simultaneously.

Another form of deviant behaviour which I regard as symptomatic of a retreatist tendency is homosexuality. (I am not referring to the occasional homosexual experimentation frequently taking place among adolescents, nor to homosexual activities resorted to under the pressures of tension and deprivation that is prevalent in jails and institutions in the United States as well as in Israel.)

The description of the retreatist youngster as perceiving himself as 'culturally and socially detached from the life-style and everyday preoccupations of members of the conventional world' (Cloward and Ohlin, 1960, p. 25) seems to apply to the youngsters who become habitually involved in homosexual activities. This form of deviant behaviour also seems to bring in its wake the kind of withdrawal and isolation from the immediate social environment that is characteristic of the drug addict.

In New York groups of teenage homosexuals who prescribe homosexual behaviour as a condition for membership, and who practise homosexual initiation rites, have been identified. I know of no such groups in Tel Aviv, but I have come across cases in which street corner groups tolerate homosexual activities between members of the group, as well as contacts with adult homosexuals for exploitative purposes. The sexual deviants are not ostracised, though they are at times the objects of derision and the targets of obscene jokes.

In comparison to this, I encountered during my work in New York a number of youngsters who, while remaining active members of thieves' groups, had entered into homosexual relations, either among themselves or with adults. In the latter case the boys were receiving money and presents for accommodating the adult deviants.

In New York small groups or cliques of Lesbian street corner girls have been observed, though little is known about them. In Tel Aviv I know of one case in which a sexually deviant girl, provokingly masculine in her dress and behaviour, 'hangs out' with a male street corner group and exerts her influence upon a few younger girls.

In New York I had occasion to observe two types of 'retreatists': One, the youngster whose foremost goal seems to be escape from the reality of his situation, withdrawal and isolation; two, the 'cool cat'[1] who assumes a pose of superiority over the 'squares' and looks down upon those who do not obtain his esoteric thrills and 'kicks'. This type of youngster, especially if he is of lower-class background, rarely succeeds in maintaining his 'cool' role, through which he seeks to stave off the spectre of loneliness and despair.

We have found traces of both retreatist attitudes in the behaviour of individual members of street corner groups in Tel Aviv. In almost all cases of retreatist tendencies, the youngsters concerned seem to have succumbed to a 'double failure' in achieving status and material success through legitimate or illegitimate adaptations.[2]

Tel Aviv street club workers have repeatedly heard youngsters who are 'heavy' hashish users, explain their self-destructive behaviour with such exclamations as: 'I don't care what happens to me, man, I'm fed-up with everything, I got no hope.' (Words which I have heard only too often from young drug addicts in New York.) The Hebrew word 'Yee'ush', meaning 'despair', crops up regularly in the conversation of these youngsters.

The 'cool', sophisticated pose has been observed among some members of Tel Aviv street corner groups who have turned to homosexual activities. There is a tendency here to assume a pose of 'superiority' and a preoccupation with personal appearances (elaborate hair-dos) and flashy, somewhat effeminate dress.

Solomon Kobrin's (1953) research in Chicago resulted in the finding that: 'Persons who become heroin users were found to have engaged in delinquency in a group-supported and habitual form either prior to their use of drugs or simultaneously with their developing interest in drugs' (p. 6). Cloward and Ohlin (1960, p. 186) observe that retreatist adaptations appear to follow failure of individuals or groups to make a successful 'criminal' or 'conflict' adaptation. Both findings have been substantiated by the experience of street club work in New York.

A recent American author states that the drug users he observed:

---

[1] Described vividly in Finestone's 'Cats, kicks and color', Stein *et al* (1960), pp. 435–48.
[2] This 'double failure' is regarded as one of the main causal factors of retreatist adaptations by Cloward and Ohlin (1960).

. . . Like most addicts who are not doctors, nurses or druggists—grew up in a crowded, lower-class neighbourhood where they were introduced to heroin as teenagers. Bored and delinquent at school, they couldn't face the prospect of starting at the bottom of the social ladder. College was unthinkable, and once school was left behind, there was little to do but hang around the neighbourhood, and no group with which to identify but one's comrades on the corner: in brief, no place to aspire to. Small wonder that, when asked why they started on heroin, almost every one of them included in his answer the phrase, *to kill time*, (Larner and Tefferteller, 1966, p. 11).

The role the street club worker can play in helping street corner youth enmeshed in the retreatist subculture of drug addiction, has been recognised for some time. A pioneering agency in working with young addicts in one of New York's worst slum areas stated:

We have long been convinced that in our neighbourhood of East Harlem, no effective work can be done with any teenagers who are in any degree anti-social unless the adult working with them is thoroughly familiar with gang structure and has a way with teenagers in their own milieu. Whether or not a youth is a gang member, gang mores are the real motivating force in the teenager's life. A person with such knowledge can work what appear to be miracles in the eyes of experts highly trained in technical fields. This generalization is as true of work with those in gangs and on the fringes. We were, therefore, pleased, but not surprised, to discover that Pat Kelley,[1] a street club worker of (the New York City) Youth Board in East Harlem, had done a competent job of helping almost an entire group of teenagers give up the use of narcotics without the help of hospitals, psychiatrists, or experts of any sort. Adolescent addicts can be reached in their own environment through their own natural group and group pressures by adults who thoroughly understand them (East Harlem Protestant Parish Narcotics Committee, 1959, p. 4).

My own experience in working with adolescent drug users tells me that a careful diagnostic distinction must be made between 'experimenters' or, as the youngsters describe it, 'kids who've started to fool around with junk', and confirmed addicts whose body metabolism has been radically changed by prolonged, habitual use of drugs, in most cases heroin. The former can still, as they often say, 'take it or leave it', and can be diverted from narcotics by the alternatives of more interesting and rewarding activities. The latter can be said to have become as dependent for survival upon their daily 'fix' as diabetics are dependent upon their periodic doses of insulin. Thorough knowledge of the facts about narcotics, as well as good diagnostic insight into the needs and behaviour patterns of the youngsters concerned, based on a long-term close relationship between worker and youngsters are an absolute prerequisite for competent work.[2] Unfortunately, much ignorance and

[1] Kelley (1959) reports on an assignment carried out between February 1957 and April 1959.
[2] For an excellent, very helpful factual account, see D. P. Ausubel (1958), a broad view, including the legal and social implications, is presented in E. M. Schur (1962).

confusion still rules even among experienced professionals. When I observed a cafe project run for 'unreachables' on New York's Lower East Side, I noticed that the supervising social worker barred a groggy-looking boy from entering the cafe. I asked my colleague for his reason and was told: 'The boy is obviously under the influence of drugs. He's a known heroin addict. We can't let boys like this in here, because they might cause trouble.' Heroin is a depressant and it is most unlikely that anyone under its influence will cause trouble of any kind. The worst that could have happened in this particular case was that the boy would have dozed off in a corner.

We cannot predict with any degree of certainty whether Tel Aviv youngsters will 'graduate' from hashish use and other relatively mild retreatist tendencies to the use of more sophisticated and destructive narcotics—whether they will move towards a distinct retreatist subcultural adaptation. If juvenile delinquency continues to increase substantially in quantity and severity in Israel such a development is not unlikely.

4 Street corner girls

Within the larger grouping of girls, Marian was constantly looking out for girls who needed more intensive help. This was not as simple as it was with the boys, who were quicker to ask for, or even demand help once they knew and accepted the worker. Marian often had to spend many weeks just chatting and being around before she could encourage a girl to talk about herself. Sometimes it turned out that she needed a new job, sometimes help with a drinking problem, most frequently help with boy/girl relationships, especially when sexual intercourse was part of the relationship. The problem could be that a girl was unable to get a boyfriend, or had difficulties in having too many. It could be that parents disapproved of a boyfriend, or that she envied her girl friends, or they envied her. A few girls were going steady for long periods with boys who seemed 'seriously disorganised', with the result that they were often acutely unhappy. In such relationships girls often had to take a good deal of violence and brutal exploitation. Although the boys seemed to talk much more about sex, it appeared to be a greater problem for the girls. They were often confused about how to behave, about the contrast between parental expectations and those of the neighbourhood, as well as about knowing who was to be pleased. In this situation it was difficult for Marian to know how best to help the girls. The one thing, however, which none of these outside expectations seemed to take into account, was that a girl had feelings and emotions, with which she had to deal. It was in recognising this that Marian was usually able to begin to help.

GOETSCHIUS AND TASH (1967), p. 77

It has been pointed out with justification that troublesome boys go in for crime, whereas troublesome girls merely go with boys.

D. J. WEST (1967)

In the United States and elsewhere attempts to apply the street club work approach to groups of delinquent street corner girls are of relatively recent origin. Information about such groups is still rather scarce. Seemingly cohesive and independent girls' street corner groups have been observed in New York. Some of these exhibit extremely aggressive behaviour, and appear to be female versions of the fighting gangs. The delinquent behaviour of other such groups consists mainly in petty theft, shoplifting and more serious crimes against property, in a few instances involving the use of violence (muggings). These latter groups can be compared to the male street corner groups of the thieves' adaptation.

We have not identified such relatively cohesive and structured groups of delinquent girls in Tel Aviv.

In New York as well as in Tel Aviv a large percentage, perhaps the majority, of delinquent behaviour of street corner girls, consists of transgressions against conventional prescriptions for sexual conduct. In both cities there is a considerable amount of sexual promiscuity and prostitution among teenage girls.

The young prostitutes in both cities, once they have passed the 'amateur' stage and started to 'work' professionally, are usually tied in with teenage and adult procurers. This form of delinquency may be classified as belonging to the 'racket' adaptation of the 'criminal' sub-culture.[1]

In the beginning of 1966 I observed a group of teenage prostitutes and pimps plying their trade in a secluded corner of a park in Jaffa. I posed as a client who would rather 'look' than 'do', I paid the regular fee (10 Israeli pounds) to one of the young men who supervised the activities, and was permitted to hang around for over half an hour before I was politely, but firmly informed that my presence made the girls nervous and was arousing the suspicion of some of the clients. The girls were mostly teenagers, but there was also a woman in her late twenties. Intercourse took place on the ground in the shelter of some bushes. A considerable number of clients, mainly adults, but including a few well-dressed teenagers, were kept waiting their turn by two procurers. These were about eighteen years old and handled the situation in a polite, businesslike way. None of the clients gave any trouble, but when one man complained that the girl of his choice had refused to satisfy him, and the girl screamed at him, one of the pimps slapped her face and ordered her to 'do her job'. Each of the girls served about half a dozen men while I was there. I noticed that, every now and then, one of the girls was permitted to take a break and left the park to have a cup of coffee in a nearby sidewalk restaurant, run by an elderly woman. A number of prostitutes, many of them teenagers, were occupying the tables in this restaurant and all seemed to be on very friendly terms with the proprietress. A number of young procurers were also hanging around. Apparently, this place served as a sort of base of operations.

In New York, young prostitutes and their teenage pimps are often found to be narcotics addicts and exhibit many of the characteristics of the retreatist adaptation. It has been observed that narcotics addiction is, in fact, in many cases the precipitating factor leading to procuring and prostitution.

In Tel Aviv there is no evidence that narcotics addiction plays a significant role as a causative or reinforcing factor of teenage prostitution, but we do not know enough at this time to rule out the possibility of drug use among these girls.

It appears that neither in Tel Aviv nor in New York have social workers succeeded to any significant degree in penetrating the subculture of the young prostitute and her male exploiter in order to gain

[1] A useful account of the social background of young prostitutes in Britain is given in a report to the British Social Biology Council, C. H. Rolph, ed. (1961).

insight and offer effective treatment. The testimonies of the police and
the probation services, as well as the experience of street club workers,
indicate that it is extremely difficult to contact and 'reach' delinquent
girls who engage in prostitution. One of the main reasons is the shame
attached to, and the severe moral condemnation of, this form of delinquent behaviour, which make it impossible for the girls to open up and
talk about their situation. Another reason is the prohibitions and the
threat of sanctions imposed by the procurers against any move by the
girls to seek help.

One of the Tel Aviv Project's female field workers established contact
with a girl who had the reputation of being a prostitute in her neighbourhood, and who appeared to have some influence among a small
group of other girls. This girl went out of her way to impress the worker
with her 'good' qualities and her sophistication during the beginning
phase of the relationship, but became more distant as she began to
realise that the worker was aware of her reputation. A second worker in
the same area who had established a relationship with a group of girls
who were not sexually delinquent, was warned by the girls to keep away
from the 'bad' girls. There are indications that it would be impossible
for the same worker to maintain contact with 'good' girls (though these
may engage in a variety of other delinquent activities) and teenage prostitutes at the same time and in the same area.

The street club worker faces the added obstacle of the girls' mobility.
Because of strong prohibitions against sexual misconduct of teenage girls
in most Oriental lower-class communities, and because the girls' clientele
is usually found in other areas of town, regular contact with the girls is
difficult to maintain.

I have encountered girls' groups in New York, who were attached to
street corner groups of delinquent boys of the 'conflict' or the 'criminal'
adaptation. In both cases the girls are dominated by the boys and are
expected to be loyal to the male group. With some exceptions, the girls
are usually less flagrantly and actively delinquent than the boys. However, the girls are expected to share the norms and values of the male
group, to play a supportive role in delinquent activities, and to stick to
the boys in times of trouble.

Some of the girls were the objects of sexual exploitation, others entered
into genuine love affairs with individual members of the male group.
Some of the girls held positions of respect and trust. In many cases the
girls constituted groups in their own right and, while they were assigned
and accepted a sort of vassal, subordinate status, they had certain rights
and privileges and exerted considerable influence. The situation in Tel
Aviv shows some similarities, although, in my experience, the New York

girls are more assertive. Two examples may illustrate typical relations between boy groups and their female satellites in both cities:

I invited the boys of a New York street corner group to a party at my house. The boys turned a deaf ear to the pleading of the girls to be taken along. Half an hour after the start of the party, the girls suddenly arrived in a body and insisted on being admitted. The boys were surprised and shocked at such audacity, but gave in meekly.

Among some of the Tel Aviv street corner groups, the girls are, at times, invited to go for walks with the boys in the 'better' sections of the city. On such occasions it is accepted practice to dismiss the girls when the boys decide to attend a movie show. The boys give as the most obvious reason for sending the girls home the fact that the girls usually don't have enough money to pay for their own tickets. The worker's suggestion that the boys should 'treat' the girls was regarded as 'ridiculous'.

There are a considerable number of girls who hang around the male street corner groups in Tel Aviv lower-class areas. At first glance, New York and Tel Aviv street corners present a very similar picture in this respect. We see the boys' group milling about on one side of the street, the girls clustered a short distance away, both groups very much aware of each other. From time to time remarks are called across and answered. Occasionally a boy detaches himself from his group and walks over to engage a girl in conversation, or else a couple of girls come to the boys' group.

In the 'mixed neighbourhoods' and in some of the less cohesive areas one can observe the 'steady girls' of leading members of the male group hanging on their boy friends' arms. In the more cohesive, close-knit communities of Oriental background this sort of thing is frowned upon by the boys as well as by the girls.

The observations of a British investigator are similar to those made in New York and Tel Aviv:

When one of their number starts going out with a girl, this inevitably poses problems. Obviously the boys are interested in the girls—they clearly talk about girls and sex a good deal of the time they are together. On the other hand, they value the group's solidarity; for most boys . . . the male group is the crucial 'primary group' in early adolescence, and friendship and loyalty die hard. As a result, many, at least to begin with, are wary of 'going steady' with a girl. The cynical 'male' view at this stage is that you go with a girl for what you can get sexually, and above all you avoid becoming entangled. (Willmott, 1966, p. 41).[1]

Especially among the younger groups, there is a certain amount of loud and rough horseplay, in which the boys seek physical contact with the girls by shoving, hair-pulling and playful chasing about.

[1] The author cites the confirmation of these observations in the west London study by D. H. Allcorn (1955), pp. 273–4.

The remarks of one of London's youth workers have been paraphrased in many reports by street club workers in New York and Tel Aviv:

There were many instances when girls were mauled and punched. Handbags were stolen and the contents thrown into the street. It was particularly painful to witness an unkind attack on a girl although the girls seemed to find it less so than I did. Although I am sure the girls would have preferred different behaviour, any attention from the boys is better than none at all (Biven and Holden, 1966).

On closer acquaintance with the youngsters, it becomes apparent that in Tel Aviv the girls do not form the relatively cohesive groups found in New York under similar conditions. The situation here rather resembles the one reported by a research project in Boston (Ackley and Fliegel, 1960). The girls form small, fluctuating friendship cliques, often with a considerable amount of petty squabbling and rivalry between them.[1]

The experience of the Boston project confirms my observations in New York and Tel Aviv, that, with some exceptions, the street corner boys expect more conventional conformist behaviour from the girls than they themselves practise. While usually even the most extreme delinquent behaviour by members of the boys' group is tolerated, girls who exhibit such behaviour in public are made to feel uncomfortable at the street corner and are often treated with contempt (Spencer, 1964). The prohibitions imposed in Tel Aviv are, perhaps, even more strict, because of the ethno-cultural restrictions imposed upon girls by the Oriental communities of our lower-class neighbourhoods.

In certain areas of Tel Aviv and New York, especially among thieves' groups, girls are still classified according to some of the categories identified by William F. Whyte (1943) two decades ago. There are the 'good' girls who are respected, and are either left alone altogether (because they are not very entertaining), or else become the objects of genuine affection and romantic attachments. These girls are expected to be virgins and not to permit 'heavy petting'. On some occasions I have observed that girls of this kind exert a restraining influence upon the boys.

One rung lower on the status ladder are the accessible girls, the girls who 'put out' only for the boy with whom they go steady. Among these we frequently find the girl-friends of the leaders of the male group. This kind of girl may either exert her influence to get 'her' boy away from the group, having her sights fixed upon marriage, or else she may be fiercely loyal to the group and strongly support its delinquent norms.

[1] See also the description of detached group work with mildly delinquent girls in Bristol in J. Spencer (1964), pp. 167 ff. The description of the girls' behaviour given here is remarkably similar to those I have read in the reports of girl-workers in Tel Aviv and New York.

Still lower in the status hierarchy are the promiscuous 'easy' girls, who are known to engage in sexual intercourse with several boys, and who may let themselves be 'handled' openly in front of the boys' group. From this stage it is only a short step down to the very bottom, where we find the girls who are sexually available to anyone, do not object to the most obscene exchanges of sex talk in front of the group, and may, on occasion, submit to sexual intercourse with groups of boys, an activity known as the 'line up' or 'gang bang'. Willmott (1966, p. 51) reports on this type of 'group sex' practised by London street corner youth. Here too, the girls who submit to this kind of activity are held in contempt. They are known as 'easy lays', 'old slags' or 'bangers'.

The relationship between the street corner boys and the girls, and the manner in which the latter are treated by the male group, is largely determined by the girls' position in the status hierarchy. 'High status' girls, among whom some of the 'good' girls as well as the steady girl-friends of the boys are counted, are frequently permitted to participate in the group's discussions and social activities and may exert considerable influence. I have found examples of this in Tel Aviv as well as in New York.

In a Tel Aviv thieves' group two girls, who were generally respected, participated on many occasions in group discussions and informal get-togethers of the boys' group. While these girls seemed to acknowledge and accept the group's delinquent norms, they were permitted to voice their disapproval of some of the more extreme and reckless delinquent behaviour.

In a Puerto Rican fighting gang of New York's Lower East Side, the high status girls regularly participated in group sessions. When the gang reached the stage of changing from the fighting adaptation to 'going conservative' (becoming a social club under a different name), these girls were formally admitted as due-paying members with full rights.

In an East Harlem street corner group, the steady girl friend of the leader exerted considerable influence over the boys and girls of the group, and was herself considered one of the leaders.

One of the Tel Aviv groups cancelled a much-desired and long-planned overnight hike, because one of the leaders had a spat with his girl friend and was too upset to participate.

In Tel Aviv, as in New York, the 'easy' girls are usually the objects of ruthless sexual exploitation. In both cities extreme cases of this kind have come to my attention. In both cities the sexual activities that take place are more clandestine and hidden in the relatively stable, cohesive communities, and more frankly and openly practised in the disorganised and mixed neighbourhoods.

For example: one of the Tel Aviv street club workers observed the sexually provocative behaviour of one of the girls 'hanging out' with a street corner group in a mixed neighbourhood. This girl engaged in teasing, exhibitionistic behaviour in full view of everyone at the street corner. She sat on the lap of one of the boys, was pushed off contemptuously, and tried again. She snatched some photos from one of the boys and hid them in her brassiere, daring the boy to recover them. When one of the boys jokingly accused her of wearing 'falsies', she opened her blouse and proved the boy wrong. The same girl, on another occasion, slapped another girl who had approached the boys' group, accusing her loudly of having intruded while she was engaged in sexual intercourse with one of the boys in a nearby park. Boys of this group, in the presence of the worker, subjected a fourteen-year-old girl to sadistic sex-play, attempting to push sticks into her vagina and handling her body brutally. The girl submitted to these attacks and entered into an obscene verbal exchange with the boys about her sexual activities. The boys told the worker that they had made use of this girl several times in 'line-ups'.

I observed similar incidents in a thieves' group in a mixed neighbourhood in New York. Here too a girl was subjected to sadistic practices in the street, and exposed her genitals when the boys dared her to do so.

A Tel Aviv street corner group in a cohesive community of Oriental background took a number of ten- and eleven-year-old girls into a hidden spot near their 'hang-out', and there engaged in sexual activities with them. A group of New York youngsters who mainly engaged in vandalism and petty theft, made use of the willingly offered services of a twelve-year-old girl, who provided oral sex satisfaction in basements and hallways. In New York as well as in Tel Aviv it has been observed that on some occasions girls from other neighbourhoods are brought to the area of certain male street corner groups for 'line-ups'. In some cases these girls offer their services free of charge, but are eventually introduced to paid prostitution.

A Tel Aviv street corner group 'imported' two girls for the use of the group, and kept them in an empty shack for several days and nights. After the group had made use of the girls, youngsters from other groups and other neighbourhoods were invited to avail themselves of the girls for payment. Most of the money was kept by the boys. The same group took two girls who had accommodated the youngsters to the working place of two members of the group. There the girls were kept overnight and prostituted themselves to adult workers under the 'supervision' of the youngsters.

I observed a comparable situation in New York. The boys of a thieves' group brought two girls into the neighbourhood and had a 'gang-bang' in the apartment of one of the youngsters whose parents were out of town. Later the two girls were offered to other youngsters and adults for payment. When the girls objected they were beaten.

Youngsters from one of the Tel Aviv groups whom I interviewed in prison told me that, on several occasions, girls who had submitted to intercourse with one member of their group were afterwards forced to service other boys of the group. The two boys who told me about this said: 'Of course you've got to slap them around a little when they don't want to do what they are told.'

In New York and in Tel Aviv the street corner boys seem to have no difficulties with maintaining a duplicity of values with regard to the girls. Sexually promiscuous and easily accessible girls are condemned and held in contempt, but it is quite acceptable, and even expected, to make every attempt to initiate girls into 'forbidden' sex practices. In both cities I have observed that the girls who 'hang out' with delinquent boys' groups are constantly aware of the possibility of getting into trouble, but seem to be titillated and attracted by the danger.

In both cities I found that the youngsters are often unaware of the fact that sex play of any kind with a female below the age of consent is a punishable offence. Youngsters who were told by the street club worker that sexual activities with teenage girls, even if the girl co-operated willingly, and even if actual intercourse did not occur, could result in arrest and charges of indecent assault, voiced their astonishment and dis-belief. Usually the boys regarded these kinds of activities as 'fun' and, in contrast to the girls, do not feel guilty about them. I met one sadly disil-lusioned sixteen-year-old New York youngster in an institution to which he had been committed after a police officer caught him with his hand underneath the skirt of his fifteen-year-old 'steady' girl.

In New York as well as in Tel Aviv, sexual relations between the girls and boys of street corner groups result in pregnancies from time to time. The consequences are similar in both cities: charges of statutory rape, fatherless children or forced marriages at an age when neither partner is ready to face adult responsibilities.

5 The social environment: society and community

Knowledge of the social environment alerts and sensitizes us to the pressures which predispose the individual, depending on his location in the social structure, to engage in one rather than another form of behaviour. And once we have defined the salient environment of a given individual, our diagnostic framework may be elaborated and refined by weaving in knowledge of intrapsychic, organic, and other relevant factors.

STEIN AND CLOWARD (1958), preface

When we look at the culture of poverty on the local community level, we find poor housing conditions, crowding, gregariousness, but above all a minimum of organization beyond the level of the nuclear and extended family. Occasionally there are informal, temporary groupings or voluntary associations within slums. The existence of neighbourhood gangs which cut across slum settlements represents a considerable advance beyond the zero point of the continuum that I have in mind. Indeed, it is the low level of organization which gives the culture of poverty its marginal and anachronistic quality in our highly complex, specialized, organized society. Most primitive peoples have achieved a higher level of sociocultural organization than our modern urban slum dwellers.

OSCAR LEWIS, (1967), pp. xlii–xliii

A foremost prerequisite for any approach to a social problem is the awareness of the social context, the social environment in which any given problem situation is located, and the readiness to seek to understand the dynamics of the multitude of factors, influences, incentives and impacts which emanate from, and impinge upon, the social environment and the individuals and groups existing within it.

The social environment is more than a source of restraint or deprivation. It is a dynamic complex of forces which participate in the shaping of personality and the determination of behaviour. If we view the individual as being independent of his environment or being set against it, or being what he is despite his environment, we will not be likely to search out and to identify the linkages, the bonds between the individual and the social structure. The social environment is not self-evident and unproblematical; in fact, it is extraordinarily complex and subtle (Stein and Cloward, 1958, p. xv).

We do well to heed this cautioning when trying to understand any aspect of the delinquency phenomenon. In our practical work with delinquent youngsters we deal at every moment with the overt and with the hidden factors of the social environment, and we ourselves as practitioners and observers, as well as our clients are part of it.

The most commonly used and most manageable term for the vast panorama of the social environment is the word 'society'. The term

implies a more or less clearly defined social structure and cultural content when we speak of 'modern society', 'western society', gradually
narrowing down the application of the word to geographic or national
boundaries such as European or American, British or Israeli society.
The term 'society' is also a dynamic, not a static concept.

Society is a system of usages and procedures, of authority and mutual aid, of
many groupings and divisions, of controls of human behaviour and of liberties.
This ever-changing, complex system we call society. It is the web of social relationships. And it is always changing (MacIver and Page, 1962, p. 5).

The term 'society' will be frequently used in this study with regard to
the relationships and attitudes of our youngsters, and it should be understood in this broad, but defined sense. When I speak of the attitudes of
individuals and groups towards societal 'institutions', I mean society's
'established forms of procedure' (MacIver and Page, 1962, p. 15),
including the organisations or agencies charged with the task of enacting
and enforcing these.

Within society, and subject to the sanctions and prohibitions of its
institutions, there are communities with their own traditions and
milieux. Delinquent subcultures and street corner groups exist in and
are, at least in part, the products of communities. The terms 'society'
and 'community' have, to the detriment of clarity, often been used inter-
changeably in the professional literature. One should distinguish between the two concepts and regard the 'community' as a living-together
unit within society consisting of a grouping of individuals and families
who live in close geographic proximity and, to varying degrees, share
cultural traditions and socio-economic conditions. The following definition is a useful one: 'Wherever the members of any group, small or
large, live together in such a way that they share not this or that particular interest, but the basic conditions of a common life, we call that
group a community' (MacIver and Page, p. 15).

In a country like Israel, which, in common with the United States, is
largely populated by immigrant groups from all over the world, many
of whom have transferred their communities intact to their new home,
while others have suffered the shock of seeing their community life
destroyed, it is especially important to be clear about the term 'community', which to many people often represents the old way of life, as
distinct from the term 'society', which represents the new.

Closely related to our concern with the dynamics of the social environment is the concept of 'poverty' which in the polite guises of 'deprivation', 'neglect', 'sub-standard', 'underprivileged' or 'lower-class' crops
up sooner or later whenever juvenile delinquency is discussed. In Israel,
as in the United States and many other countries, the word 'poverty'

often raises controversy, and the reader is entitled to an explanation of the word as it is used in this study.

Carl Frankenstein writes (1959, p. 148): 'With the concept of the "negative social situation" we mean the low standard of living, the deficient learning opportunities, the negative forms of leisure-time activities, and the deterioration of the child-rearing unit.'[1] This sums up a social situation which approaches and includes a state known as 'absolute' poverty, in which people live below the minimum subsistence level. The author's definition also includes some of the characteristics of what has become known as 'relative' poverty. The latter state has been excellently explained in an essay published in the American *Time Magazine* (1965):

People who do not suffer poverty tend to think of it in absolute, merely material-istic terms of Dickensian squalor. In fact, poverty has to be measured relative to the rising standard of living, the tenderer social conscience, the national capacity for creating wealth. Poverty is the condition—and the awareness—of being left behind while, economically, everyone else is marching forward.

This, briefly but adequately, describes the situation in which a considerable number of communities and groups in most countries find themselves today.

[1] Author's translation.

6 Delinquent adaptations and the milieu of the deprived neighbourhood

And so gangs, like most other forms of human association, need to be studied in their peculiar habitat. They spring up spontaneously, but only under favoring conditions and in a definite milieu. The instincts and tendencies that find expression in any specific form of association are no doubt fundamentally human, but it is only under specific conditions that they assume the forms and exhibit the traits that are characteristic of any existing type. And this is true of gangs. It is this that makes them worth studying; it is this that assures us that they are not incorrigible and that they can be controlled.—It is not only true that the habitat makes gangs, but what is of more practical importance, it is the habitat which determines whether or not their activities shall assume those perverse forms in which they become a menace to the community.

ROBERT E. PARK, in Thresher, 1927

The culture of poverty transcends regional, rural-urban and national differences and shows remarkable similarities in family structure, inter-personal relations, time orientation, value systems and spending patterns. These cross-national similarities are examples of independent invention and convergence. They are common adaptations to common problems.

OSCAR LEWIS (1967), p. xl

We cannot always interpret delinquency in the same way in differing social milieux. In trying to understand the meaning of a delinquent act, part at least of the process is to see the behaviour in relation to local norms and neighbourhood traditions.

J. B. MAYS (1965), p. 72

It is a well-established fact that the overwhelming majority of delinquent street corner groups in New York are found in poverty or substandard areas of that city. This seems to be the case also in Tel Aviv.

A British author, D. M. Downes (1966), notes:

The studies of Shaw and McKay, Thrasher, Hewitt and Jenkins, Watterberg and Balistrieri have all established that integrative—as distinct from isolative—patterns of delinquency are more frequent in lower than in upper social levels, and that this tendency becomes more pronounced the lower the socio-economic scale is descended. Popular impression, and both socio-cultural and statistical studies, combine to indicate that gang delinquency is a working-class phenomenon.

It has also been found that the most severe and sustained forms of delinquent behaviour exist in the lower-class environment in the United States (Bloch and Niederhoffer, 1958). That this holds true for the Israeli situation has been affirmed by my own observations, as well as by a recent research study by two Israeli criminologists. These authors conclude that lower-class delinquency appears to be sustained and perpetuated by its enmeshment in a delinquent subculture, while middle-class delinquency is of a more sporadic nature. They further report that lower-class delinquents begin to engage in delinquency at an earlier age and maintain their behaviour patterns for a longer period of time than middle-class youth. The authors found significant differences between lower-class and middle-class youth in the incidence of recidivism, the intensity of delinquent activities and the severity of delinquent acts (Shoham and Hovav, 1964).

It is widely assumed that the urban slum breeds delinquent street corner groups in New York, Tel Aviv, and probably in most modern cities the world over. The milieu of the slum everywhere seems to breathe an atmosphere of deprivation, frustration, distrust and resentment which provides fertile ground for the growth of deviant subcultures that produce delinquent groups of youngsters. The destructive atmosphere of the poverty area is intensified where its inhabitants are surrounded by, and confronted with, the material temptations and rewards of a prosperous society. The sudden onset of prosperity in Israel in recent years (although still not comparable to the high living standards of American society), appear to have increased and sharpened the resentment and discontent of lower-class youth. Cloward and Ohlin's observations (1960, p. 85) regarding the situation in the United States seem to apply to modern Israel: 'Prosperity heightens the aspirations of lower-class young people without appreciably affecting the likelihood of their achieving their goals; hence the discontent with economic position and economic prospects is intensified during prosperous times.'

Granting the differences in size and physical appearance, the atmosphere that pervades the slum areas of New York and Tel Aviv shows a considerable degree of similarity. In both cities, three major types of poverty or substandard areas can be identified:

1. the stable, cohesive lower-class neighbourhood;
2. the disorganised 'slum-in-transition';
3. the mixed neighbourhood of substandard lower-class and middle-class housing.[1]

In the United States it has been observed that different types of underprivileged neighbourhoods favour the emergence of different types of delinquent subcultures expressive of the 'criminal', the 'conflict' and the 'retreatist' adaptations (Cloward and Ohlin, 1960, pp. 20–7, 161–78). While there are some indications that similar distinct types of delinquent subcultural adaptations may be developing in Israel, the three different

[1] See also the description of an East London lower-class neighbourhood which may fit the description of the 'slum in transition' in Willmott (1966), pp. 8–15.

delinquent subcultures are, at present, not as clearly discernible as in New York.

The cohesive lower-class neighbourhood appears in two forms. One is the community whose own traditions and values, while perhaps different from those of the surrounding dominant culture, are not in conflict with societal prescriptions and norms. Chinatown in New York may be an example of such an area. There are similar ones in Tel Aviv. Where a neighbourhood of this kind neither produces nor supports a delinquent subculture, it is of no concern to us here.

Another, perhaps more frequently found, type of the cohesive lower-class neighbourhood is the one in which the community itself is the exponent of deviant norms and supports delinquent norms and behaviour patterns. While there are indications that this kind of community is gradually disappearing in New York, there are still certain neighbourhoods in Lower Manhattan representative of such areas. This type of neighbourhood often has its own adult criminal power structure and favours the emergence of gangs of young thieves and racketeers as a sort of reservoir and apprenticeship programme for the adult criminal groups (Cloward and Ohlin, pp. 161–78). The delinquent street corner groups prevalent here can be described as 'successful thieves' or 'racket' groups who have access to an illegitimate 'opportunity system' (pp. 145–148) that enables them to embark upon criminal careers.[1]

A comparison of the 'successful thieves' or 'racket' groups in Tel Aviv and New York has to take account, at least briefly, of the historical factors involved.

In the United States the racket neighbourhoods seem to have their origin in the immigration waves of the late nineteenth and the early twentieth century, when groups arrived in the large urban areas, bringing with them their own deviant traditions and their own power structures. The close-knit communities these population groups established gradually disappeared as their members found their place in the legitimate socio-economic opportunity system of American society.

In Israel the process seems to have been reversed. Here the early waves of immigrants came as elite groups inspired by ideals which did not tolerate antisocial attitudes and practices, or else, as in the case of some East European and Yemenite groups, brought with them strong social and religious values which they maintained, at times in isolation from, but not in conflict with, the official norms of Israeli society. Only

---

[1] An article by Nora Sayre (1967), 'A riot prevented', gives a vivid account of the successful co-operation of New York City Youth Board Workers with local racketeers in a Brooklyn neighbourhood dominated by a notorious group of gangsters said to be 'cosa Nostra' members, feared, respected and admired by the local street corner youth.

in recent years have immigrant groups arrived which brought with them traditions of distrust and defiance of state authority and deviant sub-cultural values conflicting with the conventional norms.

There are now indications that some initial forms of racket adapta-tions (though on a far smaller and less tightly organised scale than in the United States) are appearing in Tel Aviv and elsewhere in Israel. This development has been observed not exclusively in ethnically or other-wise cohesive neighbourhoods, but also in the disorganised slum and the mixed neighbourhood.

Two examples may serve to illustrate this phenomenon. In a sprawling slum area in Tel Aviv which shows signs of disorganisation but also contains small pockets of tight-knit, cohesive ethnic groups, street club workers came in contact with a street corner group of boys in their late teens, known as the 'B . . . Gang'. (The boys chose their name 'in honour' of a plainclothes police officer B . . . who had been especially active in tracking them down.) This group carried out carefully planned burglaries in Tel Aviv and other parts of the country, using vehicles stolen for that purpose. There are indications that this gang had connections with adult criminals who played a role in organising the crimes, disposing of stolen goods and offering shelter. In the same neighbourhood the street club workers also identified a number of loose-knit street corner groups of the 'unsuccessful thieves' variety, engaging in diffuse aggressive beha-viour, vandalism, petty theft and impulsive stealing of cars for joy-rides.

I observed small groups of youngsters of apparently uniform ethnic background in Tel Aviv who engaged in the cinema-ticket-racket. This racket is perhaps unique and bears describing. Tel Aviv movie houses sell tickets at certain hours in the afternoon and at night. When the movie shown is a major attraction there are usually large numbers of people who are turned away in the evening, and especially on Saturday nights, because seats have been sold out. These disappointed people are frequently approached by youngsters who have a wad of tickets for sale at black market prices. The youngsters I observed arrived in small groups during the afternoon ticket sales. Ignoring the long lines of ticket buyers, the youngsters forced their way in at the head of the line. When people objected, the youngsters formed a protective wedge around one boy. They offered abuse, threats and, in some cases, physical violence to persons who sought to intervene, while the boy in the centre of the group pushed his way up to the ticket office and bought a large number of tickets, to be resold at night. I was told that adults are involved and finance this racket in many cases.[1]

[1] The Tel Aviv Police has recently formed a special 'cinema-ticket-racket squad' (*Jerusalem Post*, 28 October 1964).

The disorganised poverty area or the slum-in-transition is a familiar phenomenon in New York as well as in Tel Aviv. This type of poverty or substandard area is usually found to be in a more or less advanced state of demoralisation. Two main causes for this can be identified. The originally cohesive community structure may have broken down because slum-clearance and relocation programmes, or else a natural process of absorption, have removed the most constructive and socially positive elements from the neighbourhood. In such cases a residue of low-status, hard-to-reach, multiple-problem families remains, leaderless, apathetic and in a state of anomie.

It may also be the case that community cohesion and structure, with its system of shared values and norms, have not developed in the area because a population group lacking common traditions and background has been thrown together arbitrarily or accidentally. This type of poverty area may be the result of policy or expediency in forming artificial neighbourhoods by government or municipal decree. This happens in the case of slum clearance housing projects or, especially in Israel, through the assignment of immigrant families to temporary, makeshift camps.

It has been observed in New York that the disorganised slum tends to favour the emergence of a conflict-oriented delinquent subculture in the form of the fighting gangs (Cloward and Ohlin, 1960, pp. 171–8). These groups of youngsters have received enough publicity and have been the object of sufficient professional interest to make a detailed discussion superfluous. It must, however, be pointed out that fighting gangs, while dominated by conflict norms and values, usually exhibit a secondary pattern of behaviour that is involved in petty thefts, car stealing and other crimes against property.

In the disorganised slums of New York that variety of the 'criminal' delinquent subculture which I call the 'unsuccessful thieves' group is also very much in evidence. In some cases these groups originate in the mores and traditions of a racket subculture which existed in the area before its community structure and system of deviant norms crumbled. The illegitimate opportunity system that existed previously in such areas has ceased to function. The young delinquents engaged in impulsive, badly planned and unskilfully carried out thefts, burglaries and robberies ('muggings', 'rolling' drunks, and homosexuals) that often involve the use of violence. Brawling within the group and with outsiders, the occasional beating of an adult passer-by 'for kicks' are part of the picture. Only on rare occasions do these youngsters engage in organised gang-fighting against other groups.

The disorganised slum-in-transition is a familiar phenomenon in Tel Aviv. Delinquent street corner groups observed in areas of this type fall mainly under the category of the 'unsuccessful thieves' groups. Their behaviour and their attitudes towards their own neighbourhoods and towards conventional society resemble to a remarkable degree the attitudes and behaviour patterns of similar groups in New York.

These youngsters engage in crimes against property in the same haphazard, impulsive manner as their counterparts in New York, and like the latter they are easily and frequently apprehended by the police and brought to punishment. There is, however, a difference in the degree of severity of the delinquent activities. Among the Tel Aviv thieves' groups, robberies that involve the use of violence are the exception, rather than the rule,[1] and brawling, while not unusual, is neither as frequent nor as brutal as some outbreaks I have witnessed in New York.

Weapons are usually not carried by Tel Aviv street corner boys, but street club workers have come across youngsters who habitually carry knives, among these the push-button switch-blades of Italian make which I have seen sold by street vendors in Tel Aviv and Haifa.

Only in a few cases can it be surmised that the thieves' adaptation of street corner groups in Tel Aviv slums-in-transition has its roots in the criminal traditions of one or the other groupings of inhabitants that form the population of the area. In most cases it appears as if the delinquent behaviour, and the norms that institutionalise and support it, constitute a spontaneous reaction of the youngsters to their life-conditions.

No fighting gangs have been observed in the lower-class areas of Tel Aviv and there is reason to believe that no such groups exist here. Behaviour indicative of a latent tendency to adopt conflict norms has, however, been encountered among street corner groups of the 'thieves' adaptation. The following examples may serve to illustrate comparative behaviour of this kind in New York and Tel Aviv. The incidents described took place in areas in which a considerable degree of community disorganisation and disintegration of norms and values could be discerned.

A street corner group of the 'unsuccessful thieves' variety in a Tel Aviv poverty area was involved in the first incident. One of the members of this group returned from an excursion into a slum area in Jaffa (formerly an Arab town which is now part of Tel Aviv) with a slight wound at his throat. He told the street club worker that the wound was caused by a knife thrust received in an altercation with a group of

---

[1] That the use of violence is not unknown among Israeli delinquents has been illustrated by the brutal beating administered to a police officer who attempted to arrest a group of young car thieves in Beer Sheba (*Jerusalem Post*, 4 November 1964).

youngsters who objected to his presence in their neighbourhood. The boy told the worker that he wished to keep the matter secret, because he feared that his group would invade the neighbourhood which was the scene of the attack in order to avenge him. A few days later the boy did mention the incident to other youngsters. The boys of his group expressed great anger and reproached him for not having informed them immediately. They asserted that they would have armed themselves and fought the Jaffa group. On this occasion there was a lot of bragging about previous occasions on which they had 'taught a lesson' to other groups. There was, however, no attempt to take action.

The same group was found in a warring mood on another occasion. When the street club worker arrived at the street corner one evening he noticed that the boys seemed highly agitated and on the verge of leaving the area together. Noticing suspicious bulges under their jackets and shirts, the worker made the youngsters divest themselves of a small arsenal of knives, iron rods and an axe. Questioned, the youngsters admitted that they were on their way to fight Arab youngsters in Jaffa who supposedly had 'pushed around' one of their own group the previous evening at a dance. The worker delayed the boys as long as he could, then accompanied them to the prospective battleground. The group arrived too late for action and spent the rest of the night discussing what they would have done if they had only found 'those punks'. (It is interesting to note here, that I have encountered the somewhat bizarre use of an axe as a weapon on several occasions with two different street corner groups in New York.)

A similar incident took place when I worked with the 'Emperors', a thieves' group on the upper East Side of New York. One of the boys of that group returned bruised and bleeding from an encounter with a group of Puerto Rican boys on the upper West Side. When he told his story there were outbursts of extreme anger and excitement among the boys. Knives and an assortment of blunt instruments were produced, and the group threatened to go across town to fight. It was relatively easy for me to persuade the boys to give up the idea, perhaps mainly because they knew that they wouldn't stand a chance in a neighbourhood teaming with Puerto Rican and Negro fighting gangs.

In contrast to this, an incident that occurred during my work with the 'Commanders', a Puerto Rican fighting gang, produced very different reactions. A boy in this group was assaulted by members of another gang, whose 'turf' he had entered. The 'Commanders' immediately had a meeting to discuss the measures to be taken. The boys told me that they had no desire to 'start a war' and would much rather not fight, but that they had 'no choice', as their code obliged them to avenge a slight to a member of the group. The 'Commanders' were only persuaded with considerable difficulties from engaging in 'warfare', and only after I had arranged for an official mediation meeting between the leaders of the two gangs in the presence of representatives of the New York City Youth Board.

In New York and in Tel Aviv there are neighbourhoods in which lower and middle-class housing is intermingled, often effecting a sort of checkerboard segregation-by-rent-level of lower- and middle-class inhabitants. Fighting gangs as well as street corner groups of the 'unsuccessful thieves' adaptation have been found in such areas in New York.

A street club worker was assigned to a 'mixed' neighbourhood in Tel Aviv for one year. The group served consisted of lower-class boys with a few fringe members of middle-class background. Most of the latter seemed to be cast in the role of 'patsies', rather than be accepted on an equal footing with the other members of the group. One such boy, whose father owns a factory, was constantly victimised in card and billiard games, losing substantial sums of money to other members of the group. He stole a large sum of money entrusted to him in his job at a travelling agency in order to pay his gambling debts.

The members of this group had a delinquent tradition dating back several years, a fact I verified by interviewing 'graduates' of the group serving long sentences in a youth penitentiary near Tel Aviv. The youngsters in this mixed neighbourhood street corner group engaged in boisterous aggressive behaviour, gambling, use of hashish, petty and car thefts and, occasionally, burglaries. Some of the members also had contacts with adult homosexuals from whom they received money. While the lower-class boys which made up the bulk of the group were reinforced by youngsters from adjoining slum areas who participated in their social and delinquent activities, the better-situated boys maintained relations with youngsters in middle-class neighbourhoods and, from time to time, enabled the group to participate in 'classy' parties.

In contrast to groups observed in undiluted poverty areas, where the delinquent youngsters usually refrain from carrying out thefts or burglaries within their own community, we found that some of the crimes against property were carried out by the street corner group described above within their own neighbourhood.

This situation closely resembles one I observed in a similar area in New York. The middle-class inhabitants were the targets of vandalistic, aggressive behaviour, as well as the victims of thefts and burglaries. In both cities the boys' behaviour expressed their resentment and envy of people living in close proximity who were considerably better off. The youngsters exploited the opportunities offered by the presence of middle-class people, to steal marketable valuables from the latters' apartments and cars.

The situation in the mixed neighbourhood is so similar to the picture presented by those areas where a slum sector borders directly upon a middle-class community, that the fact should be elaborated here. In New York as well as in Tel Aviv, I have observed that street corner groups of the 'thieves' adaptation are more aggressive and active in areas in which a well-to-do community lies adjacent to that of the youngsters. In both cities it happens frequently that in such areas a steady stream of complaints about crimes against property and aggressive behaviour is received by the police. These complaints are lodged by the inhabitants of the 'good' neighbourhood, and the culprits are sought, and often tracked down, in the adjoining 'bad' neighbourhood. Numerous comparative incidents can be cited to illustrate the parallels of aggressively expressed resentment of the street corner boys of poverty areas against the inhabitants of an adjacent middle-class community.

In an Upper East Side area in New York a street corner group of the lower-class sector made it a habit to urinate in the elegant and well-kept entrance foyers of the nearby middle-class apartment-buildings. The lower-class boys on several occasions exposed their genitals to women leaving or entering the well-to-do apartment houses, accompanying these gestures with obscene remarks. In some instances men living in the 'better' sector were assaulted and beaten without provocation. The situation in this particular area became so bad, that the middle-class inhabitants hired armed and uniformed private guards to protect them in the evening hours.

In comparable Tel Aviv areas the aggressive behaviour of the youngsters is somewhat milder. Here the younger boys from the lower-class sector make it a habit to vandalise the flower gardens of the privately owned one- or two-family houses of the 'good' neighbourhood and throw stones at the children of the middle-class inhabitants.

In one area the street club worker observed a lower-class street corner group from an adjacent slum loitering at a corner of the 'good' neighbourhood. The boys engaged in loud and boisterous behaviour, abused people who complained, and shouted obscenities at girls and young couples who passed by. In the latter case the young men whose female companions were insulted prudently refrained from answering or objecting in any way. People were observed to cross to the other side of the street in order to avoid the jeering youngsters.

I had occasion to gather some personal experiences of this situation from 'the other side of the fence'. I lived with my family in a new middle-class, high-rental housing project in a suburban area of Tel Aviv. This housing project is inhabited by white-collar workers, businessmen, professionals, army and police officers, etc. Across the main road to Tel Aviv that passes the project there is a sprawling slum, mainly inhabited by Oriental immigrants. Despite the close proximity, the two neighbourhoods are almost completely isolated from each other. The middle-class inhabitants frequently express resentment and suspicion with regard to the lower-class area, which is jocularly referred to as the 'Jungle'. The children of the two adjoining neighbourhoods attend schools in their own areas. Middle-class parents warn their children to keep away from the children of the slum area. The lower-class children have, on occasion, gathered in noisy groups on the well-kept lawns of the middle-class housing project and were chased away by the neighbours. (I attended a tenants' meeting in which it was suggested that 'something be done' to keep these kids away from our area.) The lower-class kids have several times threatened and thrown stones at the middle-class children. The teenagers who gather in groups in the lower-class area and sometimes wander into the middle-class sector are regarded with fear and suspicion.

In New York as in Tel Aviv, an immediate result of this type of situation is that the middle-class population exert pressure on the police to take action. This results in increased police surveillance of the lower-class areas and concerted activities by the police to break up the gangs.

In one of the mixed neighbourhoods in Tel Aviv the police responded to the complaints of the middle-class inhabitants by organising preventive actions aimed at forestalling gang activities at the beginning of every summer for the last few years. The reason given was that an increase in aggressive behaviour and crimes against property was anticipated for the summer months.

In both cities I have also observed incidents of victimising (often quite sadistic) of persons who are considered outsiders in a slum area, mainly shop owners who have their business in the neighbourhood but live elsewhere and/or are members of a different ethnic group.

The youngsters of a Tel Aviv street corner group caused a commotion near a local kiosk (the Israeli version of the American candy store). While the owner's attention was diverted, one of the youngsters removed a large glass jar filled with candy. The boys urinated in the jar, then returned it unobtrusively to its former place. The next move was to send a boy to buy some candy from this particular jar. The ensuing speculations of the kiosk owner and his wife as to how the candy could have 'melted' on a relatively cool day, and the man's attempts to analyse the cause by tasting the stuff with a spoon, provided occasions for merriment for many weeks after the incident and became one of the favourite stories of the group.

The same bored and highly inventive bunch of youngsters dressed up a baby-faced thirteen-year-old boy in girl's clothes and artistically applied heavy make-up to his face. A delegate was then sent to a local shopkeeper, an elderly man who was new to the neighbourhood. He was offered the services of 'nice, very young girl' and responded with ill-advised eagerness, locking up his shop and following his benefactors to a shack where the 'star' of the show awaited him. When the man began to fondle the 'girl', the other boys, who had hidden nearby, set upon him, flailing him with sticks, deriding him for being a 'degenerate' and chasing him down the street, whooping and laughing.

A Greek immigrant who opened a restaurant in a mixed neighbour-hood in New York quickly became the target for a street corner group's anger, although he had made every attempt to be friendly and helpful. The boys descended upon this restaurant night after night, behaving in an extremely noisy and aggressive manner, keeping other customers away. They damaged the furniture, refused to pay for their orders and stole candy and cigarettes from the counter. When the man finally lost his temper and smacked one of the boys, he was beaten severely. The next night the group smashed his store windows and he closed down. The boys' explanation for their behaviour was that the man was a 'foreigner' who had no business in their neighbourhood, that he was a 'rich guy' who was trying to 'make a fortune on us', in short, that he was 'fair game' and 'had it coming to him'.

Three major factors prominent in the social milieu of Tel Aviv's de-prived neighbourhoods seem to bear directly upon the emergence and sustenance of delinquent subcultures. The first of these is the system of lower-class norms and values, or rather the state of tension and anomie within this system, due to the pressures of modern, urban, industrialised society. The second is the ethnic factor, the inherent patterns of belong-ing to a group of the overall population which has, as yet, remained on the fringes of Israel's cultural and economic development and which is therefore subject to feelings of inferiority and of being discriminated against. The third factor is that of immigrant adjustment in a new society, dominated by new and different social and cultural values.

All three factors are so closely interrelated and intermeshed as to be nearly indistinguishable. There is, however, reason to believe that these factors are not unique for Tel Aviv's poverty areas, but follow similar patterns and exert similar influences in many other urban lower-class communities in 'neglected areas' throughout Israel, in New York and other cities of the United States, and in many other countries.

I have stressed the fact of the *lower-class* characteristics of the social milieu of the deprived areas. To sharpen the definition of the term 'class', one may draw upon the three dimensions of 'class', 'status' and 'power' through which Max Weber determined the location of any group in the social hierarchy of society. Weber defined 'class' as 'the individual's life chances in the market-place, his access to material goods and services, his wealth and income'. By the term 'status', he meant 'the individual's ability to exact deference and homage from others'. He defined 'power' in this context as 'the ability of the individual to realise his own will in communal action'.[1] The ratings of the inhabitants of the deprived areas for all three of these dimensions of social class or social position are low. This fact steeply increased the pressures toward deviance impinging upon the youth of the deprived neighbourhoods while, at the same time, making the consequences of a delinquent style of life (the belonging to delinquent subculture) and of delinquent behaviour, immeasurably more severe than these consequences would be for members of a group of higher social standing.

There are important implications for street club work here. Pending far-reaching changes in the social system of our society, the street club worker may become a key figure in the problem situation in which the youngsters find themselves. He will help them to use their own potential and society's resources to the fullest in order to increase their chances for adequate economic conditions—to raise their social status (if only from being feared and held in contempt, to being understood and accepted as they are). He will help them by mediating between them and conventional society and, perhaps most important and most difficult of all, by teaching them to know their rights and to present their legitimate demands in effective constructive ways.

Professor Geis (1965, p. 30) summarising Cloward Ohlin's position, wrote:

Disparity between cultural goals and socially structured opportunities for their achievement creates special problems of adjustment for youthful members of the lower social classes and makes them particularly susceptible to the adoption of nonconformist strategies of achievement. The precise pattern of conformity that is likely to be adopted in any given neighborhood depends chiefly upon the relative accessibility of alternative opportunity structures, illegitimate as well as legitimate. Norms of nonconformity, in other words, reflect the balance of power and the degree of integration between legitimate and illegitimate systems of opportunity.

It seems that it is this disparity between what society says you *can* and *should* be, *what you feel you are condemned to be by circumstance,* which is the most relevant factor in the emergence and the perpetuation of delinquent adaptations rather than, for instance, Walter B. Miller's (1958)

[1] Stein and Cloward (1958), p. 348.—The authors summarise a chapter in Weber (1946), pp. 180-95.

assertion that delinquent gangs are products and expressions of lower-class norms and values, or Albert K. Cohen's (1955) finding that lower-class delinquent behaviour is essentially a function of the youngsters' frustration and feelings of guilt at being unable to behave according to the middle-class values which they have internalised. Both assumptions may hold true for certain segments of the youth population. Both present a partial picture only. Street club work experience indicates that negative as well as positive aspects of the lower-class value system can be found in the dynamics and the value patterns of the delinquent street corner group. There are many youngsters (and adults) who seem to be well aware of middle-class values, assign validity to them and seek to adhere to them. Overshadowing all this there is the dichotomy between the reality of daily life in the slum and the resentment of this reality, the striving for a better, richer (not only in the economic sense) existence. This dichotomy finds its expressions in various ways, in apathy, in deviant evasion and circumvention, in rebellion and in despair. If we assume that these reactions determine the varying degrees of severity and different modes of delinquency among street corner youth, then we must, in our daily practice, be alert to their implications.

Professor Geis (1965, p. 31) summarises Cloward and Ohlin's conclusions as to the genesis of different delinquent subcultural adaptations as follows:

The criminalistic[1] pattern is produced when the organization of the neighborhood affords ready access to criminal and conventional values for individuals. The conflict[2] pattern most readily emerges when conventional and criminal controls are both absent in the neighborhood. Retreatist[3] adaptations are said to occur under neighborhood and familiar conditions where middle-class aspirations are stressed, though not accessible, and where the individual has developed sufficient inner sanctions against the use of illegitimate means or where he is restrained in their use by the external conditions of his environment.

Robert K. Merton (1958b) offered a valuable tool for estimating the adaptation of lower-class persons to the official values of the culture-bearing society (in our case European descent, middle-class society) and to the 'institutionalised means' this society offers for the achievement of the cultural goals. His 'Typology' distinguishes between five different 'modes of individual adaptation':

1. The 'Conformity' adaptation: The individual *accepts* the cultural goals and the institutionalized means leading towards their achievement.

[1] Cloward and Ohlin call it the 'racket' subculture; I find the term 'thieves' adaptation more suitable.
[2] The so-called fighting-gangs.
[3] Drug addicts, according to Cloward and Ohlin. Some patterns of alcohol consumption and homosexual behaviour also fit into this category.

2. The '*Innovation*' adaptation: The individual *accepts* the cultural goals, but *rejects* the means society prescribes to achieve them.

3. The '*Ritualism*' adaptation: *Rejection* of the cultural goals but (meaningless, ritualistic) *acceptance* of the institutionalized means.

4. The '*Retreatism*' adaptation: Both, the goals and the means which society sanctions are *rejected*.

5. The '*Rebellion*' adaptation: The individual *rejects* the prevailing cultural goals and institutionalized means, in fact he rejects the prevailing conventional cultural values, and *substitutes* his own (or his group's) goals and means (p. 253).

Applying this typology to the youngsters in the street corner groups, we find that there are hardly any 'conformists' among them. Very few youngsters who are convinced that they can attain an adequate measure of socio-economic success by studying and working hard, by minding their manners and saving their pennies, hang out at the street corner, brawl, steal cars and get into dozens of other varieties of trouble. There are hardly any 'ritualists' who quietly plod on, working, saving, doing what is expected of them day after day, for the sake of appearances or for the sake of safety and peace, but do not believe that there is a chance to 'make it', that there is any hope for their kind. We sometimes find this kind of person among the fathers of our boys. The youngsters rarely show them much understanding or respect.

At times we find the retreatist at the street corner, the youngster who has long ago given up, or perhaps has never even tried because seeing his father try and fail was enough for him. This youngster dazes himself with drugs, or drinks himself into a stupor. Sometimes he does both together because it works faster that way. More rarely he finds another of his kind and engages in the kind of sexual activity which offers some satisfaction and the illusion of shelter from the world, but which poses no challenge: he becomes a homosexual.

Most of our boys are the 'innovators' and the 'rebels'. These are the youngsters who keep things going at the street corner, the boys who *are* the group. They are the ones who want everything this society has to offer in material things—cars, elegant clothes, transistor radios, 'classy' girls, fancy brand cigarettes, parties, record-players, television sets, the biggest gold wrist watch ever made, and money, lots of money. They *know* they can't get all or any of this the way society says you should. But there are other ways, faster ways, easier and lots more fun. It takes time, sometimes years, before they finally realise that success in crime also means knowhow and skill and a good head for figures and knowing the right people, almost as much as in honest work, perhaps even more so. The others, the rebels, are a different lot, though they often look and act the same. They really don't give a damn about what everyone is shouting from the roof-tops: that you must strive for better things, that you can succeed, have your own apartment, drive your own car, open a checking account, and all through honest labour and a few good connections. Somewhere along the line they stopped believing in all of this. They frankly think that they are being lied to all the time by the adults, the 'rich guys', the police and the social workers. But they too can't live without wanting *something*, without being *somebody* in this world. So they choose other goals and other ways of getting to them. They establish a 'reputation' and the group, the gang is their audience and their mirror. They become 'tough guys', because being tough is their chosen goal. They become the most daring thieves, because achieving the fame of having 'heart' is their goal. They steal the fastest and fanciest cars and drive them as if bent on suicide, they defy the biggest policeman and tell the judge that they don't care if he puts them away for ten years, because these are the means by which *they* reach their goal: to be a big man in their own eyes and in the group, at least for a little while.

Another form of 'typology' based upon Cloward and Ohlin's (1960, pp. 95–7) categories of 'levels of aspiration' may help the street club worker to diagnose the needs and motivation patterns of some of the members of a street corner group and may help him to make the right choice in the wide range of possible approaches to any one individual youngster. Two major criteria are applied here:

1. Aspiration to middle-class social status. This includes the striving toward general social recognition by the 'better' people, socialising in middle-class circles, seeking one's entertainment and recreation in the 'better' areas of the city, having 'classy' girl friends, and actual or pretended interest in the 'higher things', such as music, art, intellectual conversation. There is often an element of contempt for the way of life and the physical environment of one's own community.[1]

2. Aspiration to middle class material rewards. This is much less complex. It means mainly a dominant desire for the trappings of affluence: expensive clothes, a flashy car and other accoutrements of 'gracious living', such as elegant furniture, sophisticated Hi-Fi equipment, the best brand of cigarettes and large amounts of money to spend on oneself and one's friends. Being most comfortable in the company of one's own kind and a certain affection for, even pride in the 'old neighbourhood', are quite compatible with this attitude.

---

[1] Attitudes of youngsters of a London lower-class area towards their own neighbourhood, reflecting different aspiration levels, are discussed in a study by Willmott (1966), pp. 18–19.

The following graph may serve as an illustration:

	Aspiration to middle-class social status	*Aspiration to middle-class material rewards*
I	PLUS	PLUS
II	MINUS	PLUS
III	PLUS	MINUS
IV	MINUS	MINUS

The PLUS and MINUS indicates the striving for, or the indifference to middle-class social status or material rewards respectively.

Seen through the eyes of the street club worker observing his group of delinquent youngsters, the application of this typology may look something like this:

I. That's Georgy alright, a real 'plus-plus' boy, always going places and getting nowhere. He's got the ambition to be somebody, to get out of what he calls 'this stinking dump'. But either he just doesn't have enough on the ball to make it, or the odds have been too heavily against him from the beginning. So he's a very angry boy, and because of that terrific drive, and because he's *got* to get what he wants, the group accepts him as the leader. He's the one with initiative and imagination when it comes to pulling a job where the loot is worth the risk. Maybe he hasn't made it the way he would want it, but he's the big man around here, respected, looked-up to, and he always seems to have some handy cash, a new transistor radio, a pair of twenty dollar shoes on his feet. No use preaching at him about a 50-bucks-a-week job in his old man's working place. 'Might as well be buried alive', he says. But if one could find a way to show him that he can still make it the legitimate way, a job with real prospects, where he can use that drive and talent for leading others. . . . The problem is, where does one find a job like that, and how long is he going to stay out of jail?

Toby is like that too, but different. Always something of an outsider on the fringe of the group. He looks strictly after 'Number one', that boy, and the others don't like him much. Always has a little racket, a little con game going and full of those stories about his 'big-time' connections which nobody believes. It's hard to get to him, break through that fantasy world of dreams of becoming rich and famous one day. Perhaps one should try to get him away from the group altogether, get him into one of those programmes in a Settlement House where he can mix with middle-class kids, join a drama group or something . . .

II. Now Jimbo doesn't put on airs. He's happiest in the local candy store or bar and very popular in the group. Made his 'rep' as a fighter in the neighbourhood. He steals because he's *got* to have things. The main task is to get him a job that pays some money and show him how to save his dough so he can buy what he wants instead of stealing it. Would be good to get him involved in some community project with the local adults. Hope they don't catch him and put him behind bars before anything can be done. If the group stops thieving he will stop too. He wouldn't want to be the 'bad' guy and lose status if his friends go straight.

III. Lou's major aim in life seems to be to get out of the neighbourhood as often as possible and find some 'classy' company. He's got a lot of charm and some-times brings some 'fancy' girls to the hang-out, so the boys like him, despite his affected way of talking. For a while he started to hang out with a 'beat' crowd downtown, but they got bored with him and he came back acting real wild, picking fights and pulling 'crazy' jobs to get back in with the group. Now he's gotten involved with a fairly well-to-do young homosexual who has an elegant flat and drives a Jaguar. I don't think Lou is really queer, but he enjoys the 'sophisticated' crowd he meets there, walks around with *Naked Lunch* in his back pocket, pretending that he reads and understands it, talking about becoming a writer, but not able to put down two straight sentences. When the boys 'sound' him, he instigates fights to show how tough he is. One should make every effort to involve him more in the group's 'legit' activities, like parties, hikes, trips, sports, perhaps put some pressure on to get him into night-school to catch up on his education.

Teddy is another one. Bright and as unstable as they come. Considers himself quite exceptional, is quite convinced that he'll become a musician. He owns a trombone and pawns it from time to time. Fact is, he can't even play the thing. The boy lives in a fantasy world and, for some time now, has sustained his dreams by taking drugs, first marijuana and now he is main-lining heroin. He's been with the group so long, the boys still regard him as one of them. I've tried to get the group to put some pressure on him to stop using drugs, but that didn't work. He let me put him 'inside' for a cure, and he held a job for a while after that, but now he's back where he was. If one could get him to really learn to play an instrument and join a band, even if he continues to take drugs. But he can't sustain the discipline and, anyway, I don't think he really has any talent. IV. 'Minus-minus' seems the best description for Dov. He had me completely fooled in the beginning. A nice kid, friendly, good-natured, easy to get to. For a while I thought we had a real good relationship. He always took my advice eagerly, always 'saw my point', did what he was told. But it's all paper-thin on the surface with Dov, nothing underneath, inside. He's like that with everybody, does anything he's told to do. The boys know it well enough and make him do all kinds of dangerous and filthy things. That boy doesn't seem to care about anything, least of all himself. But there must be something there. One has to keep digging to get it out. He steals, but not because he wants the loot. The others ask him to come along on a job, and so he goes and takes more risks than any of them. He fights like mad when the group is in it with him, is more likely to use a weapon and really hurt somebody than any of the others. When the cops question him, he admits everything with a shrug. Jail, probation, it all doesn't mean a thing to him. He shows no interest in girls, but the boys tell me that at a 'line-up' with the group he's proved himself a regular sexual athlete. And he's not stupid. No great intellect, but definitely not stupid. I've had some quite intelligent talks with him. Nor can I simply get the problem off my back by convincing myself that he is 'crazy', a pathological case. The overwhelming impression is that of complete lack of any ambition, any striving, a sort of utter hopelessness, almost cheerfully accepted. But there must be some way of shaking the boy out of this before it is too late and he spends the rest of his years vegetat-ing in a succession of jail cells. I talked to him about seeing a psychiatrist. He agreed that it couldn't do any harm talking to a 'doctor' but then he avoided me carefully for over a week. I found out quite a bit about his background. It makes your hair stand on end. There's enough reason there to understand why the boy doesn't believe that there's anything to hope or strive for. But a few days ago there was some glimmer of something to build on: I took some of the boys to the Zoo, Dov among them. The boys raised all sorts of hell, but Dov didn't do his bit this time. He was fully absorbed with the animals, seemed to know a lot about them, and, after a while all of us listened to his stories and explanations. I had no idea he knew so much about animals. The next day I brought a friend along who studied zoology. He and Dov hit it off well. Now I am investigating the possibilities of a job with animals. It seems that the Zoo hires boys from time to time. Maybe we're getting somewhere . . .

These are a few random examples of what 'typical' youngsters may mean to the worker in real life. Some of the thumbnail sketches provided above are New York boys, some of them are Tel Aviv street corner kids. A warning is in order: The worker will rarely ever encounter 'pure' types of one or another category. He should never attempt to try to fit his youngsters into slots for the sake of simplicity. Moreover, we deal with adolescents who change and develop under the influence of time and a multitude of other influences. A typology like the one given here may be useful for periodic diagnostic evaluations and for the worker's frequent examination of his own methods and attitudes toward his youngsters, but it should never be rigidly applied. It remains to be added that I, for one, have never encountered a street corner group consisting of youngsters who *all* fit one or the other 'type'. Every type of youngster is represented in most groups, and in many cases the same youngsters combine traits and behaviour patterns of several 'types' or change from one 'typical' picture to another in relatively short periods of time.

It has been pointed out by a number of modern sociologists, that contemporary Western society, the United States in the lead, stresses the success theme for *all* its members, regardless of their background or their location in the social stratification pyramid. The implication of this cultural success goal is that its rewards are available to everyone in more or less equal measure. In reality it seems that the means for the achievement of socio-economic success are rather unevenly distributed, and that those at the top and in the middle ranges of the social pyramid are first in line while those at the bottom have to wait their turn and often find that they have to make do with the leftovers when they reach the tables where society distributes its goods. This formulation appears to apply to Israel today almost as much as it applies to the United States where 'In pulpit and in press, in fiction and in motion pictures, in the course of formal education and of informal socialisation, in the various public and private communications which come to the attention of Americans, there is a comparatively marked emphasis on the moral obligation as well as the factual possibility of striving for monetary success, and of achieving it' (Robert K. Merton, 1958a, p. 542). Under the impact of recent affluence and perhaps in reaction to the austerity and the idealism of the 'time of struggle' only a decade-and-a-half ago, Israel has rapidly changed from the meritocracy of pioneering days, to the values of a prospering middle-class. Here too this value system and its widely accepted goals

lead naturally to the subsidiary theme that success or failure are results wholly of personal qualities; that he who fails has only himself to blame, for the corollary to the concept of the self-made man is the self-unmade man. To the extent that this cultural definition is assimilated by those who have not made their mark, failure represents a double defeat: the manifest defeat of remaining behind in the race for success and the implicit defeat of not having the capacities and moral stamina needed for success. Whatever the objective truth or falsity of the doctrine in any particular instance, and it is important that this cannot be readily discovered, the prevailing definition exacts a psychic toll of these who do not measure up. It is in this cultural setting that, in a significant proportion of cases, the threat of defeat motivates men to the use of those tactics, beyond the law or the mores, which promise 'success' (Merton, 1958a, pp. 542-3).

In the social milieu of the 'deprived' neighbourhood the preconditions for socio-economic failure prevail. Our experience seems to bear out the assumption that the breakdown of values, the anomie which we find dominating this milieu, is at least in part due to the widespread feeling, especially among our youngsters, that people must make a choice between admitting their own worthlessness or denying the validity of all or part of the value system, its goals and its prescribed means to reach these goals. Our observations indicate that the delinquent subcultural adaptations are, to a significant degree, the results of the preferred choice of denying the conventional system rather than the alternative of having to accept a self-image of personal wretchedness.

The feeling of being discriminated against because of ethnic origin is much in evidence among young and old in the poverty areas of New York and Tel Aviv. It is undoubtedly based upon a measure of objective fact. However, one should beware of seeing this reaction, which plays an important role in the etiology of street corner group delinquency, in isolation from the socio-economic factors and the impact of anomic pressures.

A recent investigator wrote: 'The most pressing communal problems in Israel centre on and in the "Oriental" population' (Schwartz, 1965, p. 12). The author adds: 'The proposition need not be belaboured; current statistics and first-hand observations point to this population grouping as experiencing the most severe problems and posing, for the nation, its most grave internal concern.' The socio-economic and the 'ethnic-discrimination' factors of these 'communal problems' seem to be closely intermeshed.

Just as the ethnic problem cannot be artifically isolated from the poverty problem and the social-class factor, so can it not be divorced from the immense complexities of immigrant absorption.

The findings of the Tel Aviv street club project tend to confirm those of the Agranat Committee on Juvenile Delinquency, which examined delinquency patterns thirteen to eleven years ago, from 1951 to 1953. This committee concluded (Shoham, 1962, p. 213):

The process of the social and cultural integration of the oriental immigrant boy is seemingly accompanied by internal and external conflicts which result inter-alia in delinquency. The delinquency proneness of these boys is augmented the more the receiving community[1] refrains from guiding and helping them to find their place in the new society. In that case a boy may develop a feeling that he is being discriminated against; the delinquency proneness therefore increases with the accumulation of real or illusory discrimination and failure experiences with the result that the rate of delinquency of the oriental boy increases the longer his stay in the country. The European boy on the other hand shows a better capacity for adaptation to the environment irrespective of whether the receiving community is fully prepared to assist him in the process of integration or not. The latter is therefore less prone to seek anti-social substitutes of satisfaction and consequently the longer he stays in the country, the less his susceptibility to turning delinquent.

Most of our delinquent street corner boys in Tel Aviv are native-born Israelis of Oriental descent whose parents immigrated after the War of Independence, while some of the youngsters come from families where one or both parents are native-born Israelis.

The Tel Aviv street club workers' experience in observing the social milieu of the deprived areas showed striking similarities to the American phenomenon of immigrant groups who

have faced formidable barriers to legitimate systems of opportunity. They have been relegated to the slums and the lower reaches of the occupational structure. Often for several generations descendants of the immigrants struggled to make some adjustments to the host culture. During this period, marked by acute personal and social disorganization, the young were subjected to acute frustrations stemming from limitations upon legitimate opportunity while they were relatively unrestrained by community controls (Cloward and Ohlin, 1960, p. 194).

Parent-youth conflict and the concomitant breakdown in the traditional values and the authority of the family is a frequently observed phenomenon. It is obviously closely related to the tensions of adjustment to the new and different ways of the society of modern Israel, as well as to socio-economic frustrations. We observed some differences in the impact of parent-youth conflict for boys and girls. Jackson Toby's (1962)

[1] I would substitute the term 'society' for the word 'community' here for the sake of clarity.

findings in American lower-class areas, stating that, while the disrupted family in the deprived area is most likely to produce delinquent boys *and* girls, the well-integrated family in such areas affords *more* protection 'against anti-social influences emanating from the neighborhood or the peer group' to *girls* than to boys is born out by our own experience. We saw that the traditional mores of the Oriental Sephardic family, even in cases where this family's authority has already been seriously challenged by the male offspring, tends to continue to shelter the girls from delinquency-generating influences. One mixed neighbourhood afforded us an example of the relaxation of the traditional restrictions for girls in Oriental-descent families who had lived in Israel for more than one generation, and had achieved a higher degree of adjustment to the new way of life. Here the girls seemed to be more independent and more prone to adopting the style of life of the delinquent subculture.

The Tel Aviv Project was not equipped to evaluate the intrapsychic dynamics of family disruption among the delinquent youngsters of our client group. However, because of the obvious importance of the subject I cite the opinion of a renowned psychoanalyst (Alexander, 1932, p. 146) which seems relevant to this discussion:

If the social situation gives justified reason for discontent and anti-social attitude, the early emotional conflicts are more likely to be worked out on the social level, and the earlier discontent with the family situation together with the social discontent are more apt to lead to non-social behaviour than to neurotic symptom-formation.

Professor Frankenstein (1959, p. 211) wrote:

When we speak of the externalising precipitants of child development, we observe first of all the factor of *poverty*. We have already pointed out . . . that poverty becomes etiologically relevant for the development of the child, not only *inter alia*, but primarily, as the parents' reaction to this condition. Concentration of thoughts and interests upon the missing material pre-conditions of existence, resentments, anxiety, despair as consequences of non-possession, irritability or indolence as further consequences, inadequate relatedness of parents to the child, neglect, lack of affection, thoughtlessness or even hatred for their children—those are the components of the poverty factor with which we are concerned here. It cannot be emphasised often enough that there are also parents who react differently to poverty, parents who react positively. This reaction does not only not restrict the normal development of the child, but, under certain conditions, may further it. The fact that the negative reaction is one of the most important factors in the faulty development of the socially deprived child, must not lead us to conclude that this reaction is the rule. The contrary is the case. How could we otherwise understand that so relatively few children who grow up under socially disadvantageous conditions become delinquent or show other developmental disturbances?[1]

[1] My translation.

All the Tel Aviv poverty areas are, to varying degrees, in a state of community disruption. The constantly and variously expressed concern, anxiety and tension of young and old in these neighbourhoods with regard to their community, its physical conditions, its way of life and its reputation, seems to confirm the assumption that threats to community-belonging and cohesion are among the major factors in the genesis of delinquent subcultures. I fully agree with Cloward and Ohlin's (1960, p. 211) conclusion that the strengthening of the social structure, the creation of a healthier social milieu and the reorganisation of community life in the neglected urban areas is an essential prerequisite for delinquency prevention. The street club worker can and should make an important contribution towards the attainment of this goal.

2 The search for the cause

So far I have attempted a comparative description of the milieu and the dynamics of lower-class delinquent street corner groups in the two biggest cities of one of the largest and one of the smallest nations in the world. One city, Tel Aviv, has approximately four hundred thousand inhabitants, the other city, New York, has a population of over eight million. One country, Israel, has made great strides toward industrialisation and the attainment of adequate living conditions, but is still counted among the 'underdeveloped' areas. The other nation, the United States of America, is the most highly industrialised country in the world, and its population enjoys the world's highest standard of living.

It seems somewhat incongruous to compare a specific phenomenon of social malfunction in these two, at first glance so very different, cities. Yet a comparison of lower-class juvenile delinquency in Tel Aviv and New York leads one to the conclusion that there are more similarities than differences to be observed among street corner groups in the under-privileged areas of both cities, and that the differences appear to be differences in degree, rather than in kind.

The considerable number of similarities in the milieu, the values and beliefs, the norms and the expressive behaviour of street corner groups in Tel Aviv and New York, seem to indicate that, broadly viewed, there may be some common casual factors at work in both cities.

I shall make no attempt to review the voluminous literature which deals with theories of causation of juvenile delinquency.[1] I shall, however, try to point at some of the apparent parallels in what seem to be the most basic causative factors of gang delinquency, common to both cities.

Fyvel (1964), comparing gangs and street corner groups in Great Britain with those in the United States and other countries, writes: 'All

[1] For summaries of theories on juvenile delinquency, see Robison (1960), Wolfgang, Savitz and Johnston (1962), and Berelson and Steiner (1964).

the most painstaking research has not yet really shown us why any one individual boy or girl will become a delinquent.' The observations and impressions offered here will not alter this fact, but it is possible to recognise some indications of what situations and trends in contemporary society favour the emergence of certain kinds of delinquency. The factors discussed in the following pages will be selected from a multitude of possible causes. This selection is not based on any new theoretical approach but reflects my own reactions to present theoretical thinking under the impact of practical experience in working with youngsters of lower-class street corner groups.

The wide array of causative factors and precipitating events which confronts us when we ask the question 'why?', makes it difficult to decide where to begin. More often than not the phenomena we try to look at interact so closely with each other as to be undistinguishable. We are often uncertain what is cause and what is effect, what is the symptom and what the malady. We are not always sure what leads to what, and do not know where to assign priority. Many a time, standing at a street corner in New York or Tel Aviv, watching a bunch of confused, resentful youngsters milling about, I have tried in my mind to trace the path that leads back to the source of all the trouble. I have always felt like a traveller reading a signpost at a crossroads, who finds that he is advised that his destination can be reached either by going north or south, but chances are, that it is located somewhere to the east or west.

But I shall take the plunge and start with the one thing the youngsters of street corner groups in Tel Aviv, New York or any other city have most obviously in common: their age and developmental stage, namely adolescence.

7 The strains of growing up

It seems to me that psychoanalysts are too quick to accept the statement that adolescence creates nothing really new. So Fenichel says: 'All the mental phenomena of puberty may be regarded as attempts to *re*-establish the disturbed equilibrium.' He should have said: to establish a new equilibrium. . . .

F. WITTELS (1955), p. 260

But very many people arrive in preadolescence in the sad state which an adult would describe as 'getting away with murder'. In other words, they have had to develop such remarkable capacities for deceiving and misleading others that they never had a chance to discover what they were really good for. But in this intimate interchange in preadolescence—some preadolescents even have mutual daydreams, spend hours and hours carrying on a sort of spontaneous mythology in which both participate—in this new necessity for thinking of the other fellow as right and for being thought of as right by the other fellow, much of this uncertainty as to the real worth of the personality, and many self-deceptive skills at deceiving others which exist in the juvenile era, may be rectified by the improving communication of the chums and, to a much lesser extent but nonetheless valuably, by confirmatory relations in the collaboration developed in the gang.

PERRY AND GAWEL (1953), p. 251

Aristotle once said that the adolescent is a player who dons one mask after another to see which one he likes best and which one fits best. At the same time, the youngster observes the reactions of others around him. He may even use certain masks to scare his elders. Today's adolescent tests alternative roles of a wide variety and with great rapidity. He senses, as he approaches adulthood, that he will have to make a decision to assume a relatively limited societal role.

W. C. KVARACEUS (1966)

With a few marginal exceptions, the members of street corner groups in Tel Aviv, New York and elsewhere, range in age from thirteen to nineteen. This age group roughly covers the period of adolescence, a period filled with the 'storm and stress' of growing up physically and maturing psychologically.

The fact that we are dealing with adolescents, with youngsters who are immersed in the strains and ambiguities, the mysteries and discoveries, the anxiety and the adventure of growing up, is probably the most important determinant of our successes and failures as social workers and educators in our approaches to youth. (I say advisedly: social workers *and* educators, because I am convinced that we shall always have to be both when we deal with adolescent delinquents.)

Adolescence in Israel and in the United States is not noticeably different in its characteristic psychosocial syndromes and behavioural expressions. This fact alone establishes a basic similarity in the problems of, and the approaches to, youth in both countries.

In both countries I have often found that workers tend to be so preoccupied with the delinquent youngsters' aggressive, aberrant behaviour, that they are apt to forget that they are dealing with adolescents.

I remember a seasoned social worker with over twenty years' experience in community centre work shake her head in astonishment at the antics of the boys and their 'Debs' of a New York fighting gang at a dance given at their club room. The worker turned to me and said: 'You know, it takes something like this to remind us that we are not dealing with hardened criminals, but with mixed-up kids.' Only recently one of the Tel Aviv street club workers told me: 'I never know what to expect with these boys: One moment they act and think like hard-boiled hoodlums, and the next minute they are just children, playing their games of make-believe.'

We are well reminded by Professor Matza (1964, p. 26), who has done some profound thinking on the causes and manifestations of delinquency, that:

Delinquency is after all a legal status and not a person perpetually breaking laws. A delinquent is a youngster who in relative terms more warrants that legal appellation than one who is less delinquent or not at all so. He is a delinquent by and large because the shoe fits, but even so we must never imagine that he wears it very much of the time. Delinquency is a status and delinquents are incumbents who *intermittently* act out a role. When we focus on the incumbents rather than on the status, we find that most are perfectly capable of conventional activity. Thus, delinquents intermittently play both delinquent and conventional roles. They play or act well in both situations. The novice practitioner or researcher is frequently amazed at 'how like other kids' the delinquent can be when he is so inclined.

To which might be added: and when his situation, which includes the adults who exert their influence upon him, allow him to be 'like other kids'.

The former leader of a notorious East Harlem fighting gang whom I met during a research assignment about a year before I came to Israel, put his awareness of this make-believe factor to imaginative and highly original use in his attempts to help groups of street corner kids to have fun and keep out of trouble. He initiated Cowboys-and-Indians and Union-and-Confederacy war games in Central Park, keeping fifty to sixty youngsters, among them several girls, busy with elaborate planning and manufacturing of costumes and toy weapons. The games were so vivd and adventurous, that they provided a highly satisfying and entertaining outlet for the youngsters' energies. The director of the 'friends Neighbourhood Group', a volunteer group sponsored by the American Friends Service Society who did social service work in the neighbourhood, lent additional glamour to these activities by making amateur movies of the picturesque 'raids' and 'battles'. (I was, at the time, vividly reminded of Norman Mailer's half-joking suggestion that medieval jousting tournaments in Central Park be arranged for New York's gang kids.)

Israel, more of necessity than choice, takes juvenile war games more seriously within the frame of GADNA, the voluntary pre-military youth organisation. Because of the serious application and the high degree of discipline required, the majority of our street corner youngsters are not being reached by GADNA. Perhaps a more adventurous, imaginative, exciting programme, devised with the help of street club workers and the leaders of street gangs, would attract the youngsters, channel off the aggressive energies that are often given vent in vandalism and brawling, and make them accessible to the more serious educational programmes of this youth organisation.

In New York I gained the impression that adult society had little use or patience for teenagers, was often somewhat frightened by their rebelliousness and resentful of their non-conformity with adult standards. The adult world seemed to match the ambiguity of the youngsters with their own, by vacillating between treating teenagers as children, and demanding that they comply with the expectations of responsibility and dignity of the grown-ups. It seemed, at times, as if adults regarded adolescence as some sort of mental disorder or physical disease.

The youth movement traditions of Israel, the exalted role that was assigned to youth in the pioneering effort and the defence of the country for many years, tended to imbue adolescence with a measure of dignity and self-confidence. The attitude held is reflected in a statement by the Israeli educator Carl Frankenstein (1953c, p. 253): 'As far as our society is concerned, it may be said that education can, and, indeed, must, make use of the tension inherent in the period of puberty and of the adolescent's readiness to revolt against the values of the past and the older generation, turning their readiness and the vision of the new and the possible implied in it into a creative force.'

This attitude still holds true to some extent with regard to the elite of working class and kibbutz youth and, somewhat less, with regard to middle class youth. But Israeli society has come to resemble American society to a considerable degree during the last decade, and here too the adolescent's 'readiness to revolt against the values of the past' is more likely to be regarded with fear and distrust, than to be welcomed as a vital force.

The diffuse rebelliousness of the adolescent, the striving for independence and adulthood involves our youngsters in many conflicts and forces them to face many hazards. But the 'adolescent crisis', as it has been aptly called, seems to offer a more hopeful prognosis for its successful solution to those youngsters whose socio-economic background provides a cushioning material security, and fairly good chances for adequate adjustment in the cultural and socio-economic opportunity structure of the adult world.

T. R. Fyvel wrote (1964, p. 95):

Adolescence is a time of life when young people feel uncertain and expectant, driven on by urges they do not fully understand; when they feel the need for gregariousness and for places where they can come together informally, to meet the opposite sex, to drift, to experiment, to feel their own way towards adult life, and this without supervision from their elders. Urbanized industrial society is in general deficient in providing such opportunity.

Least of all we find this opportunity in the urban slum, the deprived neighbourhood. Here it is even a major problem to find a safe and healthy place to sit and 'shoot the breeze', or to locate a room in one of the overcrowded apartments where one can invite one's friends and have a party. Here too, the facilities adult society provides, the community centres and youth clubs, are least geared to the milieu, the cultural traditions, and the needs of the youngsters these agencies serve. The planners and the staff of youth service agencies come almost exclusively from the middle class. They find it difficult to understand the values and the needs of the adolescents of their own milieu. More often than not they miss the mark completely when confronted with the sub-cultural traditions and norms of lower-class youth. I have found this to be so in New York as well as in Tel Aviv.

In the wake of prosperity, the waning of the pioneering spirit and increasing security in Israel, there came a reduction in the importance of the youth movement influence and membership. Deputy Minister of Education Aron Yadlin recently told the Council of Youth Movements that only 35,000 of Israel's 250,000 youngsters in the fifteen to eighteen age group belong to youth movements today. An additional 12,000 are members of youth clubs.[1] The great majority of these youngsters come from working-class elite and the middle-class.

In New York, as in Tel Aviv, the adolescent youth of lower-class communities find their opportunity for peer-group socialising, for experimentation, play and adventure at the street corner, more often than not in close proximity to shiftless, maladjusted adults.

The difference between middle- and lower-class youth in the chances to weather the adolescent crisis is not restricted to the reduced opportunities of the latter to work out their problems in a favourable environment. The lower-class adolescent is faced with serious obstacles not only

[1] *Jerusalem Post*, 15 November 1964.

in achieving adult status *per se*, but of securing for himself the access to satisfying, rewarding adult socio-economic status. Cloward and Ohlin's (1960, p. 107) view seems to be valid:

If the problem were simply one of achieving adult status, it would be less severe, for adolescents are well aware that adult status will be accorded them eventually. But improving one's lot in life constitutes more of a problem. We suggest that many lower-class male adolescents experience desperation born of the uncertainty that their position in the economic structure is relatively fixed and immutable—a desperation made all the more poignant by their exposure to a cultural ideology in which failure to orient oneself upwards is regarded as a moral defect and failure to become mobile as proof of it.

Except for the ideological conclave of the kibbuz, the cultural pressures towards material success aspirations appear to be as much in evidence in today's Israel, as in the United States. The frustration of the lower-class adolescent who feels this pressure but sees no chance of meeting its demands is perhaps as great in Tel Aviv as in New York. This is so, despite the fact that unemployment is minimal in Israel, and does not constitute the everpresent threat to which lower-class youth is exposed in the United States.[1]

The lower-class youngster in Tel Aviv is fairly certain he can find a job. However, for many of these youngsters the kinds of jobs they can get are limited to low-status, unskilled, sporadic ones, despite the fact that there is a shortage of skilled labour and trained white-collar workers in Israel.

The reason for this is at least in part to be sought in the lack of educational opportunities for lower-class youth living in poverty areas. To begin with, the home environment and cultural traditions of slum youth neither encourage nor support educational endeavour. Furthermore, the often inadequate and low-level elementary school facilities of underprivileged neighbourhoods do not prepare the youngsters for high school education which, in Israel, is available only to those who can meet the academic eligibility requirements. Although high school fees are graded according to income, and the lowest-income strata are completely exempted from payment, only a small minority of lower-class youngsters of Oriental origin (which constitute the overwhelming majority of the population of poverty areas) pass the high school examinations.[2] A high

---

[1] The situation in Israel has undergone a drastic change since this was written. In March 1967 it was reported that economic recession and government deflationary measures had brought about the enforced idleness of nearly ten per cent of the labour force. I have not changed the text because a return to full employment is to be hoped for within the next few years.

[2] *Jerusalem Post*, 13 November 1964.

school diploma, however, is a prerequisite for a young man's chance to move up the ladder of socio-economic success.

Anyone familiar with the school-drop-out problem in the United States, and with the serious lessening of the chances for desirable employment which faces the American youngster who has not obtained a high school diploma, will see the similiarities in the problems facing the lower-class teenager in Tel Aviv and in New York.

The limitations faced by the Israeli lower-class adolescent because of inadequate education, play so important a role in the adjustment chances of our street corner boys that they require additional explanation: In Israel the law requires every youngster under sixteen years of age to obtain employment through the State Employment Service. This service assigns youngsters to jobs with all possible consideration for the boy's (or girl's) wishes and inclinations. However, the Service determines the youngster's eligibility for certain jobs on the basis of his aptitude and his educational level. The job assignment obliges employers to regard the youngster as an apprentice who must be given every opportunity to learn a trade, including the attendance of courses at designated vocational schools. The pay is geared to the learner status of the youngster, and in some cases employers receive government subsidies to compensate them for the low out-put of beginners.

A considerable number of the members of our lower-class street corner groups have not even finished elementary school (which is compulsory), but have dropped out, or have been debarred as 'unmanageable', before terminating the eighth grade. A number of these boys have, nevertheless, the ambition to enter such trades as, for instance, automechanic, which is considered a relatively high-status one and well paid. The youth employment law, however, automatically disqualifies youngsters who have not graduated from the eighth grade of elementary school from trades which require a certain amount of theoretical studies.

In many cases the youngsters react to this limitation, and the accompanying suggestion that they choose less skilled trades, with anger and frustration. Their failure to realise their ambitions in some cases reinforces their basically negative attitude towards the long and tedious process of learning a trade, or else they find jobs that meet their needs illegally, with employers who are willing to break the law (and there seems to be no shortage of these) in order to avoid work-loss involved in giving the youngster time off to attend courses. Employment Service inspectors periodically check places of employment. Youngsters who are found working without the required credentials (their work-book), have to leave the job and the employer may be fined. The situation lowers the quality of employment and type of employer the youngsters find, and sharply increases their hostility towards authority and their readiness to make illegitimate adaptations.

Another factor must be mentioned here. In the United States the passage from late adolescence to adulthood remains in most cases vague and undefined, except through the acquisition of a steady job and marriage. In Israel adolescence is clearly 'signed off' by the induction of all eighteen-year-old youngsters into the armed forces. Because of the high status of military service and the many educational and vocational opportunities offered by the army, military service actually constitutes for most youngsters the institutionalised entry into adulthood. Lower-class delinquent youngsters have been found to exhibit a highly negative attitude towards military service. Many of them are rejected by the army because of criminal records, physical or mental ineligibility. A considerable number of the older members of our street corner groups succeed in shirking military service by a number of devious devices. These young men are deprived of the accepted *rites de passage* to adult status. In addition, a number of privileges and opportunities for employment are closed to them because they have shirked, or have been disqualified from, military service. Their chances to end their delinquent 'careers' and to make a socially acceptable adjustment are thereby further reduced.

A recent article discussing the findings of a study by Professor J. W. Eaton of Pittsburgh University and of the Tel Aviv Action-Research Project on Delinquent Street Corner Groups provides a somewhat more optimistic picture:

The real test of the army's willingness and ability to undertake a service role and to find opportunities for problematic youngsters, lies in its attitude to youth delinquents. Though it would be quite simple to turn them down, a special committee considers carefully each request for induction, taking into account the recommendations of probation officers, the recruit's social background and his delinquent or criminal record. Only those with very serious offences are not accepted, but the rest are taken into service, in the hope that it will raise their self esteem. The army keeps an eye on these youngsters, observing them over their entire service period, in an effort to find out how they react to their new status as soldiers and how many of them succeed in fulfilling their duties, or revert to committing offences. An experiment with a control group showed that about a third of them stayed in the army without further offences; another third managed to rise in rank as well, while the remainder had to be discharged early for offences or for lack of a minimum standard achievement (Levitas, 1966, p. 19).

8 Lower-class values and delinquent street corner groups

Instead of regarding the working-class delinquent as a deviant in a conformity-promoting society, it is possible to regard the working-class boy as born into a pre-ordained delinquency-promoting situation. Our task can only then be to change that situation, so that the bulk of working-class youth is freed from pressures to deviancy and heavy personal costs.

D. M. DOWNES (1966), p. 260

Searching for causative factors of delinquency in the milieu of the lower-class neighbourhood, one does best to start out by listening to the youngsters who congregate at the street corners. The careful observer will soon become familiar with a number of regularly recurring themes that can be summarised in a few sentences: 'There is nothing to do here' is perhaps the most frequently heard of these—'there is no place to go' is another. Night after night at the street corner one hears: 'I wish I had . . .' (a car, the latest style clothes, a TV set, a transistor radio, a motorbike and money, lots of money to buy all these things). One hears: 'I'm in trouble . . .' and 'I don't care what happens to me',—'you got to be lucky' or 'I never have any luck',—'I tried, but it's no use . . .' (to find a job, to stop gambling, to register for night school, to keep away from unattended cars, to save some money, to stop taking drugs).

There is an all-pervading tone of plaintiveness and helplessness, whenever the talk turns to the adjustments society prescribes, but does not always provide for; an unending chain of 'I-can't, don't-know-how, it's-no-use' is the standard response. From time to time one hears the desperate 'I got to get out of here', or the resigned 'I'll never make it.'

But there are other themes that ring out defiantly: 'I don't care what anybody says,—I don't give a damn', 'I ain't scared of nobody and nothing', 'Nobody can make me do anything', 'I don't care what happens, as long as I get my kicks', and now and then a half doubtful: 'I got my rights', or a half fearful: 'They'll never catch me.'

The tapestry of words and gestures and looks is completed by the laughter and the teasing, the cursing and the obscenities, the exchange of friendly remarks and the trading of insults, the cynical: 'You can't trust any of these guys here', and the proud: 'In our crowd we all stick together and help each other out.'

The picture that confronts us is a complex one, full of contradictions and ambiguities. I have found it to be a surprisingly similar picture in Tel Aviv and in New York.

In the more stable, cohesive lower-class neighbourhoods in both cities I have met with a pronounced ambiguity in the attitude of the youngsters towards their neighbourhood. Time and again I have heard street corner boys in such areas express their resentment and contempt for their living conditions and social background. But these same youngsters become defensive about their community and its inhabitants in the face of criticism from outsiders. I have overheard them speak of their slum with warmth and affection.

The attitude of the youngsters of the disorganised slum and the 'mixed' neighbourhood to their background and environment is almost wholly negative. However, all the street corner groups I have observed in a variety of underprivileged areas in New York and Tel Aviv appear to share and participate in a basic set of values, beliefs and attitudes that seems to constitute a common lower-class culture, a culture that cuts across national and ethnic lines.

This seems astonishing at first. It is easy enough to understand that we find shared basic attitudes and values among the inhabitants of Puerto Rican, Negro, Italian or Irish lower-class groups in New York. They all live in an American city and are exposed to the dominant American culture. The same may hold true for the large variety of different ethnic groups who populate Tel Aviv's slums. But what do the poor of Tel Aviv have in common with the poor of New York?

The answer is a fairly simple one. They have indeed much in common that could provide a basis for cultural similarities; there is the common heritage of poverty with all its age-old traditions, and there is the more recent feeling of isolation and frustration at being excluded from the affluence and prosperity of modern industrial society.

The milieu of the delinquent youth discussed here exhibits the broad characteristics of lower-class culture. In the stable, cohesive underprivileged community, the values of lower-class culture are more firmly rooted and exert a more decisive influence, than in the more frequent disorganised slums or 'mixed' neighbourhoods. It is hardly necessary to reiterate here, that lower-class culture is, like middle-and-upper-class culture in contemporary society, made up of as many negatives as positives. It may, however, be said, that the negative factors of lower-class culture tend to come to the fore, and overshadow the positive factors, with the growing disorganisation and demoralisation of the lower-class community.

Less obvious, and often ignored, is the fact that the negatives as well as the positives of lower-class culture, may become precipitating and reinforcing factors in the formation of delinquent subcultures.

It is easy enough to see how the traditional resentment of state authority, especially the hostility towards the police, which is rooted in the history of the lower classes in many countries, provides fertile ground for the development of delinquent norms. There is little difficulty in accepting the fact that such typical lower-class attitudes as the emphasis on physical toughness and combativeness, the characteristic fatalism the (often justified) readiness to seek the reason for one's troubles in external causes, may help to create and sustain delinquent adaptations.

It is a little more difficult, but essential for the understanding of lower-class delinquents, to recognise the fact that such values as courage, loyalty, solidarity, and such attributes as gregariousness and a ready sense of humour, constitute important ingredients of the delinquent subculture.

The milieu of the slum provides negative and positive lower-class values and norms to varying degrees. I have gained the impression that we find an admixture of the positive and negative lower-class values and attitudes in every delinquent street corner group. In the fighting gangs and 'thieves' groups I have observed in New York and in Tel Aviv, I found a fairly even balance of positives and negatives. However, while a preponderance of negative lower-class attitudes usually makes for a group that is likely to be more unpredictable and harder to 'reach', the dominance of positive values does not necessarily result in less aggressive behaviour or less severe delinquency. The retreatist adaptation is an example of the dominance of certain negative lower-class attitudes. The fighting gangs and the thieves' groups often exhibit a large degree of adherence to positive values and norms.

Lower-class culture does not necessarily cause or explain delinquent subcultures, though it may provide fertile ground for their emergence. While the lower-class milieu is often tolerant of certain forms of delinquency, such as brawling, drinking, gambling, etc. it is only in the most disorganised, demoralised slum that we find the community supportng the more severe forms of deviant behaviour. Lower-class culture is essentially conservative. Lower-class mores often prohibit crimes against property, the use of drugs and sexual deviance as decidedly as the middle-class value system.

In the search for the causes of delinquency we cannot stop at the analysis of lower-class culture *per se*, but have to look for additional factors impinging upon that culture.

When we listen to the youngsters at the street corners of our poverty areas we hear all the manifestations of the lower-class milieu expressed: the tendency to be impulsive, apathy, a penchant for violence, superstition, the clinging to the old and the familiar in preference to 'newfangled' ways, confusion in many areas, rigid opinionatedness, antagonism toward people from other strata of society, immoderation in consumption and seeking pleasure, directness in expression of love and anger, the assignment of responsibilities for one's woes to the outside world, preoccupation with security, fear of any kind of 'trouble', disinterest in national and public issues, preference for informal personal relationships, difficulty in distinguishing between 'personal' and 'functional' roles, ready pity and compassion and ready condemnation and contempt, prejudice, intolerance, rejection of authority, admiration of power and of strong, ruthless leaders, emphasis on personal comfort, a liking for humour, horseplay, ritualistic kidding, the division of people into 'nice guys' or 'right guys' and 'wrong', 'bad' ones, a need for excitement to break the monotony of daily existence, the desire for 'things', gadgets, insistence on immediate, concrete solutions to one's problems, gullibility, distrust of abstract ideas, preference for physical over mental activity, the enjoyment of physical manifestations of emotions, admiration for toughness and endurance, sharp differentiation between masculinity and femininity.[1]

The list is far from complete, but if we ponder each characteristic item, we come to two important conclusions. The first is that all the typical characteristics of lower-class culture, whether they are regarded as negative or positive, are reactions and adaptations to the grim reality the lower classes have had to face for many generations in a society which has always regarded and treated them as second-class, inferior beings. The second conclusion, one that is highly significant for our work with lower-class youth, is that all of these characteristics are manifest in the norms and behaviour patterns of delinquent street corner groups.

The nature of family relations and the degree of family cohesion is determined by cultural tradition as well as by the socio-economic pressures of life on the fringes of a modern urban society. There are marked similarities here between the Oriental slum communities of Tel Aviv and the Puerto Ricans of New York's East Harlem. Similarities with the Negro and while slum populations of New York are not as vivid, but still significant.

In general the family is large and includes three generations living in immediate proximity as well as uncles and aunts, cousins, in-laws, etc. Family life is crowded and noisy, most of the children's and much of the adult's social life takes place on the streets. There is a significant percentage of families in which the father is either absent, or else has ceased to function as the head of the household. This is often regarded as

[1] In the listing of the most striking lower-class cultural characteristics, I have drawn upon my own experience as well as the analysis given by Frank Riessman (1962).

the cause of delinquency and many other evils. We are well reminded by Professor Riessmann (1962):

Many commentators have placed considerable importance on broken homes as the source of emotional instability, mental illness, juvenile delinquency, and the like. The broken home, however, may not, among the deprived, imply family disorganization (nor does it necessarily have the same implications for a deprived child that it might in a middle-class home). To think of the under-privileged family as consisting of father, mother, and children alone is to miss vital aspects of this family today.

Physical punishment, rather than the middle-class scolding, 'talking-it-over' and awarding or withdrawing of parental 'love', is the major disciplinary approach. The dynamics of family relationships seem to be based on patterns of loyalty, obligations and expectations, rather than on great emphasis on love and affection (preponderant in middle-class families), resulting in a certain degree of emotional independence which is often regarded as callousness by middle-class observers.

There is gossip and friction between families in the Tel Aviv slums, but there is also a great readiness to help one another, interest and concern in each other's wellbeing and each other's children and, almost always, courtly hospitality.[1]

Describing East Harlem in New York, Dan Wakefield (1960, p. 19) wrote: 'There are beautiful things that happen here, and also terrible things.' This can also be said of Tel Aviv's slums. There is brutality here, and depravity, but also tenderness and moral strength, often under the most trying conditions.

Shaw and McKay (1962, p. 233) concluded in their study of delinquency in the deprived areas of Chicago that 'delinquency—particularly group delinquency, which constitutes a preponderance of all offences committed by boys and young men—has its roots in the dynamic life of the community'. This certainly holds true for the poverty areas of Tel Aviv and New York, and no one who has worked and lived in them for any length of time will be astonished by this observation. There are also sources of strength and manifestations of courage. Frank Riessman (1962, p. 22) is right to warn us of the profound disrespect implied in attitudes of condescension towards those we came to help:

[1] I once more point at the interesting similarities of the social milieu (*not* of the physical environment) between some of Tel Aviv's Oriental poor neighbourhoods and New York's 'Spanish Harlem'. Aside from the lower-class characteristics shared by most urban poverty areas, there are traits, like the great emphasis on hospitality and a certain dignity, pride and personal warmth which may have their common origin in the Spanish cultural heritage of both population groups. East Harlem's Puerto Ricans, as well as Israel's 'Sephardim', maintain strong traces of this heritage, the former speaking a somewhat adulterated Spanish, while most of the latter still speak Ladino, an ancient form of Spanish intermingled with the impurities of Hebrew and Arabic adopted in the Near East and North Africa.

It is often suggested that we 'accept' them and their culture, that we 'understand' their deficiencies as natural, in light of the difficult environment in which they have grown up. There is in this view a great readiness to assume that the underprivileged capitulate to their environment, until we, the teacher, the psychologist, or the social worker, come along to help them. Of course, there is nothing wrong with wanting to help people, so long as it is recognized that they can and have helped themselves. Patronization enters the picture when we fail to see the endemic efforts of the deprived, no matter how devious, to struggle with their environmental difficulties. Only by overlooking their struggles is it possible to feel sorry for them. If we emphasize their weaknesses it is hard not to be condescending.

In recent years one factor has come more and more into the foreground of the lower-class milieu: the feeling of being isolated, of being excluded and left behind by an increasingly affluent, prosperous society. Modern industrial society, while undoubtedly raising the general living standard and reducing poverty, has also raised the general level of aspirations and expectations, and has thereby increased the 'visibility' of socio-economic inequalities, intensifying and multiplying the frustration and resentment in the lower-class milieu.

This holds true for the United States and, in recent years, for Israel as well. In both countries the dominant (middle-class) values make a virtue of ambition and high aspiration and put a premium upon achievement and success, while implying that failure to live up to these values is either 'sick' or immoral.

In Israel, unlike in the United States, the limitations to the achievement of success goals are, to a considerable degree, set by the political and economic limitations the nation as a whole has to face. If, despite this obvious fact, the lower-class population, and especially lower-class youth here appears to be as frustrated, resentful and vulnerable to the destructive forces of anomie as the poor in the U.S.A., this may be due to two main causes.

First of all, there is an emphatic feeling among slum youth that, within the existing socio-economic situation of the country, it is the middle-class population that sits at the troughs of prosperity, leaving little room for those who, due to their 'inferior' social background, don't 'belong' or can't compete. There is a realistic awareness, that middle-class youth is 'first-in-line' for whatever economic advantages and social status Israel's society has to offer. There is the feeling that Israel is an 'underdeveloped country' only in its lower-class areas, while it has caught up with the rest of the world in the brightly lit, shop-lined main streets, and in the comfortable residential areas of the big cities.

Secondly it appears that, while patriotism and identification with the national goals are still important factors in many segments of Israeli society, these unifying and compensating sentiments do not seem to play a significant role in the deprived neighbourhoods of our cities. I have presented this as a cause, but it may very well be one of the effects of the frustration of poverty and deprivation in our society. However that may be, the feeling remains, that we have failed to a serious degree, to provide a large segment of our youth with the opportunities to feel involved in the national struggle, to perceive themselves as participants in the national purpose, and as contributors to the country's progress.

During the recent crisis which culminated in the six-day war of June, 1967, those street corner boys with delinquency records who were drawn into the nation's war effort, either through military service or civil defence work, are reported to have responded well. Many of the others seem to have regarded the crisis situation as one of added opportunities for joy-riding in stolen cars, for theft and vandalism. There is reason to assume that the great majority of our street corner boys and girls would have offered their services enthusiastically and worked with dedication, had an effort been made to involve them more fully. Even so, it is obvious that Israel cannot rely on the sporadic recurrence of life-or-death crises to remind the youngsters on the fringes of society that they share in the common dangers and the common responsibilities.

9 Ethnic discrimination[1]

By *prejudice* we mean essentially a hostile attitude toward an ethnic group, or a member thereof, as such. . . . By *discrimination* is meant disadvantageous treatment of an ethnic group.

BERELSON AND STEINER (1964), p. 495

A unique situation has arisen in Israel where, despite the absence of any legal discrimination, a minority ethnic group enjoys such power and prestige that it is able to constitute itself as the social and cultural norm and to imbue it with a sense of inferiority the majority ethnic group.

MICHAEL SELZER (1965), p. 14

The Agranat Committee on Juvenile Delinquency which examined the delinquency rates for the years 1951–53 found significantly higher rates of delinquency among Israelis of Oriental origin than among population groups of European descent. The Committee felt that cultural difference factors outweighed the immigrant-adjustment factors in causing this difference between the two major Israeli ethnic divisions (Shoham, 1962, p. 213).

The situation does not seem to have changed significantly during the decade after the Report. The statistics for the year 1961 (Schmelz, 1965) show the following picture:

Adult offenders (including the 16–18 age group):
        16·3 per cent born in Israel (descent not given)
        23·6 per cent born in Western countries
        60·1 per cent born in Afro-Asian countries
Juvenile offenders (9–16 age group):
        39·1 per cent born in Israel (descent not specified)
        11·6 per cent born in Western countries
        49·3 per cent born in Afro-Asian countries

Out of every 100 adult offenders (including 16–18-year-olds) born in Israel, 67·6 were found to be of Afro-Asian descent.
Out of every 100 adult offenders (including 16–18-year-olds) born abroad, 71·7 were found to be of Afro-Asian origin.
Out of every 100 juvenile offenders born in Israel, 77·7 were of Afro-Asian descent.
Out of every 100 juvenile offenders born abroad, 80·9 were found to come from Afro-Asian countries.

It may be argued that much of what has been said so far with regard to the role of the lower-class socio-economic and cultural milieu plays in the emergence of delinquent subcultures, may also be due to discrimination against new immigrant groups of specified ethnic origins. It can

[1] For a detailed discussion of the problem of ethnic discrimination in Britain see *Racial Discrimination*, Research Services Limited, 1967.

certainly be said that in Israel and in the United States the factors of
new immigrant adjustment difficulties, ethnic discrimination and lower-
class deprivation appear in many cases to be indistinguishable from
each other, occur simultaneously in the same population groups, or
overlap in many ways.

Everyone is familiar with the succession of the immigration waves
that gradually built up the multi-ethnic and multi-cultural population
of the United States. We are equally familiar with the phenomena of
discrimination against various ethnic groups in the U.S.A., and with the
'special case' of the rising-to-the-surface, the 'immigration from within',
of the American Negro, and the concomitant struggle against discrimination and prejudice.

To anyone even vaguely familiar with the history of the State of
Israel, it is well known that this country has within a decade-and-a-half
absorbed well over one million new immigrants, more than doubling its
population, and that the great majority of these immigrants are of
Oriental, Asio-African origin.

At first glance the resemblances seem striking, and indeed, many
parallels can be drawn. There are, however, some differences. First of
all, in today's United States, those groups who appear to be most
obviously the objects of discrimination, such as Negroes, Puerto Ricans
and Mexicans, are minority groups. The Oriental population in Israel
constitutes the majority of the inhabitants. A further difference lies in
the fact that, while discrimination in the United States is a public issue
today and is the object of open discussion and political action, ethnic
discrimination in Israel is still largely a sub-rosa issue and, in most
instances, hard to track down or prove.[1] This may be related to the fact
that, while in the United States one can find official and semi-official
attitudes which support discrimination, as well as laws against discriminatory practices and organisations which identify and combat
instances of discrimination, we have in Israel neither official support for
discrimination, nor laws against it, nor organisations who are specifically
set up to deal with it.

Some degree of discrimination against the Oriental ethnic groups
exists in Israel, and plays its role in the emergence and maintenance of
delinquent subcultures. The members of delinquent street corner groups
show a considerable degree of awareness of discrimination and express
their feelings about it in many ways. A brief discussion of ethnic discrimination in Israel seems, therefore, in order.

In contrast to the highly 'visible' discrimination practised against

---

[1] A great step forward in bringing the issue of ethnic discrimination out into the open
was taken with the publication of Michael Selzer's pamphlet *The Outcasts of Israel*, 1965.

certain ethnic groups in the United States, discrimination in Israel appears in more subtle and ambiguous forms. It is easy enough to see and confront instances in which American minority groups are barred from certain educational opportunities or jobs. It is more difficult to identify such instances in Israel, not only because they are, in fact, not as glaring and frequent, but because they are usually vehemently denied and 'explained away' in a hundred, often seemingly valid, ways.[1]

Except in cases of personal prejudice and biased attitudes held by certain population groups (which are universally condemned by official values), discrimination often appears to be motivated, not by irrational bias or vested interests, but caused by the realistic requirements of the state. So, for instance, it has been explained that subsidised language training, adequate housing and good employment opportunities, are more readily available to 'Western' (European and American) immigrants, because these bring with them the skills and knowledge the country needs in order to ensure its economic progress. On the other hand, immigrant groups from Oriental (African and Asian) countries, get 'second-class' treatment, because they are, in fact, used to lower living standards, do not have the educational background that enables them to adjust quickly to the requirements of a relatively advanced society, and lack modern professional skills.

The picture becomes even more complicated, when it is noted that the socio-economic deprivations which are felt to be due to ethnic discrimination, are identical and coincide with the deprivations of the lower-class population.

Michael Selzer (1965, p. 21), summarising the findings of an Israeli sociologist (Antonovsky, 1964), writes on this issue:

The unskilled labourer . . . suffers from extremely low pay, enjoys the least prestige of all occupational groups, derives little inherent satisfaction from his work, tends to have the narrowest horizons, the least self-confidence and sense of control over his life and the least ability to modify his life-fate. His children will also suffer from the same handicaps: the child of a skilled worker or small-scale businessman has a greater chance of upgrading himself into e.g. the professional classes than does the child of an unskilled labourer in becoming a skilled worker. It is for this reason . . . that 'no real advances in integration can be made' whilst ever the concentration of Orientals as unskilled labourers persists.

In the United States there is some evidence that it is considerably

---

[1] See, for instance, the statement by a young Israeli sociologist: 'We shall not propose that ethnic relations in Israel are extremely strained or even that a real potential for serious ethnic strife necessarily exists. Nevertheless, it is our feeling that if we accept Allport's definition of ethnic prejudice as "an antipathy based on a false and inflexible generalization . . . directed towards a group as a whole or towards an individual because he is a member of that group" such prejudice may be quite definitely said to exist in Israel' (Shuval, 1961).

worse to be a lower-class Negro or Puerto Rican, than to be a lower-class Italian or Irishman, that it is not quite as bad to be a 'white' slum dweller as it is to be a 'coloured' one. In Israel this difference, and with it the 'ethnic variable' that determines the degree of deprivation, is difficult to establish. The great majority of the inhabitants of underprivileged neighbourhoods here are of Oriental origin, and most of the scattered European Jews (the Ashkenazim) I have found in Tel Aviv slums, seem to have 'gone native' and become identified with their Oriental neighbours, often adopting their cultural values and behaviour patterns.

In many cases I have found it nearly impossible to establish whether certain manifestations of frustration and resentment among our street corner boys are due primarily to their exposure to ethnic discrimination, or to their dissatisfaction with their socio-economic status. I have often found it difficult to ascertain whether the youngsters' assertions of prejudice and discriminatory practices are reactions to the reality situation, or whether they represent typical projections of blame for one's own conduct.

When a Harlem youngster some years ago, told me sullenly that he grabbed a handful of candy bars and ran from a store, smashing a glass case on his way out, because the 'white' store owner called him a 'nigger', I could assume that there was at least something in the attitude of the merchant that implied the racial epithet and provoked the boy's aggressive act. When a young Oriental (Syrian, Yemenite, Moroccan, Iraqui, etc.) member of a Tel Aviv street corner group tells me that he quit his job because his employer called him a 'black animal' (the Yiddish equivalent of this epithet is used among East European Jews), I cannot be certain that the boy is not rationalising his reluctance or inability to work. In fact, there is a good chance, given the relative rarity of overt expressions of ethnic bias in Israel, that the youngster is doing the same thing other members of his group do when they claim that they steal because the police regard them as thieves, or that they engage in procuring because all the 'rich guys' make their money by dishonest means.

It has also been my impression that the implicit condemnation of poverty that is characteristic of the value system of a dynamic and prospering middle-class, is often understood, and reacted to, as a condemnation of ethnic inferiority. The contemptuous undertone of the 'you people' attitude which is frequently encountered by the lower-class person, may, in most cases mean: 'You people who don't like to work . . .' or: 'You people who don't know how to manage . . .' But the person on the receiving end of this attitude may very well hear: 'You Moroccans (or Yemenites, or Persians or Syrians etc.) . . .' On the whole, I believe that it is easier to hear the latter, because one feels psychologically on safer ground when one reacts with anger to being slighted because of one's ethnic origins, than because of one's alleged personal inadequacies and social failures.

In working with lower-class delinquent street corner groups, one has to be alert to the reality factors that impinge on the lives of these youngsters, as well as to the functions that these factors serve in the emergence and sustenance of the values and norms of the delinquent subculture. In the case of ethnic discrimination, we must face the fact of its existence and destructive influence, as well as take into account the possibility that it is, at least partly, a contributing and reinforcing aspect of the specific milieu of socio-economic and cultural deprivation that is one of the major causative factors of gang delinquency.

The youngsters of street corner groups observed in Tel Aviv, frequently claim that they are the objects of discrimination. This usually takes the form of aggressive verbal attacks against abstract entities, rather than against clearly identified individuals and institutions. The 'Western' population as a whole (the Ashkenazim or 'Vozvozim') are accused of prejudice against Orientals and of receiving preferential treatment in housing and employment. 'Government', which includes all municipal, 'Jewish Agency' and state agencies, the Histadruth (Federation of Trade Unions), the political parties and the Army, is regarded as being solidly in the hands of the 'Western' population groups. The stereotype of the Ashkenazim defines them as being wealthy, powerful, biased against the Oriental ethnic groups and out to exploit and take advantage of the latter.

The expressions of resentment against the dominant Ashkenazi population group are often as vehement as the hostile remarks about 'Whitey' that can be overheard among Negro youth in Harlem. A boy may gain the emphatic support of his group for the remark that 'all the Ashkenazim should be wiped out', another boy may burst out in violent vituperation against the 'Vozvozim' who 'run everything and give all the good jobs to their own people'.

On other occasions the expressions of resentment are milder, but no less hostile. A young youth leader of Oriental ethnic background, working in a GADNA (Military Youth Organisation) club in one of Tel Aviv's poverty areas, was told by some youngsters: 'Thank God they sent someone like you this time, and not one of those damn "Vozvozim".' When a senior probation officer met with one of the street corner groups to discuss with them their views of the probation service, one of the boys told him that, in his opinion, many of the troubles of the boys were caused by the Ashkenazim. (As the official belonged to that population group, the boy was later reproached by the group for having made an inhospitable remark, and for having antagonised an influential and powerful person.)

The youngster's complaints about specific instances of ethnic discrimination, usually involve situations which are sources of frustration for lower-class people in general. One of the major topics, for instance, is the cumbersome bureaucratic procedure and the inefficient, reluctantly offered service the boys and their parents encounter in many offices identified with 'government'. The boys, often correctly, assert that better-dressed, well-spoken and self-assured persons get preferential treatment in such places. The fact that such persons, besides being members of the middle class, are often also Ashkenazim, reinforces the conviction that there is ethnic discrimination at work here.

While open resentment may, at times, rage like a fever in one or other of our street corner groups, and result in the smashed windows of an office, a physical attack upon a 'vozvoz' store owner or the savage verbal abuse of Israeli society as a whole, there is another form of reaction which is characterised by apathy. This apathy seems to be the result of fatalistic, resigned acceptance of the pressure of a stifling combination of ethnic discrimination and socio-economic deprivation. It works like a slow poison, unrecognised and untreated.

The combination of feeling discriminated against on ethnic grounds, and being 'fated' to remain a member of a low-status poverty-group, seems often to lead to a gradual retreat into a geographic and psychological ghetto existence, furthered by the continued living in one of the isolated slums of a big city. We find this apathy, that pervades all facets of the life situation, among certain groups of parents of our youngsters. In some cases the infection seems to have spread to the youngsters themselves.

The symptoms of the apathy adaptation to 'felt' discrimination are not easily detected. Some of the more obvious signs Tel Aviv street club workers have encountered are servility and self-contempt.

My experience in working with lower-class delinquents in the United States and in Israel has left me with the conviction that, in almost all instances, the rebellious, angry youngster, who openly expresses his resentment at discrimination (whether it is, in reality, directed against him as a member of a certain ethnic group, or as a member of an underprivileged social class), is the healthier one. Whether he expresses his resentment by aggressive, abusive, or even criminal behaviour, this type of youngster is one who can be 'reached', who has potentialities to draw upon.

The apathetic youngster is often less troublesome, but he is also often 'unreachable', lost to society. It is the latter type of youngster who is easily recruited into the ranks of drug addicts in the United States.

Some of the 'heavy' hashish smokers I have observed in Israel, seem to indicate that an apathetic adaptation to ethnic and socio-economic discrimination may lead to the emergence of a retreatist delinquent youth subculture in this country as well.

Where ethnic discrimination is a flagrant and acknowledged fact, as in the United States, the street club worker, like all other socially 'up-to-date' people concerned with social problems and social justice, has sought the most direct route towards integration as the only way to reach the goal of equality of education, housing, vocational opportunities, etc. This fight for integration, wholly desirable, but by no means entirely successful in the area of legislation to remove discriminatory barriers of all kinds, has been rather anaemic in the social worker's approach to youngsters and their communities.

Community centres in neighbourhoods which contained a large concentration of Negro and Puerto Rican inhabitants bordering on a white community were proud to state that there was a significant proportion of 'coloured' youngsters among the youth enrolled as members. Of course, the young Negroes or Puerto Ricans who attended the centre's programme were those with 'good potentialities', willing and able to abide by the house rules and most likely to benefit from the use of recreational and educational facilities. But even their presence could rarely be taken for granted.

I recall a staff meeting in which everyone struggled for an answer to the increasingly frequent complaints of white parents who wanted the centre to 'draw a line at their daughters dancing with coloured boys' at the weekly club events.—I listened to the director of an old-established Settlement House in a neighbourhood which had experienced the influx of a large Puerto Rican and Negro population some years previously, explain that the agency's Board of Directors and Executive Committee did not contain a single member of the 'coloured' community, because that community had not yet reached a 'stage of maturity' which enabled it to provide suitable persons to shoulder the great responsibility. 'Suitable' in such cases usually means to be broadminded enough not to regard oneself as representing the interests of one's own ethnic group, but those of the agency, for instance in situations where the ruffled feelings of white parents whose daughters have been endangered by dancing with dark-skinned youngsters must be soothed.

I had opportunity to observe closely a voluntary agency in East Harlem. The exceptionally dedicated and highly motivated staff of this agency worked towards a kind of internal, 'emotional integration' by propagating a 'love-thy-neighbour' attitude which attempted to persuade the Puerto Rican slum dweller to 'learn to understand and to love' the non-resident, white tenement landlords and store owners who exploited the local population ruthlessly and, by their very presence, excluded the local inhabitants from developing their own commercial structure. This agency succeeded in forming close relationships with some of the most intelligent and resourceful youngsters in their immediate neighbourhood. These boys became staunch allies of the agency and used their influence and their talents to help the staff to disseminate its philosophy of 'emotional integration'. Every weekend white boys and girls from the city's high schools and junior colleges were invited to spend a day at the agency to give the local youngsters an opportunity to mingle with white middle-class youth. The Puerto Rican youngsters 'mingled' willingly. But these efforts did not change the reality of the local youngsters' slum existence and all its concomitant frustrations and humiliations in the slightest, nor did they dispel the youngsters' bitterness about ethnic discrimination. One indication of the feebleness of this approach: during these integrated social activities, the staff of the agency spent a good deal of their time in preventing the visiting white girls from getting into intimate situations with the local boys. The white girls were instructed that it was strictly forbidden for them to leave the premises alone in the company of one of the local boys.

Many youth workers have, to a greater or less degree, adopted the integration goals described above. They are often confirmed in their attitudes by the reluctance to condone hostility and to face conflict, which is so prevalent among social workers. But hostility may be a realistic reaction to unfair treatment and adverse conditions, and conflict may be the only way of bringing about change. Moreover, the drive to integrate is all too often motivated by the, perhaps barely conscious, assumption that 'white is right' and 'white is superior', which is just another aspect of the widespread premise that middle-class behaviour and values are superior to lower-class ones. Both assumptions are not false, but irrelevant. They can only serve to rob the ethnic-minority, lower-class youngster of the last vestiges of dignity and lead to further demoralisation and disintegration of the ghetto community.

East Harlem and other areas of its kind in New York, as well as some of the Oriental communities in Tel Aviv, are indeed ghettoes. But, as Professor Eaton (1967) points out in reviewing the historical origin of the American ghettoes: 'Ghettoes were more than barriers to social mobility into the larger world. They were also sources of mutual support . . . Ghettoes . . . have helped every American immigrant group to be upwardly mobile. They could attend schools attuned to their needs. They could acquire political power. And they could struggle, as a block, for a more equitable share of American progress.'

To 'acquire political power', to 'struggle as a block' for the rights and opportunities which the dominant society is withholding, holds out more promise for real integration of ethnic-minority groups, than the long-established practice of creaming off the 'most adjustable' adults and youngsters of the ghetto and granting them the privilege of associating with their white peers, or even admitting them to positions of authority and responsibility in the institutions of the dominant society, thereby depriving their own communities of their leadership and their talents. Fostering and strengthening the ghetto community's pride and dignity and therewith the ability to organise and struggle effectively for better conditions will eventually lead to integration, as these communities confront their society as equals who have something to offer in terms of their own cultural and political contributions, and who cannot be ignored or placated, because they have the power and the determination to demand their rights. Mobilization for Youth's (1961) policy in its approach to ethnic-minority areas was influenced by the recognition of these facts, implied in statements such as:

We must increase the willingness and ability of local residents to participate in the social and political life of their community. Participation by adults in decision-making about matters that affect their interests increases their sense of identification with the community and the larger social order. People who identify with their neighborhood and share common values are more likely to try to control juvenile misbehaviour. A well-integrated community can provide learning experiences for adults which enable them to serve as more adequate models and interpreters of community life for the young (p. 126).

Intergroup tensions are also a barrier to community integration. The vast mixture of peoples in the inner-city area . . . is potentially a source of cultural riches and community strength. Racial and ethnic discrimination, however, reduces it to a source of community tension, which is aggravated by other differences—i.e., the new vs. the old resident, the low vs. the middle-income neighbor. When there is congruence in the difference—as, for example, when the Negro is both new to the area and lower class—tension is increased. Mutual community interests, the common problems of lower-class people, and the common concern for a better life for their children give way to suspicion, isolation, and ultimately teenage violence.

Breaking down the barriers to community integration is conceived to be a central requirement of the Mobilization program: increasing the motivation and the ability of local residents to participate in the social and political life of their community is a major objective. The development of indigenous social organizations is emphasized in this proposal as a way of achieving this goal. Opportunity must be made available to increase the participants' knowledge of what the community (and city) offers and what it needs, as well as of effective action techniques. The dominance of middle-class styles (e.g., the formal nature of the usual community efforts) must be avoided and greater attention given to issues of interest to the lower class; a predominance of lower-class members must be ensured, and leaders actually representative of lower-income groups and influ-

ential in affecting their value systems must be identified and recruited (pp.
131–2).

The street club worker can and must play his part in this effort by
making every possible attempt to channel the energies and talents of his
youngsters into participation in the community's struggle to assert its
cultural heritage and to improve its social relations and to organise for
social and political action. The gang kids, youngsters of the street corner,
be they Negro boys and girls in New York or young Yemenites in Tel
Aviv, have the right to expect of the street club worker that he respects
and furthers their interest in their own background and their own community, or fosters such interest where it lies dormant. The alternative is
the self-contempt and apathy, the aimless frustration and erratic violence which is so prevalent among the youth of the ethnic-minority
ghettoes in our cities. The alternative is the situation described by
Stokeley Carmichael in a speech in Pittsburgh (quoted in Eaton, 1967):
'We [Negroes] don't have a concept of peoplehood. That's because we
beat each other, we fight each other, we cut up each other. This country
has destroyed the concept in us. We see ourselves as a bunch of individuals, plundering on each other, committing violence on each other.'

About a month after the 'Commanders', a Lower East Side Puerto
Rican fighting gang, had obtained their own club room and had 'gone
social', one of their members became embroiled in a fight with another
Puerto Rican group, the 'Matadors' who ruled the street corner a few
blocks away. Knives were drawn during the incident and Al, one of the
'Commanders' cut one of the 'Matador' boys slightly. I had a talk with
the 'Commanders' about the matter and warned them that they stood
to lose the club room and would jeopardise the considerable gains they
had made if they returned to gang fighting. The boys agreed unani-
mously that they didn't want to go back to their old ways, and Al was
given a severe dressing-down for 'getting the group in trouble'. But then
the 'Matadors', who had a Youth Board Worker attached to them, sent
a message that they were 'calling it on' and would not be satisfied until
the injury to one of their members had been avenged. The leaders of my
group told me that there was nothing they could do, but fight. The 'code'
demanded it. During the next few days the situation became more and
more tense. The knives which had been left at home at my request
weighed down pockets again, I overheard remarks about all kinds of
lethal instruments and emissaries from a Negro group whose members
had attended the opening dance of our club came to offer their services
as 'allies'. It felt like a scaled-down version of Central Europe in August
1939.

I asked the 'Matadors' Youth Board worker to come and meet with us. He came, he was received politely, but could not hold out much hope of restraining his group of youngsters. I asked for a personal meeting with the Youth Board worker and his supervisor at my agency. They came and brought two plainclothes police officers with them, so that I had to refuse to discuss the matter. Finally, after the first light sparring incidents between individual boys from both groups had occurred, the Youth Board agreed to the traditional 'Mediation Meeting' in its area office. Each group sent its 'President' accompanied by two lieutenants.

Both groups arrived at different times, so that they wouldn't meet at the door where a 'sounding' word or a 'bad' look might spark off a fight. The Youth Board worker and his supervisor searched my boys for weapons while I did the same with his youngsters, then the two negotiating parties sat down facing each other across an extraordinarily large and heavy table which kept the two groups at some distance.

The six boys staring at each other coldly across the table were between sixteen and nineteen years old. All of them were Puerto Ricans, 'gang kids', delinquents well known to the police. They had the same history and the same prospects, the same quick-flaring temper and the same playful charm and warm-hearted generosity, the same easily offended pride, the same fears and bitter frustrations. They, the sixty or so youngsters they represented, their parents and neighbours, altogether several hundred families, were regarded as intruders in a white neighbourhood. They were feared and hated and treated with contempt. They knew each other since infancy. Some of them had been in jail together. Both groups, and several others like them, had fought bloody battles only a year before when the large and powerful Italian street gangs of the neighbourhood tried to show them who was boss around there.

The Youth Board man, regarded as having some expertise in settling gang fights, opened the meeting. The boys were told that no introductions were necessary, as the representatives of both groups knew each other. First item on the agenda: There has been a knifing of a member of the 'Matadors' by a member of the 'Commanders'. We have to find out who started the fight, what was the cause, who was the first to draw a knife, etc. Within seconds the boys were glaring and shaking accusing fingers at each other across the table. About a minute of heated debate on 'Who started it?' and they were across the table and challenging each other to 'have it out right now'. I stopped them by yelling at them furiously to sit down, deliberately calling them 'Spics', the contemptuous term for Puerto Rican which is most likely to get any one of these youngsters fighting mad. When the word rang out the boys froze and six pairs of very cold and angry eyes stared at me. I told them: 'Yes, I said "Spics". You don't like that word and everything it means, do you? But you hear it all the time. An what does it mean? I'll tell you what it means. It means that you've got other things to think about than defending your honour by putting each other in hospital. There's plenty of need for you to defend your honour around here for all of you, every day. There's plenty to fight for, for all of you, and I don't have to tell you. You know it. If you don't have sense enough to understand that you have all the reason in the world to stick together and show some pride in who you are, all of you, that you need each other—well, go ahead then and break each other's skulls. I'm sure there are plenty of people who'll get a great big kick out of seeing you mess each other up, and the cops will be glad to take care of you when it's all over.'

I was angry and over dramatic, but the six boys listened and looked at me and at each other silently. I said: 'Now let's start all over again. Sit down and let's have some introductions. Each one of you stand up when you're called on and tell the others your name.' They did that and grinned at each other, because they knew each other's names all too well. When that was over I said: 'And now let's forget about who started what and who did what to whom. Let's just hear an answer to one question: Do you want to walk out of here and tell your men that it's your decision that some more Spanish boys have to get beaten and stomped and stabbed in this neighbourhood, or do you want to tell them that there are more important things for you to do for all of you together?' Three minutes later the six boys walked out together. Frankie, the President of the 'Commanders' and Gonzo, the 'Matador's' chief had their arms around each other's shoulders. We all spent the rest of the evening over pizzas and Coke at a nearby cafe. The 'Matadors' were frequent and welcome guests at the 'Commanders' club after that. The possibility of a fight between them never came up again.

10 Immigrant absorption

Underlying all that may be said about conditions in this country is the fact that ours is a differentiated, and to a large extent stratified, society. This means that employment opportunities, the quality of housing, the size of school classes, the convenience of school buildings, the leisure to devote time to getting things done in the community, may be differentially distributed in an English town. There are areas in our towns where the provision of many of these facilities is below the average. Here live populations who have for generations had less than their share of the good things of life which others take for granted, and who have been unable to organise themselves for the common betterment. It is into areas such as these that many, though not all, immigrants come in the first instance. They thus find themselves entering communities already overwhelmed by economic and social forces which they cannot control. Others come into areas where this possibility is a very real fear. In these areas, immigrants and existing inhabitants share a common difficulty in benefiting from the opportunities for development which the Welfare State is intended to afford.

YOUTH SERVICE DEVELOPMENT COUNCIL (1967), p. 6

Since the [1948] war . . . conditions of absorption have changed to a very large extent owing to: (1) the tempo of immigration and the decreasing ratio of the existing population to newcomers; (2) the difficult postwar economic situation, the relative unproductivity of the immigrants during their first years in Israel, and the lack of proportionate capital investment, all of which tend to lower the standard of living and to increase the feeling of insecurity and anxiety; (3) the growing bureaucratization of the social structure of the new State with the concomitant widening of social distances.

S. N. EISENSTADT (1953), p. 54

Israel and the United States have faced the complex problems of the absorption of large and numerous groups of new immigrants. With all due respect to the enormous quantitative differences involved, it seems that in both countries the adjustment difficulties of new immigrant groups from a variety of different cultural backgrounds have decisively influenced the emergence of deviant adaptations and delinquent sub-cultures among certain population groups.

In the United States the process of absorbing waves of newcomers from many parts of the globe has spread over two centuries. In Israel this process has, so far, been going on for only a few decades.

In both countries the early immigration groups have played a major role in shaping and directing the destiny of the society and in determining its dominant culture and values. In both countries each successive wave of immigrants has had to compete to some extent with the preceding and already established groups, and to struggle for its place in the socio-economic structure and the cultural life.

The vast resources and potential of the United States have, until this day, assured each immigration wave its 'place in the sun', except for relatively small, unabsorbed remnants forming islands of poverty in urban slums and certain rural poverty areas. Only in recent years have we seen indications of the waning of the absorption capacities of the U.S. (due to a variety of factors that need not be discussed here), and the most recent large groups of immigrants have encountered considerable difficulties in adjusting to their new environment and have remained unabsorbed. There is reason to assume that delinquency rates are especially high among the above mentioned hard-core poverty remnants of earlier immigrant groups, and among those more recent immigrant groups (as, for instance, the Puerto Ricans) who have remained on the fringes of American society.

Israel's resources are much more limited than those of the United States, and the process of immigrant absorption in this country has been subject to severe economic and political pressures. Although, here too, small remnants of hard-core poverty segments of early immigrant groups can be found, the main challenge to the country's absorption capacities has come from the disproportionately large Oriental immigration from Asian and African countries that took place during the last two decades. While the majority of Israel's European immigrants brought with them either some material means, or educational and vocational skills, and therefore quickly fell in step with the country's rapid pace of industrial development and urbanisation, the Oriental immigrants were largely destitute and unprepared for the requirements of a modern society. Of no less importance is the fact, that the recent European immigrant groups came from the same cultural background as the 'old-timers', and could, therefore, adjust with relative ease to the values and the culture that had become dominant in Israeli society. The Oriental immigrants in most cases brought with them traditions and a way of life radically different from that of established society. Their adjustment became consequently all the more difficult.

Already in 1953, five years after the establishment of the State of Israel, Carl Frankenstein (1953b, p. 13) wrote:

Neither the Zionist ideals of the earlier settlers nor the identification of the younger generation with an anticipated future could be adequately translated to the new immigrants (most of whom had little if any attachment to the reality and the idea of Israel), or be transformed into elements of a binding canon of evaluation and behaviour. But the greater the quantitive disparity that developed between old-timers and newcomers, the more urgent grew the need for the formation and formulation of a canon of social and moral behaviour equally binding for all.

This need for a unity of values still exists today. Perhaps more so than

ever because in recent years, under the impact of urbanisation and prosperity, a certain corrosion of the old ideals and values of the early
pioneering society has set in. The growing anomie and social isolation
among significantly large parts of the population has been helped along
by 'a most unfortunate tendency on the part of the old-timers to interpret
their functions as absorbers in terms of their own, unrelated life experience and value system' (Frankenstein 1953a, p. 14). The masses of
'Oriental' immigrants especially have borne the brunt of what Professor
Frankenstein (ibid) described as 'inadequate, aggressive evaluations (by
the old-timer population) and . . . a lack of readiness to understand
the newcomers on the basis of *their* personal and cultural background'
(p. 15). The same author states:

The complex anonymity and impersonality of bureaucratic machinery and of
bureaucratic thinking on the one hand, and the tendency towards rigid and
aggressive evaluations of everything that is 'different' on the other, inevitably
result in strengthening the force and the determining power of the cultural patterns in which the new immigrant has been reared and thus decrease his ability
and readiness to adjust.

This last statement especially, seems to point at the parallels of the
factors impinging upon the adjustment processes of the Israeli Oriental
immigrant and, for instance, the Puerto Rican population in New York.
In both cases one of the results appears to be a high degree of delinquency among the youth of these population groups, and the emergence
of deviant subcultures. The failure to absorb immigrant groups of
different ethnocultural background into the dominant culture and the
failure of the dominant culture to devise ways and means to meet the
needs of the newcomers, must be regarded as one of the contributing
factors to the emergence of lower-class delinquent adaptations.

The great majority of the approximately 200 members of delinquent
street corner groups with whom the Tel Aviv Street Club Project maintained contact over a period of three years, were the sons of Oriental
immigrants, but born in Israel. This seems to bear out Dr Shumsky's
(1955, p. 55) prediction that: 'The adjustment of second-generation
Orientals will be not smoother, but on the contrary—even more difficult
—than that of their parents.'

Cloward and Ohlin (1960, p. 194) point out the relations between
different types of delinquent adaptations, and stages in the absorption
and assimilation of immigrant groups. The authors relate three stages of
immigrant absorption to two types of delinquent behaviour of lower-
class youth. During the first, the 'arrival' stage:

Most immigrant groups have faced formidable barriers to legitimate systems of opportunity. They have been relegated to the slums and the lower reaches of the occupational structure. Often for several generations, descendants of the immigrants struggled to make some adjustment to the host culture. During this period, marked by acute personal and social disorganization, the young were subjected to acute frustrations stemming from limitations upon legitimate opportunity while they were relatively unrestrained by community controls.

This statement is based upon the observation of the American scene. It can, however, be applied word for word to the masses of newcomers, especially those from Afro-Asian countries, who arrived in Israel since the end of World War II.

Cloward and Ohlin observe that, having few other means of gaining status or satisfying outlets to their frustrations, the youth of the new immigrant groups turned to gang-fighting as a means to gain both. (A vivid account of the gang-fighting of late nineteenth- and early twentieth-century New York can be found in Asbury (1927).)

In Israel the youth of the new immigrants' slums and shackvilles did not follow this pattern. There was no emergence of organised fighting gangs in the big cities. Even vandalism and thieving among the youngsters were neither widespread nor severe during the early years of mass immigration. This seems to have been mainly due to the restraints imposed upon the newcomers by the crisis situation of political and military strife prevailing in the country in those years. In the years immediately following the Arab-Jewish War of 1948–49 there was an increase in violence and destructive behaviour, especially among newly arrived groups of North African youth. However, here too we did not witness the emergence of organised fighting gangs like those of New York and other large American cities.

Cloward and Ohlin (1960, p. 194) describe the second stage of immigrant absorption, during which the newcomers communities in the U.S. gained in organisational structure and political power. Due to the, perhaps specifically American, phenomenon of organised crime and the political machine co-operating to assimilate and integrate new immigrant groups in the host society, a 'racket' culture developed in the newcomer communities which provided an illegitimate opportunity system for the youngsters of the street corner groups. A network of adult criminal contact became available, and there were numerous opportunities for the alert youngster to learn the necessary skills and modes of operation, so as to enter upon a 'successful' criminal career. As a result, this stage of immigrant assimilation in the United States saw the emergence of the 'criminal' subculture in which teenage street corner groups served as apprenticeship settings for the rackets.

Although political corruption is not unknown in Israel, there seem to be no established patterns of co-operation between criminal elements and the political machine here. There are indications that rudimentary forms of racket adaptations may be developing among the street corner youth of some of our urban slums. In all cases where we have observed such developments in Tel Aviv, mainly with regard to the cinema ticket racket, pandering and prostitution, or hashish selling, there seem to be contacts with adults. However, I have found no evidence that this possible emergence of a 'criminal' delinquent subculture here can be regarded as a stage in the process of immigrant absorption, comparable to the American developments.

The early immigration waves, consisting mainly of Russian, East European and German Jews, had to face the 'formidable barriers' of the new arrival in a hostile environment in what was then Palestine, but could and did channel their combativeness into the struggle for ideological, economic and political stability. Their second stage of adjustment to the new country consisted of a conscious bid for power by political and military means. Throughout, the youth of these immigrant groups participated in, and was indeed in the forefront of, this struggle. There was no adult criminality or juvenile delinquency of statistical significance. The largely European (Ashkenazi) immigrants of those early years today constitute the host society of Israel, and form the major part of the middle and high income strata of the population. Later immigrant groups from Europe and North and South America came from a cultural background that closely resembled that of the old-timer population. These groups, after weathering the first adjustment difficulties, found it relatively easy to assimilate. The majority of these newcomers quickly moved into the stable working-class and into the middle-class sectors of Israeli society.

The story of the large groups of Oriental immigrants is a very different one. Coming from cultural milieu and traditions that differ widely from those of the host culture, and bringing with them very little in material means or skills, they found it, in many instances, extremely difficult to gain access to the legitimate opportunity structure. A significant percentage of these immigrant groups from Asia and Africa have not yet reached anything comparable to the second stage of adjustment. Many of their communities continue to live the marginal, pariah existence they led in their countries of origin. Those who were successful in their attempts to become assimilated to the socio-economic and political life of the country, moved out of the poverty areas, leaving behind them leaderless, disorganised communities. In most cases such communities lack the organisational structure and cohesion to offer even an illegitimate opportunity system in the form of organised crime. The 'unsuccessful thieves' adaptation is the prevalent one among the delinquent street corner groups of these areas.

The third stage of assimilation (or rather of the failure to assimilate) listed by Cloward and Ohlin, is that of 'progressive deterioration and disorganisation', the situation in which many of Israel's Oriental immigrant groups find themselves today. Speaking of the American scene, the authors predict that this stage, comparable in its frustrations and anxieties to that of the first, 'new arrival' phase, will result in a return to violence and the return to the 'conflict' adaptation as the dominant form of juvenile delinquency in lower-class areas (Cloward and Ohlin 1960, pp. 195–8).

As has already been mentioned elsewhere in this study, there are indications that violent behaviour among our street corner groups is increasing, and that some groups observed in Tel Aviv, are exhibiting some of the characteristics of the 'conflict' adaptation. It remains to be seen whether this is a passing fad, perhaps inspired by certain products of the film industries, or whether Israel will follow the American pattern.

In view of the street corner group delinquency in 'mixed' neighbourhoods which has already been discussed, it may be relevant to compare one other important aspect of immigrant absorption in Tel Aviv and New York, namely slum-clearance.

I shall once more quote Cloward and Ohlin (1960, p. 209), who speak of

the demoralizing effect of the massive slum clearance programs which have recently been undertaken in many large urban areas. Most low-income housing programs destroy whatever vestiges of social organization remain in the slum community, in part because they fail to give priority in reoccupancy to site tenants. As a result, traditional residents are displaced and dispersed to other areas of the city, while persons who are strangers to one another are assembled in the housing project. Thus the residents of the housing project find themselves in a community that is not only new and alien but lacking in patterns of social organization to which they may link themselves and through which they might develop a stake in community life.

I have had occasion to observe the destructive influence of the depersonalised and de-communised low-income housing projects during my work with street corner groups in New York. In Tel Aviv there are already strong indications that hastily and arbitrarily carried out relocation and rehousing of the inhabitants of lower-class newcomer or second generation immigrant communities tend to increase rather than reduce social conflict and heighten the tension and the frustration of the youngsters.

In Tel Aviv and in New York I have heard boys and girls from relocated families speak with resentment of their new homes, though in most cases there is little doubt that the dwellings they had left were greatly inferior to those to which they had been moved.

The key to this lies, perhaps, in the fact that these youngsters feel that they 'are being moved' without having much choice or say-so in the matter. The process of relocation is experienced as a process of dislocation, mainly because, in many cases, it is not accompanied by the socio-economic and cultural absorption into established society. Many of the youngsters and their families prefer to stay in the relative safety and familiarity of their slum, rather than to move to new, 'exposed', unfamiliar surroundings.

I remember hearing New York youngsters complain about the impersonal (they called it 'inhuman') attitude of the big stores in their neighbourhoods, where one could not hang around to 'shoot the breeze', and where credit was neither asked nor given. I have heard the youngsters complain of the many 'don't-step-on-the-grass' rules and regulations imposed on them without their agreement, hemming them in uncomfortably. I have heard the very same complaints from street corner boys and girls in Tel Aviv. In both cities slum inhabitants have actually rejected better housing because their cultural traditions were not considered and because their own wishes and preferences are not even discussed with them. The attitude of 'you should be grateful for what you are given', so often encountered by the 'objects' of slum clearance programmes, is often met with resentment and defiance. I have frequently noticed that relocated youngsters fail to adjust to their new neighbourhood and are not drawn to the existing recreational and community centre facilities in their new areas. These youngsters travel long distances to reach their old neighbourhood as that they can continue to 'hang out' with their old crowd.

11 Parents and youth in conflict

Most of the boys I've talked to in the Mental Health Service during the past five years feel that their mothers are capable. Also hostile and unpredictable. What they think of their fathers is often unprintable. One of the things that has impressed me over the past years is the contempt and hatred delinquent boys have for their fathers. 'My father is a nobody', says one boy.

M. RITTWAGEN (1959), p. 160

The younger generation, finding the ways of their parents despised in the larger community into which their schooling, their work and their play initiate them, often revolt from the family traditions and reject the family and neighborhood controls. This is notably the case among some of the ethnic groups in the large cities, such as the Italians and Puerto Ricans (though not the Chinese), but is also found in certain rural immigrant groups, such as the Poles in the Connecticut Valley. A state of disorganization of this kind is evidenced by the prevalence of delinquency and by the growth of substitute social control agencies in the form of gangs in some of the second-generation groups. The child of the immigrant has a difficult task of accommodation to a total social environment containing the diverse and sometimes conflicting mores of family and community. He must build for himself a new pattern of life.

MACIVER AND PAGE (1962), pp. 130–1

Even the most cursory study of delinquent street corner groups would be remiss in its appointed tasks, if it failed to take into account the tensions that exist between parents and youngsters. These tensions may, in certain circumstances, become important contributing factors in the emergence of delinquent adaptations.

Adolescence is a developmental stage in which the normal bid for independence and autonomy inevitably leads to a certain amount of conflict with the values and the authority of the parents. The adolescent peer group, whether it appears in the form of an athletic club, a high-school friendship group, a political youth organisation, or a delinquent street corner group, is one of the most important substitutes for the childhood security of the family setting. The peer group provides the testing ground for the first steps towards adulthood, and the laboratory for the various experiments with new values and patterns of behaviour.

It is a well-known fact that, throughout western society, the parent-youth conflict of adolescence may result in delinquent phases and episodes which the peer group tolerates, or to which it lends support. It seems, however, that the special tensions and frustrations of the lower-class milieu are most likely to provide the additional precipitating factors that lead to the formation of subcultural adaptations with pronounced delinquent behaviour patterns, perpetuated and sustained by delinquent norms and values.

Within the normal range of ambiguous attitudes towards the parents which can be observed among adolescents, the negative evaluations of the older generation, ranging from patronising pity and estrangement to open contempt, appear to be emphasised and reinforced among lower-class adolescents by a number of socio-economic and cultural factors.

Perhaps the most important of these factors may be sought in the youngsters'culture-induced material and status aspirations, and their awareness of the severe limitations set by circumstances to the realisation of their goals. Oscar Handlin (1958, p. 102) described this phenomenon some years ago, speaking of lower-class gang-boys who had learned that 'the end was to get ahead, to make good, to strive so that success might come. They must not repeat the errors of their fathers who had not made good, had not gotten ahead. The consequences of failure were everywhere apparent about them.' I have only on rare occasions encountered a youngster in a lower-class delinquent street corner group who spoke with pride and affection of his father, except in those instances where the parent provided a role model for antisocial, criminal behaviour.

I vividly remember Freddy, a member of the 'Emperors' who described his father as a 'no-good bum'. There were murmurs and nods of agreement among his friends of the street corner group, when Freddy said: 'Man, I'll have some fun robbing and getting what I want. That's better than to be like my old man. Living like he does, it's better to be dead.' It came as somewhat of a shock to me when I met Freddy's father, and found that he was an elderly German immigrant who had worked diligently for twenty years at the same job in a factory first as an unskilled, then as a semiskilled labourer. Freddy's father was proud that he had managed to bring up five children without ever becoming a welfare case. In the eyes of his children he was a dismal failure. He had 'gotten nowhere'. He hadn't 'made it'. There were many like him in the neighbourhood.

Only very few of the street corner boys I met in Tel Aviv like to speak of their parents. Questions concerning the fathers, more often than not, cause embarrassment. Here, as in New York, the prospect of following in the footsteps of the older generations is a threatening spectre from which the slum youngsters draw back in fear. Yet it is an everpresent threat, and often the only escape from the anxiety it arouses is found in the defiant life-style of the gang, in the thrill and the adventure of aggressive criminal exploits, or in the escape from reality offered by alcohol or drugs.

In New York and in Tel Aviv the (usually large) lower-class family exerts pressure upon teenage boys and girls to earn their keep and make their financial contributions to the home. In both cities this is a bone of contention between the young and the old. Due to concrete necessity, but also to the characteristic inability to plan ahead and defer satisfaction, lower-class parents often push their teenage offspring to get money-earning jobs as soon as possible, thereby preventing them from seeking prolonged schooling or vocational training. The chances of attaining a level of education and skill that would facilitate access to the legitimate opportunity system are radically reduced. The emphasis on making money to meet the immediate needs tends to devalue work as a source of satisfaction. If it is only the money that counts, there is but a short step from 'making it' by hard labour, to 'scoring' in a less strenuous and tedious way, through one of the many dishonest means offered by the illegitimate opportunity system of the lower-class milieu.

In New York the high rate of teenage unemployment, and the very limited opportunities for vocational training and apprenticeships, further reduce the chances of the lower-class adolescent to free himself from the pressures exerted by his family. Israel's labour laws prescribe apprenticeship programmes and vocational training for all qualified youngsters. Even so, parental pressure, and the necessity to provide for parents who are too old and siblings who are too young to earn their living, prevent many qualified and willing youngsters from acquiring skills which would assure them a positive adjustment in society.

There is another factor in the Israeli system which, though inspired by high moral concepts of family loyalty, contributes significantly to the parent-youth conflict among lower-class families: The allotment of financial aid to the destitute by the Welfare Department carefully takes into account the earnings of all members of the immediate family. Where there are sons or daughters who have an independent income they are put under obligation to contribute to the financial upkeep of destitute parents. Welfare policy allows for and encourages academic and vocational training by relieving youngsters thus occupied from any financial obligation to their families. However, as soon as the young men or young women begin to earn their living they are obliged to contribute. Reinforced by other negative factors in the slum environment, many of the youngsters' reaction is one of resentment against parents who have already, or may in the future, become a burden, and against state authority which imposes what are often felt to be unfair demands. Prospects for future independence and prosperity look very dim indeed to the teenage son of a large destitute family. The inner conflict and the guilt that result from being put in a position where personal interests clash with the demands of filial loyalty may very well become important factors in the search for reassurance and guilt-denial in a delinquent adaptation. One result is a tendency to refuse legitimate work altogether and turn to semi-legitimate (for instance various forms of peddling) and illegitimate means of making a living. The delinquent adaptation that results makes it impossible for the authorities to check on income, and difficult for the parents to gain knowledge of how much money is earned.

Whether cause or effect of poverty, it is an established fact that the incidence of 'broken' families and families in which the father is unable to earn a living, are very high among the lower-class strata of American society. The incidence of the 'broken' or otherwise malfunctioning family in the lower-class population has been found to be significantly higher than among the middle-class. The same situation seems to prevail in Israel.

It is unnecessary to discuss the detrimental effects of family malfunctions upon the relationship between the generations. These effects are obvious and well known. A finding by Jackson Toby should, however, be mentioned here, because it seems to describe observations on the American scene that concur with my own impressions regarding the situation in Tel Aviv poverty areas. Professor Toby (1962) sums up his examination of available research data: 'The better integrated the family, the more successful it is as a bulwark against anti-social influences emanating from the neighbourhood or the peer group. However, the difference between the protection afforded by well integrated and disorganized families is greater for girls and pre-adolescents than for adolescent boys.'

Observation of Tel Aviv street corner groups has shown that the relatively stable lower-class family, especially the family of Oriental background, is very protective of the girls, and often highly prohibitive of any contact with the other sex. A street club worker found, in her contacts with girls in two underprivileged neighbourhoods, that the girls accept the restrictions imposed upon them, although there is an undercurrent of rebelliousness. The girls make attempts to circumvent parental authority, but there is no open defiance. The majority of those girls who are involved in serious, usually sexual, delinquent behaviour come from 'broken' families.

The adolescent boys of Tel Aviv's delinquent street corner groups show a considerable degree of overt conflict with the older generation, even if their families are relatively stable. Resentment and defiance of the parents because of the latter's cultural and socio-economic backwardness seem to be the major factor here, rather than emotional conflict caused by the disintegration of the home. The social-adjustment failure of the parents, their poverty and cultural backwardness constitute a threat to the aspirations and expectations of the youngsters. This conflict manifests itself not only verbally, but is apparent in some important aspects of the life-style of the youngsters.

In a significant number of cases Tel Aviv street club workers observed that the authority of the father has been taken over by the older son. In many instances this is a youngster in late adolescence who is a member of a delinquent street corner group. In one of the groups such an 'older brother' is one of the leaders, while his three younger brothers are members. This young man has served a jail sentence for theft. He lords it at home and has expressed his desire to get away from his present environment by leaving the country and seeking his fortune abroad.

In another group the leader is a highly delinquent youngster who is now awaiting trial for car theft, injuring two children by reckless driving, and leaving the scene of an accident. The group this youngster heads meets frequently at his house. The street club worker found that the parents are relegated to the position of servants and told to keep out of the way when the gang assembles in the home. The youngsters of this group spend most of their money on clothes, and much emphasis is put upon dressing in the latest style. Parties at the home of the leader require elegant attire. In imitation of the entertainment style of middle- and upper-class circles, cocktails are served and the latest jazz hits are provided. The girls invited are brought in from 'better' neighbourhoods and the status of a group member depends upon the beauty and elegance, the 'class' of the girl he brings.

The youngsters of a small and cohesive slum area avoid exposing their background and home life, by telling the girls they pick up in other neighbourhoods, that they live in a middle-class suburban area of Tel Aviv. These youngsters prefer girls who have 'class' to the local girls and assert that these girls would not keep company with them if they knew of their home environment and their lower-class background.

The major source of parent-youth conflict and the alienation between the generations is undoubtedly to be sought in the clash of cultures between the traditions and values the parents bring with them from their countries of origin, and between the modern, emancipated, secular way of life of the new society.

In New York the rebellion of the second generation American youngsters against their parents' old-country ways is a well-known phenomenon. In New York, as in Tel Aviv, the youngsters tend to regard the values and traditions of their immigrant parents as obstacles to their adjustment in the new society, and as factors which lower their social status. In both cities the youngsters react strongly against their parents' attempts to cling to the 'old ways' and to impose their values upon them. This factor is even more pronounced in Tel Aviv, where 89·2 per cent of the fathers of poverty-area families have immigrated during the last two decades (Gluckstein, 1961).

In Israel religion plays an important role in the bid of the parent generation to hold on to the old familiar ways of life and to maintain their parental authority. Many immigrant groups come from countries where the entire life of the Jewish community was enmeshed in religious lore and determined by religious ritual. In Jewish lower-class communities especially, the main source of social status was the degree of religious learnedness and piety. The authority of the father and filial obligations were prescribed by religious dogma.

The new, modern, industrialised society relates the social status and personal authority of the head of the family to his successes and achievements in adjusting to the new way of life. Religion is relegated to a secondary position, of little importance in the struggle for access to the economic system. It can even be said that the emphasis on religious dogma and ritual in many lower-class families constitutes a withdrawal from the challenge posed by the competitive demands of the new society, a retreat into the safety of the 'old ways', where the father's dignity and authority were not dependent upon his professional skills, his economic knowhow and ambitions. Indeed, there is reason to believe that some of our delinquent street corner boys reject the religious values and rituals of their parents for just that reason. On several occasions on which religion was discussed among street corner boys I have heard contemptuous remarks about the religious piety of parents. One youngster replied, when someone remarked that his father conscientiously attended all the daily prayers prescribed by religious law: 'Sure he does, it's easier than working.' Another boy aroused the mirth of the group by saying of his father: 'He lives in the synagogue, that's why he doesn't have to worry about getting the rest of us a decent place to live.'

The rejection of religious practice, which is prevalent among Tel Aviv's lower-class street corner boys, is not only due to the influence of the modern secularised way of life of the new society to which they strive to belong. Perhaps equally important is the characteristic inability to defer satisfaction, to accept restraints, to submit to rules and regulations. The many restrictions imposed by Jewish religious ritual, such as the dietary laws and the prohibitions of smoking and driving a vehicle on the Sabbath, are rejected by the youngsters together with many secular prohibitions imposed by society. Unlike in the case of criminal or violent behaviour, legitimate society is, to a considerable degree, supportive of non-religious behaviour, thereby providing an important area in which the lower-class delinquent youngster can identify with 'respectable' society in opposition to the mores of his parents.

There is considerable pressure for religious observance exerted by the parents upon the youngsters of lower-class communities. However, this pressure is not necessarily concomitant with a parental prohibition of delinquent behaviour *per se*. We observed many instances in which a religious father was indifferent to or actually supportive of delinquent behaviour. We have encountered the case of the father who objects violently to his son's lighting a cigarette on the Sabbath, but who openly smokes, or even sells, hashish during the week. We also know the case of the father who ordered his son to grow sidelocks or else leave his house, but who makes no objections when the same youngster brings home stolen goods or money earned by unlawful means. In such cases negative, antisocial values in the slum milieu prove stronger than religious ethics. This duplicity of values makes it easier for the delinquent youngster to shrug off the demands of the parents, strengthens cynical attitudes, and reinforces the characteristic inclinations to regard all adult conventional society and institutionalised authority as double-faced and corrupt.

The girls, especially in the Oriental communities, are more conservative with regard to religious adherence, and therefore less openly in conflict with the values of their parents. They are more inclined to, or perhaps more afraid not to, obey parental demands regarding religious practice. So, for instance, on Friday nights (Sabbath eves) most of the girls, who can usually be seen hanging about at the street corner in the vicinity of the boys, stay at home in accordance with family tradition.

A unique Israeli phenomenon, military conscription for all girls at the age of eighteen, offers many girls from new immigrant families a legitimate opportunity to gain a measure of independence and make an adult adjustment in the new society. We have already recorded the observation that a significant number of lower-class delinquent boys evade army service, thereby depriving themselves of an important adjustment opportunity. A significant number of the girls of poor neighbourhoods obtain exemption from the army on grounds of religious observance.[1] Many of these girls do not adhere to religious ritual outside the home, but use religion as an excuse to avoid military service. More often than not, the girls are encouraged in this by their parents, whose cultural traditions are opposed to the important degree of emancipation implied in army service for females, and who regard this service as a loss of precious time, preventing the girls from contributing to the family income.

---

[1] Israel's Deputy Minister of Defence, Shimon Peres, stated in the Knesseth (Parliament), that 40 per cent of the country's girls of military draft age have been exempted from service (*Jerusalem Post*, 4 December 1964).

The conflict and the alienation between first generation immigrant parents and their second generation children can be summed up by a remark made in my presence by a North African street corner boy. Speaking of his own parents, and the families of his friends, this youngster, dressed in tight American jeans, stylish half-boots, pleated silk shirt and sporting a pomade-glistening ducktail haircut, said: 'I don't understand why "these people" want to come here if they want to live like in the old country. If they don't like the way "we" live here, why don't they go back where they came from?—Me, I like it here.'

A cautioning is in order: Even the most volatile and repeated expressions of resentment voiced by lower-class adolescents with regard to their parents, show only one aspect of a highly ambiguous attitude. The very same youngsters may, on other occasions, express strong feelings of family loyalty and affection. In times of crisis, and when faced with outside threat or criticism, these youngsters often are ready to defend their parents' way of life vigorously. Any treatment of their parents, considered by the youngsters to be unfair, discriminatory or patronising is likely to arouse feelings of humiliation and anger.

I vividly remember Al, one of the boys of a Puerto Rican fighting gang in a Lower East Side housing project in New York. Al strove frantically to obtain the status and appearance of an 'American' middle-class boy. He dressed 'sharp but conservative' and aspired to become a salesman, rather than a manual labourer. He constantly expressed contempt for his parents' 'old-country' ways and their inability to speak 'proper' English. One afternoon a Housing Authority Police Officer, armed with pistol and club, made a derogatory, insulting remark about his mother's appearance and way-of-life. Al flared up violently and punched the officer. Al was severely beaten and arrested for assaulting an officer. Faced with a long jail sentence he remained proud and unrepentant, sure that he had 'done right'. All his friends shared his opinion and expressed their admiration for his 'heart'.

3 The method: Detached group work or street club work

12 Street club work

A service that starts with a *problem*, not a *program*. . . .

D. M. AUSTIN (1957), p. 44

The social case-worker approach, based on the psychotherapeutic model, in which one waits for the client to give voice to his problem, simply doesn't work with youths who don't acknowledge that they have any personal problem, and who think that their troubles are all the fault of other people. More active and aggressive methods of approach have to be used, and in effect some social workers have completely reversed their technique and become what amounts to missionaries trying to sell unpopular ideas to a resident clientele.

D. J. WEST (1967), p. 247

Street-club work must be seen in the context of the broader group work approach as practised in many different settings and with a large variety of different client populations.

In order to provide the reader, and the future practitioner of street club work, with a first-glance introduction to the social group work method, I quote Professor Konopka (n.d., pp. 5–6), who offers the following ten points as 'guidelines and essential parts of the group work method':

1. The function of the social group worker is a helping or enabling function. This means that his goal is to help the members of the group, and the group as a whole, to move towards greater independence and capacity for self-help.
2. In determining his way of helping, the group worker uses the scientific method; fact finding (observation), analysing, diagnosis in relation to the individual, the group and the social environment.
3. The group work method includes the worker forming purposeful relationships to group members and the group. This includes a conscious focusing on the needs of the members and on the purpose of the group as expressed by the members and as expected by the sponsoring agency and as implied in the members' behaviour. It is differentiated from a casual unfocused relationship.
4. One of the main tools in achieving such a relationship is the conscious use of self. This includes self-knowledge and discipline in relationships without the loss of warmth and spontaneity.
5. Acceptance of people without accepting all their behaviour. This requires extraordinarily high skill, because it involves the capacity for 'empathy' as well as the incorporation of societal demands. It is the part of the method that is most closely intertwined with a high flexibility and abundance of warmth in the social group worker, as well as identification with values and knowledge.
6. Starting where the group is. The capacity to let groups develop from their own point of departure of capacity, without imposing immediately outside demands.
7. The constructive use of limitations: Again they must be used judiciously in relation to individual and group needs and agency function. The forms will vary greatly. The group worker will mainly use himself, program materials, interaction of the group and awakening of insight in the group members.

8. Individualization: It is one of the specifics of the group work method that the individual is not lost in the whole, but that he is helped to feel as a unique person who can contribute to the whole.

9. Use of the interacting process: The capacity to help balance the group, to allow for conflict when necessary and to prevent it when harmful. The help given to the isolate, not through individual attention by the group worker alone, but by relating him also to other members.

10. The understanding and conscious use of non-verbal as well as verbal material: I especially put non-verbal material first, since the group worker deals a great deal with this, especially in work with children. His capacity to use program materials, which do not demand verbal expression and yet are helpful, should be wide.

Specific group work tools—I am not too sure about the use of the word 'techniques' because to me it implies the possibility of mechanical handling, which really never is permitted in group work—are:

> The use of program media.
> The use of group interaction.
> The use of discussion method.
> The use of individual interviews (outside the group).
> The use of individual contacts (inside the group).
> The use of consultation.
> The use of referral.
> The writing and use of case and group records.
> Observation.

The above description can, in its essentials, be applied to and serve as a basis for every aspect of street club work. This is reflected in Professor Konopka's (ibid, p. 15) summary of the specific functions and goals of group work with young delinquents. She lists:

1. A strengthening of the security of the individual in the framework of the group, so that he does not feel alone and helpless, but also moves towards not being wholly dependent on it.

2. The strengthening of the individual's independence by helping him to actually participate in group decisions, not to submit to a gang leader or a powerful sub-group.

3. The introduction of an adult who represents the values of a society they (the young delinquents) reject, but who, because of his accepting attitude represents adult security and love. The delinquent can meet this adult in a group while still feeling the support of his contemporaries and relating in different degrees of intensity.

4. The opportunity of gaining satisfactions in the need for adventure and experimentation in ways that are accepted by society.

5. An opportunity for some catharsis under the protection of an adult and for gaining insight with the help of an adult and with trusted contemporaries.

6. An opportunity to gain inner resilience and status with the group through accomplishments in activities accepted by society.

[1] For a more extensive discussion of the group work method see G. Konopka (1963).

The specialised social group work service known as the 'street club work', or 'detached-worker programme' developed during the last two decades in the United States in response to the growing realisation that there existed in the urban poverty areas a large segment of the youth population which could not be 'reached' by the conventional methods of group work in the settlement house, community centre or youth club settings. These youngsters, mainly lower-class adolescents congregating in street corner groups or gangs, adhered to delinquent values and norms which they expressed by unlawful, destructive and self-destructive behaviour.

The street club worker was charged with contacting these groups in their own environment and establishing a relationship with them which would permit him to identify the structure and norms of the groups, gain insight into the sources of the problems confronting these youngsters, their modes of reacting and their motivations, and to diagnose their needs, frustrations and expectations. The worker uses the insights gained through his relationship to the group to enable the youngsters to face and cope with the realities of their situation. He attempts to strengthen the positive potential of the group, helps the youngsters to improve their relations to the community, finds alternative sources of satisfaction precluding delinquent behaviour, and helps them channel their energies into socially acceptable activities.

Working with the group in their own immediate environment, without imposing any artificial structure, the worker, while clearly and repeatedly identifying himself as a law-abiding adult and a professional youth worker, seeks the acceptance of the group through gaining the youngsters' confidence and friendship. This has to be achieved through unceasing demonstration of his ability and readiness to offer useful advice and practical help, through proving his trustworthiness and honesty in all his dealings with the group, and through his 'shock-proof' understanding (but not necessarily his approval) of the group's nonconformist behaviour.

Functioning as a knowledgeable adult and as a resource person, the worker's immediate aim is to help the group and its members to improve their capacities for establishing healthy and meaningful social relationships, and to deal realistically and effectively with the concrete problems (for instance in the areas of education, family, employment and conflict with the law) confronting them.

The worker's long-range goals are to broaden the group's understanding of the potentialities and opportunities of their life-situation, to help them emerge from the isolation into which environmental pressures and their own deviant adaptations have forced them and, eventually, to bring about fundamental changes in their values and norms, and therewith curtail their delinquent behaviour.

Some excerpts from the definition of the street club worker's role given by the Mobilization for Youth project in New York City, may help to deepen the understanding of the basic concepts of this specialised approach to delinquent street corner groups:

The intervention of a trusted adult who advises caution, settles disputes, and provides face-saving alternatives undoubtedly results in the diminution of conflict behaviour. . . . In order to change the basic values of gang members, the street worker attempts to establish influential relationships with youngsters. Through deep personal ties, the worker tries to convince youth to relinquish delinquent activities.

Another approach is to attempt to redirect the group's energies and interests into socially acceptable types of leisure-time activity. The worker gradually persuades the group to plan recreational and social events which offer satisfaction and recognition without the need for use of illegitimate or conflict behaviour. Thus 'rep' is achieved by running a local dance rather than by trying to take over another gang's 'turf'; good times are had by undertaking a weekend camping trip rather than a series of drinking parties, muggings and boppings (fights).

. . . an effective detached-worker project must use the worker as a 'bridge', relating the street gang to the major institutional orders that impinge upon it. Thus the worker becomes a channel between the group and school authorities, potential employers, the courts, the police etc. In aspiring to bring the delinquent into the mainstream of conventional society, the worker attempts to make available tangible educational and vocational opportunities which the youngster has felt are unattainable and which are vital to conventional adjustment (Mobilisation for Youth, 1961).

The staff of the Action-Research Project on Delinquent Street Corner Groups in Tel Aviv applied the street club work method to its work with lower-class delinquent street corner groups. The many similarities between such groups of delinquent youngsters in Tel Aviv and New York have led us to conclude that the American experience of street club work and the general approach and philosophy of this group work method appear to be applicable here.

13 Mandate, methods and goals

This service is *not initially requested* by the group. It is a 'reaching out' service, an assertive service. Therefore, an entire range of considerations and actions are involved in establishing the first contact with a group. Yet it is not an authoritative or protective service. It is not presented on an either/or basis—either you play football by my system of a single-wing back, or you can play T-formation at the state training school. It is a reaching-out service because the community through the worker takes the first step, takes the initiative to break through the fear and suspicion and hostility that are blocking positive communication between this group and the community.

D. M. AUSTIN (p. 45)

Street club work is one of the most recent additions to the array of specialised services offered under the auspices of the social work profession. As a professional service it adheres to the generic principles of social work and applies the group work method in its practice. Like other specialised social work services, street club work has to adapt its thinking and doing to the specific requirements of the setting in which it functions, and of the groups it serves. This process of adaptation is a continuous one in the United States and has resulted in a number of tentative concepts and experimental approaches which reflect the diversities and fluctuations of the phenomenon known as 'juvenile delinquency'.

In Israel the street club work approach was introduced by the Action-Research Project on Delinquent Street Corner Groups in Tel Aviv. In its attempt to formulate a philosophy and construct a conceptual basis suitable for Israel the Project drew heavily upon the American experience, as well as taking into consideration the local potentialities and requirements.

Apart from the similarities and differences in the characteristics of delinquent street corner groups in representative urban areas in Israel and the United States, it also becomes necessary to give some thought to the similarities and differences the street club work approach has encountered in developing a philosophy and methodology that differs to some degree from that of conventional group work practised in the structured settings of the settlement house, the community centre and the youth club.

A decisive reason for seeking new concepts and methods is that the conventional, structured group work setting deals mainly (though not exclusively) with 'artificial' groups which have entered into an agreement, albeit a rudimentary one, to accept the service on the agency's terms. The street club worker deals exclusively with 'natural' groups in the physical setting of their own choice. He specifically seeks out groups of youngsters who, because of their adherenece to delinquent values and norms, do not accept the conditions the conventional agency imposes, and are not accessible to its service.

As Professor Konopka (n.d., p. 17) has put it:

In working with such groups the group worker is forced to move out of any form of 'protection' by the agency. He or she has no outside power over the group— he cannot form it, he cannot choose the 'right' members; he cannot 'throw out' anybody, or—in our refined language—consider anybody as 'unsuited for therapy'. They are there; they are in the street; they have not asked for help and they are not apprehended. All the group worker has is his conviction that they really will be more happy people when they come to accept his help, the support of his agency which has asked him to undertake his task, and especially his own capacity to establish helpful relationships. With no props for this—not even a given room—his power of acceptance must be very great, but especially his internal security and his imagination in using every opportunity for giving help and opening the doors to confidence. In my opinion this is one of the most difficult and most highly skilled forms of group work.

The social work agency is the organisational framework within which the profession imparts the 'mandate' to the worker. Through his responsibility to the agency, the worker is held accountable to the clients which the agency serves, to the profession which determines the methods and principles of service, and to society, which sanctions these principles and methods.

Street club work, like other social work specialisations, can be carried out within the framework of a specialised agency, like, for instance, the New York City Youth Board, or else it can function as a 'special setting' within a multi-purpose agency, as do for instance, geriatric and family-counselling services in American Neighbourhood Centers.

It has been said that, in order to function effectively, 'educators and practitioners alike must create conditions in the field which will make professional behaviour possible' (Ohlin et al, 1958).

These conditions cannot be created without the co-operation of the administrator, the person who not only holds a key position in the agency, but who often plays a decisive role in evaluating and controlling the practitioner's methods and goals. Every administrative structure engenders some measure of bureaucratic procedure, which grows with the size, scope and personnel of the agency. A flexible, purpose-oriented bureaucratic set-up can make for more efficient work in the field by freeing the worker from having to deal with administrative details, and by providing a stable basis and a clearly defined frame of reference for him. A rigid, self-centred bureaucratic attitude will probably lead to some hemming in of the worker's initiative and professional growth, a decrease in his competence and a lowering of his morale. The result is usually overt or unrecognised conflict between the professional standards and prerequisites of street club work, and the administrative demands and bureaucratic expediencies of the agency. This may happen regardless of whether the administrative apparatus is manned by clerical staff, professional social workers or a combination of both.

Whether the bureaucratic structure of the agency is rigid or flexible, geared to the needs of field work practice or indifferent to them, the street club worker is at the receiving end of its policies and decisions. His work and his person are directly affected and he will therefore do well to try to understand it.

A study of bureaucratic role conceptions by Leonard Reissman describes several types of persons found in administrative positions in official agencies. While it should be understood that among all these there are dedicated and sincere people, and that all may have their function and may be indispensable to the smooth running of things in general, it must be said that experience has taught me preferences with regard to the setting up of conditions for street club work services which provide the best possible bases for efficient professional performance.

One of these types described by Reissman (1958) is the job bureaucrat who

is immersed entirely within the structure . . . He seeks recognition along departmental rather than professional lines. Satisfactions are found in the technical aspects of the work itself, and improvement of the operating efficiency of the bureau becomes an end in itself . . . He strongly adheres to the roles and the job constitutes his full centre of attention and the end to be served (p. 226).

His opposite number is the 'functional bureaucrat'

who is orientated towards, and seeks his recognition from, a given professional group outside of, rather than within, the bureaucracy. He may be portrayed as a professional who 'just happens to work for the government'. His evaluations of success and accomplishments are not measured in terms of satisfactorily fulfilling a given bureaucratic policy or aim (over and above that required of him in the position), but rather in terms of the professional quality with which he does his job. Psychologically he is facing outward and away from the bureaucratic structure . . . He is active in his professional societies and seeks appreciation and recognition on the basis of his professional specialties . . . His future plans include doing research along lines of professional interests. His standards for the 'good' civil servant are the standards of success in the profession, and not necessarily related to success in the bureaucracy. He feels no conflict between his professional ethics and his job because only the former standard exists for him. The bureaucracy imposes certain well-defined limitations upon him, but within these he is professionally biased (p. 225).

As a street club worker with an obligation to plan competent professional services for the future, with the problems of improved organisational structures and further research which this implies, I tend to be in favour of the functional bureaucrat as the kind of administrative official I would prefer to deal with. Wherever I encountered this kind of official, I found that the goals of the work were furthered. This cannot be said about my experience with the mentality of the job bureaucrat, which is by no means restricted to clerical and accounting personnel, but can also be found among professional social service staff.

Street club work is, by its very nature, a lean and fast-moving profession. It is in danger of becoming inhibited and sluggish in an obese and slow-footed administrative setting. In order to avoid this danger, street club projects should *not* be stuck away in one of the niches of large, multipurpose organisations administered by a big and complex administrative apparatus serving a large number of employees. A 'special-setting' agency with its own, separate physical accommodation, a sufficient degree of administrative independence and clearly defined, easily accessible and, above all, simply structured channels of communication and accountability to the parent organisation is greatly preferable as the organisational basis for street-club services.

A second problem is encountered in the realm of the professional, rather than the bureaucratic, setting of the street club project.

Most of Israel's social work is carried out by governmental and municipal social welfare agencies. Although some of these agencies are much more treatment-oriented than, for instance, many American Welfare Departments, the public image of the social worker, especially in lower-class communities where he is most often seen, is that of the welfare worker who investigates and determines welfare eligibility and who is instrumental in distributing financial and other material assistance to the needy. So perceived, the social worker is identified as a representative of government and authority and often encounters much distrust and hostility. The efforts that are being made to change the public image of social work are meeting with obstacles without and inertia within the profession.[1]

The youngsters of the street corner groups are notoriously hostile to, and distrustful of, established authority, in which they include the social welfare agencies. The street club worker, by presenting a new and different type of social worker, can do much to change the old stereotypes, but he would be greatly aided in this effort, especially at the beginning stages of contact with his client group, if he did *not* have to rely upon the

[1] Professor Albert Cherns (1967) points at the possible roots of the organisational problems when he writes: 'What I heard dozens of times in Israel: the complaint that government departments there are independent and warring feudalities. To the extent that this is true, responsibility must largely be placed at the door of the coalition system in which ministers regard themselves and their departments as belonging to their party, as much as to the government as a whole' (p. 13).

conventional social welfare agency for a base of operations. Wherever possible, the street club worker should be allowed to function in a 'special setting' agency, i.e. a street club project office which may remain under the jurisdiction of a multipurpose social service agency, but which has separate physical facilities. This is especially important as the youngsters visit the offices, individually and in small groups, more and more often as their relationship with the worker becomes more relaxed and taken for granted, and as they learn to use the worker's skills and resources more constructively.

None of this should be interpreted to mean that the street club worker should not be clearly identified with his profession and with a professional agency. Our own experience and that of others, as for instance the detached-worker programme described by Mary Morse (1965), have clearly shown how important this is for an unambiguous relationship between the worker and his client group. However, as Professor Geis (1965, p. 43) put it:

The lesson concerning the tendency towards inflexibility in some social agencies, their inability to respond readily to new ideas and approaches, is one that must be kept in mind in all novel and imaginative programs. Procedures and paths must be discovered to deal with such institutional inertia—and often this is quite possible—or calculated steps must be taken to bypass such obstacles as expeditiously as possible.

In New York there are a number of voluntary agencies, such as Neighbourhood Associations, Settlement Houses and Community Centers, which provide settings for street club projects. These agencies have gained the confidence of the community, and the street club worker usually benefits from their established tradition of involvement in community affairs, their good record of helping people in need, and their professional prestige, Some of these, however, have, like many of Israel's Youth Centres, shown a marked preference for the 'highly motivated', the 'well-behaved' and the 'deserving' members of their communities. They have made themselves inaccessible to the lower-class street corner youth, and sometimes have explicitly barred them from their programmes and services. The hiring of street club workers is their first attempt to 'reach the unreached', and their motives are sometimes 'mixed'. (Of the two voluntary agencies for which I worked in New York, one hired 'detached' workers after a group of upper-middle-class inhabitants complained about the increasing incidence of vandalism, pilfering, burglaries and assault carried out by the gangs of the poorer sectors of the area, the other decided to try the street club work approach after the boys of a fighting gang which had been barred from using the agency's premises threatened to break up the place and beat up members of the staff.) In such cases the worker may face the unpleasant task of overcoming the youngster's anger and distrust directed at the agency which employs him.

In recent years social service organisations have sprung up in several of the large cities in the United States, which are specifically geared to offer their services to underprivileged population groups in poverty areas. Mobilisation for Youth, on New York's Lower East Side, is an example of these. Here street club work is integrated into a network of specialised services such as community organisation, vocational training, legal aid, 'store-front' case work, teenage coffee shops, neighbourhood improvement programmes, home-help services, tutoring programmes, etc., all focused upon the needs of economically deprived, socially isolated, 'hard-to-reach' population groups. This type of agency provides the best possible setting for street club work.

Both the group worker in a structured setting, and the street club worker, are bound to adhere to the conditions of the mandate of the agency which employs them, while seeking to bring the conditions of this mandate into harmony with the needs and goals of their client groups. However, in his attempt to 'reach the unreachable', the street club worker is decisively dependent upon his success in obtaining a second mandate for his service directly from the client group. In fact the granting of this mandate by the group in itself constitutes the achievement of the first major goal of his treatment plan: the 'unreachables' have been reached. In many cases, the goals and purposes of the street club worker's agency must be kept in abeyance until the client group has agreed to sanction the attempt to offer it a service in accordance with the mandate of the agency.

Some years ago, in New York, I worked with a street corner group of thieves and drug-addicts for close to a year, before succeeding in effecting any significant changes in the attitudes and the behaviour of the youngsters. During this entire period I was rigidly opposed by Eddy, one of the leading and influential members of the gang, who frustrated most of my attempts to carry out the tasks with which I had been charged by my agency. Eddy, a heavy drug-user and accomplished thief, knew all about social workers of all varieties and did not trust any of them. He had once been invited to participate in an organised group programme in a community centre, but had left after the first session, when the conditions of participation in the programme were explained to him. He had been in jail several times, had been contacted by a number of social workers, including street club workers, and had so far refused to admit that he was in need of any kind of help. My 'break' with Eddy came one morning in a police station. He had been charged with a serious crime, which I knew he had not committed. I was able to stay with the boy through a gruelling five-hour interrogation session and give him the moral support that enabled him to convince the police of his innocence. Eddy gave me my mandate to work with him and his group in clear and concise terms that morning when we walked out of the police station together: He said: 'I had you pegged wrong, man. You stood by me, even when the cops pulled out my record and wouldn't believe a word I said because I'm on dope and a thief. I got to see things your way. Let's go somewhere and talk about what I can do about being a junkie and how to get out of the racket.'

In New York I found that there is considerable pressure upon the street club worker to adopt a role and fulfil expectations based upon concepts which reflect the group work experience in conventional, structured settings. Public opinion and the demands of institutional authority, such as the police, are significant factors in forcing the worker into the role of an auxiliary guardian of law and order, whose task it is to prevent or report delinquent acts, and to control delinquent behaviour.

Aside from the question, whether this is indeed compatible with the social worker's professional role of 'helper and enabler', practical experience shows, that it is not possible to simply transform delinquent street corner groups into athletic clubs or social activity groups in community centres, nor is it feasible for the street club worker to play the part of the Dutch boy with his finger in the dyke in order to prevent delinquent acts. There are too many holes in the dyke and not enough fingers. Results can only be obtained if the worker is given the opportunity to help his clients to work through their manifold and complex problems in their own environment and according to their own level of understanding and capacities. The foremost prerequisite for a meaningful approach in the street club work setting is, therefore, a realistic concept of the purpose of this special service, and the acceptance of suitable goals.

In Israel the conventional, structured group work setting may influence the conceptualisation of purpose and goals of street club work. Public opinion plays its part in demanding that the worker focus his efforts upon 'protecting society' from the delinquent. Official agencies, such as the police, exert a certain amount of pressure. On the whole I have found a considerable degree of understanding among leading Israeli social workers for the special problems with which street club work is faced, and an encouraging readiness to give the new method a chance to iron out its initial wrinkles and to prove itself in practice. The realistic attitude of the Police Youth Squad, and the co-operation of the Probation Service, which is primarily treatment-oriented, have been of

great help in facilitating the communication of street club work concepts to other professions dealing with delinquency problems, and in
co-ordinating street club work practice with other services.

Unlike the United States, Israel has a rich youth movement tradition.
Although it has become obvious in recent years that the youth movements have not succeeded in reaching the great majority of lower-class
youth, and have especially failed to make an impact upon delinquent
youngsters, there is still a strong tendency among educators and youth
leaders to depreciate any youth work approach which does not pursue
specific ideological goals with missionary zeal. The youth movement
tradition tends to reject the youngster who cannot live up to its high
standards of commitment and disciplined idealism. This has undoubtedly reinforced and perpetuated the isolation of a large segment of lower-
class youngsters, and may be one of the important causes of the failure
to absorb and assimilate first and second generation immigrant youth.
Nevertheless, the youth movement tradition is potentially one of the
most positive factors of Israeli youth culture. It could be incorporated
in the street club work approach and become one of its most important
assets, provided it can make realistic adaptations to the fundamental
change of values that has taken place in Israeli society in recent years,
and provided that it learns to accept the basic social work principle of
'meeting the client on his own level'.

On the other hand, street club work would, perhaps, do well to
become more receptive to the values and characteristics of the youth
movement, utilising these to guide the rebelliousness and frustration of
lower-class adolescents into more constructive activities, even though
these may involve a certain amount of defiance and agression in the
form of militant commitment to political or social 'causes.'

Several years ago I participated in a consultation meeting of the
social work staff of HARYOU (Harlem Youth Organisation) in New York.
It was the aim of this organisation, as I understood it, to provide the
organisational framework and the ideological inspiration for the found-
ing of a youth movement that would attract delinquent gang youth in
Harlem. Several of the social workers present at the meeting voiced
their concern over the fact that the gang kids who had joined the new
organisation were exhibiting a certain degree of arrogance, exclusiveness
toward youngsters who had not joined, and hostility toward conventional
society.

My reaction was then, and is now that social workers dealing with
delinquent youth will have to reformulate some of their concepts in their
search for new and effective solutions. Arrogance, exclusiveness, hostility are characteristic of the delinquent juvenile gang. They are also

significant factors in the esprit de corps of any militant youth organisation. It is much to be preferred that these characteristics be exhibited
and expressed in the frame of a youth organisation with certain cultural,
ideological and political goals, than in the setting of a delinquent street
corner group.

The delinquent street corner boy's arrogance is based upon his success
as a thief, a street fighter, a pimp, con man or a 'cool cat' drug addict.
His 'chip-on-the-shoulder' exclusiveness rests upon his membership in a
gang with a tough reputation. His hostility is diffusely and indiscrimin-
ately directed against the values and institutions of society. It may be
well worth while to consider giving the street club worker the mandate
to channel these antisocial attitudes of the young delinquent into a peer
group setting in which the youngster can be arrogant and feel exclusive
about his membership in an organisation which aims at changing unsatisfactory conditions in his community. It may be equally worth while to
have the street club worker include in his approach to delinquent youth
the channelling of the youngsters' aggressiveness into legitimate mili-
tancy directed against malpractices and inadequacies of societal institutions. We may find that this approach becomes a decisive first step in
helping the delinquent youngster emerge from his isolation and in
enabling him to find legitimate opportunities for self-expression, attainment of status and participation in the social life of his society. Eventually we may discover that arrogance and exclusiveness have turned into
pride of achievement and esprit de corps, and that antisocial aggression
has been channelled into constructive forms of social and political action.

In the United States we have in some instances seen the beginnings of
courageous and far-sighted agency policies regarding the channelling of
delinquent rebelliousness into legitimate social action. Mobilisation for
Youth in New York has done pioneering work in this area. In Israel the
policies of social service agencies still set strict limitations to similar
approaches. It is to be hoped that street club work will be able to introduce significant changes here, and that it will find an ally in the Youth
Movement tradition of this country.

A second factor that impinges upon the formulation of goals and the
implementation of methods in street club work with delinquent youth in
Israel, is the phenomenon of party politics.

Tel Aviv street club workers encountered situations in which the
competition of political parties for the membership and the votes of
inhabitants of underprivileged neighbourhoods did seriously hinder the
workers' efforts to influence the behaviour and change the attitudes of
delinquent street corner groups.[1] The ruthless methods of political

[1] Community Organisation workers in Israel have encountered similar situations.

functionaries which in extreme cases do not seem to exclude false promises, threats, vicious besmirching of public figures and societal institutions, and the offering of bribes, strengthen and perpetuate the cynicism and antisocial attitudes of the youngsters and greatly reinforce their tendency to regard conventional society as basically corrupt. The destructive results for the adjustment of the youngsters, and the obstacles put in the way of the youth worker are obvious.

One of the street club workers found himself in the centre of a power struggle between two political parties in one of Tel Aviv's slums. While both the local party representative assured the worker that they were 'against juvenile delinquency', highly reprehensible tactics were used in attempting to gain the adherence of delinquent street corner boys. The worker was told by one of the local party functionaries that his party was out to 'conquer' the community and would tolerate no interference. The worker used his professional skill in dealing with the local power structure and in establishing tolerable working relations, but his effectiveness with the youngsters, who had become the objects of manipulative corrupt practices, was temporarily impaired.

On several occasions, I have myself encountered such questions as 'What party are you from? What did you come to promise us? How much are your people willing to pay if we work with you?' when I contacted street corner groups in deprived neighbourhoods in Tel Aviv.

The political power struggle and interparty competition is a reality in any democratic country. Social workers dealing with delinquent youth have to be aware of this reality and seek to cope with it in constructive ways. However, the social service agency from which the street club worker derives his mandate should assume the responsibility of confronting political parties whose representatives employ self-serving and short-sighted methods, and seek their co-operation in stopping cases of malpractice. Where this proves futile, the worker should have access to a professional organisation, such as the National Association of Social Workers in the United States, which may be able to call upon the authority of the State or to alert public opinion to curb practices which are destructive to the country's youth.

In a country in which five major and half a dozen or so minor parties are active upon the political scene, professional social work cannot adopt an ostrich policy by ignoring the turbulence, nor should it set its workers adrift without guidance or direction to act according to their abilities and inclinations, or as luck permits. The profession's policy should at all times provide its workers with a clear and unequivocal stand on public issues that concern the welfare and adjustment of their clients. This stand should be based on professional principles and professional insight into the needs of the client, rather than any political consideration of the moment.

The street club worker must have the guidance and the backing of his agency, and of the bodies and organisations that represent professional social work, in order to maintain his professional role and act in accordance with the best interests of his clients, regardless of political interests or pressures. If the mandate of his agency does not include the necessary professional guidance and support with regard to the complex political scene, the worker is in danger of becoming relegated to a position where he appears as a rather helpless, indecisive and inadequate figure, dependent on the goodwill of this or that party functionary or local power figure, whenever his youngsters turn to him for help in such vital issues as inadequate housing, substandard schools, lack of cultural or economic opportunities, discrimination, etc. The worker will be paralysed by considerations of political expediency whenever his client group has reached a stage in which they are able to channel their energies into legitimate social action activities.

With regard to the political activities of his clients, the street club worker, backed by his agency and the profession, should let himself be guided solely by the needs and the level of his client group. Where a group of street corner boys is lured or pressured into affiliation with any organisation at a time when the group is either not ready for such a move or the affiliation may, perhaps unwittingly, serve to strengthen certain negative traits and tendencies of the group, the street club worker should seek to work through this move with the youngsters as he would any other problem of maladjustment. Where a group seems ready to make a commitment and enter into a meaningful relationship with any legal political or cultural organisation, the worker should regard this as a step which may enrich the life of the group and afford it legitimate opportunities for social activities and self-expression. Under certain circumstances such a step may signify the satisfactory termination of the worker's service to the group.

Shortly before the municipal elections of 1965, a well-known Tel Aviv 'character' toured the city's poverty areas in a white Cadillac and announced the formation of a new party under his leadership. His professed aim, proclaimed in thunderous oratory, was to abolish poverty, wipe out the slums, end discrimination, reduce taxes and many other similarly laudable things. He called upon the adults to vote for him, and upon youth to organise in his support. The man had a certain personal attraction as a national sports figure of considerable achievements, and his white Cadillac was a shrewdly used symbol of the dreams and aspirations of many of our youngsters. One of the Tel Aviv street club workers became directly involved with the 'White Cadillac' campaign, when his street corner group, actually a loose confederation of three groups of altogether fifty-two youngsters, asked him to declare himself. The question came up more and more often during the nightly meetings in one of the local cafes: 'What do you think, man, is this guy for real? Do we stick up for him? Can he really do what he claims? Who are you gonna vote for?'

The worker, himself a sympathiser of MAPAI, Israel's Labour Party, explained his own position as clearly and honestly as he could, but refused to tell the boys what they should or should not do. Instead he led a series of discussions in which the boys were encouraged to weigh the various political promises which were being made by the contending parties, and to state their own views on the issues involved and on the record and the credibility of the politicians. A growing number of the community's adults joined in. On several occasions there were heated discussions between sons and fathers on such matters as whether 'faith' or 'facts' should determine one's vote and ideological commitments, whether there were differences between what the 'party bosses' said and what they did, whether one should be guided by what seemed to be the best for the majority of the people, or whether one should support those who offered rewards and advantages to oneself and one's own kin. By the time the elections came around, the boys had learned something about the complex processes of a democratic society and improved their abilities to think for themselves. They had also discovered that they shared their ignorance and confusion about 'politics' with the older generation and could make their own contribution to sorting things out, as well as learn something from their elders. They had also discovered that 'talking politics' could be as stimulating and interesting as their usual preoccupation with car stealing, sex, fighting and the police.

I found myself in a precarious situation when I worked with the 'Emperors' in New York. The youngsters of this group, most of them of German, Irish, Italian, Hungarian and Czech descent, had come under the influence of the National Socialist Party of America, a viciously racist, Hitler-worshipping sect of the rightist lunatic fringe. My position as a Jew was self-evident. In my role of street club worker I faced the fact that the hatred and violence which the Nazis advocated openly, reinforced the youngsters' own destructive and self-destructive tendencies. In the beginning I had to listen to and see a lot of things which I found hard to take. There were swastika armbands and antisemitic leaflets, Nazi songs and talk of 'gassing Jews, Niggers and Reds'. But there were many things of more immediate concern in the youngsters' daily existence, and as I attended to these my relationship with the group grew closer and more stable. Gradually, those who had learned that I could help effectively with jobs and education, at the police station and in court, and that my intervention prevented some from risking jail, others from getting 'hooked' on drugs, became receptive to my views on race hatred, dictatorship and the 'achievements' of the 'Fuehrer'. As the youngsters learned to like and respect me and to understand that I reciprocated their feelings, they found it more and more disturbing and embarrassing to face my disapproval and, sometimes, my sharply expressed anger, when they talked about 'kikes' and 'niggers' and 'spics'. Their attendance of Nazi functions lessened, and when Nazi organisers, mainly adults, came round, more and more of the boys took my side when I engaged them in discussion. When I left this group, having worked with them well over three years, the Nazi issue was a 'dead horse' which no one needed to beat any longer.

In contrast to this, I came to the conclusion that street corner youth in the United States should be encouraged to participate in such political and social issues as civil rights, the peace movement, the Vietnam issue and other protest movements which fall under the category of 'citizens participation' and 'legal dissent' in a democratic society. It is of more benefit to these youngsters and to society to have them demonstrate against racial discrimination, than to have them wage battles to defend their 'turf' against 'whitey'. It is better for everyone if they carry banners and shout slogans proclaiming their views on Vietnam, than get their thrills stealing cars. It is better to see them wear 'Ban-the-Bomb' or 'Make-Love-not-War' buttons, than switchblades or their daily supply of heroin. All these movements offer more desirable and educational outlets for rebelliousness and noncomformity than fighting, stealing, drug addiction or just plain, bored, apathetic hanging about at street corners. So far these movements mainly involve a small minority of middle-class youth. It might not be a bad idea to get the lower-class street corner groups interested and to draw the attention of street club workers and their agencies to this possibility.

As already mentioned, Israel offers a wide range of possibilities of social and political involvement in its network of parties and youth movements. These have so far done deplorably little to fire the imagination and encourage the involvement of lower-class street corner youth. In addition to this, there is a large wasteland in the area of social action to improve the relations between Israel's Arab and Jewish youth. Arab youth is largely isolated, culturally and socially segregated in Israel, not by government decree but by public apathy. The observations of the Tel Aviv Project's only Arab street club worker showed that there is a rapidly growing incidence of delinquency and ganging among the many Arab youngsters who leave their villages to seek jobs and adventure in the cities. Youth movements and street club work could find many opportunities for co-operation in trying to involve Jewish and Arab street corner groups in bridging the gulf between the two populations.

The street club worker by accepting responsibilities in political and social action issues, adds to his already heavy burden, and faces considerable additional risks. To enable him to accept this, he must be given professional guidance concerning his own role and functions in these areas of his work, as well as a clearly defined mandate which provides him with a practical frame of reference in addition to the professional one, and which obliges his agency to give him the necessary backing and support if he encounters obstacles and becomes engaged in controversy.

Street club work does not and cannot function in a vacuum, but must be securely anchored in the solid ground of the social work profession, as well as sinking its roots into the soil of the society in which it functions. Before we can proceed to talk about the goals of the street club work approach, we must round out the discussion of the mandate for our work given by society, the profession and the agency, by clarifying the major assumptions which determine our goals. In order to do so it becomes necessary to return for a moment to the opening pages of this study, in which the definition of delinquency is discussed.

Having accepted Professor Robison's definition of delinquency as 'any behaviour which a given community at a given time considers in conflict with its best interests', the question should be asked as to what this means in terms of the goals of street club work.

A British observer (Willmott, 1966, p. 179) sums up what may be described as the average delinquency situation:

Most of the delinquency is relatively trivial—sweets or a pencil stolen from a store, a scooter borrowed, 'insulting behaviour' or 'rowdiness'. This sort of behaviour should not, of course, be condoned; but it hardly threatens the fabric of society. Most boys who appear before the Courts do so only once or twice and, in terms of their own future development as responsible adults, their adolescent transgressions are not much to worry about. The exceptions are those boys (about whom we know far too little) who commit more serious and systematic crimes, or who go on to an adult criminal career. But even the misbehaviour of the majority is a social nuisance and it sometimes leads, often unintentionally, to serious harm. Cars are stolen, windows smashed, cinema seats ripped up, public telephones put out of order, girls assaulted and other people, boys or adults, dangerously injured.

Frequency and severity of delinquent behaviour is apparently higher in the lower-class areas of Tel Aviv than in the London neighbourhood described above; it is certainly higher and gives cause for more concern in similar areas of New York and other American cities. However, even where delinquency is relatively trivial and temporary, the street club worker cannot and does not ignore the inherent dangers of such behaviour, nor is he indifferent to the damage caused to other persons or to property. One of the most important results of the worker's success in establishing a close and confident relationship with a delinquent street corner group is his ability to intervene directly to prevent dangerous and destructive behaviour. No one can tell whether the three youngsters I dragged out of a fast sports car one evening would have just taken another joy ride, as they had done so often in the past, or whether, after a few cans of beer, they would have smashed up the car, perhaps causing injury to others and themselves. In Tel Aviv, one of the boys of a street corner group ran over a five-year-old child on one of his many joy rides. A Tel Aviv street club worker found out that the boys of his group had accumulated a set of burglar's tools and were planning a 'big job'. He confronted them firmly and confiscated the tools. Another worker discovered that two fourteen-year-old out-of-town girls who had run away from home had been offered a hideaway in an empty shack on the outskirts of his group's neighbourhood. The boys had generously offered the girls their 'protection' and were looking forward to a 'line-up' that night. The worker, facing the anger of the group, enlisted the help of another social worker and had the two girls returned to their parents. In New York a young drug addict showed me a gun and told me that he had planned to hold up the owner of a nearby grocery store. I was half convinced that the boy was only showing off and not the type to commit armed robbery. But I could not take the risk and stayed with him through the night, arguing, cajoling and threatening, until he handed me the gun and a box of ammunition.

This kind of direct intervention to prevent dangerous behaviour has obvious value. It is impossible to estimate how much serious harm a street club worker prevents by direct intervention in the course of a week, a month or a year. There is no doubt that, in many cases, nothing would have happened anyway. However, even if the worker prevents one smashed-up car, one burglary, one knife thrust, he has earned his salary. The combined cost of damaged property or medical treatment, court procedure and penitentiary maintenance in each such case usually exceeds the wages a street club worker earns during one year.

But there are other, perhaps in the long run more important, considerations. Society's mandate obliges the worker to be concerned with the 'best interests' of the society that sanctions his work. The question remains, whether it is in the best interest of society to protect it from the immediate effects of the phenomenon we call 'juvenile delinquency' by

'curing' the latter's symptomatic expressions, namely delinquent behaviour. If so, our goal would be to prevent, control and suppress delinquent activities. Aside from the fact that experience has shown, and the
increase in quantity and severity of delinquent behaviour in almost every
country on the globe seems to prove, that the attempts to 'do away' with
delinquent behaviour have largely failed, it also may be assumed that
the police and other law-enforcement agencies are better suited and
equipped for this task than the street club worker.

There is, however, a more farsighted view, which regards the best
interests of society as consisting of assuring all segments of its youth the
opportunity to experience a healthy and creative process of growth, so
that they will enter adulthood in full command of their faculties, ready
to enjoy the privileges and fulfil the obligations of adult status. If we
accept this view, then the street club worker takes his place in the long
line of those who are concerned with youth, be they parents, teachers,
psychologists, physicians or social workers. The street club worker's
specific task is, in this view, to 'reach out' for those youngsters who, due
to a special set of circumstances, have been deprived of, or have been
unable to make use of, the opportunities for healthy and creative growth
a modern society offers its children. In this view, which is one I share,
the major and all-inclusive goal of the street club worker is to help and
enable the 'unreached', deprived and thoroughly confused youngsters
to grow up and become adults who can be integrated in society.

Yodi, a fifteen-year-old member of one of the Project's street corner
groups in a Tel Aviv slum, who had been alternately described by the
people with whom he had contacts as an 'animal', 'mentally retarded',
a 'psychopath', a 'freak' etc., sat in the Project office some time before his
worker arranged for him to spend a year in a youth group in a kibbutz,
and 'explained' why he was 'bad'. Yodi said: 'You see, man, it's like this
—take a tomato, it's the same like all the other tomatoes and it lies there
in a box in the market. Now a fine lady comes and buys it, and takes it
home. She puts it in the sun, because it's still green, you know, not ripe
yet. Then she wraps it up in a clean piece of paper when it's red, and
puts it in the refrigerator. She treats it nice, so it looks nice. People like
to look at it and when it gets eaten it tastes good. But now what happens
if no lady comes and buys that tomato and it gets thrown in the gutter.
It gets kicked, people step on it. It starts getting rotten and after a while
it is squashed and it stinks. People don't want to look at it, it looks so bad.
Nobody wants to take it home and put it on the table. Man, that's me,
that tomato what got thrown in the gutter.'

Yodi is a thief. He has never hurt anyone physically, but I have heard
him use the most vicious threats and the most obscene language in

speaking of people who, he feels, have 'done him wrong'. Yodi has al-most no education. He has smoked hashish and got drunk, he has had homosexual relations, and he is quite clever at planning petty thefts and burglaries for the members of his gang. Our goal for Yodi is to make him understand that he is not a rotten tomato, or any other kind of vege-table. Yodi's worker does not spend most of his time in trying to prevent Yodi from stealing or doing other 'bad things', but he does everything he can to make Yodi acknowledge the fact that he can get up, when he is 'thrown in the gutter', that he can, and indeed does, kick back, when he is kicked. The worker has 'reached' Yodi, because he succeeded in con-vincing the boy that he understands him and accepts him as he is, that he can be relied upon to help, and that he can be trusted.

There are many 'Yodis' in the street corner groups of Tel Aviv, and I have encountered many of them at the street corners of New York. Society has many powerful institutions and organisations to protect it-self from youngsters like these. These youngsters, however, have no one who protects them from the consequences of the omissions and failures of society.

The street club worker's major goal is to help youngsters like Yodi cope with their environment and with their own fears, confusions and hatreds. His immediate goal is to establish a relationship with youngsters like Yodi, and with the groups of youngsters to which such boys belong. This establishing of a relationship of mutual acceptance and trust is the first step in the long and tortuous road toward the main goal.

The mandate of the street club worker should, above all, emphasise the tasks of helping groups of young delinquents to grow up without destroying themselves and doing damage to others. The mandate should direct the worker to help these youngsters to get their rightful share of the opportunities modern society offers its youth, and to enable them to make use of these opportunities in a meaningful, constructive way.

Methods and goals of the street club work service are determined by the mandate the worker is given. In accordance with its mandate, the Tel Aviv street club Project formulated its approach and its goals as follows:

The street club worker is charged with contacting street corner groups in their own environment and establishing a relationship with them which will permit him to identify the structure and norms of the group, gain insight into the sources of the problems confronting these youngsters, their modes of reacting and their motivations, and to diagnose their needs, frustrations and expecta-tions. The worker uses the insights gained through his relationship to the group to enable the youngsters, to face, and cope with, the realities of their situation. He attempts to strengthen the positive potential of the group, helps the young-sters to improve their relations to the community, finds alternative sources of satisfaction precluding delinquent behaviour, and helps them channel their energies into socially acceptable activities.

Working with the groups in their own immediate environment, without imposing any artificial structure, the worker, while clearly and repeatedly identifying himself as a law-abiding adult and a professional youth worker, seeks the acceptance of the group through gaining the youngsters' confidence and friendship. This has to be achieved through unceasing demonstration of the worker's ability and readiness to offer useful advice and practical help, through proving his trustworthiness and honesty in all his dealings with the group, and through his 'shock-proof' understanding (but not necessarily his approval) of the group's nonconformist behaviour.

The worker's long-range goals are to broaden the group's understanding of the potentialities and opportunities of their life situation, to help them emerge from the isolation into which environmental pressures and their own deviant adaptations have forced them and, eventually, to bring about fundamental changes in their values and norms and therewith curtail their delinquent behaviour.

Stated in the form of major objectives which served as guidelines to the field-work staff, the Tel Aviv Project, set the street club worker the following tasks (Leissner, 1965):

1. The establishing of mutual acceptance and trust between the street corner group and the worker.
2. Helping the group to 'bring out' and activate its positive resources and potentialities, to de-emphasize its antisocial and self-destructive traits, and to channel its interests and energies into satisfying and socially acceptable activities.
3. Helping the group and its members recognize and face the realities of their situation in all instances, and to find realistic, workable solutions to their problems, instead of taking refuge in reality-distortions and fantasies, and instead of taking recourse to escapist, make-believe solutions or self-destructive and aggressive reactions.
4. Opening up and creating opportunities for the group and its individual members in all areas of social, economic and cultural life, and offering concrete assistance in gaining access to such opportunities in order to make meaningful and productive adjustments.
5. Helping the group and its members to deal with the complex and intricate processes of modern society through educating, counseling and direct intervention.
6. Helping the members of the group to 'work through' and cope with their personal problems concerning their physical growth, their emotional development and their social relations.
7. Guiding the group in seeking positive relations to their community and to societal institutions and mediating between the group and its social environment in order to bring about opportunities for better relations.
8. Limiting, modifying and preventing unlawful behaviour through personal influence, through helping the group and its members to gain insight into their motives, through pointing out consequences and offering satisfying and challenging alternatives.
9. Bringing about lasting changes in the delinquent values and norms of the group as a result of reaching the above listed objectives, and helping the group

to adopt new values and norms which are realistically related to their socio-economic and cultural background and which serve constructive ends in the shaping of their future.

While street club work, like any other professional approach, must provide a reference set of principles and methods, it is equally important that we heed the wise counsel that

In a practising profession a method includes the goal, the value system, the principles, and in some measure the techniques. Its main characteristic is that it gives general directions, but *never* allows the practitioner to simply follow the same rules. It is his responsibility to continually adapt it, or choose specific parts of it, or combine it with some other methods according to his diagnostic understanding of the individual or the group. If this is clearly understood, we will finally move away from giving every modification another name. It is not method, and the practitioner is not a responsible professional, if he cannot modify the basic guide lines according to the needs of the given situation (Konopka, n.d., p. 5.)

The achievement of all or any of the main objectives of street club work is a slow, often frustrating, but also frequently rewarding, process. It is, in the words of an American educator and social philosopher, '. . . a process requiring understanding and patience, sensitivity, resourcefulness, constant adaptation and the courage to confront an endless lack of finality' (Mayer, 1964, p. 40).

14 The street club worker

The concept of 'Detached Worker' envisages a worker detached from the authoritarian image of the agency that employs him, or in some cases detached from the agency structure altogether. There appear to be two motives behind this idea of detachment—one is to break down the image the client usually has of a social worker in an authoritarian setting such as a parole or a probation department. The other motive is that the worker should be given the maximum freedom and autonomy possible, and thus he needs to be detached from the red tape and traditional procedures often to be found in an established agency—particularly in a long established one.

GARY KILLINGTON (1964), p. 1

The heart of this professional service . . . is an *individual* worker. The key to success is not to be found in a type of building, a set of activities, a structured program, or even in a set of group techniques. The essential tool is the individual worker and his network of relationships with the group. His skills in personal relationships, his preparation for the job, his understanding and sensitivity are not only important, they are essentially the only things that will achieve success. This is not a team operation in the same sense that a medical team in a hospital brings a series of professional skills to bear on a patient one at a time, or sometimes jointly. While the skills and understanding of many professional persons may be used through supervision and consultation and may be required more directly for supplemental help in individual and family situations, the street-corner group worker is essentially a lone operator in working with groups. All the skill and knowledge of the team must be incorporated within his practice if they are to be of any assistance.

D. M. AUSTIN (1957), p. 44.

It has been stated (Spergel, 1961, p. 33) that 'The neighbourhood street club worker has served both in the collection of data for research and in the provision of services. He has influenced theory and practice by providing a broad group-oriented service to delinquents in a neighbourhood setting. Some concensus has been reached on what is expected of the street club worker.'

'What is expected of the street club worker', however, covers a wide range of characteristics, skills and functions. A recent action-research report raises the question of 'how good a role model the worker provides for the youngsters involved' (Los Angeles County Probation Dept, 1964, p. 65).

Gilbert Geis (1965, p. 10) wrote that: 'All the literature that we have regarding working with gangs stresses the great importance of having a worker who can demonstrate by his very attitude, his clothes, his sense of security, his behaviour that there is something to be gained by attempting to live as he does.'

Most authorities rightly stress the importance of a high degree of

ability to initiate and maintain relationships, of empathy, self-awareness, emotional and value stability, leadership qualities and a great
degree of tolerance for accepting deviant behaviour and 'alien' values.

The social group worker . . . has the professional responsibility of helping the
individuals who are in the group to fulfill their roles, and the human relationships implied in their roles, more satisfactorily. The group worker's resources
consist primarily in his ability to handle his relationships with the group and its
members. Skills in organizing leisure, recreational, or educational activities,
though useful elements in his work, remain secondary to the primary skill. The
group worker does not come to teach, but to help the members of the group with
their learning. . . .
    . . . the worker must possess two skills which do not come easily. He must know
himself and his own emotional attitudes, so that he may recognize and control
his own responses to the group and its members, and he must be able to 'start at
the level of the group' (Spencer, 1964, pp. 77–8).

Professor Kvaraceus (1965, p. 41) extends some of these basic requirements to all professionals who deal with delinquent youth:

Adults who are hired to assist in the rehabilitation process should give evidence
of emotional maturity and of valid interest in and firm commitment to young
people—even when they persist in their delinquencies. The case worker, teacher,
recreational leader, probation officer, or juvenile court judge who is unable to
cope with his own social and emotional problems represents a bad risk for
dealing with the norm violator. The child welfare army today will not stand
close inspection. Indeed, it is the rare individual who can look with professional
objectivity upon any and every youngster who has violated community norms
and who constantly thumbs his nose at official authorities. Even the best-
equipped professional can become personally involved with the delinquent and
his family either through over-identification or through retaliation and rejection
—especially when readjustments are not forthcoming in spite of the extended
help that has been provided painstakingly by the worker.

An essay by two Israeli criminologists states that 'without the charisma
in his personality structure which not only sustains moral convictions but
also conveys them to others he [the worker] will be of limited use as a
treatment man' (Shoham and Slonim, 1963, p. 157).
    The recently published report on a Detached Worker Project carried
out by the National Association of Youth Clubs in four urban areas in
England confirms our views regarding the adaptability of the 'untrained
worker' to this kind of youth-work and offers some relevant observations
(Morse, 1965, pp. 206–7):

A certain maturity of outlook is clearly required if one is to work effectively with
the unattached. This maturity is needed not only to withstand the strain of a job
of this kind but also in order to adopt the objective, non-judgemental attitude
which is so fundamental to the success of the worker. In addition, those engaged
on this project were convinced that some training was essential in the understanding of human behaviour, including 'normal' personality development and

personality maladjustment, either before or whilst actually being employed as a detached worker. Also essential is a reasonable educational level, in order to grasp the more theoretical aspects of the job. It is difficult to define exactly what constitutes a reasonable educational level for these purposes, but a formal training in youth leadership is not the only, nor necessarily the most suitable, training. . . .

It is often asked if skill in any particular activity or activities is essential. . . . [The experience of the detached-worker project suggests that] although knowledge of a special activity can be helpful in itself, it is certainly not enough and may even go unutilized if the particular group of unattached either happen to be uninterested or cannot be stimulated into developing an interest. The most helpful qualities would seem to be wide interests and a capacity to adapt oneself to activities which the unattached prefer or which strike a response in them. Skill in human relationships is the only specific expertise that can be advocated with certainty, especially if it is remembered that as much of the worker's time and effort may be spent in working with local adults as with unattached adolescents.

Indisputably the worker's personality is a vital factor contributing to success or failure in this kind of work. With a subject as complex as that of personality one is on extremely dangerous ground making any suggestions, but there is consistent evidence that the personal characteristics of warmth, ease with people, humour, imagination, and tolerance are all vital.

My own experience bears out that the prime requirement of the street club worker is the kind of personality that enables him to 'get close' to rebellious, confused, suspicious, alternately withdrawn and apathetic or aggressive youngsters, to 'get on the same wavelength' with them, to understand them and be understood by them. This, of course, has to be rooted in the kind of life experience that makes for a large measure of self-assurance about one's own values and for personal integrity, while leaving ample room for respect for different beliefs and values and tolerance for nonconforming attitudes and behaviour. These are the essentials. These alone, however, are not enough. The worker must also bring with him the ability to demand respect and to exert his leadership, as well as organisational skills, resourcefulness and considerable knowhow in dealing with the complexities of living in modern society.

These basic traits and skills of the street club worker find their application and expression through his role and functions in the work process. Professor Konopka (n.d., p. 17) wrote:

In working with delinquent street corner groups the group worker is forced to move out of any form of 'protection' by the agency. He or she has no outside power over the group—he cannot 'throw out' anybody as 'unsuited for therapy'. They are there; they are in the street; they have not asked for help and they are not apprehended. All the group worker has is his conviction that they really will be more happy people if they come to accept his help, the support of his agency which has asked him to undertake this task, and especially his own capacity to establish helpful relationships. With no props for this—not even a given room—his power of acceptance must be very great, but especially his internal security and his imagination in using every opportunity for giving help and opening the door to confidence. In my opinion this is one of the most highly skilled forms of group work.

Backgrounds and personalities of the young men and women who try their hand at street club work are as varied as are their motivations for doing this demanding and usually underpaid work. Perhaps a few brief sketches of street club workers I have known in Tel Aviv and in New York, may serve to show who is likely to succeed, and who may fail at the street corner.

A. and D. were in their early twenties when they joined the Tel Aviv Project. A. was a bachelor, studying criminology at one of Tel Aviv's undergraduate schools, D. was married, had one child and had worked on construction. His most recent job was operating a bulldozer in the Timna Copper Mines in the Negev. Both had been active as members and youth leaders in youth organisations, both had done military service. A. had been a member of a kibbutz and had attended a teacher's seminar. He is keenly interested in the study of Israel's flora and fauna and an excellent swimmer. D. worked for a short time as a counsellor in a closed institution for delinquent girls, likes to tinker with motorbikes, and has something of a reputation as a soccer player. Neither of them was ever able to state clearly just why they wanted to do this particular job, except for saying that they liked the work. Both are now in their seventh year of street club work. The youngsters in their work areas take them for granted, and boys and girls from all over the city know them and come to them for help and advice.

B., a young man in his middle twenties, chose street club work for his first job after he graduated with a professional degree in social work from one of New York's universities. Of lower-middle-class background, married, then divorced, he could be described as an intellectual, rather gentle and sensitive, and with a taste for adventure. He worked for about three years with street corner groups in New York, supervising two other workers. The youngsters of his street corner groups bullied and exploited and loved him and were very upset when he left. Several of them came to say, 'You straightened me out, man, it weren't for you . . .' B. entered law school, maintaining his contacts with youth work. 'What these kids need are lawyers who really know something about them,' he told me.

K. said that he wanted to work with 'these kids', because he had been one of them when he was younger. He was in his early twenties when he was hired by a New York street club project. Tall and muscle-packed he held a degree in physical education, was an all-round athlete, perhaps a little too serious and 'dedicated' when talking about the youngsters. Unfortunately he was assigned a supervisor who knew nothing about street club work and was too busy hiding this fact to be able to learn. At first K. seemed to do all right. He contacted a group and brought in interesting accounts of his experiences with them. Then he 'got tough' with a bunch of youngsters in his work area, and after he had made it clear to them that he 'could handle them', one of the boys swung a baseball bat at him and he was in hospital for several weeks. K. resumed his work when he came out of hospital. A few months later one of his colleagues discovered by accident that the boys whom he was supposed to work with, and about whom he wrote interesting reports, hardly knew him. An investigation disclosed that the man held a full time job as a physical education instructor in a High School and had, for quite some time, drawn two salaries while doing only one job. He was fired from the Project. His supervisor was not.

O. was twenty-five years old when he answered an advertisement for a street club worker for the Tel Aviv Project. He was married and well-to-do, owner of a large farm and active in politics. He had spent all his younger years in the youth movements, advanced to a leading position. He served in the army, edited a newspaper and published articles, and lectured at youth leaders' seminars. He opened his interview with the Project director by telling the latter that he knew all about how one ought to work with young delinquents, all he wanted was a chance to put his theories into practice. His own values were clearcut; he would demand of the youngsters no more than he demanded of himself: the will to work hard, live frugally, be a responsible citizen, etc. Everything he said seemed all wrong for the job, but the way he said it, his appearance, the way he carried himself, his enthusiasm, seemed all right. He was hired. O. started out by telling his youngsters what they should and should not do and quickly found out that he was talking to himself. He realised that he really did not know very much about this breed of kids. He began to ask questions instead of offering answers, he learned to listen. He became more patient and began to understand that what one feels may be as important in this kind of work as what one does. But he never gave up his tremendous drive to 'get things done'. Chasing about in his heavy station wagon, usually some farm produce littering the back seats, he injected some of his own energy into the youngsters. His appearance before an official in behalf of a boy demanded respect. His boys began to trust him and to work with him, and in the process they discovered potentialities no one, least of all they themselves, had known they had. O. worked two years for the Project, then took up a government appointment as supervisor of detached and youth club work with 'unreached' youth.

S. came to Israel as a tourist. A pleasingly plump twenty-two-year-old girl from the United States she had a B.A., had worked at clerical jobs, as a switchboard operator in a settlement house, and had some experience as a counsellor in summer camps. She had just begun to master the language after an intensive course in a kibbutz.The girls she was assigned to took to her almost at once. On the one hand the girls took S. under their wing, eager to teach her 'how we live here'. On the other hand they soon began to see in her a motherly sort of older sister and came to her with all those 'girl problems' that seemed either too trivial or too frightening to discuss with anyone else. The girls' older brothers, most of them highly delinquent street corner boys, 'tried it on' a few times but, to their surprise, found themselves put firmly in their place. Soon one or another of them came to grumble about his sisters' behaviour or to say how glad he was that S. was there to keep an eye on the girls. Their parents invited her to their homes and, after making excuses for their poor circumstances and voicing their concern over their children, usually got around to telling her that 'a nice girl like her' ought to get married. After a year's work S. returned to the States, worked as a teacher for a while, then applied for admission to a graduate school of social work.

C. was twenty-four when he became a street club worker in Tel Aviv. He had been a member of a youth movement, served in the army and tried his hand at a variety of jobs. Bright, and with a wide range of interests, C. came from a severely deprived background and felt that he would be well able to understand 'what these kids are up against'. A friend introduced him to the teachings of Freud and he began to attend lectures on psychoanalytic theory, group therapy, and related subjects. C. was assigned a highly delinquent and aggressive group of youngsters. They seemed to accept him readily enough, but somehow he never learned much about them, never really knew what they were up to. He was very eager to get the boys to talk about their 'deep-seated problems', their early childhood, their feelings about their mothers and fathers. He was much less eager to become involved in the numerous problems of delinquent behaviour, unemployment, boredom, hashish, etc. 'Too much talking, not enough doing', one of his colleagues described his work. There were indications that C.'s reliance on talking and reluctance to do the more practical things was partly due to his difficulties in dealing with authority figures, policemen, court officials, probation and employment officers, social workers, employers, etc., all of which had to be dealt with almost every day of the week in trying to help the youngsters sort out their messed-up situations. C.'s attitude to these people was highly ambiguous. To some degree he shared the youngster's hostility and distrust towards them, but he also envied their authority and professional status and tried to impress them by the prolific use of psychoanalytic terminology. At times he sought approval by being over deferential. It took some time before he began to understand that he was neither qualified to psychoanalyre street corner boys, nor was this approach relevant to the requirements of his job. Gradually he began to recognise the futility, even the dangers of verbal diggings into a youngster's hidden fears and emotions, before helping him deal with the immediate, practical matters. He learned that taking the boys on a hike taught him more about them than trying to organise a 'group therapy' session which discussed their motives for aggressive behaviour. He discovered that an employment counsellor was more likely to co-operate when he told him about a boy's difficulties in working without constant supervision, than when he talked to him about the boys' unresolved oedipal problems. He was well on his way to become a good street club worker when he got married and decided to look for more remunerative work.

T., the twenty-six-year-old son of a renowned Arab notable, trained and worked as a teacher, then was attracted by the challenge of street club work, the goals of which seemed to fit in with his own concern about the growing number of Arab youngsters who drifted from their villages into the cities and into delinquency. T. had grown up in a village, was deeply steeped in the tradition of his people and proud of their culture. He was well brought up and always impeccably dressed. He admitted frankly that he knew nothing about youngsters who gambled and drank, smoked hashish, stole, and lived with prostitutes. He was quite shocked when he met these youngsters and at first his approach was to tell them earnestly that their behaviour was 'not nice' and to beseech them to mend their ways. He told his supervisor that he found it very difficult to meet his youngsters in broad daylight and in places where he could be seen with them. 'There are many people who know me and my family. What will they say if they see me in the company of a group of young hooligans, what stories will come back to my village?' But T. found that his patriarchal father and his older brothers understood and accepted the nature of his work. He realised quickly that preaching made no impact on the boys, while helping them and discussing their lives with them without squeamishness did. He never gave up wearing a well-pressed suit and a tie, no matter how hot the day, but he became used to squatting on the filthy floor of a cockroach-crawling hovel while listening to a group of youngsters talk about their exploits, learned how to lean against a dusty wall at a crowded, noisy street corner, talking to a scantily dressed young prostitute who was telling him that she was pregnant and one of his boys was the father, and later to talk to the boy and his friends calmly about the matter in a disreputable cafe without moralising or being outraged. Soon the youngsters of his group brought kids from all over town to him: 'This boy is in trouble. We told him you're the man one can talk to.' T. discovered that officials and other people treated him with respect, even admiration, not because of his father's name or his well-groomed appearance, but because of the work he did.

J., a tall, very attractive twenty-two-year-old young lady, had worked as a nurse after she obtained her b.a. She did part time work in one of New York's settlement houses where she met 'detached' workers. When she heard that there were clusters of street corner girls in the area who needed a worker, she decided to give it a try. She came from an upper-middle-class family. Her father was an important government official and she had so far led what she jokingly called 'a sheltered life'. A few hours before a male colleague was to introduce her to a group of girls who had become notorious in the neighbourhood for their 'badness', J. had an attack of stage fright. 'I can't do it,' she said. 'I'll be petrified. I have no idea how to act or what to say to these girls.' Her colleague asked: 'Have you ever been at one of these cocktail parties where you don't know anybody and feel completely out of place?' 'Yes.' 'What did you do?' 'I just stood in a corner, trying to look intelligent and amused, wondering whether I was dressed right for the occasion.' 'And what happened?' 'After a while some people were introduced to me and I never did catch their names. Some made inane remarks and so did I, one asked me what I did and I told her and she told me what she did, and we talked for a while and I began to feel more comfortable.' 'Well that's about what's going to happen tonight, only without cocktails,' J.'s colleague said. 'I'll make the introductions, and then you make polite conversation. One of the girls will probably ask you what you do, and you'll tell her, and ask her what she does, and she'll tell you. You'll suffer through some of the inane talk, ignore the four-letter words they might try out on you, and when the conversation flags you'll tell them how much you enjoyed meeting them, excuse yourself politely and leave.' And that is just about what happened that evening.

Within a few weeks the girls had taken possession of J. as 'their worker' and were upset when they felt that she didn't spend enough time with them, though concerned about what it would do to her reputation 'for hanging out with us'. These girls had been at the beck and call of the tough boys of a highly delinquent street corner group. They had been the butt of the boys' bullying and obscenities, dependent on gaining the

boys' respect by their own skill in using a beer can opener to gash a face
or a bottle to bounce off someone's head, always trying to be in demand
by providing sexual satisfaction. Now they learned to rely on their own
girls' group for company and fun. J. took them on trips and to the
theatre. With the help of one of the mothers who offered her kitchen, J.
held fancy-dishes cooking sessions. Fashion designing, sewing, beauty
treatments and hair-dos became eagerly attended group activities. Sex
and personal hygiene were discussed and by the end of a year the girls
were able to use the facilities of the settlement house without being
evicted. The boys complained bitterly. The girls' gain was their loss.
But their complaints had undertones of respect and admiration, they
liked to talk to J. and about her, and when she once got into an unpleasant situation with a local adult, they rescued her forcefully. J. left when
her girls had been accepted as a 'club' in the settlement house and were
able to fend for themselves. She enrolled in a graduate school to obtain
her Master's Degree in social welfare.

These are only a few of the many different people who have become
street club workers. Some are 'naturals' for the job, others are 'unknown
quantities' when they start out, and grow into competent professionals
through hard work, conscientious training and supervision, and a certain amount of trial-and-error. A few turn out to be unsuitable for this
type of work. Except in the very general terms outlined here, there is no
fool-proof prescription for selecting the right person. The best safeguard
is the skill and experience of the supervisor or project director who interviews an applicant. Once the worker is appointed, he or she has the right
to the full support and guidance through training and supervision. A
worker's failure is very often the failure of the supervisor to meet his
obligations.

One more thing remains so be said: the assignment of the worker
should be considered carefully, and when the worker does not seem to
make headway with one type of youngster, he should be given the
opportunity to try something else, whenever possible. A young man who
is unable to cope with a bunch of very violent, 'fighting-mad' kids, may
do well with a group of young thieves. A worker who does not seem able
to establish a relationship with a group of youngsters who have adopted
the pose of hardened criminals, may do marvels with drug users. A
worker who does not get along with a group of seventeen- to eighteen-
year-olds, may do a good and much-needed job with younger boys or
girls.

15 Developing the relationship

The ease or difficulty in establishing contact, in gaining acceptance, and in developing a relationship depends on a number of factors. The age of gang members, the degree of organization, and the strength of their leadership are important considerations. The amount of antisocial activity and its motivation, as well as the amount and kind of more acceptable activity are other factors. The culture and mores of the community provide still another set of factors.

C. E. MURRAY et al (1954), p. 138

From the slowly developing confidence of the members of his group in the worker, as a result of the on-going contact made on a day-to-day basis, emerges the 'relationship' which is utilized to redirect the gang's energies. Such a relationship must at once be meaningful for the members and basically real. Very often, the beginnings of such a deep relationship between worker and gang members are manifested in the sincerity with which they solicit his advice on really serious problems, in the ways in which they may attempt to imitate his mannerisms or even dress. The more established this relationship becomes, the more easily can the worker influence the group away from the negative and toward the more positive behaviour desired.

NEW YORK CITY YOUTH BOARD (1960), pp. 8-9

When I first contacted the 'Emperors' at an Upper East-Side street corner of Manhattan, they already had a well-established reputation as a bunch of young hoodlums and thieves who terrorised the neighbourhood with their brawling, attacks on innocent strollers, muggings and burglaries. It took a few days of hanging around before the hostile, suspicious glances of the youngsters began to change to curious and puzzled ones, and the first boy came up to me to ask what the obscenity I was doing there. My explanation of my assignment was reported back to the group, and they went right on ignoring me. The following day a few of the boys came to talk. They didn't believe that 'social worker jazz'. In their opinion I was either a 'cop' or a 'faggot' (homosexual) trying to make a pick-up. So we had a little discussion about 'cops' and 'faggots', and I explained my job all over again. This exchange of opinions about who I was and what I was looking for went on for a few evenings, then the leader of the gang, a sixteen-year-old six-footer named Butch, came over and asked the boys who were talking to me, what the hell they thought they were doing. I was on my own again.

My 'break' came a few nights later: A few minutes after midnight Micky, a sixteen-year-old Irish boy, smashed his fist through a store window to grab a carton of cigarettes. I was just knocking out my pipe, ready to go home, when a bunch of the boys came running towards me, half-carrying, half dragging Micky, his arm sliced from wrist to elbow and bleeding profusely: 'You said you gonna help us, man? This guy is in trouble. Do something . . .'

Half an hour later Micky had been stitched up and made comfortable in the emergency ward of a nearby hospital. The police, called automatically in such cases, had been there and, after checking my identity, had taken my word for it that I would produce the boy for questioning when necessary, and see to it that his parents were informed. Micky's friends were waiting outside in the dark street while I talked to him. I asked: 'You mind telling me what the purpose of this exercise was?' He grinned, his face white and tired and looking much younger than his sixteen years. 'I needed a smoke, man, and there was that carton of "Luckies" staring at me.' I let that go for a moment, then said: 'The cops aren't going to take that for an answer.' Micky screwed up his face in a grimace of supplication: 'You gonna help me out, ain'tya? I'm up against it, you know, my mother is dyin' of cancer and my father is an alcoholic. I gotta take care of them.' I said 'Yeah sure, and why don't you call me Officer Krupke?'[1] He grinned as I rose to leave: 'O.K., so long man, see you in Atlantic Avenue' (New York's prison for young offenders).

Micky's friends awaited me outside in a tight, tense little group. I told them that the boy was all right and we talked about the 'accident' for a few minutes. They seemed to ignore me when I walked off, I had crossed over to the other side of the street when a voice called out: 'Eh thanks for takin' care of things . . .' and another voice shouted: 'See you tomorrow . . .'

Micky addressed me as 'Officer Krupke' for a while. His mother died of cancer a few months after the incident. I met his father and helped to get him into an alcoholic ward for a cure. He started drinking again as soon as he came out. Meanwhile Micky had taken over the old man's janitor job in order to keep their cellar apartment.

A couple of years later some members of the 'Emperors' pointed out a group of younger boys at a nearby street corner. They seemed a nice enough bunch of kids, full of pep, but relatively good-natured and well-behaved. But the older boys said: 'You better talk to those kids, man. They're getting in a lot of trouble. Soon they're gonna turn real mean.' That was my introduction to another street corner group, and I soon found out that there was plenty of work for me here: petty thefts, vandalism, a few burglaries. This group knew all about me already and were rather pleased that they would have their own worker now. I had no trouble getting to know the boys, but it took me a while to convince them that they didn't have to tell me a lot of wildly exaggerated stories

[1] A Police Officer who is the butt of a satirical song in 'West Side Story'.

about their criminal exploits to make it worth my while hanging around with them.

A group of young drug addicts welcomed me with polite detachment. They were 'very interested' in my work, very eager to 'co-operate' and 'grateful' for my offer to help them. These boys thought they had found a good-natured sucker from whom money and protection from the police could be obtained with the help of heart-rending and very imaginative hard luck stories. It took some time before I convinced them that I 'knew the score', but was still ready to help.

A tough-looking, close-mouthed outfit assigned to me because of their bad reputation had me puzzled for some time. These boys considered themselves a fighting gang. They had a president, a 'war-counsellor' and one lanky, skinny adolescent introduced himself as the 'older states-man' who did the strategic planning. These boys did some brawling, petty stealing, destroyed property and were looking for another gang they could challenge to a fight. They boasted about their hidden arsenal of weapons, painted 'keep off the turf' signs on the walls of the neighbour-hood, and called themselves 'The Chosen Few'. I was received in a cool, businesslike manner, told that my services were acceptable, as every fighting gang had to have their 'gang worker'. They displayed their weapons for me on the first night, a few knives, an old bayonet and a rusty meat-cleaver. There was mysterious talk about hidden guns. After a few days these boys began to relax and I began to figure them out. They were playing Cowboys-and-Indians and had seen too many movies about juvenile delinquents. My major concern with them was to get them to stop pilfering candy and cigarettes and go back to school.

A Lower East-Side fighting gang with a tradition of bloody warfare that reached back several years and a very justified reputation for toughness and fearlessness received me with caution and reserve. I found them sitting on a row of benches in the yard of a large Housing Project one evening and introduced myself and explained my job and why my agency had sent me to contact them. This was received in stony silence. I added: 'I've heard a lot about you and I'm impressed by your reputa-tion in the neighbourhood. I was told that you guys are one of the tough-est gangs in New York and not scared of anybody. I admire courage, and I'd consider it an honour if you let me work with you.' They liked that and there were nods of approval. But all of them gave me false names at first and carefully guarded the identity of their leaders. It took patient work and some concrete demonstrations of the kind of help I could offer, before these youngsters began to open up and give me their confidence. A year later when the group had given up their fighting and had their own club room, one of the boys reminded me of that first night: 'You said the right thing there, Aryeh, you showed us respect.'

The leader of an East Harlem gang listened thoughtfully to my description of street club work after I had introduced myself. His response was enthusiastic. The boys certainly could use help, and he, the leader, would gladly show me what was needed and teach me how to go about making myself useful. In fact, it seemed, Big Jose was quite ready to take me on as his assistant. It took several weeks before I succeeded in drawing some of the members of the group into the conversations of 'us two leaders', and convinced Jose that what his kids needed first of all was an opportunity to speak for themselves.

When I first mentioned to the 'Emperors' that the girls who were hanging out with them could use a worker of their own, the boys thought this was a good idea. 'Them girls are a mess,' one of the group's leaders told me, 'they sure need somebody to straighten them out. I mean, its different for the guys, you know—I mean we gotta get some action, get our kicks. But when the girls start drinking and fighting and acting like pigs, man, that's embarrassing, you know what I mean?'

The girls' reaction was somewhat different: 'A social worker for us?' Martha said, raising her pencilled eyebrows, 'why, we ain't in any trouble, we don't go stealing and beating up on people like the boys,' and Rita added: 'We don't want no social worker coming around giving people the idea that we're "bad" girls. Right away everybody'll think we're juvenile delinquents or something. My old man'll beat the sh . . . out of me.' But curiosity won out: 'O.K. bring her around, we'll take a look at her. But she better not get nosey, if she knows what's good for her.'

When I introduced the young woman who had taken on the job she was received with distrust and reserve. The girls didn't want to tell her anything, they wanted to know about how she lived and 'what made her want to do a crazy job like that'. A few weeks later, the girls told me proudly: 'We have our own worker now. We got our own parties and trips. The boys think we can't do nothing without them, but we do all right for ourselves.'

The worker's first contact with a delinquent street corner group, the first step toward establishing a relationship was not very different in Tel Aviv. Here too, the street club worker had to break through a barrier of distrust before the process of communication between him and the youngsters began. In most cases the hostility that accompanied the initial distrust seemed to be somewhat less pronounced than in New York. However, one of our workers was threatened by a crowd of boys when he surveyed a number of underprivileged neighbourhoods in order to identify street corner groups. The youngsters insisted that he must be a 'Balash' (youth-squad detective) and demanded to see his identification. When the worker asked why it made any difference whether he was a police officer or not, after all he hadn't bothered anyone, the reply was: 'If you're a cop you won't get out of here in one piece. We'll wipe you out.' But no action followed this ominous threat.

Tel Aviv street club workers met with the accusation of hiding their real identity, and really being plain-clothes police officers whenever they contacted a new street corner group in a lower-class neighbourhood. There was a great degree of distrust and hostility directed towards the police, and the word 'Balash' followed the worker around and was hard to shake off. Another obstacle the worker ran into was the question, 'What [political] party are you from? What's your gimmick?' It usually took some time before we succeeded in convincing the youngsters that the street club worker is neither an employee of the police, nor is he affiliated with any political party out to get votes for the next elections. But even while these questions of the worker's identity are being cleared up, the youngsters usually show their eagerness to talk about themselves, to boast about their exploits, complain about their various troubles, and ask for concrete help. There may be 'testing' of the worker that is as vicious and imaginative as similar behaviour in New York. There are attempts to manipulate and to 'snow' (deceive) the worker and to exploit him in various ways. But I found that the street corner boys in Tel Aviv are, in most instances, as 'reachable' as those in New York.

It is, perhaps, a little easier in Tel Aviv, and takes less time to lay the groundwork for a relationship: on one occasion I walked up to a group of about fifteen teenagers in a small, cohesive slum neighbourhood in Tel Aviv. I interrupted the boys' noisy exchange about the latest soccer game by introducing myself and explaining the purpose of the Project's work. The boys seemed somewhat surprised at the intrusion, but not resentful. Some of the younger kids playing nearby screamed that I was a 'Balash', but were ignored. The boys wanted to know if I represented any party, and whether I had come to make election promises. When I answered both questions in the negative, I was frankly told that the group didn't believe my story, but that they were willing to talk to me anyway. 'What have we got to lose?' one of them asked rhetorically. The boys asked what I could 'do for them', one of them adding: 'We don't need nobody to do a lot of talking. We got enough people we can talk with right here.' When I said that before I could decide what I had to offer them I would have first to learn a lot about them and their way of life, so that I would know who I am dealing with, the boys accepted this. One of them said, 'Sure, we'll tell you about us. What do you want to know?' winking at the others. Another boy laughed and said: 'All these guys here are a bunch of hooligans. They all belong in jail.' A third youngster pushed the others aside to look at me closely, angrily. 'Why don't you look at the way we live here, if you want to know about us?' he asked. 'We got nothing here. We need a lot of things.' A voice from the back of the group yelled: 'What we need is one motorcycle each, and we'll all stop stealing cars.' The laughter that followed was interrupted by one of the older boys who shouted for quiet, then turned to me: 'O.K., you want a problem? Here's one . . .' and for the next half hour I was involved in an intensive discussion about possibilities of getting certain jobs without the required educational qualifications, about the laws of workman's compensation in the case of an accident, and about the advantages and disadvantages of shirking army service.

The experience of most of the Project's field workers resembled my own. One very helpful factor was the culturally prescribed hospitality of Oriental ethnic groups, somewhat similar to the attitude I have encountered in Puerto Rican neighbourhoods in New York. In both cities the youngsters' natural curiosity soon overcomes their distrust, and all of them like to listen to a good story. In both cities the street corner boys have a vast array of concrete problems and needs and are alert to the possibility that one can, perhaps, 'get something out of this guy'. In many cases the youngsters try to use the worker from the outset as someone who can get them things or solve their problems for them.

The Tel Aviv Project's first female street club worker encountered the same attitude as her colleague in New York: 'If we get a worker, like the boys, everybody'll think we're bad girls.' Two of our workers found themselves welcomed with open arms by youngsters whose isolation was so oppressive that they were glad of any outside contact, happy and eager to sit and talk and listen to someone who seemed to accept them on their own terms. One of these two workers was told, after several months of intensive work with this group: 'You're all right with us, man. We still think you might be a cop, but we don't mind. You've helped us a lot, and we like it when you come around. You can tell us now if you're really a Balash, we don't care.'

One of the Project's workers was tested about his ability to get a job for one of the boys who had run into trouble at the Youth Employment Office. The worker helped the boy, and as a result, was immediately assigned the role of 'the guy who gets jobs for us'. He was flooded with requests for jobs for those who did not work at all, and better jobs for those who did. In order to establish his relationship with the group, this worker first had to overcome the obstacles put in his way by the limited functional role the group was trying to assign to him.

Another member of the Project staff had to undergo a number of tests as to how 'shock-proof' he was. The boys, members of a street corner group in a mixed neighbourhood, staged several exhibitions of highly aggressive, vandalistic and obscene behaviour for his benefit. When the worker neither ran away, nor began to preach and berate, the boys brought him a 'case' (the younger brother of one of the leaders) who needed institutional care, and tested the worker as to his professional competence. The worker made the necessary referrals. Then the group made every attempt to adopt him as a member, make him become 'one of us'. He was invited to private parties, offered stolen goods and treated with great and apparently sincere affection. Gradually the group began to understand and accept the worker's professional role and relate to him in an acceptable and productive way.

In New York and in Tel Aviv the street club worker is tested by the offer of sex and of presents. The sex thing is straightforward enough: sooner or later the boys offer to get the worker fixed-up with a girl or ask him to participate in a line-up. A straight refusal, accompanied by a humorous remark, is readily accepted. I found in New York that it helped to establish my position, and show that I was well provided for in that area, when I took my wife along to the group's parties, or invited them to my home. On all these occasions my wife was treated with great chivalry and respect. Tel Aviv street club workers had the same experience when they introduced their wives or girl friends to their groups, though one of the female workers was kept busy with tactfully warding off the frequent attempts by her girls' parents to introduce her to eligible young men, 'because a nice young girl like you should think of getting married'.

The matter of presents is more complicated. Especially during the beginning stages of the work, street club workers are often offered stolen goods, usually in order to involve them in the group's criminal activities, at times as a sincere gesture of appreciation and affection. Bottles of perfume 'for your wife', a carton of cigarettes, a lighter, a bottle of whisky, etc. are offered every now and then. My New York boys once brought me a stolen Christmas tree for the holiday.

Things are relatively simple if the worker is certain that the object is stolen. In such a case he will, of course, refuse, stating his obvious reasons clearly. It is more difficult to know what to do when there is a possibility that the boys have bought the gift with their own money, and a refusal may mean an expression of distrust and a rejection of a sincere expression of friendship. In some instances I have found it best to spell out my dilemma and discuss my doubts and their feelings about my attitude with the boys.

Now and then one falls into the trap. On a trip to Washington where we spent the night in a Y.M.C.A. hostel, the boys of the 'Emperors' got me out of bed in the morning and invited me to a well prepared breakfast in their room. I had put away a considerable quantity of excellent ham, and crispy rolls and several glasses of orange juice before it occured to me to ask for the source of all this largesse. It didn't help my digestion when I found out that the boys had staged an organised raid on the delivery trucks servicing the grocery stores in the neighbourhood.

A Tel Aviv street club worker, on a hike through the Galilee with his group, munched sweets and nuts contentedly, until he discovered that the boys had stolen them from the counter of a kiosk in the last little town they visited. He expressed his anger vividly and drove home the lesson by marching all the way back to pay for the stolen goods out of his own pocket.

Even legitimate gifts are, in general, to be discouraged, not only because most of the youngsters can ill afford them, but also because they tend to distort the worker's role and leave the youngsters with the impression that he is doing them 'special favours' for which he should be rewarded. Here it helps to state repeatedly at appropriate occasions that the worker receives a salary that, in fact, he gets paid for making his services available to the group and to the individual youngster. Sometimes the boys want to know 'how much' and are entitled to an honest answer. (This is another reason why street club workers should be paid adequately. It does not help the relationship if the boys have to feel sorry for him.)

On some occasions I have accepted presents gratefully, for instance when the boys of the 'Commanders' each contributed some money and bought me a bottle of my favourite Scotch at the occasion of the first anniversary of our club room. One of the Tel Aviv Project's workers received an expensive and legitimately purchased wedding gift and accepted it gladly. In such instances the worker may feel that he should reciprocate. It is advisable for workers to give presents (a game, a football, a record, food, etc.) to the group, rather than to any individual youngster.

My experience in Tel Aviv as well as in New York is that these 'hard-to-reach' youngsters are not all hard to reach, provided one tries to reach them in their own environment and on their own terms. The evidence for this is there for all to see, long before a street club worker ever contacts a delinquent group: all the groups I have observed frequently encounter problems and situations which confuse and frighten them. Even without poverty and delinquency, adolescence is a stage in life in which things are frightening and confusing from time to time, a period in which youngsters need to turn to the adults for guidance and support, no matter how hard they rebel against adult influence and standards at other times. Every delinquent street corner group I have encountered so far has had contacts and some form of a relationship with some adults in their neighbourhood. The delinquent norms of the group usually prescribe that these adults be individuals who are themselves in conflict with society, often criminal. They are the 'street corner men', who have never really left the adolescent stage and hang around, drinking, boasting, brawling, shying adult responsibilities and work. There are those semirespectable people in the community who are not averse to making a little extra cash by illegitimate means. There is the candy store or the coffee shop owner who lends money for interest, at whose place one can leave things that are better not shown at home, and who may be willing to buy a radio, a bottle of expensive liquor, a carton of cigarettes, provided the price is right and never mind where the stuff came from. There is the odd-ball character who makes his living-place available for a party, lets the fellow bring a girl there sometimes or has a boy stay overnight when he's been thrown out of his home or the cops are looking for him. There is also the adult criminal, the fence (peddlar of stolen goods), the drug peddlar and the local racketeer who may have a profitable little job for one or two of the boys from time to time.

Delinquent street corner groups in a lower-class area usually have established relationships with adults who are part and parcel of the illegitimate opportunity system which breeds and supports the delinquent subculture. The youngsters seek help and advice from adults who are today what they themselves may become tomorrow. The street club worker provides the opportunity for a new kind of relationship, one which has constructive content and positive goals. Gradually, patiently, he seeks to replace the destructive influence to which the youngsters are exposed. Patience is the key-word here.

One Saturday afternoon about six months after his first contact with a Tel Aviv corner group, nine of the boys, all about fifteen years old, invited the worker to come along with them to see a movie in the centre of the city. On the bus the boys were noisy and exhilarated and would not stay in their seats. Most of them settled down after the worker asked them to behave themselves, except for Abbi, the most aggressive and strongest boy of the group, and his close friend Arnon. These two kept ringing the bell, annoyed the driver and made fun of other passengers. The worker finally grabbed Abbi by the arm, pulled him down beside him and told him sharply to 'cut it out'. Abbi complied, but Arnon, trying to squeeze in to sit down beside his friend, stepped on the foot of a young passenger. The latter cursed him, and immediately the group was out of their seats, backing up Abbi who offered to fight the young man. Fortunately the bus arrived at the group's destination at this moment, and the worker pushed the boys off the bus, telling them that they would miss the beginning of the show if they didn't get off.

Walking to the cinema Abbi began to push Elisha, one of the smaller boys, against passing girls. The worker had hardly stopped this activity, when the boys saw a group of girls playing basketball in a school yard. All of them crowded against the fence and yelled obscene comments on the girls' anatomies. They stopped when the worker told them angrily that he would not tolerate being embarrassed that way in public and started to walk away. Abbi ran after him and promised that he would behave himself from now on. The group arrived at the cinema and tickets were bought without further incidents, everyone paying for himself.

In the movies Abbi began once more to make a nuisance of himself, shouting comments on the film, disturbing and annoying the people around him. He lit a cigarette (which is forbidden in all Israeli cinemas) and dropped ashes on the clothes of an Army officer who sat near him. The man shouted at him and Abbi offered to fight. By this time the other boys of the group were finding Abbi's behaviour disturbing and took the worker's side when he told Abbi to put out the cigarette and change seats, so that he would sit beside the worker. He told Abbi quietly that he had come to enjoy the movie and would have to leave if the rowdy behaviour didn't stop. Abbi apologised and kept quiet from then on.

After the show, on the way to the bus, Abbi apologised once more and told the worker that he was glad he hadn't forced him to leave. He said: 'I don't know what happens when I go to the city. I just go wild. I don't really want to make any trouble, but I can't stop myself.' Shortly after this, as if trying to prove his point, he picked up an empty bottle and smashed it on the sidewalk, sending glass splinters sailing off in all directions, frightening some passers-by. For the rest of the way the worker kept him walking beside him, holding on to his arm. On the bus returning to the group's neighbourhood, the worker kept the boys involved in talking about the film they had seen and the trip passed without further incidents.

Experience showed that the behaviour of the boys on that particular Saturday afternoon was the rule rather than the exception. By asking the worker to come along, by allowing him repeatedly to remonstrate with them, and to set limits for some of their outbreaks, these boys were actually telling the worker: 'We accept you and your ways now, and we think that you have accepted us. Today we'll give you a little demonstration of how we carry on when we get out of the neighbourhood. Let's see how you handle this, and whether you can help us to keep out of trouble.' The worker's relationship with his group of youngsters had reached a stage at which they not only were inviting him to become closely involved in one of their favourite activities, but were bestowing upon him the authority to intervene, to reprimand and to set limits.

The establishing of a relationship with an understanding, knowledgeable and law-abiding adult is in itself one of the major goals of street club work, the first breach in the barriers of distrust and hostility that isolate the delinquent group. The process that takes place in establishing the relationship between the worker and the group consists of two parts: the gaining of mutual acceptance and trust, and the clear definition of the worker's role and function.

A great deal of confusion rules with regard to the latter: the clear definition of the worker's role and function, especially in Britain, where 'detached work' is still in its embryonic stages. Mary Morse's (1965, pp. 203–6) report on a National Association of Youth Clubs project carried out some years ago described some unfortunate and unnecessary attempts by detached workers to disguise their identity. The confusion on this subject which still prevails is reflected in a recent article by Dr Cyril S. Smith (1966, p. 48), who writes:

When a youth worker enters a working-class area with the object of contacting potential offenders he is faced with the task of defining his role. This is not only necessary for his own mental health but also to make it possible for people to know how they should react to him. It is common for him to be suspected of being a 'queer' on the make. Where the worker conceals his identity, he develops almost unbearable feelings of guilt and his incapacity is increased by the absence of help from other agencies in the community who are unaware of his existence. But what role should he adopt? It is difficult to assume the role of caseworker since that role often carries the obligation to wait until your help is requested and the caseworker can only begin when the individual assumes the role of client. (This is a problem which also faces other types of community care.) In this situation, however, it may do more harm than good for the young person to assume the role of delinquent, for this self-perception is often a stage in the career of a criminal. It is also difficult to play the usual role of youth leader since their activities are usually carried on inside more formal settings. Has he then to be satisfied with a very diffuse role like friend (as in the Cambridge-Sommerville study) which can mean everything or nothing depending upon the situation? But when did friends keep process records of their relationships with each other? Or interfere with each other's lives? Perhaps the answer to these questions will only come with time and experience; trying out a role will indicate its acceptability.

Surely we know the answer by now: The worker must identify himself clearly and, if necessary, repeatedly, as a youth worker with special tasks which can be spelled out in detail, employed by an agency or organisation and charged with working toward certain goals with a group of youngsters who have given indications that they are in trouble and cause trouble to others. There can be no concealment or subterfuge here, and an honest and constructive relationship cannot be built on any other basis. A worker who does not know what his professional identity and function is has obviously not been trained for his job, nor received the necessary supervision and guidance from his agency. He should not be sent out into the street to contact youngsters.

16 Learning to accept each other

Essentially, a worker must begin by accepting a group of street corner boys not as a collection of perverse and bad individuals or as a group of innocent but misunderstood children, but as a group of individuals operating within a framework of values which reflects their views of the world and the view of much of the community around them—a framework of values that brings them into frequent and often harsh conflict with the larger community. This framework of values may be opposite to that which the worker uses to guide his own life, but he must, nevertheless, accept its reality and the validity it has for the group members.

D. M. AUSTIN (1957), p. 50

The first prerequisite for gaining the trust of any group is honesty. A recent article by Professor Hallek (1963), an American psychiatrist, discusses the need for professional honesty in dealing with 'disturbed adolescents'. The subject is of such fundamental importance in working with delinquent youth, that some of the main points of the article must be mentioned here.

Professor Hallek (1963, pp. 49–50) points out that dishonesty in declaring and spelling out the mandate and goals of the worker will lead to a reaction of distrust and disbelief on the part of the youngsters. The pretence of altruistic, disinterested helpfulness which makes no demands and expects no returns, is based on the assumption that delinquent adolescents are naïve and inexperienced in the ways of the world. Neither in New York nor in Tel Aviv have I found this assumption to be borne out by the facts. The youngsters 'know the score', and they want to know 'What's in it for you'. It is best to tell them from the outset that the worker has certain expectations regarding their delinquent behaviour and hopes to change some of their attitudes. It is also best to admit right away that the worker has been sent to this or that particular group because their behaviour has caused concern. This does not have to take the form of preaching and admonishing, but can be stated in simple direct terms. I have time and again told a group of youngsters who asked me the reason of my interest in them: 'I heard that you guys made a bit of a name for yourselves around here. You get into a lot of trouble, scare people, the police have an eye on you. My agency, the people who pay my salary, think maybe you and I can work together to get things straightened out, help you with some of your problems, and maybe you'll teach us how some of the trouble here starts and how it can be stopped.' I have found that the youngsters accept this kind of an approach and are willing to discuss the issues implied.

Professor Hallek (p. 49) warns that it does not engender trust if the

worker maintains the pretence of the infallibility and high moral standards of conventional adult society. My own experience leads me to
believe that nowadays it is rather difficult even to convince six-year-olds
of this myth, not to mention adolescents who have grown up in slums.
The worker is much more likely to gain the confidence of the youngsters
if he helps them face reality as it is and deal with it as constructively as
possible. It is not only hypocritical to hold up models of propriety and
righteousness for emulation, it is impractical. The people we try to help
are usually not cut out for the roles of saints. The worker is more likely
to earn confidence in his judgment and methods, if he conveys expectations that are geared to the realities and potentials of personalities and
life situations.

Professor Hallek (p. 51) speaks of the 'lie' of telling the youngster that
giving up delinquent behaviour will end all his troubles, that conformity
brings its own rewards. He points out the implicit dishonesty of asking
the youngster to exchange the 'bad' for the 'sick' role. These are issues
of great significance to street club work, because they are pitfalls the
worker must learn to avoid if he wants to establish a relationship that is
based upon trust. Their avoidance demands an honesty that goes deep
beneath the surface of everyday politeness. The kind of honesty demanded here must be based upon more than the will to tell the truth,
it must be based upon the readiness to seek true understanding of the
needs of the youngsters. The worker must first truly understand the
reassuring, satisfying role delinquent behaviour plays in the lives of these
boys, he must gain insight into the important defensive function of being
'bad', before he can be honest about telling the youngster how much he
must give up in order to conform, how little he may gain, and that,
nevertheless, circumstance demands a certain degree of conformity from
anyone who wants to stay within the framework of this society rather
than be, sooner or later, destroyed.

The worker must also be straight about his own limitations, his own
values and feelings. The temptation to pretend to know more than one
really does is great, but this pretence can only lead to disappointment and
distrust. By being evasive about his own values the worker causes confusion and reinforces the cynicism of the boys. He neither should nor
can impose his own values upon the group, but he should be clear and
direct about them, in order to afford the youngsters an opportunity for
comparison and a frame of reference that is different from that of their
immediate environment.

One of my New York colleagues who had upheld the liberal, enlightened view of the equal rights of all men, no matter what their race,
creed or religion in his discussions with a group of boys who believed in

'white supremacy', was pinned down one day: 'O.K., man, we've heard all that jazz you talk before. Now tell us one thing: Would you let your daughter marry a nigger?' His reply was: 'No, I would not, but that is because people like you, with your opinions, make it so difficult and humiliating and even dangerous to live in a close relationship with a person of different race or skin-colour.' I thought this a rather clever answer at the time. For the street corner boys it was perhaps a little too clever. Their reaction was: 'Never mind the speeches. Fact is you wouldn't let your daughter marry a black man, because deep down you think like us, you're a white man.'

I was asked the very same question: 'Would you let your daughter . . .' by the boys of the 'Emperors' one evening after a heated discussion on civil rights and segregation. I thought of giving my colleague's well formulated reply. Or else I could have easily evaded the question, especially as I have no daughter. But there were about a dozen boys challenging me to declare myself. Some of these boys were so deeply rooted in the traditions of race hatred and prejudice that nothing I or anyone else could say would change their attitudes. A few had expressed doubts about what they had been taught since infancy, the generations-old contempt for those who were 'different' and therefore inferior. Among these were some who had learned respect for a Puerto Rican youngster in a fight, or had found a friend in a Negro boy in jail. For most of the youngsters my opinions on a variety of matters had become important, not necessarily to be agreed with, but at least to be considered. I said: 'Yes, I would.'

For a while it looked as if I had destroyed what had taken me so long to build up. I met with a kind of derision and contempt I had not encountered even during the first weeks of my contact with the group. I was pointed out to strangers as 'the guy who'd let his daughter . . .' I tried to carry on as usual. On several occasions I said: 'Well, I've told you where I stand. I'm as entitled to my convictions as you are to yours. You can argue with me about them, but you can't force me to deny them. Now do you want to talk about that job you were offered (or your court case, the loan you have to repay, the driving test you're afraid you won't pass, your father's refusal to see a doctor, the hike we're planning, etc.), or would you rather 'go it alone' because I think differently than you do about certain things?' Nobody refused my help and advice. A boy came up to me and said: 'You know, that wasn't too smart to say what you did in this neighbourhood.' Another youngster drew me aside to tell me that he'd been thinking about what I said, and that he thought I might have something there. He'd met a Puerto Rican girl and 'man, she was the sweetest . . . and intelligent too, talks better

English than me'. One night Freddy pointed his thumb in my direction once again: 'You know what that guy said, he said he'd let his daughter . . .' and Butch told him: 'Why don't you shut your f . . . mouth. The guy's got a right to his opinion, don't he? It's his daughter, ain't it? It didn't bother you when you stole ten bucks from your old man and Aryeh lent you the money to put it back before your old man found out and beat your brains in.' That was the last I heard of this. My relationship to the group was not disrupted. On the contrary. I had reason to believe that it had passed a crucial test and had come out of it strengthened and deepened.

It is perhaps hardest for the worker to be honest about his own feelings. Anger, disappointment, frustration, are feelings that are difficult to hide. The pretence that, as far as the worker is concerned, they do not exist, usually does more harm than good. Of course the professional is expected to learn to control his feelings and let his reason rather than his emotions determine his actions. But in asking a group of youngsters to enter into a meaningful and constructive relationship with him, the worker is also asking them to let him gain insight into how they feel about their own persons, their behaviour, their environment and about him as an individual with a certain function and purpose. This gives the youngsters the right to know how he feels about them, to be aware of his affection, as well as his anger.

Any meaningful relationship must be based upon mutual acceptance and trust. If these qualities are demanded by only one partner and granted only by the other, manipulation and exploitation will rapidly become the dominant factors. Manipulative and exploitative relationships, however, are part of the delinquent milieu and support the system of antisocial norms and values we seek to change. Only an honest, creative relationship can be regarded as one of the major goals in reaching and helping a group of delinquents.

Gaining the youngsters' trust is one essential prerequisite for establishing the relationship between worker and group, conveying acceptance of the group's values, norms and behaviour is another. Sophia M. Robison (1960, p. 511) describes this aspect of establishing the relationship in simple terms: 'Getting acquainted means sticking around in the gang's hangout and trying to make friends no matter what happens.'

The clue lies in the words 'no matter what happens'. It is not easy for the worker who has his own values and his own standards of behaviour, to stand around and not interfere or even voice his disapproval when a group of delinquent youngsters behave and express themselves in their accustomed manner. I remember vividly how difficult it was for me to bear with one particularly unpleasant form of behaviour exhibited by a street corner group I contacted in New York. This group of boys found a special delight in spitting on the sidewalk, until the area surrounding them was covered with their saliva and it was hard to find a place to stand without stepping into the stuff. A nasty habit, to be sure, but *their* habit. No one had given me the right to object. If I didn't like it, I could always leave. If I wanted to work with this group, I had to accept their ways, no matter how obnoxious these were to me personally.

A Tel Aviv street club worker found the group he contacted engaged in throwing eggs at buildings and at people who were foolhardy enough to come within range. The boys had obtained a case of raw eggs somewhere, and found them ideal missiles. The worker found this behaviour very disturbing, and the thought that he himself might become the target didn't help his peace of mind. Yet the worker did not interfere.

Behaviour may put the worker's shock-resistance and patience to even more severe tests, and is often designed to do just that. One of the Tel Aviv street club workers sat on a park bench surrounded by a group of youngsters he had contacted the preceding day, while the youngsters engaged in obscene and sadistic sexual activities with a fourteen-year-old girl. The worker could have objected and interfered, undoubtedly with the result that he would have been told to mind his own business, or challenged to 'try and stop us'. Or else the worker could have got up and walked away. He may very well have walked away from his chance to reach this group and work with them.

I encountered a very similar situation with a New York street corner group, when I was invited to a party which turned out to be a line-up in which a dozen youngsters made use of two girls. I neither tried to intervene, nor did I leave. The Tel Aviv worker was asked by boys what he thought of their behaviour. He admitted frankly that he did not quite know what to say, that he had never seen sixteen- and seventeen-year-old boys mistreat a fourteen-year-old girl in this manner, nor had he ever known a girl who would submit to this kind of treatment. The boys began to 'explain' their behaviour and talk about the girl. A discussion ensued which taught the worker a number of things about the norms of the group, which permitted such behaviour, and the values and beliefs which sought to justify it. The New York youngsters wanted to know whether I had enjoyed the 'party' after the girls had been dismissed. I asked them to explain to me, what kind of kick they got out of this activity, how the girls felt about it, and in what way this form of sexual gratification differed from masturbation, an activity I knew they considered childish and embarrassing. We talked until the early morning hours and I learned a lot about these boys that night.

Cloward and Ohlin (1960, p. 91) state: 'Delinquents have withdrawn their support from established norms and invested officially forbidden forms of conduct with a claim to legitimacy in the light of their special situation. They recognize that law-abiding persons regard their behaviour as illegitimate and they accept the necessity of secrecy and circumspection.' In other words, the delinquent youngsters tell conventional society: 'To hell with what you think is right. We get our kicks our way. We know you are out to hang us, but first you got to catch us.' When these youngsters exhibit their behaviour openly, they are telling the worker: 'We'll show you who we really are, let's see if you can take it. You say you want to work with us? We don't know what that means. Let's first see if you're going to accept us as we are, of if you're going to start preaching at us or run for the cops.'

The street club worker's ability to 'take it' and to show that he accepts the boys on their own terms, that he is honestly, and without prejudgments, trying to understand who they are and why they are that way, this ability determines whether the group will permit him to challenge their values and criticise their behaviour. If the worker is unable to accept the boys on their own terms and convey an understanding attitude to them, two things may happen: either the boys walk away from the worker and refuse to have anything to do with him (which is frequently the reaction of delinquents to the conventional group work setting in community centres, youth clubs, etc.), or else they remain secretive and defensive about their values and their behaviour, but seek to manipulate and exploit the worker for their own purposes.

The youngsters are at times rather ingenious in hinting at their own problems and confusions, groping for the worker's understanding. Learning to listen 'with the third ear', to 'read between the lines', offers many opportunities to the worker to reach the boys and to demonstrate his own accessibility.

One evening when I arrived at the street corner, I found the 'Emperors' sitting huddled together on a stoop. I had known the group for only a relatively short time and was surprised when a welcoming 'Hey, man, we been waiting for you, we gotta ask you something' rang out as I approached. The question they were so eager to ask was: 'Do you know anything about Christian religion, the New Testament and all that?' I said, yes, I did. 'What we want to know is, do you believe in the Immaculate Conception?' I puffed my pipe, trying to gain time to figure out what this rather unusual question might imply. I hadn't noticed any great concern with theological questions among these boys. They knew that I am a Jew, and this was a Catholic neighbourhood. I asked: 'You mean do I think a woman can get pregnant and have a child without sexual intercourse?' Joey giggled: 'Yeah, when the Holy Spirit makes out with her.' Chuck said: 'You think that stuff is true?' When the guy really doesn't do it, you know, how can she get a kid from that?' I thought I had it: 'What you want to know is can a girl become pregnant when you do it between her thighs, what they call a "brush job", maybe when you take her home in the evening and stand her up against the wall in the hallway. Is that what you want to know?' There was an excited, surprised reaction from everybody: 'Yeah, man, you know about things like that?' I said, yes, I knew about the practice and that quite a few of the girls could be persuaded to permit this kind of substitute copulation. I also knew that quite a few marriages in the neighbourhood were hitched because the Judge gave the boy a choice between a jail term for statutory rape and a wedding. I said: 'You got reason to worry about things like that. When you get a girl under the age limit pregnant, you're in trouble.' I sat down on the stoop with the boys and explained the physiological processes of conception and assured them that it was practically impossible that impregnation could occur if the male organ was not inserted in the vagina, especially if the activity was carried out standing up. I voiced no opinion as to the 'moral' aspects of this sort of thing but mentioned, during the ensuing discussion, that the girl was unlikely to derive any pleasure and that the unavoidable pollution might make her feel dirty and humiliated.

This incident turned out to have been an important first step in enabling the group to discuss with me openly the many sexual problems they encountered, problems which are normally encountered in adolescence, all the more disturbing in a society which exposes its youth to an overwhelming onslaught of sex titillation, while condemning youthful sexual experimenting as indecent and immoral.

One of the Tel Aviv workers listened with growing discomfort to a group of street corner boys discussing their techniques of avoiding army service. The worker himself was convinced of the educational value of military service, and had strong feelings about the immorality of shirking one's duty to defend the country. Although he had met the boys only recently, he entered into an argument with them about their attitude towards the army. Seeing that one of the members of the group was a soldier on leave, wearing his uniform, the worker called upon this young man to confirm his statements about the positive aspects of army life. The soldier refused to take the worker's side in the argument, and instead backed up the negative attitudes of the group. The worker found himself facing a solid front of hostility and scorn. During the weeks following this conversation, the worker made very little headway in his attempts to learn more about the youngsters' feelings and behaviour patterns. The group did not break off contact, but tried to manoeuvre him into a 'useful-but-harmless' role in which he would do what the boys wanted without being able to establish more than the most superficial relationship with them.

During my work with the 'Emperors' in New York, I was set back on my heels once and made to realise that I had, after several months of intensive work, as yet failed to understand and accept the norms of this group. Members of the 'Emperors' had held up a gas station attendant, beaten him brutally and robbed him of his money. I visited the boys in jail and helped them obtain legal representation in court. I also visited their victim and his family. Soon after this came Thanksgiving Day and I helped the group to organise a party at a local restaurant. The atmosphere was warm and friendly. The boys and their girls were talking about the group members who had been jailed for the hold-up and I felt accepted and secure enough to tell the boys that we should give some thought to the victim. I suggested that we 'pass the hat' and collect some money to send this man's family a Thanksgiving present, to show that we were not indifferent to his plight and shared the responsibility for what had been done to him by our friends. The reaction to my remarks was an icy one. One of the leaders of the group wanted to know 'where I got that "we" stuff from', and Joey, the boy who 'did the talking' for them, said: 'Man, I thought you know the score by now, and you come us with that social-work jive. You think we're in the Y.M.C.A. or something? We don't give a sh . . . about that guy and his f . . . family. We look out for ourselves, for our own guys, nobody else. We wouldn't give that guy a dime. Don't you understand man, that's how life is. One day this guy gets his head broken, and the next day it may be one of us. That's the way the ball bounces. And the guy's a Nigger, anyway, so who cares?' I had been told in no uncertain terms: 'That's the way we are, and you ought to know that by now. You can take it or leave it.' It took quite some time before I recovered the ground I lost that night.

In New York as well as in Tel Aviv, I found that, in order to learn to accept the group on their own level, the worker must learn to recognise and respect the major defence mechanisms of the delinquent group. He must learn to accept the 'techniques of neutralization' that help the youngsters deal with their guilt and that sustain their delinquent behaviour. This is a precondition for establishing a relationship that may eventually enable the worker to bring about changes in this behaviour and in the underlying attitudes. Briefly summarised from the article by Sykes and Matza the investigators who coined the term, these 'techniques of neutralisation' are:

'Denial of responsibility': Others are to blame for what and how we are. If it weren't for the cops, we wouldn't be thieves. If the probation officers would leave us alone, we wouldn't refuse to work, if people weren't prejudiced against us, we wouldn't use violence . . .

'Denial of injury': We didn't mean any harm when we smashed the window, we were just having fun and the window was cracked anyway. We didn't mean to hurt the guy, we were only kidding and nothing much happened to him. He didn't even need stitches.

'Denial of the victim': He deserved what he got, he had it coming to him, he was asking for it, because he was looking for trouble, cheated us when we bought things at his store, is a homosexual, belongs to this or that ethnic group . . .

'Condemnation of the condemners': Politicians are corrupt: 'respectable' people are worse than we are only they don't get caught, policemen are crooks . . .

'Appeal to higher loyalties': We wouldn't have done it, but we had to help out our buddies. We had to do it to defend our gang.

Last but not least, the worker who asks a group of young delinquents to 'open' up and give him access to all aspects of their lives, to share with him their values and beliefs, and to discuss their behaviour frankly and honestly, must under all circumstances seek to guard the confidentiality of the information he thus gains.

This is not always an easy task and will, at times, bring the worker in conflict with the demands made upon him by law-enforcement agencies. Once the street club worker has established a close relationship with a delinquent group, he will unavoidably become their confidant in matters pertaining to unlawful behaviour and gain knowledge of delinquent activities. While it may be his duty as a citizen to inform the police and assist them in apprehending the offenders, his role as a street club worker and the treatment goals of his job do not permit him to function as an ordinary law-abiding citizen in these matters. (This does not preclude the worker's attempt to use his relationship with the youngsters to prevent delinquent acts, or to persuade youngsters who have committed a crime to face the consequences.)

It has been my personal experience in New York that, while the police frowned upon any work with delinquents that did not include furnishing information to law-enforcement agencies, local police precincts showed considerable understanding and willingness to co-operate when the nature and purpose of street club work was explained to them.

However, the New York City Youth Board, the organisation that pioneered in street club work in the United States, has in recent years given in to pressure and adopted the policy of providing the police with information regarding the activities of their clients (New York City Youth Board, 1960, pp. 255–9). This has undoubtedly greatly reduced the effectiveness of their workers. While it is possible to prevent gang fights and break up gangs under this policy, it is impossible to establish relationships of mutual trust and acceptance that enable the worker to go beyond the treatment of symptoms to the change of the underlying values and attitudes.

In Tel Aviv the Youth Squad of the police has greatly facilitated the work of the Project by their readiness to consider the views of the street club worker and to extend their co-operation.

There are exceptional circumstances, such as activities that endanger human life, where the worker is obliged to inform the authorities if all his efforts to prevent such behaviour have failed. In such cases the worker must make his decision in consultation with his supervisor and his agency, and inform the youngsters involved of what action he intends to take. In no circumstances should the worker lie to the group or seek to hide his actions.

Once the street club worker has succeeded in demonstrating to his group that he is honest with them, that he can be trusted and that he understands and accepts them, he will not find it difficult to get the youngsters to be honest with him and to accept him. The worker will have to define and explain his role and his functions patiently and repeatedly. Moreover, he will have to demonstrate by his actions what his role and functions are. Even so, all the most erudite explanations and the greatest efficiency in carrying out his tasks cannot replace his acceptability as a person. Especially in working with lower-class youth, the personal factor supersedes all intellectual explanations in the process of becoming accepted and establishing relationships. As Frank Riessman (1962, p. 28) points out, the lower-class milieu produces a person who 'has an informal, human quality of easy, comfortable relationship to people, where the affectionate bite of humour is appreciated. The factory "horseplay", the ritualistic kidding, is part of this pattern. He emphasizes personal qualities. It is the man, not the job that is important.'

I have found this statement confirmed by the experience of the Project staff in Tel Aviv, as well as by my own experience in New York. In both cities lower-class street corner boys demonstrate their need for a relationship with a knowledgeable, resourceful, trustworthy and accepting adult, by confirming the worker in his role. After the initial attempts that test the worker's ability to define his functions by trying to assign him roles he cannot accept, either because they are not compatible with his status as an adult, because they are in conflict with his professional mandate, or because they involve him in unlawful activities, the young-sters usually help the worker to maintain a role that is compatible with the image he has created. Sometimes this takes forms that are touching or amusing. In Tel Aviv and in New York I have observed that a member of a street corner group is severely reprimanded by the rest of the group for having made unfair demands upon the worker: 'Man, why are you asking the guy for money? He ain't here for hand-outs, he ain't no bank', or (after a boy suggested that the worker participate in an unlawful acitivity): 'Don't be stupid, You know he can't do that, he's a social worker. You talk like he's a thief.'

In New York I once appeared at the hang-out of the 'Emperors' in a pair of new shoes which I thought were rather 'stylish'. After some polite remarks about my new footwear, one of the boys drew me aside and said: 'I hope I ain't gonna hurt your feelings, but the shoes you're wearing, don't get me wrong now, they're nice shoes, but they're the kind of shoes the guys here wear. They ain't right for you, they make you look like one of the kids.' After I helped the 'Commanders' obtain their own club-room and we had furnished it with odds and ends of furniture, the only comfortable chair was always reserved for me and no one else would use it when I was present. When I asked the reason for this preferential treatment, Frankie, the leader of the gang, said, 'It's only right that you should sit in the big chair, you're our worker,' to which another boy added, 'and we got to consider your age, man', which let some of the air out of my expanding ego.

In Tel Aviv I observed that the boys usually see to it that their worker has a seat, when the gang meets around some park benches or in a coffee shop. Due to the cultural traditions of hospitality among the Oriental population the worker is always welcomed when he visits one of the youngsters' families and treated as an honoured guest. The same treatment is accorded the worker when he attends parties given by the boys. It is very important that the worker knows on such occasions to find a balance between the required etiquette expected of a guest, and his professional role, which may call upon him to exert his leadership and set limits.

The process of establishing mutual trust and acceptance between the street club worker and a delinquent street corner group is in itself an educational procedure that may lead to important changes in the atti-tudes of the youngsters toward conventional society, and that may improve their abilities to establish positive social relationships. Mutual respect is one of the prerequisites for any learning processes in this area. The worker should not only demand respect and earn this respect by his appearance and behaviour, he must also show respect for the group and its members. That includes respect for their cultural traditions, their opinions, their abilities and potentialities, their needs and their problems, as well as respect for their right as a group and as individuals to make their own decisions and to be left alone when they want to be.

17 Helping in concrete ways

The variations in rates of officially recorded delinquents in communities of the city correspond very closely with variations in economic status. The communities with the highest rates of delinquents are occupied by those segments of the population whose position is most disadvantageous in relation to the distribution of economic, social, and cultural values. Of all the communities in the city, these have the fewest facilities for acquiring the economic goods indicative of status and success in our conventional culture. Residence in the community is in itself an indication of inferior status, from the standpoint of persons residing in the more prosperous areas. It is a handicap in securing employment and in making satisfactory advancement in industry and the professions. Fewer opportunities are provided for securing the training, education, and contacts which facilitate advancement in the fields of business, industry and the professions.

SHAW AND MCKAY (1962), p. 234

Yet the streetworker may be alone, or have only little company, in being close to the daily living of the youngsters, to their crises, to their sense of trust. He is part of their lives in a way that is often unique. He can be a connecting link between them and services and opportunities. Whatever other programmes are designed for alienated groups in our slums, the street-worker should be central, the point of contact.

S. BERNSTEIN (1964), pp. 29–30

George Brager (1962), director of 'Mobilization for Youth' in New York City, has pointed out that the street club work or detached worker approach which relies solely upon the worker's relationship with, and personal influence upon the group, does not meet the requirements of the situation. The author distinguishes between this relationship-oriented approach and the approach that is focused upon the redirection of the group's energies and interests into socially desirable recreational activities. Mr Brager (pp. 32–3) points out that neither approach is sufficient in itself, and suggests a third approach, described as follows:

One conception of the role of the street-corner worker is as a mediator through whom the street-gang can relate to the major institutional orders that impinge upon it. Thus the worker becomes a bridge between the group and school authorities, potential employers, and so forth. He makes young people aware of vocational and training resources and in some cases he provides 'connections'. He may introduce the youngsters to people who are 'one rung up the ladder' (of socio-economic success), so that routes to mobility become visible and are perceived as accessible.

This role of 'mediator' which the street club worker adopts is, in essence, one of a resource person who offers concrete assistance in coping with practical problems, who helps the youngsters to gain access to, and make use of, existing legitimate opportunities, and who seeks to improve or create such opportunities where they are insufficient or where they do not exist.

My practical experience and my observations in working with delinquent street corner groups in New York and Tel Aviv lead me to subscribe fully to the concrete, realistic approach George Brager advocates. However, I can see no discrepancy between such an approach and the roles of the worker as an adult who creates a personal relationship with the youngsters, and as a professional who helps the delinquent group redirect and channel its interests and energies. Far from being mutually exclusive or incompatible, the three roles mentioned here complement each other and are, indeed, integral parts of the same group work method. One cannot establish a constructive relationship with a delinquent group without offering the youngsters something more tangible than a friendly and permissive attitude. Experience has shown that members of a delinquent subculture are very unlikely to give up their delinquent adaptations in exchange for conventional adjustments, unless a personal relationship paves the way. On the other hand, it is obviously futile to attempt to use the relationship and to exert personal influence in order to change delinquent norms and behaviour without providing legitimate alternatives.

The channelling and redirection of the group's interests and energies is part and parcel of the effort to provide such alternatives. Socially acceptable recreational leisure-time activities for adolescents are certainly not the only, or even the most important, means to help delinquent youngsters to relinquish their destructive and self-destructive behaviour patterns. They can neither replace nor supersede the attempt to enable these youngsters to gain access to the legitimate socio-economic opportunity system through academic and vocational training and suitable employment. Nevertheless, we cannot ignore the fact that we are dealing with adolescents, and that helping them to have fun in a socially acceptable manner is both desirable and essential.

The function of the street club worker should neither be restricted to that of 'understanding friend', nor to that of recreational group worker or employment counsellor. The worker's role should encompass these and other functions. In the United States some difficulties have been encountered in gaining acceptance for this broad, multifaceted image of the street club worker. This may be due to the frequently found misconception of specialisation as a narrowing and limiting of the worker's functions. Specialisation should, however, be conceived of as leading to the enrichment of the worker's functions and resources through the disciplined inclusion of a wide range of relevant knowledge and approaches, all geared to the needs of the client group and focused upon the goals of the service.

In Israel we can draw upon the tradition and the model of the *madrich noar*, the 'youth guide', evolved in the educational settings of the kibbuz and the Youth Movements. Hanoch Reinhold (1953, p. 217), one of the directors of 'Youth Aliyah', an educational network that trains new-immigrant youth for kibbuz life, described this type of youth worker as an educator who 'is not selected with a view to becoming a "specialist" in education, but rather because of certain personality traits which seem to mark him out as suitable for youth guidance'. This *madrich* combines the functions of educator, group worker and resource person. He is skilled in counselling and programming, he acts as mediator between the values and mores of the new-immigrant cultures and the new way of life of the host society. He helps his group of adolescents to deal with their social and psychological problems as well as to cope with everyday practical matters.

Provided we avoid the pitfalls of equating the disciplined, ideologically motivated Youth Movement setting with the delinquent street corner group, and provided we add to the equipment of the *madrich* the principles and methods of social work as well as the specific methods and techniques of the street club worker, we may be able to develop the type of worker who is ideal for our specific tasks.

In New York as well as in Tel Aviv, and possibly in urban areas of modern industrial society all over the world, the delinquent youngster who grows up in the milieu of the slum lacks a great many opportunities which are, more or less, taken for granted among his more fortunate, better-adjusted peers. The physical environment of these youngsters, their socio-economic and cultural background leave gaps in the range of possibilities for healthy, constructive adjustment which, in most instances, cannot be filled without outside help.

If we confront these youngsters with the demand that they bridge the gaps themselves, under their own power, drawing upon their own resources and by their own will, we align ourselves with those conventional attitudes which are largely responsible for the situation we seek to remedy. These attitudes, implicit in the value system of a prosperous, ambitious middle-class society, assert that a successful social adjustment depends solely upon the moral fibre and the will-power of the individual.

These attitudes rest upon the false assumption that the opportunities for adjustment are equally available to all members of society, and that those who do not take advantage of these opportunities are either innately incapable, or else they are immoral or sick. Many contemporary social-welfare approaches in the United States as well as in Israel still reflect the above described attitudes and assumptions. Wilensky and Lebeaux (1958, p. 138) have coined the term 'residual' for this conception of social work, in contradistinction to the 'institutional' conception of social welfare. The latter recognises that the existing societal system with its socio-economic opportunity structure and its institutions does not provide equally for all its members, and that for a considerable number it does not provide at all. The 'institutional' conception regards social welfare and its professional organ, social work, as 'essential components of modern life, as "normal" and "proper" as the more traditional institutions' (Kahn, 1959, p. 9). Social service for those individual members and segments of the population who are underprivileged in their access to society's opportunities for adequate adjustments is, in this view, regarded as a basic human right that must be as continuously and unconditionally available as is the protection of law or the guarantee of adequate sanitary conditions, education, etc.

The implications of the 'residual' and the 'institutional' conceptions of social welfare for social work in its many areas of practice cannot be discussed in this context. It is, however, relevant to our theme to point out that many of the attempts to provide services for delinquent street corner groups in lower-class areas seem to be rooted in 'residual' thinking. This thinking runs along the following lines: society provides universal education for all: let these youngsters avail themselves of this opportunity. Community centres, youth clubs, youth movements afford everyone the chance to join and avail himself of the opportunity to form satisfying social relations and enjoy wholesome cultural and recreational activities; let every youngster take advantage of this. Youth employment offices and apprenticeship programming see to it that those who have finished their education make adequate vocational adjustments: let everyone make use of these services. The law and its judicial and enforcement organs prescribe equal and fair treatment and offer protection to every citizen: the youngsters have nothing to fear or worry about, as long as they behave lawfully, and even if they run afoul of the law, their rights are guaranteed.

It has already been stated in the preceding pages, and it is well known to everyone who has worked with delinquent youth in any modern city, that the services and societal institutions available to these youngsters are not sufficient in quantity, nor qualitatively geared to the needs of lower-class youth, nor easily accessible to them. The result is not only that these youngsters do not receive the services which, according to the standards of modern democratic society, are rightfully theirs, but also that the assertion that they do enjoy all rights and privileges implicitly condemns them for failing to make adequate adjustments and throws their failure into their frightened, confused, and increasingly resentful faces, saying, in effect: 'What's wrong with you? Society does all this for you yet you continue to wallow in your morass of ignorance, frustration and hate.' What we see happening here is, to use a term coined by Professor Cloward of the Columbia University School of Social Work, the creation of the 'illusion of service' in which many societal institutions, including the social work profession, participate.

Street club work, adhering to the 'institutional' conception of social service, has a unique chance to help delinquent street corner youth free themselves of some of the destructive effects of this 'illusion of service'. The first concrete service the street club worker can offer his client group, is his presence in their immediate environment, his knowledge of the reality they face, his readiness to show understanding of this reality and his ability to accept and, in some instances, even share their feelings about their situation.[1] The street club worker is the man-on-the-spot who sees with his own eyes what is happening, who does not have to be told what the reality is by youngsters who have learned to expect that they will not be believed. Through the establishment of a constructive relationship with the street club worker, youngsters who welter in a Kafkaesque labyrinth of confusions, fears, frustrations and resentments as adolescents, as inhabitants of slums, as members of this or that 'inferior' ethnic group and as delinquents who are in conflict with the norms of society, can learn to relate to a representative of conventional society who accepts them as they are, who sees their situation as it is, and who is there to help them cope. In New York and in Tel Aviv I have heard street corner boys speak with pride and confidence of 'their' worker. My experience in both cities leads me to believe that the very presence of the street club worker, his readiness to listen and to talk things over, and his availability for advice and help in times of crisis, constitute a concrete service which enhances the chances of these youngsters to emerge from their isolation, break the patterns of their destructive and self-defeating behaviour and make socially acceptable adjustments.

[1] One of the pioneers in working with delinquent youth went so far as to say that 'in the case of the child who is in open conflict with society' the worker (in this case the therapist), 'must take the child's part, be in agreement with his behaviour, and in the severest cases even give the child to understand that in his place he would behave just the same way. . . .' Aichhorn 1955, p. 95.

18 Employment

Employment was a problem for the young people and to us during the whole of the field-work. The difficulties included finding jobs, keeping them, giving them up, getting the sack when they didn't want it, not getting the sack when they did, deciding on reasons for keeping a job, wanting to work and not being able to, having to work and not wanting to. These and a hundred other variations on the employment problem were the largest single activity in working with the boys.

Employment gave us the point of contact with the boys that most often deepened into their asking for other help, advice or guidance. It was our ability to deal and/or help with employment problems that provided the strongest link between the boys and ourselves. On the whole the boys disliked the set-up at the youth-employment service, and normally refused to ask them for help. This attitude was both the cause and effect of using the grape-vine to get information about jobs.

G. W. GOETSCHIUS AND M. J. TASH (1967), p. 68

Dear kindly social worker, they tell me get a job,
Like be a soda jerker, which means I'd be a slob,
It's not I'm anti-social, I'm only anti-work,—
Glory Ivy, that's why I'm a jerk.

Song in 'West Side Story'

Finding and keeping a job is one of the major areas of concern to street corner boys. In New York I have spent many an hour 'talking jobs' with the youngsters of street corner groups, listening to their views of what is and what is not a 'good' job, discussing their expectations, questioning them as to their qualifications and experience. Tel Aviv street club workers engage in the same discussions, often in the same manner, with their groups. Although jobs are more easily available here, the worker is confronted with the same problems: How to motivate the boys to want to work at all, how to get them to go through the often tedious and complicated procedure of looking for employment, how to get them to keep the job longer than a week or two. The fact that the special relationship between the worker and the youngsters enables the latter to speak frankly about their inadequacies and difficulties is especially important here.

For instance, the youngster who has been fired for the third time in a row from a job to which he has been referred by the employment office, may resort to rationalisations or outright lies when questioned by an exasperated employment agent. He cannot admit to behaviour which he knows to be unacceptable to the person across the desk. However, the same youngster, surrounded by other members of his group who have the same or similar problems, will tell the worker: 'Man, I don't know what to do, I can't make it to work in time. I tell myself every day I'm gonna get up at six and catch the bus, but somehow I never make it.' This frank admission offers the worker the opportunity to explore the reasons for this, quite common, weakness with the boy and his peers, to work through the problem with him and to help him find a solution.

There are some differences in the situation in New York and Tel Aviv. In Israel the boys leave school officially at fourteen, although there are a considerable number of school-drop-outs before that age. In New York the youngsters are expected to stay in school till the age of sixteen, but every street corner group I have known had a significant number of boys who had dropped out before that.

In New York jobs can be obtained through personal contacts, private employment agencies and the State Employment Service. In Tel Aviv all youngsters are obliged by law to use the Youth Employment Service of the State, where they undergo medical checkups, vocational testing and are assigned to professions for which they seem qualified and which offer them an apprenticeship programme that includes theoretical studies in evening schools. In practice, however, many lower-class youngsters shun the official channels and get jobs which while they do not teach them a trade, offer better pay and are more to their liking than the ones to which they may be assigned by the Youth Employment Service. The same situation prevails here as is reported by Peter Willmott (1966, p. 105) in his investigation of East London adolescents:

With the first job, informal contacts through relatives and friends were about as important as the youth employment service. But when the boys came to change their jobs—and over half of them had been in more than one since leaving school—then the 'youth employment', as the boys called it, was less important, the influence of family and friends more.

In New York it is rather difficult for a lower-class youngster to find an opportunity to learn a trade, especially if he has grown up in a slum milieu, is a school drop-out and poorly motivated for regular work.

The lower-class delinquent youngster is characterised by what is known as 'poor work attitudes' which are part of the vicious circle of cause-and-effect, symptom-and-malady in which the youngsters find themselves trapped by their socio-economic and ethnic background, their frustrated aspirations and their delinquent adaptations. The 'poor work attitudes' of the youngsters appear to be products of the traditions of the slum milieu in which 'people who are denied access to various social resources soon lose the capacity to make use of them';[1] the delinquent street corner group in many cases constitutes one of the slum milieu's 'organised patterns of living which become barriers to the utilisation of opportunity'.[2]

[1] Mobilization for Youth Proposal, 1961, p. 89.   [2] Ibid, p. 89.

Helping the youngsters to make better adjustments in the area of work cannot be regarded as an isolated function. It is part of the process of helping the street corner group to gain a realistic view of their situation, to find satisfying alternatives to their antisocial behaviour, and to change their values and norms. In New York as well as in Tel Aviv I have found that the popular formula, 'Get them to work and they'll keep out of trouble', is somewhat too simple to meet the requirements of a complex reality. More often than not it is necessary to work through the whole range of problems that face these youngsters and to help them re-evaluate the unrealistic and self-destructive solutions which they have chosen, before the concept of work takes on meaning and moves from a marginal to a central position in their lives.

For reasons already mentioned, the objective obstacles the street club worker encounters in his attempts to help the youngsters make positive work adjustments are greater in New York than in Tel Aviv. During my work with delinquent street corner boys in New York, the headway I made in the process of changing the youngsters' attitudes towards work was often rendered futile because no suitable jobs could be found

In Tel Aviv we have, for the time being, a manpower shortage, and youngsters who are willing to work are usually able to find employment.[1] In both cities the worker has to deal with the youngster's unrealistic expectations of work that promises all those things that are only rarely available for the lower-class teenager without adequate schooling and without vocational skills: status, good pay, good working conditions and an occupation that is interesting and offers the chance to build a vocational career.

In both cities I have found that even the most cohesive group consists of individuals who differ to some extent in their potentialities, their levels of aspiration and their personal emphasis upon one or the other life expectation. Most common is the boy whose sights are set upon making the most money in the shortest time and in the easiest manner possible. The environmental pressures that impinge upon the street corner group in the lower-class milieu, as well as the delinquent subcultural adaptations of the group, cause and sustain this basic attitude. Characteristically this type of youngster works only sporadically, spends his money as quickly as he earns it, and lives only for the moment. He fatalistically shrugs off all thoughts of the future, relies on his luck and waits for the 'break', the big miraculous chance, that will bring the hard cash that means status and the joy of living. In the delinquent group, he is usually quick to respond to opportunities for making a 'fast buck' (or

[1] As already mentioned, the situation has changed in this respect since the beginning of 1967, when unemployment began to rise steeply.

Israeli Pound) by illegitimate means. I have found that the youngsters
are most comfortable in jobs that have a minimum of dull routine, present something of a challenge and adventure, and can be done in the
company of their own kind of youths or adults.

In Tel Aviv these youngsters seem to prefer auxiliary jobs in the
markets, helping to sell fruit, vegetables or other items, carrying crates
of merchandise. The surroundings are colourful and lively and there is
often a chance to make some extra money, though not always by lawful
means. In many cases members of the same street corner group work
together, the adults who employ them are neighbours or relatives, and
sharp practices, stolen goods, peddling without a licence are much in
evidence and reinforce delinquent patterns. The borderline between
delinquent activities and this kind of work is often so vague, that the
street club worker is inclined to discourage this form of adjustment and
to try to influence the boys to find other types of employment.

There is another reason for regarding this kind of work adjustment as
undesirable: The 'peddling-adaptation', at present still very widespread
in Israel, is a relic of the past. With the modernisation of Israel's cities,
the advent of the supermarket and the shopping centres, the filth-
ridden, traffic-obstructing open-air markets will soon disappear. There
is no future in this sort of thing, and the youngsters waste the years
during which they could acquire a trade that would assure gainful
employment as adults.

Many of our young men take advantage of the shortage of labour on
construction. The building boom that is sweeping the country provides
opportunities for temporary unskilled labour. The youngsters prefer to
work in contracting arrangements in which a job (such as carrying a
certain number of bricks or bags of cement, unloading a specified
number of trucks, etc.) is paid for in a lump sum. There is something of
a challenge in finishing the job with maximal speed, and this sort of
arrangement offers opportunities to share the contracted work with
other boys of the group. The atmosphere of the construction site is
undoubtedly a healthier one than that of the market, but here too the
chance to learn a trade is lacking.[1]

The street club worker's task is to encourage the gradual development
of work habits that enable boys to keep jobs for reasonable periods of

---

[1] Note the observation of an American Sociologist who speaks of 'the tendencies toward the evasion of work which are so characteristic of the American factory worker
and which today obsess all workers. The big lure of escape remains the hope of "being
one's own boss". The creed of "the individual enterprise" has become by and large a
working-class preoccupation' (Bell, 1956, p. 34). Among the youngsters, the preference
for contract work may be regarded as a sort of striving for 'individual enterprise', a
compromise form of 'being one's own boss'.

time, and to try to direct the boys towards jobs that offer a chance to acquire specific skills that may lead to a trade. Here, as in all other areas of his work, the street club worker must beware of letting his demands outpace the level of readiness of his clients. Special consideration should be given to the needs of the youngsters to work in a congenial, familiar environment.

Tel Aviv street club workers found it helpful to encourage those members of a group who have a job, to obtain employment at their own working place for others boys who are without work. In such cases the youngster who helps a friend to get a job gains status, while the boy who is helped finds it easier to adjust in familiar company. The group as a whole can be brought to take an interest in this process, and therewith be led to modify its norms regarding work. We have found that the worker who has established a close and creative relationship with his group, can engender a spirit of positive competition by directing the group's attention to the achievement of the boy who has succeeded in keeping a job for an unusually long period of time, or who has begun to acquire professional skills. In some instances the worker's praise becomes an important source of support and status and motivates other boys to gain approval in the same way.

In New York the street corner boys find it much more difficult to obtain well-paying temporary jobs of the type described above. The push towards criminal activities is all the greater, as opportunities for occasional odd-jobs are limited. Unlike in Israel, where the trade union (mainly the Histadruth) is open to anyone who applies, I found that the Unions in New York tend to be exclusive and reluctant to admit new, and often unreliable, members, at a time when a percentage of their own membership is in line for job-openings. For the same reason it was difficult to find an apprenticeship for a youngster who seemed sufficiently motivated to learn a trade. Mobilization for Youth was, to my knowledge, the first social work agency to negotiate with the unions as well as with employers for job openings which could serve to gradually lead the boy with poor work attitudes to make better vocational adjustments.

In the majority of cases, helping the street corner boy to learn how to obtain and keep a job is a combination of the worker's relationship with the youngsters, his personal influence and direct intervention. Frequently it does not suffice to tell the boy what to do, but to do it with him. In New York I took four of the strongest members of a street corner group with me to the house of a personal acquaintance who wanted some furniture shifted from one floor to the other. We worked together and the boys had fun showing off their muscles and their skill. One of them showed a special knack for this kind of work, and I succeeded in getting him a job as helper on a furniture-moving van. I dragged some other boys out of bed at five in the morning and went with them to some of the big department stores who need daily labourers to load and unload trucks. With some of them I made the rounds of the large grocery stores and flower shops in search of job-openings for delivery boys. In some cases I found it necessary to dissuade youngsters from taking undesirable or unlawful jobs: during a hospital strike that occurred a few years ago, a number of the boys of the 'Emperors' were recruited as strike-breakers with the promise of high wages and an opportunity to use their fists on picketing strikers. A boy of another group obtained a job as a truck driver without having a driver's licence.

Tel Aviv street club workers use a similar approach in helping young-sters with 'poor work attitudes' to get and hold jobs. A special problem is posed by the law, in itself positive and desirable, that obliges all youngsters under sixteen to register at the Youth Employment Office and obtain work through that agency. I have found it necessary to ignore this ruling temporarily, in order to help those who are not ready to seek steady employment and learn a trade, gradually to acquire work habits that will raise the standard of their work attitudes and therewith their employability. A great number of our youngsters obtain jobs on their own. It seems more fruitful and realistic to encourage these boys to stick to their jobs and 'prove themselves', than to insist on the letter of the law with the predictable result that they will shun work altogether.

In both cities I have found that it is effective if the street club worker encourages boys who work in the same neighbourhoods or in the same place of employment, to go to work together in the morning. Getting up in the morning, especially after a 'wild night', is one of the major obstacles to keeping a job. It helps if two or more boys go to work together and assume the responsibility of getting each other out of bed.

In New York as well as in Tel Aviv the worker does well to establish contact with employers and visit the youngsters at their places of work from time to time. I found that the boys welcome this, and that employers usually prove to be co-operative and helpful, provided the worker is tactful in explaining his interest. The worker can be very help-ful in creating understanding and a positive relationship between the youngsters and their employers, but he has to be especially careful not to leave the employer with the impression that the boy he visits is a potential troublemaker, or else arouse the suspicion that he is seeking to interfere in the employer's way of handling his business. One of the street corner groups in Tel Aviv asked the worker to visit each one of their employed members at their working place at regular intervals, and the employers have in each case welcomed his interest. In New York I succeeded in enlisting the unstinting help of the head of a large firm in enabling a teenage narcotics addict to keep his position as an office-boy and eventually begin to learn draughtsmanship.

In both cities the street club worker fulfils an important function by helping the youngsters deal with the complex process of job-hunting. In many cases the worker has to do a thorough educational job in preparing the boys for the job interview with employment agent and employer. In New York I frequently used a role-playing technique in which I 'starred' as the employer, while the boys, often in the presence of the entire group, acted out how they would enter an office, sit down, answer questions, etc. This method was applied in Tel Aviv. The worker also advises on such procedures as filling in forms, taking tests, locating the right offices and officials and so on. The important, perhaps exaggerated, role the questionnaire plays in the employment procedures was brought home to me when I discussed the applications for admission to a pre-military training programme with the commanding officer of a naval base in Haifa. The officer showed me the boys' application forms and told me that they had been refused an interview because of the lack of neatness and the spelling errors made in filling out the questionnaires.

Many times the worker will have to accompany the youngster to the employment office and teach him on the spot such simple facts of life as the necessity of waiting for one's turn, going through the prescribed formalities and making a good impression generally. In Tel Aviv street club workers have been greatly helped in these matters by the co-operative attitude of the staff of the Youth Employment Service. It must be stressed here that the simple matter of waiting one's turn (which, due to the pressure of work and the complex bureaucratic procedures, often consumes several hours) is a major obstacle for street corner boys, who quickly become fidgety, noisy and troublesome. They cannot sustain the tension of sitting around doing nothing for long and often react to reprimands with hostility. I have often found that it makes all the difference if the worker can spare the time to stay with the youngsters, undergo the ordeal of waiting with them, and exert a restraining influence. At the same time, the presence of the worker and his knowhow in dealing with officials often helps to cut some of the red tape and assures a more understanding official attitude.

Not infrequently we find among the members of delinquent street corner groups boys of a somewhat different orientation. These youngsters, who may be found in the highly delinquent core of the group or among the more passive fringe, appear to have their sights set on status and on getting out of the lower-class milieu, in addition to making quick and easy money and getting their 'kicks'. The street club worker should be alert to the presence of such youngsters and ready to help them use their specific motivation and their potentials to realise their aspirations.

I have found that it is especially difficult to help this type of youngster make satisfying work adjustments, as the opportunities to which he aspires are usually barred to him because of his socio-economic and cultural background. He often rejects unskilled or semiskilled manual or service jobs (construction labour, factory work, delivery jobs, elevator operating, dishwashing and cleaning jobs in restaurants, etc.) and demands jobs with higher status, such as skilled blue-collar or white-collar work. Despite their aspirations to leave the slum milieu and improve their social status, these youngsters are often as ill-prepared for steady work as their less ambitious friends. Their frustration is even more severe, because the gulf between their aspirations and their qualifications is wider and more difficult to bridge. Here the street club worker has to make special efforts to motivate the youngsters to take advantage of educational and training opportunities, and to make such opportunities accessible to them. Both in New York and in Tel Aviv I have found that the aspiration for upward mobility and middle-class adjustments are especially prevalent among street corner girls.

In New York there are at times opportunities to introduce those with ambition into the educational, cultural and vocational training programmes of community centres and settlement houses. In many cases this kind of youngster is more able to adapt to the middle-class milieu and conduct norms of such agencies than the rest of the group. In Tel Aviv the Department of Culture and Sport of the Municipality has recently begun to experiment with similar programmes in the youth club setting, but it is as yet too early to tell whether these programmes will be able to reach lower-class street corner youth of this potentially more upwardly mobile type.

The New York lower-class teenager is especially hard hit by the unemployment situation, and it is therefore extremely difficult to find adequate employment for those who have their sights set on high status jobs. In one instance I was able to help two boys of a Puerto Rican street corner group to obtain jobs as floor-boys with an opportunity to become salesmen in a 'Junior Men's Fashion' store. I spent some time advising them on suitable dress and behaviour and wrote personal letters of recommendation. On another occasion I enabled a bright youngster of the 'Emperors' to be admitted to City College through a period of preparation and tutoring and a personal discussion with the director of admissions of the school. This youngster had a record of thefts and assault and had begun to use narcotics. He held out for a year, then succumbed to the pressures of his environment and dropped out, but was able to obtain a white-collar job.

Tel Aviv street club workers in most instances seek the co-operation of the Youth Employment Service in trying to help certain youngsters obtain jobs that respond to their needs for status. There is, so far, no adequate solution for those who demand jobs that require higher academic qualification than they can offer. What is needed here, is a special apprenticeship arrangement which includes an academic tutoring programme that enables the pupil to attain the obligatory level of education while training him for the profession to which he aspires. In some instances the armed services offer opportunities for acquiring desirable professions, and it is therefore especially important to use the worker's influence to counteract negative attitudes toward military service and to facilitate positive adjustments in this area. One worker used his personal contacts to obtain a civil service job for one of the girls hanging out with a street corner group. This girl exhibited a high degree of aggressive and sexually promiscuous behaviour and seemed to be well on her way to becoming a prostitute. Another worker negotiated with the relevant authorities to enable several boys of his group to obtain training opportunities in the Navy and the Merchant Marine services.

The status-oriented youngster who seeks work adjustments which will enable him to leave the lower-class milieu poses an additional problem. In order to help him to realise his ambitions, it often seems necessary to help him also to sever his ties to the group to which he belongs. In most cases the delinquent street corner group exerts pressures that make it very difficult for a 'different' member to attain status in a socially acceptable way. Instead the group frequently offers opportunities to gain status in accordance with the group's delinquent values and norms. There is, however, no doubt, that the departure of a member who reaches a higher level of adjustment in a socially acceptable way weakens the group and deprives it of a positive influence. In many cases there is no alternative to helping the aspiring youngster to cut his ties, even though this may lead to an increase in the feelings of isolation and hopelessness among the boys who remain at the street corner. Wherever possible the worker should try to sustain the bond of mutual acceptance between the boy who made a positive adjustment and the rest. The goal of the worker should be to help the group as a whole to strengthen its positive potential through enabling individual members to make better personal adjustments, not to lower the general level of the group through depriving it of its most positive and successful members. There are important implications here for the street club workers' use of available community centre or youth club facilities. My experience leads me to believe that it is preferable to wait until a street corner group is ready to join a structured setting of the above kind in a body, rather than to syphon off the potentially most adjustable youngsters by referring them to any agency, leaving behind a maladjusted hard-core.

I have heard much talk about teaching delinquents 'good work habits'. When the phrase is used in penal settings (and I include in this category some American and Israeli institutions for delinquent youth whose professed approach is treatment and rehabilitation), it usually means in practice the use of hard work as a punitive device. Even some of the more enlightened people who deal with youngsters who have poor work attitudes seem to feel that good work habits can be instilled by any kind of work, no matter what its content or significance to those who are compelled to do it. This view appears to be implied in the approach of certain work camp programmes in the United States where, for instance, teenage boys are engaged in felling trees. The director of a youth prison near Tel Aviv expressed this attitude explicitly when he told me, during one of my visits to this institution, 'It doesn't really matter what they do. The main thing is that they are taught to acquire regular work habits.' This was in reply to my question about a number of youngsters I had found pasting coloured paper on book covers. They disliked their job, regarded it as more suitable for girls or invalids, and did not believe that they could or wanted to make a living by doing this kind of work. In New York I talked to several boys who had returned from work camps. Some of them laughed when I asked them if they had learned a useful trade: 'Sure, you lead us to any tree in Manhattan and we'll chop it down scientifically.'

A report written for Mobilization for Youth has this to say with regard to the work training offered to delinquents in institutions:

Many of the vocational skills taught are relatively useless if not absurd, since the learnings that derive from such training can rarely be translated into real jobs. A Puerto Rican youngster living in the Lower East Side of Manhattan reported that his main employment during the winter months of last year was milking cows at 4 a.m. In his eyes, this was not only onerous but wasteful work. There is surely no way in which this activity can be translated into useful employment (Ontell and Jones, 1963, p. 4).

I doubt that work which is meaningless to a youngster can improve his general attitude towards work. I am more inclined to believe that this kind of activity, especially if it is done under compulsion, may very well reinforce the youngsters' negative feelings about work. Attempts to bring about positive changes in the poor work attitudes of delinquent youth have to take into account the youngsters' need to find some creative interest in their work and their realistic wish to see some practical use for their own future in their occupation. The street club worker should take this fact into consideration in his attempts to obtain jobs for the boys and girls of his group.

Tel Aviv street club workers have on several occasions arranged for individual members of their groups to spend a period of time working and living in a kibbutz. These placements have usually been effected in order to give the youngster a chance to temporarily leave his oppressive environment and be exposed to a different way of life. The jobs the boys are assigned in the kibbutz should be geared to their interests and their future expectations upon their return to the city. Unless there is reason to expect that a youngster will choose agriculture as a profession, there is not much sense in having him do farm work for a prolonged period of time. There are many kibbuzim today who engage in a variety of industrial work which could offer these boys a chance to learn a trade that may help their future adjustment.

In New York Mobilization for Youth has come up with some ideas which, with some modifications, could be adopted elsewhere and constitute important tools for providing meaningful, interesting work, a chance to acquire useful skills and an opportunity to teach better work habits in a manner geared to the level and the needs of delinquent street corner youth. One such idea is the organisation of an Urban Youth Service (Mobilization for Youth, 1961, p. 98). This is a subsidised work programme in which youngsters do repair and neighbourhood improvement work, as well as set up small workshops in their communities. Examples of work that can be done and skills that can be acquired are: construction of playgrounds, building repairs, landscaping, manufacture and repair of furniture for private homes, community centres and schools, etc. The work is done under the supervision of professional instructors and with the guidance of youth workers.[1] It is conceivable that street club workers could not only play an important role in organising and supervising such programmes, but that entire street corner groups could be given jobs which are contracted out to them, and which they do under the guidance of a professional instructor and their street club worker.

I have seen many examples during my work with lower-class delinquent street corner groups in New York and in Tel Aviv that show that these youngsters, who are usually poorly motivated for steady work and who rarely have the staying power that is required for the long process of learning a trade, can nevertheless work enthusiastically and patiently when the job they do holds their interest and has meaning for them.

[1] A national programme 'to provide work experience and training to young people from low-income families' is reviewed by Saxton (1967) pp. 156–61.

In New York I worked with the 'Commanders' for many weeks cleaning, painting, decorating and furnishing an utterly filthy and neglected
storage chamber that had been offered to them as their club room. In
one of Tel Aviv's slums the worker saw, to his amazement, that a group
of delinquent street corner boys had volunteered to help a local young
adult who had befriended them to build a small house for himself in the
courtyard of his parents' home. The boys, among them youngsters who
shunned all regular work and heavy hashish users, worked diligently and
well under the supervision of the future owner and a professional builder
until the job was completed. In these instances work was without re-
muneration. An organised work programme of the kind initiated by
Mobilization for Youth would, of course, have to assure the youngsters
adequate pay. The money might prove to be well spent, not only in
terms of some of the badly needed work done, but also in terms of the
improvement of their attitudes towards work.

The youngsters' own interests and potentialities, their motivations,
their aspirations, their level of readiness in terms of physical and psychological development and chronological age must be taken into account.
This becomes especially important at the time of transition from late
adolescence to young adulthood, a time when many agencies pressure
their 'detached' workers to terminate their services to a group because
most of the members have reached the age of eighteen. This is often a
thoroughly mistaken view. The last phase of adolescence is often a
crucial period of anxiety and crisis, offering the first and the last real
opportunities for helping them to 'put aside childish things' to begin to
face adult responsibilities and make a lasting vocational choice.

In one of Tel Aviv's destitute neighbourhoods on the outskirts of the
city, a group of eight boys, aged seventeen to twenty, split off from a
large delinquent street corner group, left the neighbourhood and 'squat-
ted' in an empty shack on a nearby beach. These eight boys had been
among the most highly delinquent members of their crowd and were
considered the most 'disturbed', not only by social workers and police
officers who had come into contact with them, but also by the adults of
their own community, people who themselves were notorious for their
deviant attitudes and their involvement in criminal activities. All had
criminal records and most had spent some time in jail. They had a long
history of brawling and stealing. Some of them had 'worked' as procurers. (The mother of one of the boys was a prostitute.) None of them
had held a legitimate job for longer than a few weeks; all had either been
rejected by the armed services as 'unfit', or else were shirking military
service.

The 'beach boys' had settled down at the sea-shore shortly before the street club worker came to their old neighbourhood. He learned about them from the other street corner boys, who feared and admired them. The worker became aware of the beach boys' continued influence over the main group, their recruitment of youngsters from the neighbourhood for their criminal exploits, and the fact that they frequently sheltered younger boys who had run away from home or were wanted by the police, providing them with opportunities to smoke hashish, consort with prostitutes and meet a variety of deviants from other areas. This led to the decision to seek out the beach boys and establish a relationship with them with the goal of helping them to make some more desirable adjustments.

The worker overcame the beach boys' initial distrust and soon spent an average of three evenings a week with them, sharing their meals (which at one occasion, consisted of steak from a giant turtle which had drifted ashore) sitting around a fire telling and listening to stories, and generally entering into the adventurous atmosphere of their Robinson Crusoe existence. He was able to help them effectively with a variety of matters, and successfully negotiated with the police to call off the frequent midnight raids, searches and interrogations. The police, who rightly considered these boys a potential source of trouble and danger to the public, especially the tourists they were apt to prey upon, were persuaded to 'lay off' for a while and give the street club Project a chance. Very soon the worker became a welcome and eagerly awaited visitor.

While the beach boys' delinquent activities continued for a while, the worker discovered that they had got hold of an old boat, patched it up, and engaged enthusiastically in offshore fishing. He hitched on to this, encouraging them, spending nights and weekends with them at sea. He helped to get them odd jobs which, together with the fish they sold, enabled them to buy nets and other equipment, and he learned with them to repair nets and catch fish. He persuaded them gradually to give up their delinquent involvements and to stop encouraging the delinquent activities of the younger boys from their old neighbourhood. When the boys met his conditions, he obtained a loan for them which enabled them to buy a bigger and better boat, equipped with an outboard motor. When it became apparent that several of the boys were illiterate, the worker brought a friend who volunteered his time to teach them to read and write. Several of the boys were frequently ill because they lived and worked in a state of near-nakedness in all weather, saving the few items of clothing they owned for their excursions to the city. The worker persuaded them to use some of the money they earned to buy waterproof overalls, rubber boots and other suitable clothing. As a result of all this less and less money was spent on drinking, hashish and whoring, delinquent activities stopped and the group itself began to impose strict discipline upon its members. The boy who had become most skilled in fishing and keeping accounts was elected 'manager' and the group began to discuss the possibility of forming a licensed fishing co-operative.

A number of crises occurred: youngsters from a nearby middle-class suburb damaged the boat one weekend and received a severe beating, upon which their irate parents demanded police action. This was settled by negotiation. Rival fishermen from Jaffa came out at night in their boats and stole the nets. The boys wanted to get guns and retaliate, but, after heated discussion, decided to keep better watch and enlist the worker's help in obtaining another loan to buy new nets. The municipal authorities discovered that the boys were illegal squatters and sent a force of inspectors to drive them off. There were threats and scuffles but, with the determined backing of the agency, the municipality was persuaded to let the boys stay after they agreed to dismantle their shack and move it to a more remote part of the beach.

At the end of one year of the street club worker's association with the beach boys, negotiations were opened with the Co-operatives Division of the Histadruth (the Association of Trade Unions) and the Fishery Department of the Ministry of Agriculture, to enable the boys to receive professional training and be registered as a co-operative. The response of the official agencies was excellent. Officials visited the boys at their shack and convinced themselves of their competence and sincere motivation. The military authorities and the police co-operated in removing the stigma of criminal and 'unfit for military service' records which would have disqualified the boys from working aboard a ship. The group was assigned to a training ship of the fishing fleet for a six months' course of training and, after successful graduation, given very substantial government loans and subsidies which enabled them to work independently as a fishing co-operative.

There are many ways in which these youngsters on the fringes of society can be helped and guided to give up their self-defeating attitudes in exchange for creative and meaningful adjustments that promise them access to the legitimate opportunity system. The job cannot be done without investing the will as well as the means to create new opportunities and new channels for absorbing the youngsters into the labour force of the country. Of all the people who deal with lower-class delinquents in one capacity or another, the street club worker is perhaps in the best position to identify and evaluate the limitations and the potentialities of the street corner boys and girls. His job brings him face to face with the obstacles put in their path towards adequate adjustments in the areas of vocational training and suitable employment. It is part of the street club worker's responsibility towards his clients to use his insight to help initiate programmes and approaches that offer concrete solutions to to the crucial problem of work adjustment for the youngsters he serves.

A word of caution: it has been my experience in New York and in Tel Aviv, that work is not necessarily a cure-all for delinquent adaptations. Satisfactory work adjustments are indispensable prerequisites for any attempt to change the values and norms of the delinquent subculture. However, even steady employment and satisfying work does not always preclude the adherence to delinquent norms and the pursuit of delinquent activities. There is a wide range of other factors, some of them discussed in the preceding pages, which impinge upon the situation of the delinquent street corner group, and which must be tackled in order to bring about lasting changes towards socially acceptable adaptations.

19 The need for a place to be

Even when the old-law tenements were brand new—that is before the turn of the century—they were far from being anyone's dream of Home. The rationale of the design was to provide the greatest use of the lot. Neither the comfort nor even the sanitation of the tenants was taken into consideration. At the time these structures were built the indoor toilet was still something of a luxury, and in the buildings where toilet facilities were installed they were rarely in each apartment, but more often one to a floor—a hall toilet for the use of all the families on the floor. Inside rooms, normally cited for use as bedrooms, had no windows and depended on the adjoining room for fresh air. On the outside, no thought was given to making the face of the building attractive, or even uniquely ugly in a way that at least was different from the rest. The standard city tenements are too familiar to need any further description; you have seen their faces.

DAN WAKEFIELD (1960), pp. 233, 242–5

The projects are hideous, of course, there being a law, apparently respected throughout the world, that popular housing shall be as cheerless as a prison. They are lumped all over Harlem, colorless, bleak, high and revolting. The wide windows look out on Harlem's invincible and indescribable squalor: The Park Avenue railroad tracks, around which, about forty years ago, the present dark community began, the unrehabilitated houses, bowed down, it would seem, under the great weight of frustration and bitterness, they contain, the dark, ominous schoolhouses from which the child may emerge maimed, blinded, hooked, or enraged for life; and the churches, block upon block of churches, niched in the walls like cannon in the walls of a fortress. Even if the administration of the projects were not so insanely humiliating (for example: one must report raises in salary to the management, which will then eat up the profit by raising one's rent; the management has the right to decide who is staying in your apartment, the management can ask you to leave, at their discretion), the projects would still be hated because they are an insult to the meanest intelligence.

JAMES BALDWIN (1962), p. 351

What are these elements of housing that affect poor people? Three are largely physical in nature. City space (how generously it is provided and how it is used) affects everyone and affects the poor in special ways. Congestion interferes with their lives. Space that is planned, as it is tending to be planned, for openness and for challenge overlooks their needs. The neighborhood is a second significant physical element. It should provide at least three conditions that are important to self-improvement: it should allow families to choose whom they see and how frequently; it should foster a feeling of local identity; and at least some neighborhoods must be financially and ethnically diverse. The final significant physical element is the design and adequacy of the house or flat itself.

A. L. SCHORR (1964), pp. xv—xvi

In the course of my work with the After-Care Department of the New York State Division for Youth I visited a family in Harlem in order to investigate the chances for readjustment of a youngster about to be released from a State Training Camp. Having located the family on the third floor of a filthy, rat-infested tenement building, I found nine people living in a dingy two-room apartment. While the boy's mother told me that the gang to which the youngster belonged was hanging out at the next street corner, and that the entrance hall of the building served as a meeting place for drug addicts and pushers, her sixteen-year-old daughter sat hunched over a book in a corner, her hands over her ears to shut out the noise of the other children, trying to prepare for a school examination. Another daughter was nursing an infant, two younger boys were playing cards on the floor and the oldest son, a young man in glaringly effeminate dress, was applying make-up to his face in front of a mirror. The woman told me that her efforts to find a larger apartment in a better neighbourhood had been rendered futile because the Welfare Department would not permit her to pay the higher rent that was demanded everywhere. Reporting to my agency I stated that there was no point in discussing the readjustment of the boy unless immediate steps were taken to provide adequate living conditions for his family.

During my work with the 'Commanders' in a low-income housing project on New York's Lower East Side, I found that the defeatist, demoralized atmosphere that pervaded the housing project strongly affected the attitudes and behaviour of the group. This atmosphere was to a great extent caused by the Housing Authority management's disregard for the cultural background and traditions of the tenants, the discouragement of any community spirit (tenants' committees were regarded as dangerously subversive), the disrespect for the privacy and the dignity of these people and the punitive attitude expressed in the excessive use of the Housing Authority Police. In order to help the youngsters to emerge from their highly destructive and self-destructive delinquent patterns it was necessary to show them that I understood and accepted their frustration and their anger about their living conditions, and that I was ready to help them find legitimate ways to expose and remove oppressive attitudes and unfair measures to which they and their families were being subjected. I helped the youngsters to gain access to a radio programme, where they could air their grievances, and enlisted the help of my agency on their behalf to negotiate with the Housing Authority Management.

A cursory glance at some statistics will show the magnitude of the problem in Tel Aviv: 14·2 per cent of the entire population of Tel Aviv reported 'household density' conditions of more than three persons per room, while only 1·1 per cent of the inhabitants of the city's best residential sector (North Tel Aviv) lived under such conditions. On the other hand the statistics for three of the Tel Aviv Street Club Project's work areas show respectively 40·2, 53·3 and 58·5 per cent of the inhabitants of these neighbourhoods living in a density of more than three persons per room. These figures do not include the significant number of people in these areas from whom no answer as to their living conditions could be obtained.[1] Conditions in such notorious slum areas as New York's Harlem and East Harlem are if anything worse, and the contrast between housing conditions in New York's underprivileged areas and the middle-class residential areas are even greater.

In New York as well as in Tel Aviv I found it especially difficult for the street club worker to offer concrete help in the area of housing and living conditions. Here we deal with vested interests (such as real estate business, local chambers of commerce and political factions) and bureaucratic power structures, which are not easily accessible, nor subject to influence or persuasion. The worker needs the strong backing of his agency and of the professional social work organisations in order to intervene effectively on behalf of his clients.

In 1965 a worker became concerned with the situation of one of the members of a street corner group in a Tel Aviv slum. Some probing among the members of the group and talks with the boy himself showed, at first, that the deterioration in the boy's behaviour and attitudes was due to his feelings of shame and guilt over having engaged in homosexual activities. The worker's first reaction was to deal with this as a problem of sexual deviance that demanded a psychotherapeutic approach. Inquiries, however, showed that the boy had not slept at home for several days, and that the homosexual episode had occurred one night when he sought shelter in a shack inhabited by a vagrant who introduced him to this practice.

Further talks with the boy and visits to his home resulted in the following information. This fifteen-year-old youngster lived in a one-room house together with nine other members of his family. Toilet, washing and sleeping facilities were highly inadequate, and the youngster had, for some time, rebelled against his discomfort and lack of privacy. The boy shared a makeshift bed with a thirteen-year-old sister. One night the girl menstruated for the first time, and the boy awoke finding himself spotted with blood. He ran out of the house in a state of anger and disgust and refused to sleep at home from then on, finding shelter wherever he could. The worker discussed the situation with the parents, who showed a deeply concerned but defeatist attitude. The mother said that the family had saved enough money over a number of years to buy a

---

[1] The figures are based upon the population census of May 1961. Conditions may have improved slightly since then, but there is no indication of significant changes.

small piece of land adjoining their present home. They had applied to the municipal authorities for a permit to build an annex to the house that would give the family more living space, but had not received an answer to their request. The worker made some inquiries at the municipality and then helped the mother compose a letter explaining her situation to the relevant authorities.

Several months passed without any conclusive reply to the family's request for a building permit. To the group of youngsters the matter had become a sort of test case that would prove whether people in their situation could expect any help and understanding from the authorities. Many families in this neighbourhood faced the same problem, but were so deeply convinced that 'nobody cared', that they would not even make the attempt to apply to the authorities for help. Here was the case of a family who had, under very difficult conditions, shown itself resourceful and diligent enough to save the money necessary to improve their living conditions. Other people in their situation would not seek a law-abiding solution by applying for a permit, but go ahead and build without a licence, risking that municipal inspectors and the police would tear down the structure as soon as it had been erected. The worker's readiness to help was not questioned by the youngsters, who had established a close and warm relationship with him. But now it would become apparent whether the worker's assertion that 'the best way is the legal way' was right, and whether the worker commanded resources that were sufficient to help in a situation as decisive as this one.

The worker contacted the relevant authorities at the municipality and, after some initial difficulties, was given the opportunity to plead the case of his clients. Attempts were made to find a way to either grant the family a building permit, or else assign them to a housing project. However, all efforts on behalf of this hard-pressed family failed and no immediate solution could be found which would not run counter to the municipal authorities' city planning and slum clearance programme.

The family who had sought the worker's help in their predicament, reacted with bitterness and an 'I-told-you-so' attitude of resignation. The worker, in consultation with his agency, sought legal advice as to what other means the petitioning family had to improve their living conditions. The street club worker's relationship to his group did not suffer, but the youngsters' confidence in his ability to provide concrete help in situations of pressing need had been shaken. The boys' belief that laws and regulations are mainly devices which are used against them, rather than for their protection and welfare, was reinforced, strengthening the negative values with which they confront society.

Life in an overcrowded household where the lack of elbow room is often aggravated by shabby furnishings, inadequate toilet and washing facilities, incessant noise and a general aura of neglect, is one of the most frustrating and depressing aspects of the lives of a great many lower-class street corner boys. The adolescent's growing need for some measure of privacy is often the direct cause of an unending series of family rows. The youngsters' feelings of resentment and embarrassment caused by a seedy home which contrasts sharply with the high living standard upheld as a measure of status and success by an affluent society, often turn a natural phase of rebelliousness into an attitude of open contempt for the parents, leading to severe conflict or final estrangement between the two generations within the family. Street club workers often become aware of this situation by a youngster's reluctance to allow them to visit his home. It is a gauge of the worker's relationship and his acceptance by the youngsters when they begin to loose their inhibitions about this.

The habitual hanging-about at the street corner, in candy stores or cafes is, at least partly, a result of the lack of a home where one can spend an evening in comfort. The youngsters are often aware of this and say so. When an exasperated police officer who for several nights in a row had chased the boys of a New York street corner group away from the stoop in front of one of the buildings said: 'Why don't you boys go home instead of hanging around here?' One of the youngsters answered: 'Man, if you lived like I do, you would be looking for a stoop to park your ass on too.' The officer's reply, 'Well, why don't you tell your old man to get a decent place to live', didn't help matters either. Another boy was ordered by his probation officer to be home at ten o'clock every night. He was told that his probation would be rescinded and he would be sent to jail if he disobeyed. The boy told me angrily: 'I said: go ahead and turn me in. I ain't going home at ten. With all the racket going on, I don't get to sleep before midnight anyway, and I'll go off my mind sitting in that rat-hole I live in every evening. I'll go to jail, serve my time and be done with it.'

In New York and in Tel Aviv I have found that many of the youngsters periodically stay away from home for a night, several days or even weeks. Invariably this 'absenteeism' is most frequent among those youngsters whose living conditions are most inadequate and crowded.

Twenty-six out of a group of fifty-two street corner boys in a Tel Aviv slum neighbourhood ran away from home repeatedly during two years of a street club work assignment. Without exception, every one of these boys lived in highly inadequate conditions. Six of them spent the night in an empty shack on the outskirts of the neighbourhood on such occasions, at times alone, sometimes two or three of them together, and from time to time with a runaway girl from another area or with a homeless prostitute. One boy slept in an empty well, another in a junkyard, a third in a garage. One boy camped in the back room of the cafe in which he worked occasionally. Several of the boys found shelter in cellars or made a makeshift lean-to in a field. Two boys found that they could get into a nearby school at night. One boy was sheltered by a middle-aged prostitute. Three boys found temporary lodgings with adult homosexuals.

During these runaway periods the youngsters are especially vulnerable to the influence of unstable, sometimes criminal, adults and homosexuals, and they find many opportunities for stealing and other delinquent activities. The street club worker assigned to the above-mentioned group therefore made a special effort to locate runaway boys as quickly as possible, often enlisting the help of other members of the group, and to return the youngster to his home after discussing the situation with his family, or else staying in contact with the boy and helping him to find adequate shelter and to keep out of trouble.

In eleven of the above-mentioned cases, the worker persuaded the youngsters repeatedly to return home with him, after having made sure that he would find somewhat improved living conditions at home, and that he would not be punished. The worker helped two youngsters to find furnished rooms, agreeing with them that their continued living with their families had become impossible. One boy gained admission to a communal settlement (kibbuz) upon the worker's recommendation.

It is my impression that the need for 'a place of one's own' where one can enjoy some measure of privacy, independence and comfort either alone, or in the company of one's friends, is an expression of the youngsters' need to get away from the squalor and crowding of their own homes. This may very well be one of the main reasons for the notorious inability of most of the street corner boys in slum areas in New York and Tel Aviv, as in many other cities, to become acceptable participants in the programmes of conventional community centres, youth clubs and settlement houses. Some of the major objections the youngsters raise is, that they have to share a room with other groups, that the adults who 'run the place' make the rules for the uses of the room and its furnishings, and that these adults have the right to supervise, interfere and hover about at all times.

In New York I have seen numerous instances in which street corner groups set up their own club rooms in basements or put up some flimsy structures in a hidden corner of one of the roof-tops. The good results of providing the 'Commanders', a Lower East Side fighting gang, with their own club room in a storage chamber have already been mentioned. The boys worked untiringly in removing large piles of junk which had accumulated over several years. They showed a range of unsuspected talents in painting the walls, repairing various pieces of old furniture which was collected from many sources, doing carpentry and putting up lavish decorations. The girls helped with the decorating and made curtains. The club was kept spotlessly clean at all times. The group made its own rules and statutes which they posted on one of the walls. These were considerably more strict than those usually prescribed by conventional youth clubs, and they were rigidly enforced. A very similar process took place in a basement in East Harlem which became the home-away-from-home for a street corner group after their leader had called upon the services of his two older brothers, both known and feared racketeers, to 'persuade' the landlord not to raise any objections. In this case a kitchen was installed in a corner and the girls frequently cooked meals for the boys.

I have recently read an interesting account of a self-maintained club in an English town run by what is described as 'by their own description, "rather a rough lot". As a gang of about 15, they used to roar around town in an old jeep, creating their own havoc. They had a rather checkered history in and around town. The police knew them all well after several encounters . . . They had generally "done" all the clubs in the town and were asked by most not to come back . . .' (Waldorf, 1967).

In the semi-rural environment of some of Tel Aviv's poor neighbourhoods, especially those located on the outskirts of the city, the youngsters build shacks which serve as club rooms and often provide shelter for one or several youngsters at night. Building material consists of old crates and petrol tins which have been hammered flat, and old pieces of board and planks which have been begged, borrowed or stolen from various sources. One of the Tel Aviv groups laid a very presentable floor, using half a truck load of tiles stolen from a construction site. The boys thoughtfully constructed a secret cache for 'loot' under the floor, and put in two doors so that they could skip out through one when the police came in through the other.

The shack-building craze was rampant in the two cohesive lower-class communities to which the Tel Aviv street club project assigned workers, as well as in that neighbourhood which can be described as a disorganised slum-in-transition. In the latter the street club worker found that shack-building started already with the eight- and nine-year-olds, who built low little contraptions resembling dog-houses with great enthusiasm. There were almost no shacks in the two mixed neighbourhoods of interspersed lower- and middle-class housing which, as our statistics showed, provided somewhat better housing for the families of the street corner boys. Although the shacks were used for all sorts of undesirable purposes, such as hashish smoking, the planning of burglaries and sexual activities with willing girls or prostitutes, the street club workers did not discourage the shacks as such. Instead, they exerted their influence to turn the shack into the group's club room, made use of it for discussions and other positive activities, gradually reducing the negative use. In one instance the worker persuaded the group to offer their shack as temporary accommodation to one of the boys who had found living at home unbearable and was on the verge of running away. This youngster became a sort of resident caretaker and used his influence to prevent the other boys from using the shack for delinquent purposes.

What I have seen in New York and in Tel Aviv has convinced me that in many, though not in all, cases the street club worker should try to help his group to get their own club room, whether this is a cellar, an empty store (as in East Harlem), a flat or a shack they can erect themselves. In many cases this is more realistic and more geared to needs than the usual attempts to get the group into one of the conventional youth clubs or community centres. In some instances the group's 'private club' can be regarded as an interim step towards adjustment to a more conventional youth club or community centre programme. This is what happened in the case of the 'Commanders' who, after running their own club successfully for a year, participated fully in the 'young-adult' programme of the same settlement house which had previously disbarred them because of their delinquent and highly aggressive behaviour. The Israel Ministry of Education has recently embarked upon a youth work programme which provides shack clubs for individual street corner groups in lower-class areas under the direction of a former staff member of the Tel Aviv Street Club Project.

20 The law

A combination of impoverished economic position, a marginal scholastic record, a particular kind of disrupted family situation, a current infraction of burglary, and two past citations for auto theft yields a disposition. What disposition? If we ask court agents, they will honestly and appropriately answer that it depends. On what does it depend? It depends on other factors. On what other factors? Well, perhaps on a diagnosis of the child's personality, but that too depends. On what does that depend? Ultimately it depends on the need of the child. And on what do these needs depend? And eventually we come to the final and only possible answer. It depends on the professional training, experience and judgement of the court agents.

D. MATZA (1964), p. 116

The vast and complex network of law enforcement agencies and procedures plays an important role in the lives of the delinquent street corner group. Its intricate and rarely even half-understood processes are a constant topic of conversation and throw their shadow over all aspects of the youngsters' lives. In New York as well as in Tel Aviv I have found that hardly a day passes without the street club worker being called upon to offer counsel and direct help in dealing with a situation in which the police and the courts are involved.

Space does not permit a detailed discussion of the police and the judiciary systems of Israel and the United States and their procedures regarding juvenile offenders.[1] However, some significant points must be mentioned in this context. In both countries juvenile offender treatment in police, court and probation procedure is limited to boys up to the age of sixteen.[2] The age limit for girls is eighteen. Aside from the question whether it makes any sense to maintain that an adolescent of seventeen is legally regarded as an adult, this age division poses some special problems for the street club worker. Street corner groups often consist of youngsters whose main age range lies between fifteen and eighteen. In helping the youngsters to understand and face frequent involvements with the law, the worker has to deal with two different systems and approaches. In almost all cases, it is considerably easier for the worker to gain the understanding and the co-operation of police, probation and court officials when dealing with offenders below the age of sixteen.

On the whole it can be said that I have encountered an understanding, flexible and co-operative attitude among police officers (especially the

---

[1] For a detailed view of the legal system with regard to juvenile delinquency see Rosenheim (1962) and Aloni (1964).
[2] For information on the Israel Youth and Adult Probation Services see articles by: Yona Cohen and M. Horovitz in Drapkin et al (1965). See also Yona Cohen (1959).

Youth Squad), probation officers and judges more often in Tel Aviv, although I have met with some outstanding examples of insight and humane attitudes on the part of police, probation officers and judges in New York.

His special relationship with the street corner group gives the street club worker a wealth of information and a degree of insight into the nature, the context and the motivation of delinquent behaviour, which usually is not available to law enforcement or judiciary officials. Provided he gains the co-operation of the law enforcement and judiciary authorities, the street club worker can use his specific knowledge and his relationships for a number of purposes: To enable the youngsters to gain a realistic understanding of their obligations and their rights with regard to the law and its representatives; to help law enforcement and judiciary officials obtain a more inclusive picture of the background and the characteristics of the young offender; to help law enforcement and judiciary officials determine approaches, punishments and rehabilitative methods which are most likely to prevent recidivism and a hardening of criminal adaptations and to contribute to the valid prediction of the effects of legal procedures upon the youngster and his peers; to help the youngsters better their relations with law enforcement officials and bring about changes in their (at times reciprocated) attitudes of hostility and distrust towards the latter.

Attitudes of hostility and distrust towards the police have deep roots in the traditions and norms of the lower classes everywhere. These feelings are often reciprocal. Most street corner boys consider the police their enemy. The reaction of the individual police officer depends to a great degree upon 'whether the officer is able to control his impulse to use physical force', upon his ability to 'consider misbehaviour not as a personal threat to his dignity' and upon the extent to which police officers 'share the points of view and prejudices of the ethnic group to which they belong' (Robison, 1960, p. 211).[1]

While the street club worker has many opportunities to discuss with the youngsters their attitudes and behaviour towards the police, he does not always find it easy to obtain a hearing for their problems and views with law enforcement officers.

It may be of some interest here to mention a similar situation reported by the staff of a London Cafe Project, working with 'unattached' youngsters in an area with a high delinquency rate. The authors (Biven and Holden, 1966) describe the local community's relationship with the police as follows:

[1] Peter Willmott (1966, pp. 151-3) describes the same kind of hostility and distrust towards the police among the youngsters of a London lower-class neighbourhood.

Deep mistrust exists on both sides. The police are of course recruited from outside the area and Shuttleton[1] is an unpopular station. Police tend to walk about
in pairs, they are on the look out for trouble and prepared to see it almost anywhere. Any teenager tends to be viewed as a potentially dangerous 'mod' or
'rocker'. They adopt a peremptory manner with any group of youngsters whom
they chance to find and are unable to see how this provokes them into behaving
in just the manner they expect. They look for the worst in people and they soon
find it. It would of course be wrong to blame the police for the high incidents of
petty crime in the district but we believe that their attitude is one of the factors
that perpetuates it.

This description fits the situation in Tel Aviv remarkably well. In New
York relationships tend to be even more tense. Working with street corner groups in neighbourhoods as different as Yorkville and the Lower
East Side, I found that it was common practice for police officers to walk
up to groups of boys hanging about at a street corner or sitting on the
benches provided in the courtyards of the housing projects, order them
sharply to 'get moving', often accompanying this command by a shove
or a jab with the nightstick in a boy's stomach. The boys were often
ordered to line up facing a wall to be searched for drugs and weapons,
and the whole procedure was frequently punctuated by insulting and
obscene remarks by the officers. At the slightest show of reluctance to
obey orders, the nightstick was used freely, and on several occasions guns
were drawn.

In New York I found that street club workers must seek to establish
a personal relationship with the personnel of the local police precinct
in addition to the official contacts that exist between the precinct and
the worker's agency. The key people here are the patrolmen assigned to
the area of the worker's client groups, the youth patrolman attached
to the precinct and the detectives who investigate offences and inter-
rogate the offenders after an arrest has been made. The degree of
understanding and co-operation which the worker obtains depends upon
a number of factors: his ability to explain his professional functions and
to convey his understanding for the responsibilities and complexities of
the policeman's job; the personal attitudes of the individual officers with
whom he deals; the attitudes of the commanding officer of the precinct
and, last, but not least, the public pressure exerted upon the police at any
given time due to dramatic incidents of youth crime, press campaigns
against 'young hoodlums', etc. I have encountered attitudes ranging from
very bad—instances in which police officers seemed to be ruled primarily
by their own hostility and contempt for the youngsters and by their over-
riding intent to obtain a conviction in court—to excellent, where police
officers showed an impressive understanding of the need to prevent the

[1] The name of the London neighbourhood was changed in the text of the article.

hardening of criminal values and norms among the youngsters of the street corner groups.

In one of New York's underprivileged neighbourhoods the youth patrolman of the local precinct helped me greatly in my work by his fair and co-operative attitude. This officer's wide range of experience and his thorough knowledge of the youth problems of the area made his counsel in all matters concerning the planning and carrying out of youth services in the neighbourhood invaluable. On several occasions he met with a group that seemed to be heading for serious troubles to 'talk things over before it is too late'.

When I began work with a New York fighting gang some years ago the relationship between this group and the police had reached a record low. Police officers openly expressed their intention to 'wipe out' this particular gang and to 'get everyone of these punks behind bars'. The boys were told to 'keep moving' whenever a police patrol found them hanging around in the vicinity of their homes. Insulting and humiliating language was frequently used by police officers on such occasions and any reply or show of reluctance to obey resulted in the use of the nightstick and arrests for 'resisting an officer'. Simmering hatred for the police threatened to come to a boiling point and there was much talk about 'japping a cop' (ambushing a police officer). After working through the intolerable and dangerous situation with the youngsters as well as with the police, and after the boys and girls of the group were given the opportunity to air their grievances on the radio, several of the police officers could be persuaded to visit the group's newly acquired club room, have a cup of coffee with them and convince themselves that they were not dealing with 'animals' or 'psychos' after all. The boys were hospitable and polite on these occasions and conceded that the officers 'weren't so bad, once you got to know them'. When dangerous tension arose at a dance given by this group because the pocket-book of the girl-friend of the leader of a rival gang had been rifled, the boys themselves agreed to call in the 'cop on the beat' in order to help settle the matter without violence.

Two youngsters of a thieves' group I worked with in New York came to me one evening and told me that the owners and employees of a local store had accused them of stealing a tape recorder and had filed a complaint at the precinct. The boys had been ordered to appear at the police station the following morning to be questioned. Both youngsters had police records and had stolen in the past, but vehemently denied having carried out this particular theft. My relationship with these boys was such that it seemed very unlikely that they would lie to me about this matter. The boys felt that, because of their bad reputation, there was no chance that they would be believed and they were afraid that a confession would be 'beaten out of them' at the precinct. On the promise that I would 'stick to them', I persuaded the youngsters to give up their plan to go into hiding, but to appear at the police station at the appointed hour.

Because of the good relations I had established at the precinct, I was permitted to remain with the boys throughout the interrogation which went on for over four hours. I impressed on them that I would not help them in any way to cover up if they had indeed committed the theft, but advised them not to admit to anything they had not done in order to 'get it over with', as often happens in such cases. In the course of the interrogation by two detectives, at one point interrupted by an outburst of defiance by one of the boys which earned him a slap in the face, I gained the feeling that the boys were holding something back. I talked to the detectives about my doubts and my conviction that the boys were innocent in the particular case, but was told that the testimony of the store owner and three of his employees was enough to convict the youngsters in court. I asked, and was granted, permission to speak to the boys alone and told them that I felt that they had information which they were keeping from the police. After I had promised to guard their confidence, the youngsters told me that they knew that one of the employees had stolen the tape recorder, but that their code of honour forbade them to 'fink' (inform.) We sat there in the squad room of the police precinct and discussed the thieves' code to which these boys and their friends adhered. The boys finally conceded that the young man they were protecting had himself broken the code by adding his signature as a witness to the complaint against them. This matter cleared up, the boys told the officers what they knew. The detectives were sceptical, but agreed to question the man in order to show the boys that they were willing to make every effort to be 'fair' with them. The four complainants were brought in and the young man whom the boys had accused confessed to the theft after a short interrogation. The two youngsters and the detectives shook hands and assured each other that there were 'no hard feelings'.

This incident was discussed at great length by the group to which these two youngsters belonged and contributed considerably towards loosening up the atmosphere of rigid distrust and the deeply rooted feelings of not being given a chance by the authorities.

One of the Tel Aviv street club workers experienced a somewhat different situation. Investigating a motorcycle theft, the police picked up two boys of the workers' group. One of the boys had actually stolen the bike and confessed. Both boys were questioned about the unsolved theft of a car in the neighbourhood. They claimed that they were threatened and beaten into giving their interrogators the name of the alleged thief of the vehicle. They picked a name at random, and the police arrested a youngster who was a fringe member of the group. This boy had a police record, but had not been involved in delinquent activities for some time and was working steadily. He was arrested at his place of work and held for interrogation for ten days.

When members of the street corner group informed the worker of the boy's arrest he requested, and was granted, permission to speak to the youngster at the police station. The worker's impression that the boy was innocent of the charge was reinforced by conversations with the boy's employer, his mother, and the other members of the street corner group. The interrogating police officer discussed the case with the worker and gave him permission to speak to the youngster alone. Although the police suggested that the worker should persuade the boy to sign a confession, he advised the youngster to stick to the truth, even though the promise of being permitted to go home the moment he confessed seemed tempting. After having seen the boy the worker talked to the two members of the group who had given the arrested boy's name to the police. They both assured him that they had picked the name at random and had made the accusation because they were frightened.

When the worker returned with this information to the police station, the interrogating officer conceded the possibility of the boy's innocence. The conversation between the worker and the interrogating officer took place on a Friday morning. When the worker asked for the boy's release, he was told that the pressure of work and the complex bureaucratic procedure would make it impossible to set the boy free before the following Sunday. The worker remonstrated with the police and other agencies whose assistance he sought, but was told that there was nothing wrong with leaving the youngster in jail for an additional two days and two nights. The worker then asked for the intervention of the Project Director and the boy was released that same day.

When several members of the 'Emperors' were charged with assault and their pictures appeared in the New York daily press under such captions as: 'Teenage Hoodlums' and 'The Law of the Jungle in Our Streets', I enlisted the help of two Youth Squad detectives to find witnesses who would back up the boys' story that they had acted in self-defence and under extreme provocation. The two young officers were Negroes and well aware of the racist attitudes of the notorious gang to which the accused youngster belonged. Nevertheless they were willing to listen to my pleas and sacrificed their off-duty hours to give the boys a 'fair shake'. The boys' acquittal and the subsequent charging of their 'victim' with perjury was largely due to their efforts. I used the occasion for rubbing in the group's racist attitudes, and the boys thanked the two detectives humbly and sincerely.

Cases in which the street club worker intervenes with the police on behalf of a youngster who is innocent of the accusation levelled against him are the exception rather than the rule in both New York and Tel Aviv. In both cities the street club worker is called upon on many occasions to stand by boys who have run afoul of the law and have to face the consequences. Many times the worker is instrumental in enabling a boy to face the reality of the situation, no matter how difficult that may be, and to refrain from making matters worse by trying to evade arrest or by attempting to lie his way out.

The most useful and decisive moment for the street club worker's help and intervention is the time immediately after an arrest. At that time the boy is usually in a stage of crisis and near-panic and can be made to face the realities and consequences of his conduct as well as the true meaning of his system of values and norms. The street club worker often faces considerable difficulties in his attempts to see the youngster immediately after his arrest. It usually depends upon the individual interrogating police officer whether the worker is permitted access to his client. My request for official permission for the Project staff to interview our youngsters at this time was refused by the Israeli police.

The Tel Aviv Youth Squad, whose jurisdiction is limited to youngsters under the age of sixteen, holds an enlightened attitude which stresses prevention and an educational approach. The Project staff and their client groups greatly benefited from the understanding, co-operative attitude of this organisation.

In New York I have found it very helpful that street club workers are issued with official identification cards obtained on recommendation of the employing agency and signed by the Police Commissioner. These cards serve to identify the worker as a bona fide professional to police officers and court officials, and state explicitly that the worker is authorised to interview his clients in prison.

Although the street club worker has no official legal standing in the court proceedings in New York or Tel Aviv I have found that on most, though not on all, occasions judges are willing to authorise his presence and consider his opinion. The lower-class delinquent youngster is ill-equipped by his background and upbringing to face the power and majesty of a court of law. He is frightened, at times defiant, and usually thoroughly confused. 'The juvenile delinquent is additionally confused because, unfortunately, he hardly understands most of the words that are used in court. Like Camus' stranger, he is frequently a mystified observer at his own trial' (Matza, 1964, p. 133). Whether or not he is guilty as charged, the youngster is entitled to the same adult support and counsel which is usually accorded a middle-class youth. The street club worker, by his very presence and his availablity for help and advice can do much to make the court experience understandable, meaningful and even beneficial.

It was recently reported in a publication of the United States Children's Bureau (1967) that:

The Supreme Court of the United States, by an 8-to-1 decision, ruled on May 15 that the constitutional guarantee of due process of law is applicable to court cases involving minors charged with being 'delinquents'. In a detailed opinion, written by Justice Abe Fortas, the Court ruled that in delinquency hearings before juvenile court judges children must be accorded the constitutional protections of due process in regard to the right to remain silent, to receive adequate notice of hearing, to counsel, and to confront witnesses, and the privilege against self-incrimination. That is, they must be given specific notice of the charges and adequate time to decide on a course of action and to prepare a defence; be clearly advised of their right to counsel and be provided with counsel by the State if the parents are unable to afford a counsel; be warned that their testimony can be used against them; and have an opportunity to face their accusers.

This decision is specially significant in view of its implications regarding the heretofore prevalent usage under which the basic constitutional rights guaranteed to every adult offender, no matter how trivial or how serious his crime, were frequently ignored in the case of a juvenile delinquent. It should be added that this was mainly due to the wish to prevent the youngster from being treated as an adult criminal, rather than motivated by any punitive bias. The results, however, were very frequently that a youngster was punished severely for an offence which would have resulted in a relatively light sentence for an adult offender represented by a lawyer. In a number of cases a minor was found guilty when an adequate court procedure would have established his innocence.

The worker's presence in court is specially important in New York, where the overwhelming pressure of work rarely permits the judge or the harassed legal-aid lawyer to delve deeply into the background, motivations, and perspectives of the youth before the bench. In Tel Aviv I have found that, on the whole, judges are inclined to give a considerable degree of individual attention to a boy (or girl) who appears before them. In both cities, I have observed on numerous occasions that the very fact that the street club worker, as a representative of a youth service agency, states his interest and concern, influences the severity of the sentence.

The above statement may demand elaboration. In both cities delinquent youth is judged and sentenced not only in accordance with the nature and severity of the unlawful act that has been committed, but also, and often decisively, with due consideration of the question whether the young offender is likely to repeat the offence and become an habitual criminal.

The judge, in passing sentence, is not solely concerned with punishing or rehabilitating the young offender. He also assumes the responsibility of protecting society. The middle-class adolescent who has broken the law in most cases appears in court with his parents, friends of the family and legal counsel. Unless the boy has committed an exceptionally serious crime or is known to the court as an habitual offender, the judge has every reason to assume that the boy's background, his family's concern, resources, and standing in the community offer reasonable hope that the youngster will be more closely supervised and is unlikely to embark upon a criminal career.[1]

The situation is in most cases radically different where a youngster from a slum milieu is concerned. Here the Judge often takes into account the fact that the poor resources, and the inadequate living conditions of the boy's family as well as the destructive environmental influences to which the youngster is exposed are conducive to a repetition of the offence and may demand incarceration in the interest of society. The street club worker's presence, his testimony in court or his submittal of a written statement may in certain cases signify to the judge that the interest and concern of a trained youth worker warrants a rehabilitative sentence such as probation or a suspended jail term.

I know of a number of instances in which the street club worker not only helped a youngster to be receptive to the moral significance of his arraignment in court, and prevailed upon him to honestly admit his offence rather than lie to the judge (thereby either increasing his chances for more severe punishment or else lull him into a sense of falsely 'having gotten away with it' leading to a repetition of the offence), but where the worker also used the occasion of a youngster's court appearance to involve the street corner group in a thorough discussion and reappraisal of unlawful behaviour.

The arraignment of one of the youngest members of a street corner group in New York's Children's court may provide an example of the street club worker's functions on such an occasion. Eric was brought to

[1] The following item appeared under the 'This England' column in the *New Statesman*, 21 April 1967: 'Two boys who threw a 10-year-old boy into the canal were ordered today at Burnley juvenile court to go to an Attendance Centre for the maximum of 24 hours. . . . The magistrate's chairman, Mrs B. C. L. Bruggen, told the boys it was a disgraceful affair which might have had awful consequences. If they had not come from good homes a different course might have been taken' (quoted from the *Manchester Evening News*).

court on charges of habitual truancy and petty theft, the probation officer who conducted the pre-trial investigations knew the boy mainly from interviews that took place in his office. Focusing upon the youngster's delinquent behaviour, the official recommended commitment to a state training school. Having worked with this youngster's group for about a year I was able to draw the attention of the judge to the following facts: one, that the group to which the boy belonged did not engage in severely delinquent activities and was on the verge of being absorbed into the programme of a community centre; two, that this particular boy was somewhat effeminate and most likely to become the subject of homosexual exploitation in a closed institution: on the other hand, the norms of the street corner group to which the youngster belonged would not permit him to become engaged in homosexual activities. My recommendation to assign this boy to probation even though he would probably persist in his misconduct for some time was accepted on the above stated terms.

A more dramatic but not highly unusual incident took place when four boys of the 'Emperors' were arrested for assaulting an adult.[1] Each of the four youngsters had a previous conviction for assault and had to expect a severe sentence. I had invested a considerable amount of intensive work in trying to change this group's preoccupation with brawling and physical violence, and was therefore surprised that, according to the victim's testimony and the newspaper reports, they had behaved in a manner which they seemed to have given up some time before. A talk with the boys after their arrest led me to believe that there was more than reasonable doubt of their guilt and that the complainant had actually been the aggressor. The reputation of the 'Emperors' had been so bad for so many years that I found it rather difficult to convince anyone that these four youngsters deserved help. Nevertheless, my agency made the services of a lawyer available. Despite the lawyer's able defence things looked black for the youngsters until I enlisted the help of two Youth Squad detectives. Witnesses were subpoenaed, the complainant's main witness was proven to be untrustworthy and the man had to admit in court that he was drunk and had attacked the boys without provocation. In asking for a dismissal of the charges, the District Attorney informed the Bench that the man would be indicted for perjury and that another case in which the same person had obtained a conviction against three other adolescents a few months previously, was being reopened.

[1] The incident was reported in all New York daily newspapers on 3 August 1959. The pictures of the boys were published and they were described as 'brutal punks' and 'teenage hoodlums'. Their alleged victim was described as the 'son of an anti-communist hero' from one of the Balkan countries. No report of the exoneration of the youngsters ever appeared in any New York newspaper.

Although this is a somewhat exceptional case, it demonstrated clearly that a street club worker who can draw upon his knowledge of the behaviour patterns of a group of young delinquents may, in certain circumstances, become instrumental in helping the court to arrive at a correct conclusion. The impact upon the youngsters is obvious: as long as the boy is at large, he is accessible to the guidance and help the worker can offer him. Once the youngster is behind bars the worker will visit him and co-operate with any social service and rehabilitative programme available, but opportunities for helping the youngster to work through his problems and make positive adjustments are severely limited, and he is exposed to the considerable impact of the well-known criminogene influences of the prison environment.

David Matza (1964, p. 121) states categorically: 'The pressure exerted on the judge by his social work underlings is, to state it simply, for *mercy*.' This reflects a widespread public bias which is all too familiar to the street club worker. Experience indicates that the facts are not as simple as Professor Matza's statement. Neither in New York nor in Tel Aviv nor, to the best of my knowledge anywhere else, do judges have access to adequate numbers of qualified and experienced 'social work underlings'. Nor do social workers, when they are consulted by the court, which is by no means always the case, have a uniform attitude towards juvenile delinquents. There are indeed some social workers who seem to be motivated by a charitable attitude based on pity or false sentimentality, rather than on professional judgment. I have met others who express a strong belief in the therapeutic value of severe punishment, especially when a sullen young culprit is 'unco-operative', hiding his fear and confusion behind a pose of indifference or arrogance. There are social workers who make sincere attempts to figure out what kind of court action is most likely to prevent a young offender from becoming a recidivist and hardened criminal. These workers, if they have the necessary specialised training and experience, are sometimes able to help the judge to gain wider perspective on a case. There are others who hide their own confusion behind a welter of pseudoscientific verbiage which leaves the wise judge distrustful and exasperated and the gullible one utterly confused.

The street club worker becomes one of the court's 'social work underlings' when he requests permission to advise the court or furnish information relevant to the case, and the judge authorises him to speak up or submit a written statement. He does not seek to exert pressure for 'mercy', but he can, provided he is certain that he knows the youngster well enough, help the judge decide whether the boy will, perhaps with the worker's own or other suitable help, be able to desist from further criminal activities, and he may venture a prediction of how a term in a reformatory or approved school, a jail sentence, probation, conditional discharge or a suspended sentence will affect the youngster's future conduct and attitudes.

A Tel Aviv street club worker explained to the judge that the youngster appearing before him for an act of vandalism would gain prestige from the short jail sentence the law prescribed and reinforce his group's tendency to adopt the role of dangerous criminals, while an order to apologise to the owner of the damaged property and a weekly deduction from his wages to pay for the damage under the supervision of a probation officer, would serve to show him and his friends that his behaviour had been 'stupid' and humiliating. Another worker had to tell a boy who asked him for help in court: 'We both know that you've done a great number of "jobs" [in this case burglaries] but were lucky enough not to get caught until this time. When the judge asks me whether he should give you another chance, whether I think that you won't do it again, I have to say that if you get away with this one too, you'll probably go on the same way.' Naturally, the boy was upset, but he and his friends in the group accepted the logic of the worker's statement. On more than one occasion I have had to tell a boy who asked me to 'speak up' for him in court: 'I can't do that. I don't know enough about you. I don't even know whether you're telling me the truth now. I'll help you get a lawyer. You're entitled to that, like any other citizen, but I can't tell the judge that I really know what makes you tick.'

Judges differ in their attitudes to street club workers according to their personal bias, their experience with social workers, the public attitude towards young delinquents prevailing at any given time, pressure of work and even the momentary mood they are in. I have been curtly refused permission to have my say by the same judge who, on another occasion, invited me to his office and listened to me with interest and patience. I have encountered a judge who told me in no uncertain terms that he had a deep distrust for people of my calling and would, on principle, not consider my opinions. More often, both in Tel Aviv and in New York, judges have listened to the street club worker's remarks carefully, asked searching questions about his work, and consulted him repeatedly with regard to a boy's background and prospects.

On one occasion in New York I asked the judge for 'permission to approach the bench' and told him in a voice audible only to him and to the prosecuting attorney who had joined us, that Floyd, the tall blond boy in the dock had, in my opinion, given all the signs of serious mental disturbance. Floyd, a fringe member of the 'Emperors, who had just been described as an 'arrogant young hoodlum' by the District Attorney, was shunned and known as 'crazy' by the other members of the group. He had, over a period of several years, engaged in increasingly violent and self-destructive behaviour. His latest exploit was a lone excursion to Harlem, where he was caught molesting a thirteen-year-old Negro girl, offering her money for having sexual intercourse with him. He did this in full view of a group of Negro teenagers and was saved from a severe beating by the timely arrival of a patrol car. The police officers found an assortment of sleeping pills, benzedrine tablets and marijuana cigarettes when they searched him. I told the judge that I had discussed the situation with the boy's parents and with himself, and all had agreed that a thorough psychiatric examination and possibly commitment to a mental hospital should be requested. Having listened to me attentively, the judge turned to the boy and asked in a booming voice: 'Young man, your social worker here says that you are crazy. Are you crazy?'— Floyd shrugged his shoulders: 'How the f . . . do I know.' he said, 'If I'm crazy I don't know it, do I?' That seemed to satisfy the judge. He ordered a psychiatric examination and the boy was subsequently committed to a mental hospital for treatment. Another judge embarrassed me and, to some extent defeated my purpose, by telling a group of youngsters on an assault charge: 'I'm convinced that you are incorrigible and belong behind bars. However, your social worker here is working very hard to help you, so I don't want to render his efforts futile. I'll put you on probation, as he recommends. But remember, I'm letting you off lightly only because I am impressed by this man's efforts on your behalf. I hope you show him some gratitude for getting you off the hook.' I had just spent the best part of a year trying to make these boys understand that it was *not* one of my functions to 'get them off the hook' when they beat up people or committed other delinquent acts.

In Tel Aviv judges found the court appearances of street club workers so helpful and informative that, on several occasions, workers were invited to meet with a judge privately to tell him about their work and discuss the youngsters' attitudes and the effects of various types of court procedures upon their behaviour. The Israel Legal Association invited me twice to speak about street club work and the role of the street club worker in court at their meetings, which were attended by a substantial number of judges.

The degree to which the street club worker can fulfil a useful function helping the court and his clients is, of course, largely determined by the worker's ability to express himself clearly and honestly, to speak to the point without wasting the court's time, and to pay due respect to the dignity of the occasion in his appearance and behaviour. No one expects the street club worker to be an amateur lawyer or psychiatrist, but he is expected to know what he is talking about when he describes the boy's attitudes and behaviour, his role in the group, the milieu in which the youngster and his group exist, conditions and prospects of employment, education, family relations, housing conditions, etc. The prerequisites for this and many other aspects of street club work are training and professional supervision.

The street club worker who goes to court with one or several of his youngsters does *not* ask for 'mercy'. This is a point so important that it bears repeating. His task is to help the court understand those facets of the youngster's life which more often than not remain obscured, mainly because the court officials can only see the boy in a crisis situation and as an isolated individual, out of the context of his social milieu and his peer group associations. It is in this area that the street club worker can provide information which may help the court to arrive at a decision which furthers the youngster's chances for constructive adjustments, rather than confirm and perpetuate his delinquent role. The worker defeats his own purpose and distorts his own role if he fails to convince the judge as well as his client that this is what he is there for, that he is not trying to get anyone 'off the hook'.

The probation services in Tel Aviv emphasise treatment and rehabilitation to a greater degree than their colleagues in New York, where more weight is put upon the supervisory and penal functions of the assigned officers. Because of the emphasis on treatment relationships and goals, delinquent youngsters here seem to regard the probation officer more often as a helpful, trustworthy person, than the New York youngsters. In both cities it appears to hold true that:

The difficulties which the social worker [in the Probation Service setting] encounters with his caseload are further complicated by lack of familiarity with the criminal and delinquent sub-cultures from which most offenders emerge. Social casework emphasizes the importance of identifying the social environment with which the client is interacting in order to understand how he perceives and feels about his situation and how he may be helped. This requires knowledge and familiarity with the cultural and social backgrounds from which the offenders come, a familiarity which the officer does not usually bring from his own background and knowledge which his formal education does not specifically give him (Ohlin *et al.* (1958), p. 256).

The street club worker's relationship to the street corner group, his close ties to the daily lives and the environment of the youngsters and his regular presence in their milieu offers him opportunities to be of service to the assigned probation officer. In New York the worker has to establish a working relationship with the individual officer with regard to a specific youngster. In most cases co-operation and mutual consultation were extended and received gladly and proved of value in the concerted effort to rehabilitate the youngster. In Tel Aviv the probation service made co-operation with the staff of the street club Project a matter of policy. The staff of the two services met regularly and probation officers and street club workers consulted frequently. In several cases probation officers have met with the client groups of the Project in order to discuss with the youngsters the means and purposes of probation.

Neither in New York nor in Tel Aviv does the commitment to an institution or the penitentiary necessarily put an end to the relationship of a delinquent to his street corner group. In most cases, this relationship is perpetuated and even strengthened by the imprisoned youngster's loneliness and need to cling to something beyond the walls that shut him off from the outside world. On his return to the community, the group he left behind at a street corner of his neighbourhood are often the first to welcome him back. Here the boy does not have to hang his head in shame or try to hide the fact that he has been in jail. On the contrary, he can boast about his experiences in front of his peers, enhance his status and contribute what he has learned to the group's lore. In most cases, he returns to the same milieu and way of life from which he has come and there is no one to help him cope with his experience in a meaningful way. The street club worker can help the youngster and his group work through and evaluate the prison experience realistically and render concrete assistance in making positive adjustments with regard to employment, family relations and the attitudes of the community.

21 Social relations: getting out of the delinquency rut

The social creation of the delinquent character is a matter of the very highest importance and deserves a book to itself. Consider what happens. There are a number of quite different behaviours, some really harmful and anti-social, some indifferent and even performed innocently, yet all forbidden. When, however, they are all tarred with the same brush, the salient fact about them all becomes their defiance, culpability and punishability. Vice becomes 'vertical'; if a boy masturbates, smokes, plays truant, he might as well steal, joy ride, hustle, use narcotics, commit burglaries etc. Such a boy no longer has friends, but mutually blackmailing accomplices. . . . When the conceit, the being cool, the mask-face, are taken away, the kids at once appear in their variety, colour, lyric speech, and graceful and vigorous poses, very different from either the usual delinquent sullenness or the conventionality of the resigned Beats.

PAUL GOODMAN (1960), pp. 211, 213

There are many other areas in which the street club worker's role of mediator leads to concrete help to the delinquent street corner group and its individual members. In some instances this consists mainly in enabling them to make contacts which help them to obtain a more realistic view of their own situation and which broaden the range of their interests. At other times the worker can offer his group opportunities to gain new experiences and try out new forms of behaviour in situations to which they have not been exposed previously. 'The worker gradually persuades the group to plan recreational and social events which offer satisfaction and recognition without the need to use illegitimate or conflict behaviour' (Mobilization for Youth, 1961, p. 166).

Tel Aviv street club workers were constantly aware of the feelings of isolation which pervaded the atmosphere of our work areas. The young, as well as the adults of these poor communities identify themselves as inhabitants of their own immediate neighbourhoods. But they say that they are 'going to Tel Aviv', when they leave their own areas to attend to some business in other parts of the city, sometimes only a few minute, walk or a short bus ride away. They distinguish between shops, cinemass cafés, etc. in their own neighbourhood and 'in Tel Aviv'. Although their own communities are geographically and administratively integral parts of the City of Tel Aviv, the people who live in these communities do not seem to feel as if they are.

There are times when this finds expression in more flagrant ways. During the 1965 municipal elections, for instance, nearly everyone we talked to, adults and youngsters alike, made contemptuous, cynical remarks about the sudden interest of the authorities in the slums, the appearance of public figures and the loud expressions of concern over deprivation and neglect. Almost all attempts at implementing positive improvements by representatives of official or semi-official bodies during the pre-election months were shrugged off as part of the vote-getting campaign. 'You won't hear from "them" again after the elections', people told each other. When a street club worker contacted a street corner group a few weeks before the elections one of the leaders of the group told him: 'We don't mind you coming around, but you better wait till after the elections. Now all kinds of "government characters" and busybodies from Tel Aviv come around to help us. None of the guys is gonna believe anything you say right now.' The same remarks can be heard, the same attitudes expressed, in New York slums.

During the 'disorders' in one of Tel Aviv's slums in October 1965[1] we overheard many remarks, such as: 'All year round you don't see a police-man here when somebody is in trouble or when there's an accident. Now all of a sudden they can spare hundreds of them.' Or: 'There have been "drag races" and car stealing for years all over, "even in Tel Aviv". Now "they" are making a big deal of it, just to give our neighbourhood a bad name.'

It is always 'they,' 'them' and 'theirs' as against 'us' and 'our', and often a deep sense of isolation and resentment underlies the use of these small words which I am tempted to call 'rejective' instead of 'possessive' pronouns. There is a general feeling of frustration at the visible advan-tages 'they' seem to have, and the apparent success and prosperity of those who live outside the underprivileged neighbourhoods, often just across the road 'in Tel Aviv'. The same feeling prevails, and is vociferously ex-pressed, in the slums of New York.

I contacted a group of youngsters milling about near the main road 'to Tel Aviv' which divided their slum from a modern middle-class neigh-bourhood. When I, the stranger who had come to talk to them about

---

[1] Between 10 and 15 October 1965 the police prevented driving stunt exhibitions with stolen cars (comparable to the American 'drag races') from taking place in the main street of this area. Frustrated youngsters engaged in acts of hooliganism and threw stones at passing vehicles and at the police. The police reacted in force, dispersed the hundreds of spectators of all ages who had assembled, and made well over a hundred arrests. A few months earlier what became known as the 'bus riots' occurred in the same neighbourhood, when the Tel Aviv Bus Co-operative which serves the entire city moved one of its bus stops, forcing local users of this particular bus line to walk some distance to the next stop. On this occasion youngsters from other deprived areas came to the aid of the local youngsters and participated wholeheartedly in the 'fun', during which several buses were smashed. On this occasion the inhabitants of the area voiced the opinion that they were victims of discrimination by the bus co-operative. People claimed that ' "they" wouldn't have dared to do this in Tel Aviv', and that the slum areas were intentionally given the worst kind of bus service in the oldest, most incon-venient buses.

their 'problems', asked questions, one of the boys pointed his finger at the well-to-do community across the road: 'You want to know about our problems?' he asked in a tone of exasperation, 'You need new glasses or something? Look at the way "they" live over there and' (jabbing his thumb over his shoulder at the slum area behind him), 'look at the way we live. That's our problem, man.' There was a rumble of assent from the youngsters clustered around us.

On the 'other side' the feelings of the poverty areas are often reciprocated. In New York and in Tel Aviv one often encounters responses of fear, contempt or ignorance with regard to 'these elements' or, among the more enlightened, a pitying, patronising attitude. Only rarely have I come across expressions of respect and understanding.

During my work in Tel Aviv I was invited to speak to the senior grades of one of the most modern, best constructed and most exclusive high schools in Israel. The assembled group of bright, healthy, lively teenagers reacted with warm, eager interest and concern to what I told them. Yet I felt like an anthropologist explaining the strange customs of an exotic tribe to an audience who had heard vague rumours about their ways of life, but had never had any direct contact with these people. I timed the walking distance between this school and the nearest lower-class area to which one of the Project's street club workers was assigned. The time needed to walk from the school to this community is about four minutes. A sixteen-year-old student said that her teacher had once taken the class to visit a school in a poor section of Jaffa. She said that she had felt uncomfortable and embarrassed at the time. 'It was like being taken to the Zoo. My heart ached at seeing these kids and the place they had to use for a school.' One of the teachers later mentioned that some boys from the nearby poor area had, on occasion, raided the school grounds. He looked worriedly at the well-kept lawns and flowerbeds, the spotless buildings and tiled floors, and said that something would have to be done about it. Perhaps a select number of these youngsters should be allowed to use the grounds for supervised activities after school hours, rather than risk their resentment and destructive reactions if entry into the school grounds was forbidden them altogether.

In New York I once spoke to a group of young adults, members of the congregation of one of the city's wealthiest churches. This group, led by their minister, had asked my agency whether there was something useful they could do to help us in our work with the gangs of an adjacent neighbourhood. I suggested several ways in which the young men and women in the audience could 'do something', all of these involving some personal contact. I had the feeling that I was not 'reaching' them. Finally a young man in his early thirties, a junior executive with children of his own, spoke for the group. He said: 'We hadn't envisaged any direct personal involvement with these boys. I don't think any of us would be able to communicate with this type of youth. I'm a little ashamed to say this, but I think we should honestly admit that we are afraid of these violent young people.'

When the staff of the Tel Aviv Project discussed the delinquency situation in one of our work areas (a mixed neighbourhood), with a senior official of the municipality, his opening remarks were: 'This place has a very bad name and people in the decent neighbourhoods around it are very upset. We have done all we can for these people. We have given them a park, a youth club, even a basketball court. They don't seem to appreciate everything we are doing for them. The behaviour of the youth of this area is getting steadily worse.' I could sympathise with the man's exasperation. But when I asked him in what manner and to what degree the municipality had done all these, in themselves admirable, things in consultation and with the participation of the youth and the adults of the community, we stopped speaking the same language. I am afraid the (no doubt well-meaning) official had no idea what I was talking about. A glaring example of the gulf which exists between 'them' and the people of the poverty areas: A large and expensive youth centre was opened with great fanfare at the outskirts of one of Tel Aviv's largest slum areas. A bevy of distinguished guests, an orchestra, boy-scout troops and the mayor himself were there. Not only had there been not a trace of community participation in the planning and construction of the centre, but at the elaborate opening ceremony uniformed municipal guards kept the local population at a safe distance and none of the local community 'elders' were invited.

An American writer (Wakefield, 1960, p. 85) who described East Harlem, one of New York's worst slums, quotes one of the youngsters there as saying: 'You envy—you get to envy and hate.' There is undoubtedly a cause-and-effect relationship between the feelings of isolation and resentment described above and this boy's words. The similarities between Tel Aviv lower-class areas and East Harlem should not be overstated. But similarities exist. In the deprived areas of cities the world over, youngsters learn to envy and hate. This is part of the reality the street club worker has to face.

Still, this is not the whole picture. Things would be too simple if it were. The youngsters of the deprived areas go 'to the city', in some cases quite frequently. They often feel uncomfortable and insecure when they do. They strut belligerently, look for trouble (and all too often find it), make a nuisance of themselves in public places and shock and anger the people they encounter with their loud and boisterous behaviour and their obscene language. But looking for trouble is not the main motive. Many of the boys want to escape the dreariness and boredom of their own environment, to gain status and move a rung up the social ladder by being accepted or tolerated in a middle-class neighbourhood; last but not least, to establish and maintain contact with young delinquents and adult criminals or deviates in other areas of town. Some of the youngsters from well-to-do districts seek contacts with lower-class street corner boys because they are attracted by the apparent romance and adventure of 'gang life', or because they in turn seek status, in ways which may mean a step down to their parents and teachers but which may give them prestige, a sort of romantic nimbus, with their more timid peers in their own environment. Much of the *Bnei Tovim* middle-class delinquency in Israel seems to be due to these kinds of motives.

The opposite sex is a magnet which draws both sides. Middle-class boys seek the company of the slum kids because they hope to get 'fixed-up' with an 'easy lay'. Some of the pimping careers of boys from our Tel Aviv projects started that way. Boys from the lower-class areas look for access to 'classy' middle-class girls with whom they can show off. For some of the youngsters coming to a party in his own neighbourhood with a girl from one of the better residential areas of town carries the same prestige as showing up with a stolen Jaguar or Thunderbird, rather than with an old 'Chevy' or jeep. Some efforts by Negro youngsters of New York's Harlem to 'make out' with white middle-class girls which I observed seem to be related to the same sort of motivation. Some middle-class girls date boys from the poor neighbourhoods because of the thrill, the adventure, and because of the opportunities for illicit sexual experience which is more easily detected and may lead to more complications in their own environment. Many of the slum girls look for boy friends in the middle-class areas in the hope that they will find a better kind of husband than is available in their own neighbourhood. In some cases the girls are encouraged by parents with middle-class aspirations who actually push the girls to seek boy friends in the better areas of the city, and forbid them to date the 'no-good' youngsters of their own communities. Some of the teenage prostitutes from lower-class areas start their careers this way. In many cases the young men from the other side of the tracks are willing to pay for their pleasure, but they marry girls from their own backgrounds, just as the boys from the lower-class areas may have some fun with middle-class girls, but usually end up marrying girls of their own kind.

All that has been said in the preceding paragraphs is by no means intended to imply that *no* sincere lasting, and mutually beneficial friendships and love relationships can spring up and be maintained between youngsters of different strata of the population. What has been emphasised are the delinquency related aspects of the basically unsuccessful attempts of our youngsters to break out of their isolation, to make themselves known, to become accepted, to be seen and heard outside their own confined areas. The street club worker can do much to limit the dangers in this area, point out risks and consequences, and to guide such activities into desirable and realistic channels.

There are occasions on which the worker can enable the youngsters to use the mass media of communication (radio, television, the newspapers) to tell their story, air their grievances and express their feelings. There are certain dangers here, which can be minimised through the sincere and understanding co-operation of broadcasting and television staff. It is the worker's task to guide the latter in their planning of the programme and to assure their understanding of the purpose. The dangers are obvious: Sensationalism, glamorising of the 'gangster-pose' resulting in the enhancement of the value of the delinquent way of life; or else a patronising, or even contemptuous, sarcastic attitude by the interviewer, which will make further dents in the already beaten and battered self-respect of the youngsters. My own experience proves that this does not have to happen. I have on several occasions arranged interviews on radio and TV for groups of New York and Tel Aviv youngsters; the boys and girls were treated with respect and understanding, and came away proud of their performance, and with a new awareness of the possibilities of making themselves seen and heard by more effective and more exciting means than by raising hell at the street corner.

The function of the street club worker must be twofold in order to be effective: on the one hand he has to invest much patient effort with the street corner youngsters in order to make them receptive to new contacts and experiences, on the other he has to explain the youngsters' traits and customs, their problems and needs to such persons and agencies who are willing and able to take an active interest in them.

I met Jim, a young engineer, at a party in the house of friends in New York. After a while our conversation turned to my work. Juvenile delinquents and 'what to do about them' seems to be a subject in which everyone is interested and on which everyone feels entitled to voice strong opinions. Bill was no exception and, if anything, his opinions were based on even less personal experience and information than those of the average man. He had only recently left school, was eager to make a success of his new job at one of the giant steel construction firms and his views were a bit too superficial and conventional for my taste. But I perked up my ears when he mentioned his interest in sailing and a very tricky collapsible boat he had just bought. At that time I had started work with a new group of thirteen- to fifteen-year-old youngsters who had actually been 'referred' to me by the 'Emperors' who felt that these younger boys were getting into trouble and needed 'somebody to straighten them out like we did when you first came around'. These youngsters had become involved in some petty stealing, there had been a few cases of vandalism and brawling and two of the boys had attached themselves to an older addict and were experimenting with marijuana and barbiturates. I felt that this group needed a break in the routine of the street corner as soon and as often as possible and thought immediately of Jim and his boat. When I talked to him about the boys he made it quite clear that he had no tolerance for youngsters who 'don't behave themselves'. With some hesitation he agreed to give up a weekend to come along with us to one of the big lakes in Connecticut and let the boys use his boat.

The trip was a great success. The boys' enthusiasm about the boat was boundless. They were very appreciative of Jim's generosity in trusting them with such a valuable possession and treated the boat with great care. They accepted Jim's somewhat straight-laced attitude towards them without a murmur and made it a habit to add 'sorry, Jim', when airing their feelings with the usual four-letter words. Jim was finally and completely conquered when he found himself the centre of an attentive group of youngsters listening to him talk about his work, asking intelligent questions, seeking his advice on their difficulties with maths, geometry and technical drawing. Throughout that spring and summer Jim and his boat came with us once every month. These outings and the good, healthy fun they had, was probably one of the main factors preventing this group from going the way of the 'Emperors'. The sincere interest and friendship with a 'straight guy' whose uncompromising opinions on how boys should behave were not always realistic but demanded respect, certainly made a lasting impression on many of the youngsters.

I had a similar experience when I enlisted the help of a very spry and forceful seventy-year-old gentleman, a retired master carpenter, who agreed to teach a few of the boys of the 'Commanders' to work with wood in the workshop provided by the settlement house which employed me. Mr Ward made it quite clear from the outset that he would tolerate no 'horsing around' and no 'bad language', and that he had no intention of wasting his time reasoning with the boys or trying to 'educate them', as he put it. They, by all standards 'highly delinquent' boys, treated the old gentleman with the greatest respect. He told me repeatedly how much he enjoyed working with them, how he couldn't understand all the dire warnings he had received, and could hardly believe all the 'wild stories' he had been told about these youngsters. I was eventually able to get one of these boys a steady job as a carpenter with a man who pro-duced very fine handmade furniture.

These and other experiences, for instance a no-nonsense football coach one of the street club workers enlisted for his group in Tel Aviv, show clearly the great benefits of finding opportunities for street corner groups to meet and associate with people who have something to give, whether in the areas of sports or professional skills, rather than expose them to, no matter how well-meaning, adults who see their main contribution in 'being nice' or in 'reforming' the boys. This has been spelled out by Makarenko (1955) one of the greatest educators of 'wayward' young-sters:

You can be as dry as you like with them, severe to the point of captiousness, you can give the impression of being completely indifferent to their sympathy, you can ignore them, even if they are under your very nose; but if your work is good, your knowledge ready and accessible, you can set your mind at rest; they are all for you, and will never let you down. It does not matter how your skill will show itself; it does not matter in the least what you are, whether joiner, agronom, blacksmith, teacher or truck driver.

On the other hand, however kind you may be, however much you may like to chat with them, however sympathetic you may be either in work or play; if all your work results in failure or disaster, if every step you take shows that you do not know your own business, if everything you do turns out to be rubbish or 'junk', you will never get anything out of them except contempt, sometimes ironical and condescending, sometimes angry and resentful, sometimes capri-cious and importunate (quoted in R. S. Cohen, 1955, p. 211).

It goes without saying that this applies to the street club worker himself in every aspect of his work.

It may be added that the street club worker's attempts to relate his group to conventional society do not always meet with success. On one occasion a prestigious youth organisation in New York, whose pro-gramme emphasised 'citizenship education', offered their co-operation and sent a personable young man to explain the aims of his organisation to the boys of the 'Emperors'. He met with cold stares when he suggested that the youngsters should meet with him to listen to a police official talk about crime prevention illustrated by an exhibit of finger-printing equip-ment. The boys, who all without exception had their own experiences with the New York City Police methods of crime prevention, and were all too familiar with finger-printing equipment, made it unpleasantly clear that they were not interested. The group of youngsters who did so well with Jim and his boat, worked with me willingly when I formed a theatre group with the aim of having them act out a play. A local church was persuaded to make a basement room avilable and assigned a young priest to keep an eye on us. This young man did not make any concrete contribution, but frequently asked the boys to discuss 'their problems' with him and often found occasion to do a bit of 'preaching'. The boys were not comfortable with him and I failed to establish friendly relations with the man. We did all right for a while, acting out the parts of *Mr Roberts*, a play with a sense of humour and some mild rebelliousness which appealed to the group. Then, one afternoon, we were unceremoniously thrown out because one of the boys had been discovered smoking a cigarette in the toilet. My explanations that this fourteen-year-old youngster had smoked regularly for over a year, and that our progress with the 'theatre group' was surely more important than this minor infraction of the rules were to no avail. The boys were very angry and their anger included 'that whole phony idea' of the theatre-group; *Mr Roberts* remained unperformed.

All these activities may happen on the spur of the moment, in response to a crisis situation, they may be initiated by the question of an interested adult who has something to contribute and asks: 'What can I do to help?' or they may be the result of long-term careful planning.

A street corner group in a Tel Aviv slum which was contacted by one of the field workers of the Action-Research Project engaged in extremely provocative, vandalistic behaviour in their own community. A favourite sport of the youngsters was throwing raw (usually stolen) eggs at buildings and people, and running up silently behind women returning from the market with heavily laden baskets of victuals, shoving them, so that their purchases spilled into the street. This behaviour did not serve to endear the boys to their harassed neighbours, and as a result the youngsters were treated with hostility and contempt by the adults of the community which, of course, included their own parents and relatives. The street club worker's relationship with the group enabled him to 'work through' their rowdyism and their low standing in the community with them and to bring about positive changes in their behaviour. By this time, however, the attitudes of the adult community had become intransigent. People told the worker that they knew 'these kids' too well to believe that they could be reasoned with and could change. The youngsters, well aware of these convictions of their elders, showed a tendency to persist in, or return to their aggressive behaviour because: 'They hate us anyway. Everthing we do is wrong as far as they are concerned. Just listen how they talk about us, nothing but "these hooligans, these filthy animals" all the time.' The worker, having failed in his attempts to get the adults and the youngsters to sit down together and discuss the situation, gave the boys an opportunity to air their feelings by 'publishing' a news-sheet in which members of the group expressed their feelings in anecdotes and stories which were either dictated to, or tape-recorded by, the worker. This helped to release tension for a while.

Then, during the heavy rains of the winter, when the neighbourhood underwent its annual flooding by rain-water due to lack of canalisation and paving, the worker seized his opportunity. On a particularly bad night, when the houses and the belongings of the inhabitants were endangered by inundation, he called upon the group to 'show the neighbours who you really are'. He led the boys in a hard night's work in helping to prevent damage to houses, make repairs and salvage property. The boys worked hard and enthusiastically. At dawn the adults of the community thanked the youngsters warmly and produced two bottles of brandy to celebrate and to help the boys revive their wet and frozen bodies. The worker, who usually urges the group to abstain and does not drink himself, participated in the little impromptu celebration, and there was a feeling of friendliness and solidarity that greatly improved the relationship between the group and the community.

As a result of this night's work the neighbours became more accessible to the worker's efforts. A community club house, from which the group had been barred long since because of their destructive, undisciplined behaviour, was opened to them on two evenings every week, and the group elected a committee which worked out the conditions for using the club facilities with the neighbourhood committee of the adults.

The 'Commanders' of New York's Lower East Side, obtained a club room in a more direct way. When I contacted this group, its behaviour was sullen and aggressive and its spirit defeatist. Beaten, but still vengeful and defiant after a recent 'war' against the Italian gangs of the neighbourhood, these Puerto Rican youngsters felt cornered, humiliated and without hope. They snarled and hit out at anyone who approached them, and some of them, among them their toughest 'warriors', had begun to look for relief of the tension and the frustration in the deceptive, temporary peace of heroin. Their 'turf' where they had strutted proudly, had become no-man's-land patrolled by 'cops' with ever-ready clubs.

Discussing their situation and the weather, which had begun to turn cold, with the boys at the street corner, I found that a safe, dry and warm place to meet was their most immediate need. Their reputation for violence had barred all doors, but a meeting with the programme director of my agency brought results. The 'Commanders' were given permission to clean out and renovate an old storage room, decorate and furnish it and turn it into their very own club room. For the next year this room became the centre of activities and the focus of interest of the group. Decorated lavishly and kept meticulously clean, it enabled the boys and girls of the 'Commanders' to break away from their destructive past and establish a new and different reputation in their neighbourhood.

Parties and a monthly dance attended by up to one hundred gang youngsters from that area, were the most satisfying and rewarding activities of the 'Commanders'. Other street corner groups with whom I worked in New York could not obtain their own room, but had to hold their parties wherever a suitable location could be found. In New York, as well as in Tel Aviv, these occasions, whether they take place in a private apartment, a room made available by a community centre, or a restaurant, give the youngsters a chance to have fun and to experience that feeling of relaxation of tensions that is so hard to find at the street corner. Taking the group out of their milieu on such occasions, having them meet other people and learn how to adjust to a different, unfamiliar environment, helps the youngsters to broaden their horizon, gain better perspective on their own situation and learn to accept certain restrictions and controls in exchange for pleasure and comfort.

Finding and using opportunities for a group of 'notorious' street corner boys to show them that conforming behaviour has its advantages, is by no means simple. Such an attempt may look like this:

One evening in New York I was walking down the street with six boys of the 'Emperors'. We were discussing some 'hot' issue and had left the neighbourhood. A hectic evening behind us, we all felt the need for a cup of coffee. The boys were reasonably well dressed ('sharp but conservative'), so I suggested a nearby cafe that was somewhat expensive, but famous for its pastries. The boys hesitated. Joey said: 'I don't know, man, I don't think they'll let us in.' Phil added: 'Yeah, one look at us and they'll yell for the cops.' We discussed this noisily for a while. In the end I said: 'They can't refuse to let you in just because you're under eighteen; this isn't a bar, it's a cafe. If you go in quietly and behave like gentlemen, nobody is going to say a word. You behave like any other customer, and you'll be treated politely. You pay and leave a tip for the waiter like everyone else.' My judgment was accepted with some scepticism. We had no trouble entering the cafe. The boys were on their best behaviour and sat quietly around one of the long tables which lined the walls, commenting admiringly on the elegant decor. A waitress came over and took our orders politely. Then the manageress came, an impressive elderly lady, who wanted to know whether I was 'responsible' for 'these boys'. I said no, I wasn't 'responsible' for them, but that I was 'with' them. The manageress said that she had no objection to us at all, but would we please have our coffee and cake and leave as soon as possible, as she needed the tables. I saw the faces of my boys get that familiar resentful look and pointed out politely that there were no 'reserved' signs on our tables, that we had no intention to stay for an unreasonable time, but that I assumed that we had the right to eat and drink at our leisure. The lady, by now seconded by an equally impressive elderly gentleman, said that if I took 'that attitude' she would have to ask us to leave. Looking at my boys' narrowing eyes I had a fleeting vision of a newspaper headline: 'Teenage Vandals Raid Cafe'. I said firmly that I believed that we were entitled under the law to be served in any public commercial catering establishment, that I insisted on service and that we would not leave. The lady mentioned the police and I heard Freddy say dreamily: 'I get a feeling this place is gonna be redecorated real soon.' To which Chuck added: 'Yeah, definitely, and then we'll do ninety before the man gets here.'[1] I asked the boys to 'keep cool' and told the manageress and her assistant that she was free to call the police, but that I would take legal action to test whether she had any right to refuse service to a group of perfectly well-behaved clients in a half-empty cafe. She departed with the gentleman in tow, and for a while we were the objects of considerable interest from the other clients. Then the waitress came with our orders. While serving us she said under her breath: 'Sorry about that, I just work here.' The outsize tips and extra-polite treatment this remark earned the waitress showed how vulnerable these boys were behind their tough posturing, and how appreciative of a friendly word.

One of the Tel Aviv street club workers took members of his group to a restaurant on the other side of the highway which formed the 'frontier' between their own slum neighbourhood and one of the city's middle-class suburbs. Here too the boys predicted that they would not be welcome, and here too the worker's judgment was wrong and they were right. As in the incident described above, the boys were served reluctantly on the worker's insistence. On their way back the boys were flinging things into the fields near the road. The worker, unable to see what they were throwing away in the dark, asked them. He was told: 'Oh, just a lot of spoons and knives and forks we took from the place to teach the guy not to treat people like dirt.' The worker pointed out that this behaviour would certainly convince the restaurant owner that he had been right to regard them all as hooligans. Motke, one of the leaders of the group, said: 'He's convinced, man. He told us: "I know all about you and I don't want you in my place . . ." didn't he?'

The lesson to be learned from these and many similar experiences is that the street club worker must recognise the limits set to his efforts to establish better relations between his youngsters and conventional

[1] Translation: 'And then we'll run away at ninety miles an hour before the police arrive.'

society. These limits are all too frequently set by people who are most vocal in deploring the behaviour of 'these kids' while, at the same time, they are unable or unwilling to accept the youngster's efforts to break out of the rut of their usual behaviour and demonstrate that they are willing to conform.

Trips and overnight hikes are great opportunities for fun and adventure for American as well as for Israeli youngsters. They afford the worker many opportunities for teaching rudimentary principles of planning and organisation, and for demonstrating that discipline is not just a bother and a burden, but has a useful function in getting what one wants out of life.

My first weekend trip with fifteen boys of the 'Emperors' to a forests-and-lakes district in up-state New York became one of the legends of the street corner. Richly embellished with tales of Homeric exploits and adventures, the trip rivalled, and often out-shone the usual stories of fighting, stolen cars and 'gang-bangs'. The fifteen youngsters who participated in this outing ranged in age from fifteen to nineteen. Not one of them had ever spent a night in a tent in the woods before. After dark they needed reassuring that there were no wild animals, and all of them stayed very close to me, listening to the strange silence. During the day they were, to my regret, more adventurous.

Most of our first night in the woods was spent trying to prop up our tents, after someone had fed most of the tent-poles into the fire as easily available fuel. The next morning there was an attempt to fell a tall pine, which led to considerable difficulties with some State Troopers. That afternoon half a dozen tins of meatballs which I had, very unwisely, included in the provisions, were used as ammunition in a meatball fight. The following morning I had to rescue two boys who wanted a closer look at the inmates of a girl's camp they had discovered and were being chased by a formidable lady armed with a double-barrelled shot-gun. I took the group to a rather elegant beach at one of the lakes and found that none of them could swim. A group of very pretty, very poised, bikini-clad young ladies had me rather worried when they showed unmistakable interest in my youngsters. To my surprise, the boys were quite overwhelmed by the advances of the bathing beauties. They showed off like mad, but no one dared to make a 'pass'. Later I had to mediate when Neilie, eighteen years old and richly tattooed with snakes, daggers, skull and crossed bones etc., had an altercation with the father of a two-year-old. It seemed that Neilie was building a sandcastle, the toddler had promised to lend him his pail and shovel, but then changed his mind. Our return to the city was held up for a while because Ken, the oldest and most influential member of the group, a former boxer who had just finished serving a jail term for burglary, could not bring himself to pull down the tent he had erected with much care and inventiveness.

A more detailed report of a weekend trip was summarised from the process records of one of the Tel Aviv street club workers. The group concerned consisted of adolescent youngsters who had a well-deserved reputation for brawling, vandalism, petty and vehicle thefts and burglaries. Many of them smoked hashish and several were involved in homosexual activities. The following is an abbreviated version of the worker's account:

Mr S. the street-club worker, first brought up the idea of an overnight trip during a group meeting in April 1964. The boys were very eager to go, but had no idea how to go about organising a trip and expected the worker to do the planning and organising for them. Mr S. insisted that the group take responsibility for all preparations and, for the next three months, a great part of the group's life centred around the planning of the 'great event'. The numerous group discussions about the trip afforded the worker much insight into the structure and the dynamics of the group.

Abbi was charged with the task of drawing up a list of the boys who would participate. His list clearly reflected his own preferences and pointedly excluded all of the fringe members, except for Arnon. Abbi also ruled that Aron couldn't come along because he would be sure to get the group into trouble. The question of who would and who would not come along became the subject of heated discussions. Abbi tried to impose his will upon the group, at times by threats of beating up youngsters who objected to his decisions. This finally led to a rebellion headed by Avshi, Adi and Aron. Abbi was forced to make a number of compromises and relinquish some of his responsibilities to Avshi.

The question of money was another source of much discussion and controversy. At first the youngsters made a half-hearted attempt to get the worker, or rather the worker's agency, to foot the bill. Mr S. firmly rejected this, saying that all the boys could easily raise the necessary cash if they worked and didn't spend their money on hashish or lost it gambling. The worker also laid down an 'iron rule' which forbade the use of any stolen money. Contributions would only be accepted from boys who worked, as others could only obtain the necessary cash by stealing. The boys agreed on a substantial sum (20 I.L.) to be chipped in by each member and to be paid into the 'kitty' in weekly instalments. The boys all felt that it was 'safest' to have the worker collect and keep the money. Mr S. refused, pointing out that the youngsters would have to learn to trust each other and handle their own affairs. His decision was accepted reluctantly, but the youngsters were unable to agree on a reliable banker. When Mr S. suggested Adi, there was an uproar, summed up by Elisha in the words: 'That's like letting a cat watch the milk.' After a number of meetings and arguments the group finally settled on Abbi and Arnon as 'bankers', admonishing them to keep an eye on each other. The group seemed inclined to trust Arnon more than Abbi but the former had little standing among the youngsters and needed Abbi's authority to back him up. Adi was very pleased when Mr S. suggested that he take responsibility for the money, and quite hurt when the group rejected the suggestion. He announced that he wouldn't participate in the trip.

The detailed planning of the trip proved very difficult for the youngsters. There was great impatience and a constant demand to forget about all the preparations and discussion and just get up and go. Quite a few boys became exasperated with the unexpected amount of planning that had to be done and the many difficulties the group encountered in organising the trip. Outbreaks of delinquency, arrests, family problems etc., intervened, and gradually the number of participants was whittled down to eight boys: Abbi, Avner, Avshi, Uri, Elisha, Eliezer, Arnon and Etnan.

There was much discussion and poring over maps in order to decide where to go. The boys first wanted to go to the Negev, but because of the heat in that part of the country, the Galilee was finally chosen. Tasks were distributed and redistributed, lists of camping equipment and other items were drawn up, menus were planned and, finally, the complicated task of renting a suitable vehicle was tackled. The trip was set for a weekend because the worker insisted that none of the participants should lose a day's work.

On the appointed day in July, about three months after the first mention of the trip, the boys who had decided to participate showed up punctually at the appointed hour and piled into the station-wagon which Mr S. had driven into the centre of the neighbourhood. Despite the worker's repeated insistence on suitable clothing, all the boys appeared in their customary 'sharp' dress: tight chino pants, fancy shirts and pointed, high-heeled shoes.

The whole group was there to give the hikers a noisy send-off. There was also a large crowd of other youngsters and many adults, but none of the parents showed up. Trouble arose over who was to sit in the front of the car beside the worker. When Abbi and Avshi started to fight. Mr S. dispensed with democratic procedures and ruled that the boys would take turns sitting beside the worker, according to his instructions. This was accepted without a murmur. The hikers departed singing and waving, those youngsters who were left behind running behind the car yelling advice and ribald remarks.

After leaving the city, Mr Saad stopped the car and gave the group a last peptalk on behaviour, making it quite clear that he would enforce safety rules and a reasonable degree of discipline. Except for minor infractions, Mr Saad's authority was respected and his rulings obeyed throughout the trip.

When the car passed the Tel Mond Youth Prison the boys waved and shouted excitedly. The worker vetoed a demand to stop and visit the six boys of the 'Gang' who were imprisoned there. As the jail was left behind, the boys were singing 'prison songs' which were part of the repertoire of the street corner groups in Tel-Aviv's slum areas.

That evening the group arrived at the shores of the Kineret Lake and camped there for the night. Mr S. had some difficulties getting the boys to work together to arrange the evening meal, but finally everyone sat around the camp fire, singing and telling stories. The boys listened with avid interest to Mr S.'s stories about the history of the area, the battles fought there during the War of Independence, fishing and boating on the Lake and his own experiences as a member of the kibbutz at the shores of the Kinneret. Later the boys were given a chance to race around and play games—but all of them were afraid to leave the vicinity of the camp and would not go anywhere without the worker. Later that night Elisha complained to the worker that Avshi had molested him and proposed homosexual intercourse. This led to a lot of kidding and mutual accusations of being 'queer', but ended in a serious discussion on homosexual behaviour.

It was three a.m. before the youngsters were exhausted enough to get to sleep, nevertheless they were up bright and early, eager for new adventures.

After breakfast the group walked around to look at the landscape. After this Mr S. took the group to a kibbutz where they witnessed a platoon of paratroopers engaged in a training exercise. The boys were impressed, but in an ensuing discussion about military service they said that the army was 'not for them and their kind'. All the youngsters claimed that the army did not want them because they were delinquents, and that they too felt that they weren't suitable for military service because they couldn't stand the rigid discipline. Abbi, feeling the need to show off, made some provocative remarks in earshot of the soldiers and bothered one of them who was resting. When a tough-looking paratrooper called him over and told him to shut up and behave himself he backed down, visibly shaken, and none of the other boys came to his aid. Later he told the worker that the soldier wouldn't have gotten away with it in the neighbourhood but here, in the kibbutz, the boys were outnumbered and couldn't win a fight. Trying to regain status with the other boys, Abbi began to run about wildly and fell into one of the trenches that were part of the defence system of the kibbutz, scraping some skin off his arm and banging his head. The worker helped him get out of the trench but then warned him to calm down, unless he wanted to bring the trip to a premature end.

During the day Mr S. visited several other kibbutzim with the boys. As the border was only a short distance away, the boys became very cautious, stuck close to the worker and expressed their admiration for the kibbutz people who lived and worked under the guns of the Syrian border fortifications. At one point there was a bit of an argument about taking 'only a few' grapes from one of the vineyards, but the worker was obeyed when he objected.

After the noon meal the boys went for a swim. Except for Elisha, Etnan and Arnon none of the youngsters could keep themselves above water. They were embarrassed, but delighted when Mr S. gave them swimming lessons.

In the afternoon the group visited the town of Tiberias and then reached a monastery near an Arab village. Here the boys had many questions and were amazed when the worker suggested that they visit one of the churches. Cautioned firmly to behave themselves the boys were quiet and subdued in the strange surroundings and listened attentively to Mr S.'s explanations about the symbols and rituals of Christianity. Abbi, however, couldn't stand the peace and quiet for very long and started to ring an unattended church bell which he had discovered. Mr S. had barely dealt with this, when the boys discovered the collection-box and began to speculate on how much cash it might contain. They asked the worker, half-jokingly, what he would do if they broke it open and were somewhat shocked when he said that he would hand them over to the police.

The group had left the monastery area and was getting into the station-wagon, ready to depart, when Abbi showed the worker two picture postcards he had stolen from the souvenir-stand of the monastery. Mr S. lectured Abbi but the boys seemed to be honestly puzzled about the fuss over such a puny item. Abbi said he didn't regard the snatching of the two postcards as stealing and the other boys remarked that they would have taken much more important and valuable things if they wanted to steal. Mr S. demanded that Abbi return with him to the monastery and pay for the two cards. The boy agreed and the whole group walked back to witness the transaction. Luckily the monk in charge of the souvenir stand had a sense of humour and, while he accepted the money, only made a joke about the pilfering of the postcards. Mr S. insisted on a discussion of the incident and all, including Abbi, finally agreed that he was right and promised to keep their hands off things for the remainder of the trip.

The group had another swim in the Kinneret in order to cool off, and then ate in an Arab restaurant. Having eaten, the boys cleverly cheated the waiter out of paying for some of the things they had ordered. Mr S. let it pass while the waiter was at the table in order to avoid a scene and a possible fight. When the man had moved away, he told the surprised boys that he knew what they had just pulled off and demanded that they pay every penny they owed. Upon his demand the waiter was called back, told that the boys had discovered their 'mistake', and given the money owed. He praised the boys for their 'honesty' and everyone thought that this was the best joke of the season.

After an evening excursion into the mountains and another meal around a fire Mr S. drove the boys back to Tel-Aviv, where they arrived close to midnight, exhausted and happy. While most of them had fallen asleep on the last lap of the trip, they all perked up when they approached the neighbourhood and arrived singing at the top of their lungs. Despite the late hour all the other members of the group who had stayed behind and many of the youngsters from other groups were there to welcome the hikers and to listen to the richly embellished accounts of their adventures.

The trip became part of the lore of the area's street corner groups and is still a favourite subject of nostalgic reminiscences when the boys get together to talk of their adventures. The planning of the next trip, this time including boys who hadn't participated in the first one, began the following day.

Programming for fun and adventure should play an important part in street club work. Under the impact of the many, often severe, problems our youngsters face, we are often led to underestimate the significance of just plain doing things that are fun, the more so, as our experience shows that we cannot expect trips, parties, sports and games to counteract directly and immediately the pressures and events which precipitate delinquency. Imaginative programming may not be a cure for delinquency, but it fulfils important needs and offers alternatives. Most important of all, it helps to thin out the heavy concentration on destructive behaviour and the preoccupation with the deviant values and norms of the delinquent street corner group.

An English writer reports:

Many of the boys wanted to do things which were exciting and new, yet the only possibilities seemed to be all night drinking parties or breaking into a warehouse. They talked of going to the south of France, or a West End club, as if they would do it next week and yet they knew that they were extremely nervous as soon as they stepped out of their own neighborhood. There were the two extremes, the day-to-day aimless activities, and the dreams of exciting adventure. The workers had to live with the aimlessness, and to use all the ingenuity they had, to make the exciting happen, and help the young people to the point where they could enjoy it (Goetschius and Tash 1967, p. 63).

Specific problems can be faced directly and may lead to new insights regarding the youngster's own attitudes and needs in relation to society. Some examples have already been given in the areas of employment, housing and the law. There are other areas in which the youngsters' difficulties stem to a great degree from ignorance and lack of information. Here the worker can help by making information and sources of knowledge available.

Tel Aviv street club workers asked a physician to meet with their groups in their own neighbourhoods, in order to tell the boys about the dangers, the symptoms and the treatment of venereal infections. Employment counsellors were asked to speak to the groups about vocational opportunities. Probation Officers were invited to discuss the goals and procedures of probation. Police officers showed their willingness to meet the boys on their home ground, listen to their views and discuss the problems and methods of law-enforcement with them.

The significant factor here is that the youngsters are not asked to attend lectures or present themselves at the desk of an official, but that these men, who represent authority and whose approach is usually regarded with fear and suspicion, come to the street corner with the street club worker, sit down on a park bench or in a coffee shop, listen to the youngsters' questions and grievances and give them their opinions and the facts as they see them.

22 Social action: the wider issues

It is the political task of the social scientist—as of any liberal educator—continually to translate personal troubles into public issues, and public issues into the terms of their human meaning for a variety of individuals. It is his task to display in his work—and, as an educator, in his life as well this kind of sociological imagination, and it is his purpose to cultivate such habits of mind among the men and women who are publicly exposed to him. To secure these ends is to secure reason and individuality, and to make these the predominant values of a democratic society.

C. WRIGHT MILLS (1959), p. 189

Liberals and welfare workers have a tendency to complain about the local inadequacies of administrative arrangements and resources. No doubt, there usually is much more that could be done within existing programs. But often the criticism involves a scapegoat mechanism of vulnerable officials while ignoring the major culprit: ourselves. In a democracy, planned social changes require ideological and political support.

J. W. EATON (1967)

Incidents of the work process are liable to bring the street club worker into conflict with power structures that cannot be dealt with by the worker alone, or even by the agency which has given him his mandate. In such cases the question arises how deeply the worker should become involved in matters which may force him to 'buck the system' in the interests of his clients. I am well aware that the issue is a controversial one and faces the social work profession as a whole. This is not the place to go into such fundamental problems as whether the social worker should and can attempt to change the existing situation, when the latter is detrimental to the positive adjustment of his clients, what are the limits of 'social action', and how far the social worker may go in testing these limits. However, in assuming the task of offering concrete help to delinquent street corner groups, a task which he cannot evade without rendering his service largely illusory and ineffective, the street club worker must squarely face the questions of his obligation to the youngsters, and decide what risks he is ready to take to meet these obligations.

When the street club worker attempts to reach the 'unreachable' youngsters of the slum community, he always encounters the question: 'What can you do for us?' The worker's task is to lead these distrustful and defiant youngsters to understand that there may be very little that he can do for them, but that there are a number of things he can do with them and that one of his foremost goals is to enable them to do things for themselves. This cannot be done solely by endorsing the status quo, by telling the youngsters to take a positive view of the negative aspects of their life situation, and to adjust to things as they are. This approach is one that has become obsolete in view of the realities of modern industrial society. It is based upon the old 'residual' concept of social work that seeks to ignore or hide the fact that there are inconsistencies, injustices and lacunae in our system of society that must be faced, no matter how frustrating and uncomfortable this may be. Inadequate educational facilities, ethnic and social class discrimination in the access to the legitimate opportunity system, exposure to destructive, corrosive influences in the slum milieu, substandard housing—all these are realities that cannot be ignored or talked away. The delinquent adaptations of our client groups are in themselves adjustments to the situation in which these youngsters find themselves. The worker will be hard put to convince them that these adjustments are undesirable and, in the long run, unrewarding, even though they seem to provide many satisfactions, adventure, status and all sorts of 'kicks', unless he is willing to help them to seek constructive ways to change the situation.

George Brager (1962, p. 40), who rightly stresses the need to integrate street club work with an approach of larger scope which seeks to change the milieu of the underprivileged neighbourhood by strengthening and organising the positive resources of the community, writes in this context:

The tendency of social workers to emphasize the amelioration of conflict and the reduction of tension, while often appropriate and helpful, may discourage the participation of lower-income groups in such an organization. With issues smoothed over and differences minimized, there may be little to arouse the interest of a group that lack the predisposition to participate. Matters sufficiently vital to engage the interest of slum residents are almost inevitably controversial, or challenging to some powerful community interests. If a community organization avoids these matters, it can be expected to be avoided in turn.

This dictum is applicable to street club projects in New York as well as in Tel Aviv. Unless the street club worker is willing to restrict his functions to that of a friendly adult who, as the youngsters often put it, 'helps us out sometimes', and unless the worker is willing to minimise his chances of affecting lasting and deep changes in the values and behaviour of the delinquent street corner group, he must be ready to help them face the concrete issues, even though that may entail acknowledging conflicts and accepting risks.

That these risks are not negligible has been illustrated by the experience of Mobilization for Youth in New York. This organisation has, during the last few years, helped its lower-class client groups, youths as well as adults, to engage in organised social action against ethnic discrimination, substandard conditions in the local educational system and inadequate housing. This resulted in a witch-hunt for alleged communists against the directors and the staff of Mobilization, initiated by certain newspapers. Despite the destructive influence that the smear campaign has undoubtedly had upon the work of Mobilization, it is encouraging to note that the National Association of Social Workers and the Columbia University School of Social Work (in whose Research Department the Mobilization for Youth programme was initiated and planned) expressed their support for the organisation which was called 'one of the nation's most promising antipoverty programmes' by President Johnson (*N.A.S.W. News*, 1964).

Mrs Alt, Chairman of the New York City Chapter of N.A.S.W., stated (ibid): 'As social workers we believe that evaluation of the Mobilization for Youth program should be related to its over-all goals and accomplishments. To place the entire program in jeopardy because of some real or alleged actions of an unpopular or even an improper nature is a disservice to the entire city.' She added that 'with New York City's great need for methods to meet social problems, social inventions cannot be developed unless there is toleration for risks.'

Dean DelliQuadri of the Columbia University School of Social Work wrote that the Mobilization programme has 'Aimed to increase the power of low-income people to effect community decision making processes. A major rationale for this objective stemmed from the personal sense of powerlessness felt by many lower-income people who, as a result, have little motivation to learn or to change' (*N.A.S.W. News*, 1964). The Dean quoted an M.F.Y. report as stating that: 'People who have effective ways of shaping their environment are not likely to strike out against it.'

The need for new methods to meet social problems is as great in Tel Aviv as it is in New York. The street club work approach which has been introduced by the Action-Research Project in Tel Aviv may provide one of these new methods. Our success will in part depend upon our readiness and ability to help lower-class street corner youth to participate in the endeavour of changing intolerable conditions in their environment. The Israeli tradition of making full use of the idealism, the daring and the natural rebelliousness of youth in shaping the future of the nation, seems to have become defunct. Perhaps the street club worker can help to revive this tradition by helping to channel the rebelliousness of street corner youth into social action in the many areas where what is needed is not adjustment, but change. By doing this, the worker can help his client groups to emerge from their social isolation, shed the self-destructive adaptations of apathy and diffuse aggressiveness and make an important contribution to society. The chances for success would be better, if street club work could proceed within the framework of an integrated community organisation approach and enjoy the backing of a strong, confident professional social work organisation. Both are still lacking in Israel. It would furthermore be of great help if we could enlist the support and active participation of the youth movements, who seem at present more concerned with the rituals of the past than with building for the future.

I know of no better way of stating the issue that confronts the street club worker in his task of offering concrete help through enabling street corner youth to invest its energies in social action, than to quote once more the words of George Brager (1962, p. 38):

We must frankly recognize the barriers faced by lower-class people generally and by participants in delinquent gangs in particular. Angry youngsters (and adults) must be shown, not that their anger is without basis, but that there are conforming, if controversial, ways to express such sentiments. Programs in which youngsters learn to come to grips with issues that effect their lives and develop skill in acting collectively to correct abuses should be emphasized. Persuading slum youth to join in efforts to expand legitimate opportunities for all people in their social category is a difficult task because of the alienation of the youngsters and the relationship of sponsoring group-service agencies to other special-interest groups. Group programs so oriented can, nevertheless, be developed. For example, a youth organization composed not only of the lower-class 'elite'—youngsters on their way up and out of their class—but also of those for whom working-class life may be a more permanent expectation, an organization that treads the thin line between adult guidance and adolescent autonomy, that gives a hearing to the largely submerged point of view of adolescents, that visibly and dramatically provides an outlet for adolescent culture and capers, can open channels for the expression of grievances and the creation of hope.

The delinquent youngsters I have met and observed seem to be badly in need of a 'cause', that often elusive intangible something in a person's life in which one can invest one's hopes, for which one can fight and make sacrifices, and which not only offers an idea or a set of beliefs one can identify with, but which helps a person to establish and assert his identity. The delinquent adaptations of our street corner youth are, perhaps, above all attempts to answer this need for a cause. For society as well as for the youngsters themselves, these answers remain unsatisfactory, destructive and sterile.

Paul Goodman (1960), discussing America's troubled youth, wrote: 'When one does nothing, one is threatened by the question, is one nothing?' That terrifying question also threatens youth without a cause. No matter how great the obstacles, it is relatively easy for the street club worker, through concrete assistance in finding jobs and through creative programming, to help delinquent youngsters to do something. It is immensely more difficult in a society pervaded by attitudes of disillusion, narrow self-interest and cynicism, to help these youngsters to find something to believe in, something that tells them who they are and what they stand for.

In the United States the national scene is so vast, and the social and political issues (with the notable exception of the Civil Rights issue) so vague and undefined, that there it is very difficult indeed for youth to develop a sense of belonging and identity (which is the meaning of 'patriotism' in the creative, ennobling sense), or to find causes that challenge and inspire. It may very well be that the preponderance of the fighting-gang adaption among American lower-class delinquents is in part a direct, and perhaps a relatively healthy response to this great gap in these youngsters' lives.[1]

Other, more destructive opportunities are provided by the political 'lunatic fringe'. It seems that in New York and other American cities the 'Black Muslims' have succeeded where the more responsible Negro Civil Rights Movement leadership missed their chance to draw upon the potential of the Negro gang youth.[2] I worked with a highly delinquent 'white' street corner group which became involved with the American Nazi party.[3]

When I took a group of Yorkville street corner boys to Washington some years ago and showed them the monumental symbols of their country's history and power, the youngsters expressed neither enthusiasm nor pride with regard to the traditions and the institutions of the nation. On the other hand, Negro and Puerto Rican youngsters who participated in the Civil Rights march on Washington in August 1963 seemed very conscious of being 'Americans' and of being part of something big

---

[1] I strongly disagree with Lewis Yablonsky's thesis, that the fighting gang is a conglomeration of psychopaths (see Yablonsky, 1962).

[2] An American writer wrote recently in an article on the 'dissenters' movement against the Vietnam War: 'It is pitiful but true that by an overwhelming margin it is the young who are crying out in horror at what we all see happening, the young who are being beaten when they stand their ground, and the young who have to decide whether to accept jail or exile, or to fight in a hideous war' (Chomsky, 1967). It is important to note that, among the tens of thousands of American youngsters who have joined the movement of dissent and resistance against what they consider to be an unjust, murderous war, there are almost no young people of the lower class. Almost no attempts seem to have been made to reach lower class youth. In contrast, most of the youngsters who marched in 'Bomb Hanoi' counter demonstrations organised by the American Nazi Party and other such organisations, were recruited from the slums.

[3] The recent eruption of the Black Power movement upon the American scene is altogether a different story. When social injustice drives its victims to take recourse to such desperate measures as looting and burning, social workers, street club workers included, become irrelevant. They must stand aside and admit failure, until such time when they can honestly offer a constructive alternative to open rebellion. For the background of the Black Power rebellion (and the implied effect upon Negro youth) I refer the reader to the excellent article in *The Sunday Times*, London, 30 July 1967.

and important, something that transcended, and at the same time gave more meaning to their everyday reality.

Israel is a small country with a population which is topped by many of the world's larger cities. It is a country that owes its existence as much to the fierce ideological struggle and the profound personal commitments of its inhabitants, as to any of the global political factors involved. Its economic and political situation is still a precarious one today. It is all the more surprising that, after only a few years of relative (and perhaps illusory) prosperity and security, one must today say of Israel what a British writer on youth problems said of England a few years ago, namely that 'what one might call the sense of national purpose has become unusually dimmed' (Fyvel, p. 323). This fundamental lack is evident among the youth of our urban poverty areas. It is one of the major causes of the social and cultural isolation of these youngsters and results in the highly detrimental lack of a sense of identity among them. What Paul Goodman (1960, p. 97) wrote of the American scene holds true here:

> Our rejection of false patriotism is, of course, itself a badge of honor. But the positive loss is tragic. . . . A man has only one life and if during it he has no great environment, no community, he has been irreparably robbed of a human right. This loss is damaging especially in growing up, for it deprives outgoing growth, which begins with weaning from Mother and walking out of the house, of the chance of entering upon a great and honorable scene to develop in.

Neither in New York nor in Tel Aviv have I found that the entity of the nation or any of the various political parties which constitute different trends and issues within that entity, have succeeded in making lower class youth feel that they too are represented, that their interests are matters of public concern and that they too are involved in the effort to build and maintain the society. In both cities there is pronounced apathy and cynicism among the street corner groups with regard to national, political and cultural issues and goals. While the street club worker can neither deny nor ignore the valid reasons for these attitudes he should use his relationship to the youngsters and his resources in order to help modify and change them.

A recent study by two Israeli investigators (Kreitler and Kreitler, 1964) confirms the obvious conclusions that among Israeli youths the readiness to realise ideals is related to the personal attribution of importance and relevance of these ideals to one's own life, as well as the awareness of realistic opportunities and means for ideological involvement. The street club worker's relationship of mutual trust and acceptance with a group of delinquent street corner boys offers a unique chance to discuss and explore their attitudes with them, and to help them find access to opportunities for commitments and participation in issues that transcend the narrow individual interest or the gang mentality of the group.

There appears to be a tendency among most political parties and social action groups to take it for granted that lower-class street corner youth is not accessible to ideas and issues outside the immediate scope of the gang milieu. My experience leads me to believe that in many cases this is not so. However, anyone who seeks to reach these youngsters with regard to any matter of interest and activity will have to be ready to understand and respect their values and needs, and to meet them on their level and conditions. The street club worker can fulfil the important function of mediator here, not only initiating contacts with his group, but using his insight and his relationship to ensure that such contacts result in the establishment of communication and opportunities for new channels of interest and involvement.

4 The tasks of supervision

23 The process of supervision

The importance of professional supervision in street club work cannot be stressed often enough. The experience of street club projects and similar programmes confirms this at every step and has been corroborated by recent reports. A British project, for instance, cites 'adequate support and guidance whilst on the job' (Morse, 1965, p. 207) as one of the essentials of effective operation and stresses that the workers' problems in the areas of acceptance, self-awareness, values etc., demand a process of structured supervision by trained personnel (ibid, p. 90). An American project reports:

As seen by the research team, the lack of professional training among the workers has been mirrored by the lack of professional supervision available to them. In addition to its low professional level, supervision has been sporadic, self-contradictory, and complacent with respect to program enhancement and research co-operation. This has left the workers in a series of unfortunate quandaries, wondering where to concentrate their time and efforts, bickering about differing styles and preferences of work, and expressing great ambivalence over commitment to the research process (Los Angeles C.P.D., 1964, pp. 41–2.)

It can be said with some certainty that the qualifications of the street club project supervisor must include professional graduate training in social group work and experience in supervision as essential prerequisites, and that thorough practical experience in street club work is indispensable. The Tel Aviv project 'built in' professional supervision as part of the programme's structure. The field workers met the supervisor (in this case the project director) once a week in a group-supervision-and-training session which lasted a minimum of two, and sometimes as long as four hours. In addition each worker met the supervisor once a week for a personal discussion lasting about one hour. Throughout the week the supervisor was informally available for an occasional chat and for direct assistance in emergencies which demanded his advice or his intervention. Formal meetings with the staff of other services and agencies, such as the

Youth Probation and the Adult Probation Services, the Police Youth Squad, the Youth and Child Care Division of the Municipal Social Service Department and the Family Service field offices were regarded as an additional significant aspect of the supervision and training process.

Margaret Williamson (1961, p. 19) defined social work supervision as 'a dynamic enabling process by which individual workers who have a direct responsibility for carrying out some part of the agency's program plans, are helped by a designated staff member to make the best use of their knowledge and skills, and to improve their abilities so that they do their jobs more effectively and with increasing satisfaction to themselves and to the agency'.

This definition is acceptable, with the addition of one substantial factor which is basic to the supervision process and provides the frame of reference for all other goals, namely the focusing upon the needs of the client. All other purposes of the supervisory process, such as professional effectiveness and growth of the worker, the enhancement of his skill and knowledge, the development of self-awareness in the worker, his accountability to the agency, and even the goals and functions of the agency itself, are subordinate to this.

The scope and purpose of this study does not permit a detailed discussion of the principles and methods of social work supervision.[1] We shall limit ourselves to touching upon some major aspects of the specific requirements of street club work supervision, the integration of training in the supervisory process and the special problems of supervising the untrained worker.

The process of supervision begins with the interviewing of the new worker, outlining for him his duties and responsibilities, acquainting him with the structure of the agency and introducing him to the staff. This constitutes the first phase of an orientation period in which the new worker is also provided with a rudimentary understanding of the philosophy and the basic principles of social group work and the street club work approach. The new worker then spends a number of evenings with group workers of the Project already experienced in the field. Here he is introduced to the youngsters and to members of the community as a new man who has joined the Project to do the same kind of work as the worker who brought him along. These evenings in the field afford the new man an opportunity to observe the youngsters and the 'old' workers in action, to gather impressions and to ask for explanations.

During this initial phase, the new worker participates in meetings

---

[1] For useful expositions of social work supervision see Reynolds (1942) and Williamson (1961).

with the staff of other services and agencies, where he has an opportunity
to get some idea of the methods and opinions of professionals with whom
he will later be in contact.

The supervisor may have to introduce the street club worker to his specific tasks
by acquainting him with the sociocultural peculiarities, the geographic and
demographic features of the community in which he will work, as well as the
agencies and institutions with which he may have to deal, such as social agencies,
police, courts, schools, employment agencies, etc. It may be necessary, as part of
the 'orientation period', to introduce the worker to key figures in the neighbourhood, as well as have informed community persons speak to him about specific
problems involving his future client groups. The supervisor should also outline
for the worker, as clearly and thoroughly as possible at this stage, the responsibilities with which the worker is charged, the limitations of his functions and the
results he can realistically expect.

An essential part of 'orientation' is a frank and unambiguous description of how
the supervisor sees the supervisory process and the relationship between himself
and the worker, what the worker can expect of the supervisor, and what the
latter expects of the worker (Leissner,1961, p. 11).

The orientation period comes to an end when the worker is assigned to
a street corner group. In some cases the new worker is introduced to his
client group by a member of the field work staff who is already acquainted with the youngsters. In another case the project director may first
strike up an acquaintance with a street corner group and then introduce
the new worker. A new worker may contact a group which has been
identified as highly delinquent directly and without preliminaries. In all
instances the manner of introducing the worker to his group should be
guided by the supervisor's estimation of the worker's personality and the
predicted reaction of the particular group.

With the assignment of the worker to a group, the supervisory process
becomes geared to the day-by-day requirements of the job. The first point
of departure is always the client, and the learning process is based on
the recurrent questions: 'What happened in this or another situation,
and what did you make of it? What did you do about it and why? What
were the alternatives, what other interpretation of the situation is possible, and what else could you have done about it? What were the youngsters or the group trying to say to you, how did you understand it and
how did you react? What effect did your response or action have upon
the youngsters? What effect did the youngsters' and your own actions
and responses have upon you? What can we learn from what happened?
How can the supervisor help you in dealing with this or another specific
problem? What conclusions for future action should we draw from what
we observed?' Again and again the pitfalls of manipulation and expediency have to be pointed out and discussed. Such typical problem areas

as the worker's acceptance of the youngsters' deviant values and delinquent behaviour, the timing and methods of setting limits, the imposing
of the worker's own values, his acceptance of his own limitations, his
frustration in the face of failure, his anger at destructive outside interference, the tendency to become overconfident after some initial success,
the dangers of losing perspective by becoming over involved with the
youngsters' own confusions and problems, all these have to be worked
through over and over again. Analysing and discussing the work step by
step, the worker has to be led to understand the traits and personal
characteristics of individual youngsters, to gain insight into the structure
and the dynamics of the group, to recognise needs and motivations, to
diagnose behaviour, and to identify emerging patterns. He has to be
helped to become aware of the norms which rule the conduct of the
group, to evaluate influences and to utilise the resources of the community and of societal institutions. Concurrent with this whole range of
complex phenomena and processes, the worker has to be brought to
awareness of his own needs and motives, his own weaknesses and
strengths so that in the end he will be able to function effectively and
securely in his professional role.[1]

One writer on the subject of supervision states: 'Supervision is on the
one hand an intellectual experience which includes in its scope an evaluation of feelings as a part of the factual basis of knowledge, and is on the
other hand an emotional experience which includes the subjective feed-
back from learning about feelings in people and thus in oneself' (Houwink, 1967, p. 114). The author of a British 'report of a two-year training
project in which selected youth workers acquired skill in supervising'
wrote:

While learning from and about the situation, the worker is looking outside himself, but is also becoming increasingly aware of his own behaviour, feelings
and values. Perhaps an important aspect of supervision is that it should help
such learning to be an interesting process, rather than a deflating, unhappy one.
Inevitably, increased awareness brings discomfort or depression at times, and
workers would confirm this. But if learning from the situation is geared to
building on to what a worker knows and is aware of, then the awareness of new
factors to be recognized and understood can be gradual and acceptable; recognition of a weakness can be balanced with recognition of strength, understanding
lack of a skill can be seen in terms of acquiring that skill (Tash, 1967, p. 79).

---

[1] The often used, but rarely fully understood quality of 'self-awareness' which is basic
to the social work concept of professional competence, was aptly described by Professor
Grossbard (1954, p. 15): 'Self awareness grows from within and may be described as a
process that is midway between knowing and feeling. It is possible for a person to be
aware of something without being able to describe it. Awareness often precedes con-
ceptualization. It is a close cousin to intuition, a quality that cannot be translated or
brought into existence through didactic methods.'

All this cannot be done through mechanical instruction or lecturing. The worker's professional stature has to grow out of a process of close co-operation between him and the supervisor in which both contribute equally, a process which is based upon a relationship of mutual confidence and shared commitment to the common goal. The aims of this process were lucidly summarised by Charles A. Beard (1932, p. 96) who wrote: 'In the wider ranges of social relations it is not words that count, but capacity to understand, analyze, bring information to bear, to choose, to resolve, and to act wisely. Competence in the individual, not dogma, is our supreme objective.'

In a concise, pragmatic manner, the New York City Youth Board (1960, p. 127) has outlined some of the characteristics of the beginning phase of street club work supervision:

Supervisor continues to assist the worker in purposefully listening and observing and acquiring the kind of knowledge necessary to planning future work. Around such fears and concerns as are expressed by the worker regarding his mode of dress, talk, what he should say, how he should stand, the supervisor is supportive and assists the worker to overcome his self-doubts as to whether the group will ever make something significant of his presence on the scene. The supervisor can invariably point out the important though inconspicuous developments which provide the kind of reassurance necessary. He can assist the worker in planning his approach to the group in a systematic fashion, with special emphasis on the beginning structuring of his role.

The street club worker, perhaps more than any other youth worker in more conventional settings, is especially in need of a continuous sustaining influence and practical support by the supervisor. The following was written in the United States, but was found to apply fully to the Israeli scene:

The street club worker's function is still far from clearly defined in the public eye, yet he is under public scrutiny in the community in which he works, as well as in society at large. Demands are made upon him to provide services incompatible with social work principles, and unrealistic in view of the vast problems confronting him. He is under fire for 'coddling' young offenders and under pressure to suppress symptomatic behaviour that causes fear and annoyance to the citizens. People expect him to 'lower delinquency statistics', and he is asked to furnish proof of how many delinquent acts he has 'prevented'. His work is romanticized and sensationalized by some, while others disparage it as 'do-gooding'. In a status conscious profession he is the low man on the totem pole, and often, where he is 'detached' from a conventional social work setting, his own agency regards him as something of an odd-ball. He needs the supervisor's backing in the face of these pressures and he must be able to call upon the supervisor's direct intervention through the determined use of the latter's own professional status, his authority and his connections in the profession and in the community. He continuously needs his supervisor's reassurance with regard to his own worth as a professional and with regard to the validity of his work (Leissner, 1961, p. 17).

Street club work, perhaps more than any other social work discipline, demands an atmosphere of informality in the relationship between worker and supervisor, with the greater accessibility and the direct involvement which this implies. In a way this reflects the demands for informality and immediacy of relationships made upon the worker by the street corner setting. It is of great importance that the supervisor should recognise the specific requirements street club work makes upon his ability to maintain the kind of relationship to his workers which is conducive to the spontaneity, flexibility and depth of personal investment characteristic of this type of work. The fact that this kind of relationship cannot be taken for granted in the conventional agency, is discussed by Professor Cloward (1960, p. 40) in a thought-provoking passage.

Psychiatric thought, which has had a profound impact on social work, has probably contributed to increased formalization because of its stress on controlled relationships. At the level of staff relationships, the psychiatric orientation has led to increased structuring of relationships between individuals occupying different positions, but especially between the supervisor and the person supervised. Relatively informal relationships have been supplanted increasingly by professional relationships. One consequence of the professionalization of relationships is, of course, that there are fewer ways in which people relate to one another, and the limits of these relationships are more stringently drawn.

The demand for informality of relationship and for easy accessibility and a large degree of direct involvement of the supervisor in the work process should, however, not be understood as a depreciation of structure in the street club worker's job, nor should it be interpreted as advocating that the supervisor follow the worker around, look over his shoulder while he is with his group and interfere in the group work process.

Careful structuring of the worker's responsibilities, his use of time, his conception of his own role and of that of the supervisor is of the greatest importance in the 'unprotected' setting of street club work. It can be adequately maintained without recourse to rigid codes of behaviour and tangles of rules and regulations. Here too the needs of the client and the demands of effective work, rather than mechanical procedures, are the best criteria.

The following job description drawn up by the director of the Tel Aviv Project in consultation with the field work staff and the Professional Advisory Committee, may serve as an example of the structuring of the worker's responsibilities and the safeguarding of his professional role.[1]

1. The worker's job is to help and enable naturally formed street corner groups and their members to increase their abilities, as individuals and as groups, to

[1] The unusually large time allotment for recording is due to the fact that the Tel Aviv Project was committed to research.

deal realistically and adequately with the social and emotional problems confronting them. Where the values, norms and behaviour patterns of the client groups are found to be in conflict with the norms, values and behaviour expectations of society, the worker has the task of attempting to modify delinquent behaviour patterns and effect changes in the group's attitudes toward itself and its obligations to society.

2. In order to carry out his assigned tasks, the worker shall contact street corner groups in low-income areas of Tel Aviv–Jaffa and establish with these groups a professional social service relationship, using the generic social work approach, as well as the specific methods of street club work.

3. The worker's job is, furthermore, to furnish the action-research project with the bulk of its observational, descriptive and diagnostic material through observing and selective recording of the client group and the effect of his own work upon it.

4. In order to serve the research tasks of the project *and* in order to increase the effectiveness of his work, as well as assure his own professional growth, the worker shall seek to gain insight and understanding of his client group's structure, values, norms and behaviour patterns. He shall seek insight and understanding of the needs, motives and problems of the individual members of the client group, and of the environmental and psychological pressures impinging upon the group and its members.

5. The worker shall attend supervisory and staff-training sessions and be prepared to make full use of these sessions to obtain help in coping with immediate problems, in evaluating the on-going process of his work, in obtaining insight and knowledge that will improve the effectiveness of his service and assure his professional growth. The worker shall also make full use of the availability of the project director, the research assistants and the project secretary in order to obtain all necessary assistance in carrying out his tasks.

6. The worker shall be on duty 42 hours per week, these working hours to be spent in the following manner:

(a) The worker shall spend four evenings a week, four hours each evening and altogether 16 hours a week in personal contact with his client groups or in contact with individuals affiliated with these groups.

(b) The worker shall reserve 7 hours per week for individual contacts with members of his client group during the day in cases of special problems, help in seeking employment, assistance in dealing with courts, police, etc.

(c) The worker shall reserve 4 hours per week for community contacts, home visits and contacts with other agencies.

(d) The worker shall spend 5 hours a week in supervisory and staff-training sessions.

(e) The worker shall spend 10 hours per week in selectively recording the process of his work, *all* referrals and contacts with other agencies as well as individual and group evaluations.

The worker is expected to show flexibility in arranging his working hours, in special circumstances, but shall *normally* adhere to the above cited schedule. He shall *under no circumstances* spend the hours allotted to recording for other purposes.

The worker shall *not* spend any time *beyond* the obligatory working time in service to his client group or any work connected with it. When he does spend additional time on duty, he shall deduct this from his regular working hours with the exception of the hours allotted to recording.

7. The worker shall channel *all* interdepartmental and outside-agency contacts through the project director.

8. The worker shall at all times guard the confidentiality of *all* matters concerning his client groups and their individual members and shall not divulge *any* information regarding his client groups and their members to persons not directly employed by the project or members of the Professional Advisory Committee, without the permission of the Project Director.

As to the degree of direct involvement of the supervisor in the work process, this involvement is an integral part of the close agreement of supervisor and worker regarding their commitment to the job, and to the supervisory process as one of the main tools used in getting the job done the best possible way. It does *not* imply the practice of 'direct observation' practised by supervisory staff in some group work agencies. As Anne W. Lindsay (1952, p. 142) pointed out:

Individuals in the group and the group leader himself need as free an atmosphere as it is possible to establish. It takes time to build a natural relationship between a group and a leader and its growth depends upon lack of self-consciousness. When a supervisor enters a group solely as an observer, the leader may become too aware of his presence and his relationship with the group may be affected.

To this I added in an earlier paper (1961, p. 14):

In the street corner setting we have the additional factor of the initial inaccessibility of delinquent street corner groups, the usual distrust and, at times, the open hostility with which they regard strangers. It is enough of a task for the worker to gain the trust and the acceptance of the youngsters, without burdening him also with the job of making his supervisor acceptable to them. However, after a solid relationship between worker and group has been established, the supervisor may want to arrange occasional get-togethers with worker and group for various reasons, such as acting as an outside mediator in a special crisis situation, helping to prepare absorption of the group into a conventional setting, assisting the worker in preparing an exceptionally ambitious bit of programming (such as a big party or an extended hike), or in order to support the worker in the, usually difficult, process of terminating his service to a group.

Such direct contacts between the supervisor and the worker's group should be worked out as the need arises and always in full agreement with the worker. Such contacts should *not* become a routine part of the supervision process, nor should direct observation be used as a device of accountability.

Whenever the relationship between supervisor and worker provides no other way of making sure that the latter is doing his job than checking up on his work in the field, it is time to consider whether the worker, or the supervisor, are really suited for this type of work.

The Tel Aviv street club Project succeeded in establishing the kind of relationships between worker and group and worker and supervisor, which made occasional field visits of the latter both helpful and welcome. As the relationship between workers and groups grew closer, more and more of the youngsters began to visit the Project's office in order to discuss special problems, out of curiosity about the worker's agency, or just to have a cup of coffee and a chat. On such occasions the supervisor was usually introduced to the youngsters and, at times, asked to sit in on a talk about an especially serious or complicated matter.

Group supervision played an important role in the work process of the Tel Aviv Project. Much impressed by what we knew about this relatively recent approach to supervision, we thought at first that it would gradually replace the individual supervision meetings altogether. Our experience did not diminish our enthusiasm for group supervision in the least, but we learned that the individual sessions remain indispensable and can only be complemented, not replaced by group meetings.

Group supervision, as we conceived it,[1] is, like individual supervision, focused upon the client group and the daily process of street club work. 'It is not a "seminar" in which the leader's primary responsibility is to the whole group and where the exclusive aim is to convey knowledge. Nor is it "peer" supervision in which each member of the group makes a contribution, but no one helps the worker to integrate the various contributions.' Leadership responsibility is vested in the supervisor who provides guidance and direction. 'The central concern of the group is client need—it does not primarily focus on the group process (within the staff group); it is not group therapy. The sessions are case focused, and are related to the worker and his helping role.' However, the supervisor must know the weaknesses and strengths of the individual workers and be aware of their patterns of interaction, and alert to dangers which may arise for the individual worker through undue exposure to destructive, uncontrolled criticism. Workers are called upon to present their work and formulate specific problems clearly for their colleagues and for the supervisor. 'Since immediacy of response is an essential quality in the direct treatment process, the worker—in group supervision—develops flexibility and the ability to examine and test ideas quickly when exposed to a variety of approaches and concepts. The worker is exposed to many sources of knowledge; he sorts out what is usable and integrates it for himself. This affords additional help in learning to sift ideas. Knowing the work of one's colleagues produces mutual respect and enables the worker to see the many different ways in which a client can be perceived and helped.' The supervisor determines the emphasis of discussion, synthesises, evaluates and communicates the professional approach to problem-solving. The supervisor is less protected in his authority. He must be flexible in using the roles of teacher and participant.

[1] I am indebted for guidance in group supervision, and for the following description (with the exception of remarks based upon my own experience) to Judd, Kohn and Schulman (1962), pp. 96–8.

Some of the dangers of group supervision should be mentioned here: While the exchange of ideas and opinions should be frank and informal, damaging forms of criticism should be kept in bounds. On the other hand, the supervisor must beware of not letting the group deteriorate into a mutual shoulder-patting club. The cautioning of Professor Abrahamson (1959, p. 100) should be heeded: 'It must always be kept in mind that discussion itself is a slow process and is ineffectual as a means of disseminating information that is needed immediately. If the learners have little or no information about a topic and the leader remains passive, the group merely pools its ignorance about the subject matter.' Group supervision is invaluable in developing the kind of team spirit and esprit-de-corps which is a major asset to any street club project.

It must be added here that group supervision proved itself to be especially valuable in furthering the competence and professional developing of relatively inexperienced, untrained workers. The process lends itself uniquely to giving this type of worker, who will remain our mainstay in the foreseeable future in Israel and in many other countries, confidence in his abilities and in the value of his contribution, in offering mutual support, reducing anxiety and gaining perspective. The remarks of Margaret Williamson (1961, p. 137) are of some interest in this context:

It is to be remembered, particularly with young beginning workers, that there may be more familiarity with the use of the group for problem solving, than with individual consultation; faced with a new kind of work, the impulse is strong to seek out others doing the same kind of job, to find out what they are doing and thinking. It has been noted, in the case of young first-year students in the professional school, that learning, in the one-to-one setting, is the essentially new experience and that it can be threatening.

Account should be taken, too, of the prevalence of the grapevine in worker groups; the need for help is great, and an astonishing amount of misinformation and misdirection can get going in the pursuit of it. The importance of having this situation organized by the supervisor himself, seems obvious.

A few words must be added about the problem of keeping records, the teaching of which is one of the responsibilities of supervision. Keeping records and writing good descriptive and evaluative reports is indispensable in street club work, as in any other form of group work. Like everyone we ever heard of in the field of social work, street club workers also have their problems in this area. As Maas and Polansky (p. 129) so understandingly stated: 'Compared with process records in casework, good process records in group work have seemed both more difficult to write and less likely to be written in view of the inter-personal complexities, lesser controls, and multiple pressures of practice in group-work settings.'

The consistent keeping of records and the regular submittal of written reports is one of the main areas of difficulties for the untrained worker. It is, at best, an arduous, time-consuming task, which becomes all the more perplexing when one has not had occasion to acquire the habit of describing one's observations and expressing one's opinions in writing. Lack of experience in the kind of mental note-taking during the work process, which becomes a sort of second nature to the seasoned group worker, tends to make the duties of recording a burdensome, worrying task, which can actually become an impediment to comfortable, unself-conscious relations with the group. Such technical aids as tape-recorders or the taking of notes during group meetings, which can, at times, be used in conventional group work settings, are out of the question in the street corner setting.

In Tel Aviv I asked the fieldwork staff to jot down notes every night after returning from work and after each significant meeting or activity concerning the group or its individual members taking place outside the street corner setting, for instance at the employment office, in court, on a trip, etc. About twice a week the worker had to sit down, go over his notes, sift his memory and write down what happened in a descriptive, narrative report. The only guidelines he was given were the well-known ones of the journalist: 'Who? What? When? Where? How? and Why?' The supervision process was used to lead the worker gradually to understand the importance of describing behaviour as well as verbal expressions, of stating clearly who the persons were who interacted, to point out what the rest of the group was doing when this or that incident involving certain individuals took place. The greatest difficulties were encountered in getting the workers to 'put themselves into the picture', to describe what *they* did and said, or, equally important, why they did *not* do or say something, to state *why* they acted in a certain manner and, finally, to talk about their own responses and feelings and to risk an interpretation of the behaviour, the responses and feelings of the youngsters.

Especially in the beginning we were very careful not to arouse anxiety by demands for self-critical analysis of the worker's actions and responses in the reports, but left this to the more comfortable and supportive exchange of the individual and group supervision meetings. I refrained throughout from using the written material submitted by the worker as a device to detect mistakes or for the award of 'medals' for success. The aim was to get a frank and uninhibited account of what was going on in the field and how the workers felt about what they observed and what they did. We tried to avoid causing the worker to write 'for effect', to put down what the supervisor might want to hear or what would impress his colleagues. The latter is one of the reasons why workers' records were not read aloud in the group supervision meetings.[1]

The gradual development of acceptable standards of recording is aided by occasional requests for a written summary of an especially interesting inter-actional process or event which may have been mentioned by the worker during a supervision meeting, as well as reports on meetings with key community persons or the representatives of other agencies. This encourages the worker to discuss his views of certain aspects of the work process in writing. In addition to this, diagnostic summaries on individual group members should be obligatory. The quality of the content of the reports does, of course, reflect the advances the individual workers made in the learning process and in their professional growth.

Some of the major points I have tried to make here are supplemented by the remarks of Anne W. Lindsay (1952, pp. 6–7):

The actual writing of the process record often seems a hard task for young workers, . . . while workers may complain of their lack of skill in writing, the real problem is lack of practice. The writing of a record for literary purposes has little value in our field. The sound basis for good record writing is the capacity for seeing and interpreting, feeling and understanding.

When a worker has faith in what he is doing, an honest desire to grow to professional maturity, a forthrightness in setting down on paper what he sees, according to his knowledge and understanding, the record he writes takes on a reflection of his own skill and spirit. . . .

The self-involvement of the worker is an important part of the recorded material, if in later analysis the record is to serve him as a basis for appraisal of his role. It is necessary that he include his awareness of his role if the self-evaluating process is to have significance. . . .

There is no quick formula by which we teach workers how to write good records. Workers learn to practice group work by doing and the record is the narration of this practice.

A useful tool in learning to write reports on the work process is what has become known as the 'critical incident' technique, which I would like to rename the 'significant incident' technique.[2] In using this method of reporting the worker selects what he considers one of the most significant incidents of a work period, which may be as dramatic as a savage fight between two or more youngsters, or as subtle as a chance remark by one boy addressed to another, such as: 'Nobody's asking you for your opinion, man,' which may have alerted the worker to the fact that one of the leaders of the group has been 'demoted'. The worker is given a

[1] For an interesting and useful account of street club workers' records and a critical discussion of the latter see National Federation of Settlements and Neighborhood Centers (1967).

[2] I would like to give credit to whoever originated the 'critical incident', but am unable to identify him.

set of questions and asked to write his report in the form of answering them. This set of questions can be worked out between supervisor and worker. It may look like this:[1]

1. *What happened?*
Nine of the boys were standing around discussing how to spend the evening. Joe suggested going to the movies. Chuck said: 'Nobody's asking for your opinion, man.' Joe said: 'F . . . you, I'm going to see a show' and walked away.

2. *What did the group (or individual members of the group) do?*
Some were looking at each other, as if embarrassed or uneasy. Chuck and Mokey grinned at each other as if they shared a private joke. Then the guys continued to argue about what to do, finally decided to go to Mokey's apartment to drink and listen to records. They asked me to come along and I agreed.

3. *What did or didn't you do, and why?*
I didn't say anything until we got to Mokey's apartment and had settled down. Then I asked Chuck: 'What's with you and Joe?' Joe said: 'Oh, nothing man.' So I left it at that, because I had a feeling that they didn't want to discuss it with me. We talked about Mokey's new Miles David record, about Toni's new job and what his probation officer had said about it and whether women like sex as much as men. I stopped Mokey from having his third beer, because he should be wide awake for his new job in the morning. On the way home I walked with Mitch and asked him why the boys had given Joe the cold shoulder. He said: 'It's between him and Chuck. You better ask him about it.' I didn't press him.

4. *What, in your opinion, led to the incident, and what is its significance?*
I've no idea what led to this. Last night Joe was still the boss. I've never seen the boys react to him that way. He's always been something of a leader and the boys say that he can beat any one of them in a fight. Chuck has rubbed him the wrong way once before and got a punch in the mouth from him. Joe must have done something to lose status. I'm worried about it, because Joe was a steadying influence, often put a damper on when the boys came out with some wild schemes. He's been in jail for armed robbery, so he doesn't have to prove himself and can veto 'crazy jobs'. If Chuck and Mokey take over, the group might get out of hand again. Chuck is always out to prove how tough he is, and Mokey is so dumb, he can be talked into anything that promises some fun. I had Joey pretty much on my side. Chuck is always nice and polite, but I don't think I have really gotten through to him yet.

5. *What do you intend to do about the incident and why?*
I'm going to try to get Joe and Chuck, each by himself, and find out what happened between them, or between Joe and the group. I can't do anything definite until I know what's going on. In the meantime I'll keep close to Chuck and watch out for any signs of trouble. My relationship with the boys isn't stable enough yet to allow me to poke my nose too deeply into their affairs, so I'll have to be careful not to seem too nosey and be told to mind my own business.

[1] The incident is adapted from one of my own reports on work with a New York street corner group.

6. *What help do you need?*
None at the moment.

A final word on recording: instruction, gentle persuasion and repeated demands are not all that is needed to get workers to maintain consistent and useful records. The workers must also be provided with the necessary facilities and tools. An experienced youth worker R. M. Wittenberg (1949, p. 112) wrote:

It takes time to write things down, particularly if one is selective in what he writes. If an agency is interested in records, it will have to give the leaders (youth workers) time to write them. They will need opportunity to concentrate, which means a quiet place. In addition, it may mean stenographic help, because records, to have value, should be kept in such form that it is possible to look back at them after a period of time. It means a folder for the records of each group; it means a file where they can be kept, because if they are worthwhile they will be full of confidential information.

In New York and in Tel Aviv I was lucky enough to work for agencies which provided street club workers with adequate office facilities, a dictating machine, filing cabinets and, most important of all, a project secretary who looked after the typing and filing.

On-the-job training of the staff is part and parcel of the supervisory process, integrated with all other aspects and phases of this process, and like these focused on service to the client group and geared to the day-by-day demands of the work process. Here too the danger of a split between training and practice must be guarded against. The California study mentioned earlier reports upon some detrimental effects of such a split. This study points out that 'it is sheer folly to attempt to introduce any type of training program without consensus among action personnel, research staff and trainers as to the *objectives* of the action program' (Los Angeles C.P.D., 1964, p. 70).

Some of the comments of the action staff quoted by this study serve to illustrate the effects of a staff training programme which is conceived as a separate service, rather than an organic part of the supervision process. Street club workers stated that:

The training was not pertinent to our type of work . . . most of the material did not relate to working knowledge that the officer [the street club worker] could apply in his everyday work with the youth on the streets . . . the group type of [training] session . . . did not give any new ideas or concepts or approaches to working with gang groups . . . too much time was spent teaching our instructor about the intricacies of gang work . . . instructor was psychologically oriented and did not give full treatment to social structure and gang theory . . . (Los Angeles C.P.D., 1964, p. 80).

In the case of the Tel Aviv Project staff training was one of the responsibilities of the supervisor (the project director). The main areas of instruction were:

(*a*) generic principles of social group work,
(*b*) group dynamics,
(*c*) methods and techniques of street club work,
(*d*) psychological and socio-cultural aspects of personality development,
(*e*) norms and values of delinquent subcultures,
(*f*) problems of adolescence,
(*g*) techniques of referral to, and co-operation with, other services and agencies.

None of this material was delivered in the form of lectures. In the main, the supervisor made use of the opportunities arising out of the discussion of 'live' practice issues during the group supervision sessions and, sometimes, during individual sessions. The following are typical examples of this process.

One of the workers has told the group how he got his youngsters to organise a trip, partly by using all the weight of his personal influence, partly by doing most of the preparatory work for them. The supervisor uses this to give a brief talk on the concepts of helping the client by 'enabling' him to do things for himself, and upon the issue of 'self-determination', which may be infringed upon by undue use of personal influence just as much as by the use of physical force. The supervisor's statements are followed by discussion.

A worker 'confesses' his confusion over the fact that the youngster whom he had identified as the leader of the group, meekly obeyed the orders of another, less 'important', youngster in a certain crisis situation. Other workers cite similar instances in their own experience. The supervisor talks about the concepts of 'leadership' and 'group structure', points out the differences between 'leadership' as a personality trait and as a function of the given situation. The workers are called upon to interpret their experience in the light of these two views.

A worker tells the group that he is worried about the increasing involvement of his youngsters with prostitutes. He says that he would like to talk to them about this, but isn't sure how they will 'take it' if he broaches the subject. They may resent the intrusion into their most intimate personal affairs, or they may deny any knowledge of the subject out of embarrassment. Yet, the worker feels that he would be remiss in his duties if he avoided this matter altogether. The supervisor asks the other workers whether they feel that this matter should be 'handled', and what techniques they would use. If the group itself does not supply adequate answers, the supervisor talks about the need to evaluate at each point whether the present stage in the relationship between a worker and his group is 'ripe' for the direct broaching of 'touchy' subjects. He may then draw upon his own experience in the field to relate how he handled a similar situation, for instance by bringing a newspaper clipping dealing with the arrest of a prostitute or with the rising rates of venereal disease, read out this item or pass it around while having a cup of coffee with the boys, gearing his next step to the youngsters' reactions and remarks.

A worker tells the supervisor that he is very upset about the fact that in the community in which he works children are beaten up by their parents for the slightest infraction. The worker expresses his disapproval and compares it to the experiences of his own childhood, in which physical punishment was a rare exception. The supervisor talks about the 'socialisation process', the 'withdrawal-of-love' device which is the alternative for physical punishment in many middle-class groups. He points out characteristic differences in the child-rearing practices of different social classes and different ethnic groups. Using the youngsters of the worker's client groups as examples, the supervisor then traces with the worker the possible effects upon the youngsters' personalities of the child-rearing customs to which the worker objects.

To the group's amusement a worker relates how he tried to 'get to' one of the youngsters in a highly delinquent street corner group, by telling him that he, the worker, regarded him as a 'good boy', not as involved in delinquent behaviour as the rest of the group. To the worker's amazement the youngster was enraged by this 'compliment' and insisted vehemently that he was as 'bad' as they come, the proud owner of a long and severe record of delinquent activities. Here the supervisor has an opportunity to question the workers about their own observations regarding the willingness of their youngsters to admit that they are not as delinquent as the next fellow. The supervisor talks about the values and norms of the delinquent street corner group, the origins of these and their ambiguous relationship to the values and norms of conventional society. There is an opportunity here for discussion of the differences in the norms of various groups (Why did Yossy have to leave his group and become a member of another 'outfit' when he 'advanced' from petty theft and annoying little girls to stealing cars and procuring? Why didn't Amy, a bright likeable boy who had never been in trouble with the law, 'make it' with this particular group, until he finally went on a pilfering spree and was caught?) and the supervisor may talk about the concept of the 'delinquent subculture' and the different forms this may take.

One of the workers is puzzled because he has been rebuffed when trying to chat with a youngster with whom he had established a close and warm relationship. Another worker reports that a boy flared up violently when he kidded him good-naturedly about his latest change in hair style. A talk about the many personal crises to which adolescents are subject, the many confusions of this developmental stage, and its physical and emotional problems may be called for here. The supervisor will point out that the worker should respect the adolescent's need to be left alone when he needs privacy, that there are times when the need to rebel against all adult interference and authority will include the worker, and that a teenager is often preoccupied with, and highly sensitive about his physical appearance.

A girl has approached her worker for help in learning to type. The supervisor consults the other workers about the best way of referring her for vocational training. If no one has the necessary information, the supervisor may be able to supply it himself, or obtain it by making a few phone calls on the spot. He may decide to write a letter to the relevant agency, asking them to accept the girl. But it may not be so simple. The worker may express some doubts about the ability of the youngster to do the kind of work to which she aspires. Here the supervisor will have to talk about the techniques of preparing the youngster for referral. Perhaps the worker is mistaken and her reluctance to credit the youngster with the necessary requirements for an office job stems from insufficient discussion of these requirements with the youngster. Or else the worker is right. How is she going to make the girl understand that she is not suited for this kind of work, help her bear the brunt of her disappointment, perhaps have to face her anger. This particular youngster may be so 'shaky' that she should not be exposed to the possibility of failure. Can we find an alternative which would be acceptable to her? Or else this youngster is sturdy enough to be brought face to face with reality, and too stubborn to accept the worker's advice. Let's get her what she wants then, arrange for an appointment for her and let her find out herself that she is not equipped to pass the tests or not able to submit to the dull routine of typing-class.

Another worker has to be in court a few days hence. He wants to know how far he can go in helping the youngster who has been caught riding a stolen motor-bike. The other workers will probably explain all the technical details to their less experienced colleague: contacting the probation officer to discuss the case with him, presenting one's credentials to the judge and asking permission to say something about the boy's background, etc. The supervisor may have to spend some time on the principles involved. What is the worker's role in court? He is *not* an amateur lawyer. He is there to support the boy in a crisis situation, but *not* to help him get away with it regardless of whether he is guilty. He is there to help the court to obtain information about the youngster's background, the possible motives for his behaviour. He can help the court gain some perspective on the youngster by learning more about his environment. Most important of all, he makes it known that he represents an agency which is taking an active interest in this boy and will participate in any effort made to rehabilitate the youngster and prevent him from becoming a hardened recidivist. The supervisor's task here is to equip the worker with the information he needs, guide him in preparing his 'case', make him aware of his professional responsibilities and limitations and, last but not least, to help him gain self-assurance and confidence in his own competence.

One of the great advantages of this integrated approach to staff training is that none of the often difficult and complex material is presented in one-shot lectures which, as so often in academic settings, absolve the student from continuous working through of the information that has been ladled out to him. The basic issues and principles which are being taught in the integrated manner, arise again and again in the discussions and analyses of the work process. Material that has not been digested by the workers, that has been omitted altogether or has been presented too abstractly to permit practical application, is presented repeatedly in different forms and in response to different facets of the dynamics of the ongoing work.

The staff training of the Tel Aviv Project was supplemented by occasional reading and discussion of relevant excerpts from the professional literature. Occasionally lecturers on specific subjects were invited, as, for instance, Ministry of Health experts on narcotics and venereal diseases. The staff also had frequent opportunities to hear professionals of other services and agencies talk about their experiences and methods. The workers' own contributions to each other's and to the supervisor's knowledge, especially in the areas of local customs and ethnic peculiarities, proved invaluable. Moreover the problems which confronted the workers and the experience they gathered in their daily practice in the field found an echo in the practical street club work experience of the supervisor. This helped considerably to provide a solid basis for professional growth and to forge the bond of a common learning experience between workers and supervisor. It is this bond which ensures success because, as Gordon Hamilton (1954, p. 11) put it, in the process of supervision, 'at best, student and instructor learn together'.

Mary Richmond (1930) wrote many years ago, when social group work was still groping uncertainly for its professional image, that 'the supreme test of a trained worker is the ability to turn to good account the services of the relatively untrained'. This is a maxim which will have to guide supervisors of street club projects for many years to come. The test can only be met if we accept the fact that carefully planned, structured and consistent professional supervision and on-the-job training are as essential to the worker's success as his own enthusiasm and commitment, and that he has as much right to expect high standards of supervision and training, as he has the right to be adequately paid.

Some final remarks: the supervision process must be carefully geared to the workers' level of readiness and needs, so as to be conducive to his professional growth and stature. Especially with the untrained worker it is important to be wary of the fallacies of 'psychoanalysing' the worker in the individual sessions and from confusing group supervision with group therapy, in order to avoid confusion between the roles of worker and client. Peter Leonard (1966) has drawn attention to the widespread role confusion in supervision practice. Leonard (pp. 12–13) quotes Wilensky and Lebeaux (1958):

> Since sensitivity to the motivational and emotional states of the client—perhaps the prime objective of social work training—must be preceded by self-awareness, the student is himself subjected to a near psychotherapeutic experience. He is persistently called to account for his own behaviour, not in cognitive but in emotional terms—not 'Why do you think this way?' but 'Why do you feel this way?'

Leonard (1966, p. 83) quotes from a study of a social work agency (Blau and Scott, 1963):

> Workers whose judgement frequently differs from that of their supervisors might be accused of being 'unable to accept supervision'. The practice of questioning the worker's unconscious motives tended to elevate the super-ordinate into an omniscient power. Workers found that they could not be right in any disagreement since their arguments were not accepted at their face value but dismissed as being rationalizations to mask unconscious resistance.

This state of affairs is all too prevalent. I have always felt that the attitude it reflects is one of lack of respect for the worker's judgment. The street club worker must frequently rely upon his judgment to cope with the intermittent crisis situations which are part of the routine of his work. He rarely has time and opportunity to consult his supervisor or seek advice elsewhere when he is called upon to react to a street corner situation, to give immediate assistance to a youngster in trouble, or to intervene in order to prevent dangerous or unlawful behaviour. His own calm, self-assured stance, his self-confidence, are often the only resources at his command and the only stable rallying point for his youngsters. The worker's self-assurance and his confidence in his own judgment can be seriously undermined by a supervisor who seems to be mainly concerned with the mysterious processes which may or may not be going on in the dark recesses of the worker's subconscious, or who prefers to seek the reasons for a worker's opinions and decisions in the worker's own childhood, rather than in the ascertainable facts of the street corner situation. Moreover, the complex and often unpredictable situation and behaviour of a street corner group make mistakes of all kinds unavoidable. The worker must be able to risk making mistakes. He must be able to experiment with various alternative attitudes to the boys' behaviour and with different courses of action in helping them to cope with different situations. The only alternative is an extremely cautious, indecisive or largely passive role. The worker may be rendered timid and ineffective if he is led to expect that his errors and occasional failures will be interpreted as symptoms of his own unresolved personality problems.

When the supervisor finds it necessary to assert his authority by laying down rules, he should do so in a direct, unambiguous manner, explaining the reasons frankly, without taking recourse to manipulation or the subterfuge of 'therapeutic' reasons. For instance: a supervisor informs the worker that agency policy forbids the lending or giving of money to clients. He explains that the project's limited budget does not permit compensating the worker for such expenses, and that experience has shown that the youngsters tend to exploit the availability of loans or gifts of money which, in turn, may lead to a distortion of the worker's role. This is the straightforward way. The 'psychologistic' way: The supervisor analyses the worker's (rationally quite understandable) inclination to 'help a boy out' by giving or lending him some cash, in terms of 'giving material things as a substitute for "love",' a defensive device indicating a lack in the worker's own emotional equipment. He hints darkly at the symbolic 'anal' propensities of money and suggests that the worker should examine his own childhood experiences to identify the reasons for his 'need' to hold out a couple of dollars to a boy who is upset because he cannot attend a local dance with the rest of the group having spent all his money on something else. This approach, when it becomes an established pattern in the relationship between worker and supervisor, is likely to turn a young and impressionable worker into an introspective bundle of complexes and doubts who sees neurotic symptoms in anything that occurs in his relationship to his client group.

Evaluation of the worker must be handled carefully. It takes a considerable amount of professional sophistication and self-assurance to accept and use periodic full-scale evaluations constructively. Especially during the first year, ongoing evaluative remarks on the worker's attitudes and performance which are geared directly to the work process are preferable, arouse less anxiety and defensiveness and teach the worker to regard evaluation as a helpful and practical aspect of the supervision process.

I regard a two-year period of intensive and sustained supervision and training as the minimal requirement for creating a competent professional street club worker, starting with the 'raw material' of the untrained worker. Following this period the intensity of supervision can be reduced, though not discontinued altogether. The worker should be ready to provide supervision for other untrained workers, while still himself receiving guidance.

Throughout the supervision process, the supervisor must be aware of the ever-present temptation to take over and do the worker's job himself, or to interfere unnecessarily. The supervisor's support must at all times be given on the basis of respect for the worker's abilities and potentialities, and must neither deprive the worker of his independence, nor stunt his initiative. The worker should neither be overprotected by the supervisor and sheltered from the dangers of his profession, nor should he be exposed to the 'sink or swim' approach and made to feel inferior when he has to be saved from drowning. We might well heed the dictum of the great Russian educator Makarenko: 'The utmost possible demands on a person, but at the same time the utmost possible respect for him' (quoted in R. S. Cohen, 1955).

It is in educating and guiding the street club worker, in supporting and sustaining him throughout the daily process of his work, that the supervisor meets his own responsibilities and gains his rewards. The supervisor's functions make him an integral part of the job, the tasks, the problems, the failures and successes of the worker.

24 Termination

When terminating with the group involves referral into a structured agency program, the group and the agency that will be giving continued service are involved. There is gradual movement into the agency with the support of the worker. The agency that is receiving the group is provided with information on the group and its individual members, and the worker has a continued commitment to assist the agency in helping with initial minor problems of adjustment which might occur.

When the group members are left on their own, efforts are made to assess their familiarity with neighborhood resources, the degree and extent of group cohesiveness, and the degree to which there is a system of mutual responsibility and obligation toward each other. Finally, there is a follow-through on a periodic basis, either on the part of the worker or the agency, to assess their current status and their continued progress and growth.

NEW YORK CITY YOUTH BOARD (1960), p. 149

As it turned out this termination phase of the work was much more important than we had anticipated. Despite our determination from the very beginning of the enquiry to 'make termination a part of the day-to-day operation in the field', we left the whole process until much too late because we did not appreciate either its full significance or the amount of work and kind of knowledge and skill it would require.

GOETSCHIUS AND TASH (1967), p. 72

There comes a time when the street club worker begins to unravel the many and intricate knots which have been tied between him and his group of youngsters. The web of relationships which has grown over the years has to be loosened, thinned out and finally severed, so that worker and youngsters can begin to move away from each other and eventually walk off in their chosen or appointed directions, the young men and women acknowledging the end of their need for, their dependence upon the worker, and he being released from his responsibilities toward them.

The process that takes place at this time is a subtle and complex one. In group work terminology it is know as 'termination'. The word is another of the many unfortunate choices which make social work jargon offensive. It has, to me at least, a smell of disinfectant about it. It is a coldly clinical, artificial word used to describe what should be a natural development culminating in an experience of satisfaction and a sense of achievement for the youngsters and the street club worker. Unfortunately the poor choice of a word only too often reflects poor practice. In all too many cases termination is brought about by factors which have very little to do with the goals of street club work or with a valid evaluation of the group's situation and needs. Quite often work with a group stops more or less abruptly because the worker leaves his job. Sometimes this is unavoidable. Young men and women do get married, decide to take advantage of an opportunity for travelling, or simply change their minds about the kind of career they want to pursue. At best, agencies frankly admit that work with a street corner group has ended due to circumstances not related to the needs of the group. At worst, the breaking off decision is elaborately rationalised in pseudo-diagnostic terms.

There are two different conceptions of street club work which influence from the outset the forms termination will assume, and the problems it will present. The first I shall call the 'open-ended' conception, the second may be described as the 'time limited' approach. Both have their uses and applications, but on the whole I believe that the open-ended approach is the better one.

The time-limited approach is at the basis of such statements as that of a Canadian report: 'At the beginning of our contact with delinquent groups it is made clear to the boys involved that this is a service with a beginning and an end' (Ottawa Youth Services Bureau, 1963, p. 24). The report recommends a two-year period of service for highly delinquent groups in poor housing areas, and a one-year period for groups in neighbourhoods where housing, family and community controls are more adequate (ibid, p. 25). A degree of flexibility in the application of these time limits is implied, but experience has shown that there is a danger here of an undue preoccupation with these limits which may inhibit the worker's flexibility and influence his judgment of the group's needs. In some cases the time-limited approach is rigidly applied, and the agency decides from the outset that a group will be served for a clearly defined period. This decision cannot be based upon a valid diagnosis for a number of reasons. It takes a considerable length of time, allowing for the gradual development of a relationship, before the worker can identify the characteristics and needs of his group. The wide range of influences exerted by the youngsters' own growth and development during the age of adolescence, as well as by environmental, external factors can not be predicted with any degree of certainty. Moreover, if the time-limited approach is rigidly applied the evaluation of the results of the work becomes irrelevant. A group which shows a marked decrease of delinquent behaviour at the end of a one-year period of street club work, may be up to their necks in trouble within a few weeks after termination, or drift towards a different delinquent adaptation, as has so often been the case with New York fighting gangs who have been induced to stop their violent behaviour and then took recourse to narcotics. On the other hand, a group which did not appear to benefit from a one- or two-year period of service may show how much it has gained some time after the worker has departed.

The time-limited approach seems to have something of a residual tinge. It seems to be related to a concept of social work which aims at repairing a social or psychological situation in which a breakdown has occurred, taking it for granted that the service can be terminated when the repair, the 'cure', has been affected. Another aspect of this line of thinking is that the recipient of the service may be pronounced 'unde-serving', 'unco-operative' or, in the case of delinquent street corner groups, 'unreachable' if the desired change in attitudes and behaviour is not brought about in the allotted time period.

The open-ended approach appears to fit better into the 'institutional' conception of social work. This approach tells the street club worker to make his services available to the group until the changes which take place in the group and in their environment gradually reduce the need for his presence and his guidance and until the point is reached where he can withdraw. There is no need for a predetermined decision for termination. The situation of the group determines the changes in the intensity of relationship between worker and group and the timing of his withdrawal. This attitude makes it unnecessary for the worker to stress as a point of departure and as a basis for his relationship the fact that this is a service with a beginning and an end. This obvious fact should be conveyed to the youngsters continuously by the limits the worker sets to his relationship to the group and by the unambiguous way in which he defines his role as a professional youth worker, rather than as someone who has 'joined the gang', a 'nice guy who likes kids', a parent substitute, etc. Just as it is the group, not the worker which, by 'opening up' and accepting help and guidance, determines when the 'period of service' begins (which rarely takes place at first contact), so it is the group which should indicate when the time for parting has come.

The reasoning here is something like this: Although it is obviously difficult to make a clear distinction between the tasks of 'prevention' and 'rehabilitation' in dealing with delinquency, the emphasis should clearly be on prevention. Prevention, however, cannot be timed in advance. One cannot predict the future date at which a group of mildly and sporadically delinquent youngsters will have been prevented from becoming 'chronic' delinquents, rigidly adhering to the norms and behaviour patterns of a delinquent subculture, or when a highly delinquent group will have been prevented from drifting into even more destructive ways of life (for instance, from being thieves or street fighters to becoming drug addicts) or become recruits for the adult criminal underworld. More-over, if we accept the well substantiated findings that the deprived

neighbourhood, the slum, the non-community housing project, breed
and perpetuate delinquent subcultures, then we also must accept the
need for street club work as a permanent institution for as long as the
breeding ground exists. In other words, a street club worker in a high-
delinquency area may not reach a clearcut 'termination' at all. As the
boys of his group leave adolescence behind them and become young
adults, the worker may find that his relationship to them loosens gradually and changes while he begins to concentrate on serving the next
generation of delinquents, often the younger brothers of his first group.
The older group will usually drift apart, as the adolescent need for close
peer associations disappears. But as the worker remains in the area, his
contacts with his 'old boys' will continue and may even become a source
of support to him in his work with the young ones.

It would, of course, be much better if we could wipe out delinquency
by a period of street club work with a delinquent group in a lower class
neighbourhood. Unfortunately all experience indicates that this does
not happen unless we can eliminate the sources of frustration and anger
and the concomitant needs for youngsters to find deviant solutions to
their problems which exist in such areas.

My own experience in New York and in Tel Aviv has convinced me
that this approach to street club work as an 'institutionalised' method of
helping youngsters in trouble areas is, if one takes the long term view,
the only effective one. A precondition to its implementation is a radical
change in the professional status of the street club worker. The latter
must be ensured well-planned and structured working conditions which
include training, supervision, chances for advancement within the profession and, last but not least, an adequate salary. If this is achieved,
'termination' on the basis of expediency (usually meaning that a group
of troubled youngsters, after having received implicit or explicit promises of help, is left high and dry because their worker has decided that
six months or a year are more than enough, and that it is time for him to
settle down to building some sort of a career) will become the exception,
rather than the rule. Conditions must be created which will ensure that
a street club worker is as unlikely to regard his responsible and demanding work as a youthful escapade or a stop-gap job to be given up at the
first chance of a better offer, as a young doctor or lawyer is unlikely to
take this attitude towards the practice of medicine or law. Until this
comes about, any discussion of termination of service in street club work,
and the closely related evaluation of the results of this type of group work
with delinquent street corner groups, will continue to end in a measure
of frustration and doubt.

Almost all reports on street club work point out that termination is most likely to lead to some manifestations of crisis in the group. Saul Bernstein (1964, p. 87), for instance, writes: 'Strong feelings are generated, especially that of being deserted by the worker, and there have been threats that they will act even worse than they used to, thereby to show how essential it is to continue the service.'

The Canadian report cited above states that the announcement of termination 'causes some boys to threaten to return to past behaviour patterns' (Ottawa Youth Services Bureau, 1963, p. 24).

I know from experience that there is usually some emotional reaction when the street club worker leaves a group of youngsters he has known and, in a manner of speaking, lived with for some time. The worker's own feelings are by no means unaffected. It is rather astonishing that all studies I have read tend to dissect these feelings in coldly clinical terms, instead of acknowledging the simple, natural fact that the worker gets to like the youngsters and they have grown to like him, and that both sides may feel somewhat upset and sad about ending a close and warm relationship.[1] However, if these, quite normal, reactions assume crisis proportions, the question must be asked whether the youngsters are not expressing a quite rational and justified resentment at a termination which is dictated by expediency or unrealistic demands upon their abilities to change at a pace prescribed by the worker (or his agency) rather than determined by their own situation and needs. Those feelings of being deserted, let down or given up as a lost cause may be justified. Allowing the worker-group relationship to dissolve naturally in the course of a gradual development which has the growing-up process of a group of adolescents at its basis, makes it quite unnecessary to offer such explanations as:

The Detached Worker understands the reasons for these threats but is not deterred from his decision. He impresses upon the boys that whether or not they get into trouble again is their own business but that it will not cause him to continue working with them. He also tells them that if they should get into more trouble it will be evidence that our work, instead of being worthwhile and of lasting value, was only a delaying measure (Ottawa Youth Services Bureau, 1963, p. 24).

Such explanations sound contrived and have very little meaning to the youngsters.

In New York I worked with the 'Emperors' for well over three years. The intensity of service gradually diminished towards the end of the second year, and during the third year I began to work with a younger

---

[1] I feel inhibited about using the word 'love', in this context, ever since I heard social workers of standing and influence speak about 'using love as a tool', reflecting an attitude which I regard not only as immoral, but as downright obscene.

group hanging out at the same street corner while the older group gradually drifted apart, the boys having become young men and finding other interests. I left the younger group at the end of a year's work after having introduced them to another worker. I had to leave the 'Commanders' at the end of one year, due to circumstances beyond my control, rather than because I felt that they were ready to stand on their own feet. Fortunately my agency was able to absorb most of the boys and girls of the group into a 'young adult' club at the Settlement House. We had a lavish farewell party at which our adventures and achievements together were reviewed at length and we all aired our feelings freely. Individual members of the 'Emperors' and the 'Commanders' kept in touch with me and sought my help with personal problems for about two years after I had withdrawn from their neighbourhoods.

Street club workers of the Tel Aviv project remained in the same neighbourhoods from the start of their work in 1963 to the present day, working with three 'generations' of delinquent and delinquency-prone youngsters loosening their ties to the older groups gradually while shifting the emphasis to the younger ones.

In New York as well as in Tel Aviv the problem of why, when and how to end service to a street corner group has, in many instances, been found difficult to solve. Termination on the grounds of expediency or unrealistic expectations still occurs at least as often as the more desirable gradual withdrawal which grows out of a changing situation.

25 What are the results?

Evaluation refers to the procedures of fact finding about the results of planned social action, which in turn move the spiral of planning ever upward. It is the proper methodological accompaniment to rational action.

HYMAN, WRIGHT AND HOPKINS (1962), p. 3

Not many programs have been evaluated. Some have perhaps been evaluated too soon. Most of the evaluative studies that have been conducted do not meet the criteria of good evaluation. They do not make clear exactly what the preventive measures and processes under consideration are, toward what manner of youth they are directed, how well they have been carried out, and with whom or in what measure they succeed or fail.

HELEN L. WITMER AND EDITH TUFTS (1954), p. 47

The kind of change that may result from this is an internal rather than an external one and perhaps it cannot be measured in terms of either the present or the immediate future. The Committee's hope is that as a result of the young people's experience in the cafe the adult attitudes they eventually assume will be less narrow and restricted than those of their parents and that they will be able to allow themselves to take some responsibility for the conduct of their own lives and for the life of their community.

B. BIVEN AND H. M. HOLDEN (1966), p. 8

Street club workers tend to answer the question as to the results of their work somewhat vaguely and evasively. One of the reasons is that the question is quite often a 'loaded' one. The questioner's mind as to what answer he wants to hear is already made up. He expects to hear an impressive and soothing column of statistics rattled off: the delinquency rates for the area reduced by so and so much, x number of gang fights or thefts prevented, so many drug addicts 'cured', so many boys in full employment. When the worker obliges with the 'right' answers, the questioner is satisfied. He is usually not unduly worried about the origin and validity of such statistics. But when the desired reply is not given, the questioner, who may be someone with considerable influence upon the future of the service, is quite likely to dismiss years of painstaking, soul-searching work as a waste of time and money.

At a 'benefit' party in New York a lady who contributed generously to the agency which paid my salary wanted to know how many boys I had helped to 'adjust' and become 'decent, law-abiding youngsters' that year. She was not very happy when I was unable to give her a straight answer. An Israeli police official left me in a somewhat better frame of mind when he told me: 'As far as I can see, the issue is a simple one: if one of your street club workers manages to keep two boys out of jail in the course of one year, he's earned his annual salary. It costs the state about that much in legal procedures and prison maintenance.'

A more sophisticated line of enquiry raises even more difficulties. A gang has stopped fighting, but what alternatives have the youngsters been given which will prevent them from taking recourse to even less desirable adaptations, even more disruptive or self-destructive behaviour? A third of the members of a group have been enabled to join a community centre and are doing well there. But what happened to the others? Isn't their situation even more hopeless now, after the most stable youngsters have moved away? Two dozen youngsters with a bad work record are now fully employed. But what kinds of jobs do they have? Is there any future in what they are doing, any challenge and interest? Or are they condemned to a life of boredom and frustration? Some people approach the matter of results with admirable broadmindedness, a version of the 'virtue is its own reward' attitude. A young detached worker in London told me happily that his agency has assured him that he would not be held responsible for any results, but had their unqualified blessing to go forth and work with 'unattached' youth. Work to what purpose, towards what goals?

Any evaluation of the results of street club work is logically related to two main factors: one is the kind of youngsters we serve, the other the goals we have set ourselves for our work. Both factors are interdependent, both raise problems with regard to the evaluation of the results.

Witmer and Tufts (1954, p. 2) outlined three basic conceptions of delinquency prevention, pointing out that 'each has different implications for program planning and for likelihood of successful results'. To this may be added: each implies a shift in emphasis in the selection of the client population.

One approach is focused upon predelinquent or potentially delinquent children and seeks to provide specialised individual and group treatment services for these. This approach is based on the assumption that potential delinquents can be identified, that delinquency can be predicted at an early age. One should be very cautious in basing any prevention programming upon so doubtful an assumption. May it suffice here to mention Professor Toby's (1961, p. 13) warning of the 'boomerang effects of early stigmatization'.[1] Street club work's preventive approach is concerned with the effects of the delinquent subculture and its exponent, the adolescent street corner group, upon any of the youngsters who grow up in a deprived, delinquency-generating environment.

[1] Professor Toby's article offers an excellent, concise critical discussion of the practice implications of delinquency prediction theory. Delinquency prediction theory is expounded, *inter alia*, in Glueck (1959) and Stott (1960).

Experience indicates that even the most conforming, well-behaved nine-year-old child in such an environment may grow into a highly delinquent street corner boy with the onset of puberty and adolescence. One of the most important and lasting results of street club work may very well be the prevention of a rigid delinquent adaptation of the 'next generation' of youngsters, following in the footsteps of the older groups in the neighbourhood. A solid relationship and intensive work with the older groups is a precondition for this preventive work, sometimes resulting in an effective alliance between the worker and the older groups in preventing the young ones (called 'little nuisances' or 'little bugs' with affectionate derision by Tel Aviv street corner boys) from 'getting into trouble'.

Unfortunately the street club workers' intensive involvement with the often severe problems of the older groups leaves little time to concentrate upon direct preventive work with the young ones. It is therefore to be highly recommended that a second worker be assigned to work in close co-operation with the first, but to concentrate exclusively upon preventive work with the seven- to eleven-year-olds. This 'second generation worker' would concentrate primarily on play group and other recreational activities and maintain close liaison with parents and schools. This worker, who might be described as a neighbourhood play-leader rather than a street club worker, would also co-operate closely with existing community centres and settlement houses in order to effect an early integration of the 'young ones' into their programmes, in the hope that an established tradition of participation in structured, supervised programme activities will weather the storms and upheavals of puberty and adolescence and will later counteract the pull of the delinquent gang.

It may be added that even where such a highly necessary second generation worker is not assigned to help the street club worker bring about lasting changes in a delinquency-generating neighbourhood, it can safely be assumed that the latter's long-term, intensive work with the local street corner groups has a preventive effect on the younger children. If for no other reason than because the street club worker's influence dilutes what would otherwise be a rigid model of a delinquent senior group and presents the potential apprentices of a deviant subculture with the alternative of coping with tensions and frustrations through the help and guidance of a trusted, knowledgeable adult.

Another conception of delinquency prevention 'stresses reducing recidivism and lessening the likelihood of serious offences rather than reaching children who have not yet offended against the law. What is chiefly to be prevented, in this view of the problem, is the aggravation of delinquent behaviour, its continuance rather than its onset. Programs operated on this basis accordingly deal largely with youngsters who engage in behaviour that is illegal and that may already have led to court action' (Witmer and Tufts, 1954, p. 3). Street club work clearly is a program of this type, based largely upon this conception of delinquency prevention. The results of this type of work have been implied or spelled out throughout the pages of this book and it may be unnecessary to elaborate further. Let us, however, take a brief look at what other writers on the subject have to say.

First of all it must be stated, that many reports on the results of 'detached work with delinquent gangs' are, upon closer examination, neither talking about street club work as it is defined in these pages, nor are they dealing with the types of client groups with whom we are concerned. The Ottawa Youth Services Bureau (1963, p. 25) report lists as criteria of success which have been met the following achievements:

No arrests for a period of six months to one year.

Community members report that '. . . the boys are behaving and not making a nuisance of themselves . . .' and the group '. . . is involved in constructive pursuits. . . .'

The youngsters' school performance is satisfactory.

The members of the group have gained a '. . . constructive but realistic self-image . . .' and have become associated with non-delinquent friends.

Status within the group is related to 'positive' factors.

Members take responsibility for their own behaviour, rather than have the group dictate their behaviour.

The youngsters are able to '. . . get along with normal-acting boys and girls in normal school settings . . .

. . . There is no indication of wanting to get into further trouble.

. . . A loosening of group cohesion occurs simultaneously with members' participation in normal activities outside the group.

The seven groups who are reported to have come close to show these remarkable results consisted almost entirely of pre-adolescent youngsters who were only mildly and sporadically delinquent. The largest group consisted of ten, the smallest of four members, while most counted five to seven youngsters (Ottawa Youth Service Bureau, 1963, pp. 26–32).

Oswald (1963, p. 13) records an Australian agency with one middle- and one lower-class client group:

The detached work programme had more effective results with youth of a higher educational level. This group stated their initial problems more often as familial and personal ones. They showed a better capacity for verbalising and for developing insight into their problems.

The programme has emphasised the difficulties involved in attempting to assist and bring about change in youth with established delinquent patterns. While this programme had low success with them, it is worthwhile to point out, firstly, that these youths were the failures of other agencies; and, secondly, the detached worker had achieved some success where others failed. . . .

The report left me with the impression that, while some valuable and conscientious 'detached' work had been done with these two groups, the method used was not group work of any kind and certainly not street club work as defined here, but a sort of on-the-spot case work and individual counselling.[1]

Saul Bernstein (1964, pp. 79–82), reporting on a survey of 'street work' with lower-class delinquent street corner groups in nine major American cities, summarises four major categories of results criteria:

Public Behaviour [The prevention and reduction of fighting, stealing and vandalism] . . . was consistently reported as the area of greatest achievement [Professor Bernstein points out:] Probably one significant reason why decreases in public delinquent behaviour are relatively achievable is that consequences tend to be quick, visible and in terms which the youth understand. In this category are injuries, arrest, and retaliation by enemy groups. Unfortunate results in relation to other kinds of behaviour, such as drinking, sex, and the use of drugs, are not so immediate and clear to the teenagers.

Private Behaviour [This includes sexual activities, drinking and drug use]: While the responses were far from completely negative in this area, they were mostly discouraging. The resistances to change in relation to sex, drugs and alcohol seemed to be as strong, if not stronger, in the youth than those to other kinds of change. They are accessible escapes from drab and frustrating living, and they provide exciting enjoyment. They also symbolize adulthood. Whatever successes were reported were usually linked to other changes, such as obtaining a good job, improved family relationships, developing ability and interest in athletics, strong identification with the worker, and the like. The low batting average of success indicates that new knowledge and methods are needed.

Interpersonal Relations [This is defined as:] . . . How the youth treat each other, whether they show concern about the misfortunes of their fellows, pleasure in their good fortune, and other forms of what is generally regarded as highly socialized and mature behaviour. [Having pointed out that the level of mutual loyalty and 'camaraderie' in street corner groups is often impressively high, while the more disturbed groups are likely to engage in mutually destructive behaviour, Professor Bernstein writes:] The group work method has rich contributions to make toward improved inter-personal relations. After the worker becomes trusted and liked by the members, and shows active concern about what happens to every one of them, there often is a shift, over a period of time, in their attitudes and behaviour toward each other. Time, patience, devotion and skill are essential, but many workers reported substantial changes.

[The author adds:] in our legitimate interest in tangible goals like stopping violence and delinquency, promoting school attendance and jobs, there is the

---

[1] This view was confirmed by a conversation I had with a member of the staff of the Service to Youth Council, the Australian agency which issued the above cited report.

danger of overlooking or slighting the less obvious goal of helping these young people experience more satisfying and mature relationships. The worker often provides their first opportunity to enjoy in a meaningful way the richness and depth of trusting and considerate interdependence with their fellows.

This theme does not ring the tocsin of public relations and fund raising, nor was it emphasized by all the agencies visited. Nevertheless, it was gratifying to find it stressed by many, with good results reported. Insofar as workers are successful in moving towards this aim, the quality of living in large segments of our population will improve, with ample implications for the way these teenagers will bring up their own children.

School and Jobs: [The author sums up a thoughtful discussion of this most important subject by saying:] Success is influenced but not controlled by the workers. To solve these problems for large numbers calls for far-reaching changes in education and in economic opportunity for youth.

Finally it must be emphasised that street club work with groups of delinquent youngsters who already have an impressive and extensive history of conflict with the mores of society and with the law, cannot be expected to produce miracles of regeneration and conversion. I cannot put it better than the Chicago Youth Development Project worker who told Professor Bernstein (1964, p. 83):

'When problems change from very, very bad to very bad, and then to bad, that is progress. A lifetime of experience is behind the behaviour and the values of alienated youth and destructive forces continue to operate while the worker tries to stimulate change. Movement is not even; it tends to occur in jerks, with some forward and some backward. It is easier to modify behaviour than it is attitudes, although the two are closely inter-related. Change usually does not happen across the board; the old and the new get mixed up together, with strong pulls toward the old. Miracles should not be expected, but healthy changes can be achieved.'

Under pressure of public opinion it is often very difficult for the street club worker to have to admit that all he has to show for his work with a particular group of youngsters is some kind of successful 'holding operation', in fact applying to all types of delinquent adaptations what some of New York's best and most dedicated workers with young drug users had to say about their work:

The goal of treatment of most addicted adolescents cannot realistically and honestly be considered abstention, in the light of almost all present knowledge and almost all methods of treatment observed. Rather, the goal must be to help the youth to grow and develop as best he can in the light of his recurring addiction so that he will stop using somewhere along the line (East Harlem Protestant Parish Narcotics Committee, 1959, p. 3).

But there are also forces at work, some of them known to the street club worker, some of them outside the range of his awareness, which in themselves lead to desirable changes in individuals or groups. These

may take the form of a boy's first great romance, or a group's involvement in a crisis situation which transcends their own narrow preoccupations, such as a political movement or an upsurge of patriotic fervour.
The most common is simply the process of growing up and coming face
to face with adult responsibilities and mature interests. Most authorities
agree that juvenile delinquents outgrow delinquency, rather than become adult criminals.[1] That is if they are lucky enough to avoid serving
a period of apprenticeship in our great schools of crime, the State Training Schools and Youth Prisons.[2] In almost all cases in which a street club
worker, often with the co-operation of police, probation and Court
officials, succeeds in keeping a youngster out of jail and shepherding him
through adolescence without incarceration, this in itself constitutes a
major achievement. I refer once more to Professor Bernstein (1964, p.
79):

Each instance of the prevention of damage to property and the hurting, even
killing, of people is an achievement of great value. With each such episode, there
are apt to be the further consequences of arrest and incarceration, which have
serious implications for the youth and their futures. A goodly number of them,
if they can be helped through the turbulence of adolescence, may well settle
down to a more regulated and law-abiding adulthood. But a dramatic conflict
with the law can set forces in motion which portend a dismal future.

A third conception of delinquency prevention outlined by Witmer
and Tufts (1954, p. 2) sees delinquency as caused by a wide range of
detrimental environmental factors (such as poverty, inadequate housing
conditions, family and community disruption, lack of recreational and
educational facilities, ethnic discrimination, etc.), all or most of which
can be found in the lower class milieu.

From this point of view, activities looking to the reduction of prejudice against
minority groups are a form of delinquency prevention. So too are efforts to
improve home life through raising the income level of poverty stricken families,
providing better houses and neighborhood facilities for them, improving job
tenure and work arrangements, and in other ways reducing economic uncertainty and increasing the security and self-esteem of the parents. Similarly,
efforts to help parents feel and be more adequate in child rearing and to make
schools, recreational programs, health and welfare services more adequate to
their task of promoting the healthy personality development of children are also
regarded as delinquency prevention measures.[3]

The target of prevention measures is, in this view, 'the children who

[1] See, for instance, Bernard (1957), pp. 421–44; McCord et al (1959), p. 21; Dunham
and Knauer, (1954).
[2] The Staff Psychiatrist, Children's Division, Domestic Relations Court of the City of
New York stated: 'In 1956, thirty-six state penitentiaries reported that some 52 per
cent of their inmates were state training graduates' (Rittwagen 1959, p. 141).
[3] The prevention-oriented policies of many of Britain's local authority children's
departments which have, in recent years, resulted in the setting up of family advice

live in some particularly disadvantageous situation, such as extreme poverty or a particular minority group or some other form of social isolation' (ibid). As has been pointed out earlier, street club work does indeed seek and find its client groups in these strata of the youth population.

His work with a delinquent street corner group involves the street club worker to a large degree in the activities which are rightly described as 'preventive' in the above quote from the Witmer and Tufts study. The worker's range of possibilities in this endeavour is, however, limited.

Cloward and Ohlin have stated that: 'Delinquency is not, in the final analysis, a property of individuals or even of subcultures; it is a property of the social systems in which these groups and individuals are enmeshed. The target for preventive action, then, should be defined, not as the individual or group that exhibits the delinquent patterns, but as the social setting that gives rise to delinquency.'[1]

Together with the entire social work profession, the street club worker is the object of the serious criticism that he, like his colleagues in case work and other social work disciplines, not only fails to bring about the fundamental social changes which are essential, but helps to perpetuate the *status quo*. Peter Leonard (1966, p. 30) pinpoints these views neatly in his discussion of the 'conflict' theory in sociology. The author summarises the particular sociological view of the social stratum in which delinquent street corner groups originate and thrive:

Here, we might say, is a stratum of society alienated from society as a whole, competing unsuccessfully for scarce resources and producing a disproportionate number of social problems especially those of poverty, illness, child neglect and delinquency. This stratum of socially and economically disadvantaged individuals and families does not form a group conscious of its common manifest interests whose goal is to attack the existing power structure. Rather, it forms a quasi-group of people who have similar latent interests in changing the status quo, but with no class consciousness to make this interest manifest. The dominant groups in society are concerned to dilute the conflict without making any substantial change in the socio-economic structure, and so individuals within this stratum who come into conflict with the wider society are termed 'maladjusted', 'deviant' or 'abnormal' and therefore the object of social work. Within this analysis social work is seen as a means by which society can ensure that underprivileged individuals are manipulated into adjusting to their position in society.

There is no doubt in my mind that social work *can*, and often *does*,

services, are a step in the direction of broadly conceived preventive approaches. The potentialities for co-operation with 'detached' youth workers in this type of service have not yet been recognised (see Leissner, 1967). For information on the growing interest in such services in the United States, see: Kahn *et al* (1966).

[1] Cloward & Ohlin, *Delinquency and Opportunity*, above cited, p. 211.

serve as the means for manipulation of the underprivileged and discontented, the means which befog the issues of social conflict and induce docile adjustment to unjust and intolerable conditions.[1] But so do the members of many other professions, such as doctors, psychiatrists, lawyers, teachers, clergymen, city planners, architects designing public housing, the people who run our radio and television programmes, produce our movies or write our newspapers. All have the option of using their knowledge and powers to maintain an undesirable *status quo*, or help people to change it. The results of their activities depend upon how they make use of this option. The street club worker is no exception to this rule.

Some of the examples given in these pages will have shown that the street club worker can and does become the initiator of change not only in the attitudes and behaviour of individual and group, but also in the youngsters' environment (their social setting) and in the attitudes society and its institutions adopt toward them. Effects are minute if compared with the vast range of problems which remain unsolved. But if far-reaching, profound changes, which go beyond dealing with symptoms and strike at the precipitating factors in the social environment of the street corner group, are rare, this is mainly so because street club work as a professional method has rarely been precisely defined, and adequately equipped in terms of staff, professional status, training and supervision, to give it a fair chance to prove itself. Moreover, even under the best conditions, street club work is not a panacea for delinquency. As J. D. West (1967, pp. 298–9) and other writers before him have pointed out, this is as unrealistic as expecting 'any one explanation or treatment method to solve all health problems'. We must also take into account that:

The causes of delinquency are numerous both in toto and within the individual case. This makes it unlikely that any program will achieve spectacular results. Most programs are single-focused. They aim at the elimination or amelioration of some condition that the backers regard as especially important in delinquency causation. Since, however, these conditions do not operate in isolation—either in the community or within the individual child and family—it is not to be expected that any single approach to delinquency prevention will be strikingly successful (Witmer and Tufts, 1954, p. 8).

It can be said that, within the limited and clearly defined setting of the street corner in a deprived neighbourhood, street club work encompasses as wide a range of causal factors and objectives as possible. However, the worker's success in tackling as many of the precipitating factors as necessary, and in bringing about a significant and lasting change in

[1] A British observer of the American scene remarks: 'Social work seems, in fact, to be one of the scapegoats for a more general failure within society' (Jones, 1967, p. 151).

the attitudes and behaviour patterns of the youngsters, does not depend upon his own isolated effort. In the long run, the success of the street club work method is assured only if society shows itself willing to back up this one specific and, of necessity, limited, effort by making its own resources available. Experience shows that such a concerted effort, in which street club work functions as part of a powerful, co-ordinated team, has so far not been consistently applied anywhere.

Most prevention programs describe single agency thrusts. It is true that there is some interdisciplinary programming visible in some countries and many reports of interagency co-operation. But what is not visible in any of the countries is a grand design or a mosaic of meaningful effort in which the social systems of the school, the police, the courts, the recreation and sports agencies, the clinic, the welfare agency mesh smoothly in a network of service to vulnerable youth and endangered family (Kvaraceus, 1965, p. 20).

The process of street club work includes a wide range of contacts with those individuals, agencies and institutions which impinge more or less directly, upon the daily existence of the street corner group and its individual members. The worker's success in bringing about positive changes in the group's situation and attitudes depends largely upon how creative and constructive he is in initiating, maintaining and using these contacts. The evaluation of the results of his service will be greatly influenced by items on a 'things done' list, such as the following:[1]

A compromise was reached in the conflict between Joey and his parents over his financial contributions to the household. Now Joey can save up to buy his own motor-bike and stop using other people's machines.

An arrangement has been worked out with Tommy's married brother for the boy's room and board, as Tommy has found no way of resolving the conflict with his father.

Mr Jenkins, owner of the local grocery store, has been persuaded not to press charges against Nick after the boy agreed to pay off the value of the things he stole in weekly instalments.

Ronny's employer, who discovered that the boy is an addict, has become the worker's ally in trying to keep the youngster from ending in the gutter. He is keeping Ronny on the job under his personal supervision and enables him to make up the working hours he misses from time to time. Ronny has shown some talent in drawing, and his employer has agreed to let him attend a draughtsman's course at the company's expense.

Mr K, the neighbourhood 'loanshark', has been induced to 'freeze' the

---

[1] The examples which follow are selected from my own experience and observations in street club work practice in New York and Tel Aviv.

interest on Richie's loan and let the boy pay it off in reasonable instalments.

Eddie, who has finally admitted that he can't read or write, was introduced to Mr Starkman, a retired sales manager, who has become his tutor.

Police Officer M, who 'had it in' for Chuck ever since the boy threw an egg at him, met with M and the worker and, after accepting the kid's apology, agreed to bury the hatchet.

A group of parents who had become very upset about their daughters' association with the street corner boys were invited to a party the boys gave and came away saying that they had enjoyed themselves and that the youngsters had behaved very nicely.

The Principal of a nearby secondary school arranged with the worker to meet the street corner group. He discussed their hostility to the school and the damage they had caused to school property with them, listened to their grievances and gave them permission to use the school's gym once a week.

Mr Tomas, owner of a neighbourhood restaurant, who had barred the group from his premises, was persuaded to meet with the boys, explain his own problems to them and establish friendly relations, permitting them to enter his place, provided they were dressed decently and kept the noise down.

A local racketeer who is greatly admired by the youngsters promised the worker to support his efforts to 'straighten the kids out'. He met with the group and lectured them sternly about their 'fooling around with drugs'.

Mrs L, a public health nurse, met with a group of girls and talked to them about personal hygiene, sex and birth control, showed them slides and arranged for personal consultations with individual girls.

An amateur 'body-building' club invited the group to a demonstration and discussion and agreed to let them use their equipment once a week under their own and the worker's supervision.

A housing authority official agreed to meet with the group and discuss with them ways and means to better the relationship between them and the housing authority, listing his complaints about their behaviour and listening to their grievances.

The Commanding Officer of the Youth Squad spent an evening with the group at their 'hang-out', listened to their complaints and discussed their attitudes toward law and order with them.

The worker brought Probation Officer P to the local cafe and he talked with the boys about the purposes of probation and the ways in which the demands of probation clashed with the 'code' of the group.

Representatives of the local Tenants' Council agreed to meet with the group to talk about how the boys could help the community improve living conditions.

The two rival political parties active in the neighbourhood were persuaded to invite the group for a discussion of their ideologies, methods and goals.

The worker introduced a journalist to the group and he talked to them about how a newspaper is run and why the papers were 'down' on delinquents.

After members of the group had become involved in strike-breaking activities, the worker brought a union official to the street corner and he told the boys about the trade union movement and the way in which workers fight for their rights and for better pay and working conditions.

These are only a few, arbitrarily selected, examples of the large number of activities which may serve to break through the social and psychological isolation of a group of delinquent youngsters, loosen up deviant subcultural patterns and effect changes in attitudes and behaviour. The results are likely to be neither dramatic nor immediately apparent, but the very fact that the worker has succeeded in initiating and carrying out such activities proves that change is taking place.

The list of accomplishments must, however, be further extended to include the worker's efforts to play an initiator's role in bringing about some measure of co-operation between the various agencies and institutions whose functions and activities are relevant to the situation of the street corner group. If we accept the dictum that: 'to promote the welfare of children is not the prerogative of any one professional discipline but depends on the co-operation of many different people', and the indispensable need to 'improve the lines of communication among all the disciplines professionally concerned with promoting healthy child growth' (Pringle, 1965, p. x), then it is obvious that the street club worker's contributions in this area of endeavour must be taken into consideration in evaluating the results of his service.

Opportunities for initiating or facilitating co-operation between different agencies in relation to the problems of the street corner groups arise frequently as part of the work process. If the worker is alert to these opportunities and skilful in making use of them, he may be able to add to the list of 'things done' such items as:

Worker arranged a meeting with a local youth club leader, the gym instructor of a neighbourhood school and adult members of the community in order to discuss recreational programmes for street corner youth.

Monthly meetings between the street club worker, local clergymen, Y.M.C.A. staff, and a volunteer group organised by a nearby settlement house were held to discuss the co-ordination of recreational, cultural and educational activities for street corner youth.

A meeting was set up between a local physician, doctors from a neighbourhood clinic, the social welfare worker assigned to the area, the neighbourhood pharmacist and the youth squad of the police to establish channels of communication regarding prevention and treatment of venereal disease among the youngsters, and to discuss methods of handling V.D. cases in a way which removes the threat of police intervention.

Probation officers, police officials and a representative of the Youth Employment Office met with the street club worker to discuss the youngsters' complaints that police and probation officers contact individual boys and girls at their places of employment, endangering their relationships with colleagues and employers and jeopardising their jobs.

The worker brought about a meeting of local social workers, probation officers, staff members of youth prisons or state training schools, parents and members of the street corner group in order to discuss the adjustment problems of youngsters who are about to be released from jails or institutions.

Meetings were arranged between influential members of the community, clergymen, police officials, settlement house staff and representatives of youth movements and political parties to discuss racial tension in the neighbourhood with members of the street corner groups.

'Case conferences' were scheduled to discuss the socio-economic and mental-health problems of specific youngsters and their families with the relevant social workers, health department officials, teachers and housing authority officials.

Last but not least, the street club worker who has proved his competence, skill and knowledge in his relations with the representatives of other agencies will be able to include in his list of positive results instances of success in enhancing the understanding of the special problems of delinquent street corner groups and in exerting a constructive influence upon the attitudes other professionals and agencies hold with regard to these youngsters. In a way, the street club worker becomes the 'spokesman' for the 'gang kids'. In New York street club workers have been asked to address groups of interested citizens from all walks of life on their work with street corner youth. They have given talks to the staff of community centres and settlement houses, have led discussions on the problems of teenage drug users with groups of hospital nurses and have lectured to classes of social work students. Radio and television, the daily press, professional and other magazines have encouraged street club workers to tell the public about their approach.

The Tel Aviv Project found Israel even more receptive. Street club workers were invited to address meetings of youth workers and educators, judges and lawyers, police officers, social workers, doctors, trade union officials and army officers. Street club workers gave single lectures, seminars and courses in schools of social work, criminology and sociology faculties of universities, training institutes for youth leaders, youth and adult probation departments and the Police Training School.

Here too, the results are usually neither dramatic nor immediately apparent. But the changes in attitudes which occur have far reaching results for the youngsters of the street corner, whether such changes become manifest in chance encounters between ordinary citizens and street corner boys, whether they show up in the school room, a youth club, the office of a probation officer, the police station or the court room.

The following Appendix contains the summarised records of the results of eighteen months of street club work with a cluster of highly delinquent street corner groups consisting of fifty-two youngsters located in one of Tel Aviv's poverty areas.[1] The records cover the period from January 1964 to July 1965. Work with these groups continued after the records provided here were concluded and Mr S, the street club worker assigned to the area, is carrying on his tasks at the present time. Although these records cannot be regarded as 'final results', it is hoped that they will offer the reader some concrete examples of the intricate mosaic of 'successes' and 'failures' which the street club worker has to learn to live with, and of what the worker is up against when he is called upon to answer the question: 'What are the results?'

[1] This is the same grouping of youngsters described on pp. xiii–xvi at the beginning of this book. The records are taken from Leissner, Rubin and Bors (1967), vol. ii, pp. 221–66.

Appendix

Street Corner Groups in a Tel Aviv lower-class community

A descriptive evalution of the results of an eighteen-month period of street club work

1. The street corner groups

We identified four groups in the neighbourhood. These groups can be regarded as separate, loose-knit friendship groups. They congregate in close geographical proximity, and most of the youngsters of the different groups are in frequent contact with each other. Interaction between the different groups was, at times, so intense that we tended to see them as subdivisions of the same group, rather than separate entities. In order to show the intergroup connections, we have marked the name of each member with the number of the *other* group with whom he has maintained frequent contact. A member of Group I who maintained close relations with youngsters in Group III, will therefore have the marking g/3 after his name.

During the eighteen months work-period the Project's street club worker focused his major efforts upon Group I, and spent most of his time with this group. Because of this, there was a tendency to see the other three groups in relation to Group I.

The worker served fifty-two youngsters. This number was arrived at during the first six months of the eighteen months work-period, after the unrealistically large number of boys in the neighbourhood with whom the worker had been in relatively loose and unfocused contact for several months previously was greatly reduced. Until the end of the eighteen months work-period there were, however, about twenty-five youngsters who did *not* belong to any of the groups described here, but who had been in contact with the street club worker and continued to ask for his advice, intervention in family matters and assistance in obtaining employment, settling court cases, military service problems, etc. This 'legacy' from the beginning phases of the Project continued to make demands upon the worker's time and energy, at times to the detriment of his intensive service to his client groups. Outright rejection of the 'surplus' youngsters proved impossible because (a) this would have endangered the positive image and reputation of 'helping person' which the worker had gained in the neighbourhood; (b) because the youngsters of his own groups often exerted pressure upon the worker to make himself available to outsiders who were know to them; and (c) because the worker often found it personally difficult to refuse his help in cases of serious need.

GROUP I

This group counted twenty-one members in the fourteen to eighteen age range. At the time of our first contact this group was greatly influenced by Group III, but was, on the whole, less severely delinquent than the Group III boys. Partly due to the influence of the street club worker, partly due to the arrest of a large number of the Group III boys in April and May 1964, the youngsters of Group I became more cohesive and identifiable as a separate street corner group, developing along the patterns of their own needs and goals, rather than adopting the 'style' and behaviour patterns of Group III.

The youngsters in Group I engaged in petty theft, vehicle theft and, more rarely, in burglaries. Brawling and vandalism were of almost daily occurrence during the early months of service. Several of the youngsters used hashish and several were involved in homosexual activities. It is significant to note here, that the most delinquent boys had the most frequent and closest contacts with members of other groups in the neighbourhood, and often co-operated in delinquent activities with the latter. Common interest in the use and obtaining of hashish provided one of the foremost motives for interaction with other groups and other areas.

Most of the youngsters in this group had poor work adjustments. Many rarely worked at all and those who did obtain employment preferred temporary work for a few days or weeks, mainly on construction.

A few of the youngsters of this group were in severe conflict with their families and, from time to time, stayed away from their homes for several days or weeks.

Membership list of KS-I

'Core' Group	
	1. Abbi
	2. Avner
	3. Avish g/4
	4. Adi g/2/3/4
	5. Aron g/3/4

'Regulars'	
	6. Ofir g/2
	7. Uri
	8. Achi g/2
	9. Eli g/2
	10. Elisha
	11. Eliezer g/3
	12. Amnon g/3/4
	13. Amitai g/2
	14. Assaf
	15. Ephraim g/2/3/4

'Fringe' Members	
	16. Arnon
	17. Itai
	18. Etnan
	19. Binyamin
	20. Boaz
	21. Baruch

Personal profiles of members of Group I

ABBI

Personal. Born 1947 in Israel. Second oldest child. Attended elementary school, failed in high school. Bright, strong, good talker. Brother: Didya (Group IV).
Delinquency. Vandalism, brawling, a few motorbike thefts, gambling. Police record for gambling, assault.

Family. Immigrated pre-1948 from Egypt. 7 children. Poor but bearable living conditions. Some conflict with parents. Parents semi-literate.
Group status. Leader of positive elements. Tends to bully. Alternately well-liked and resented. Admired for daring.

Remarks. Very close relationship with worker. Worker prevented his drift into more severe delinquency, helped him improve work adjustment, improve relations with family, make fair adjustment in military service.

AVNER

Personal. Born 1947 in Israel. Attended elementary school. Fairly bright, strong.
Delinquency. Vandalism, brawling, a few motorbike thefts. Has police record for driving without licence, disorderly conduct.

Family. Immigrated pre-1948 from Syria. 7 children. Relatively well-to-do. Father building contractor. Good relations with parents.
Group status. Influential, well-liked. Respected because of high family status, ability to get jobs for others.

Remarks. Good relations with worker. Worker prevented his drift to more severe delinquency. Work adjustment good from outset. Worker helped him make good adjustment in military service.

AVSHI

Personal. Born 1947 in Tunisia. Second youngest child. Elementary school drop-out. Moody, unstable.
Delinquency. Petty theft, vehicle theft, burglary, assault, drinking, heavy use of hashish. Long police record. Probation refused. Jailed autumn 1963–spring 1964.

Family. Immigrated 1955 from Tunisia. 6 children. Extreme poverty. Parents semiliterate, religious. Father died 1958. Fairly good relations wth mother.
Group status. Leader vacillating between positive and negative elements. Well-liked.

Remarks. Worker sent him to kibbutz in summer 1964 where he stayed 2 months. Found unfit for military service. Married steady girl friend, Sabra (member of Project's girls' group) in spring 1965. Very good relation with worker. Worker helped him sort out numerous court cases, helped him improve work attitudes, reduce use of alcohol, hashish.

ADI

Personal. Born 1946 in Israel. Youngest child. Drop-out from elementary school.
Delinquency. Brawling, vandalism, petty

Family. Immigrated pre-1948 from Syria. 4 children. Parents separated, Adi lives

theft, vehicle theft, burglary, assault, incendiarism, gambling, heavy use of hashish, drinking, homosexual activities. Long police record. On probation. Short jail terms in March and November 1964.

with mother. Mother is retarded, illiterate. Extremely poor conditions. Father has police record. Conflict between siblings.

Group status. Major delinquent influence. At times well-liked at others withdrawn.

Remarks. Very close relationship with worker, but periods of evasiveness. Worker spent much time in personal counselling because of self-destructive tendencies (suicide attempt in jail). Worker helped him to improve use of probation period, prevented third jail sentence because of homosexual tendencies. Found unfit for military service. Worker counteracted his influence upon other boys. Helped him reduce hashish use, improved his work attitudes.

ARON

Personal. Born 1948 in Iraq. Second oldest child. Drop-out from elementary school. Fairly bright, strong. Homosexual tendencies.

Delinquency. Vandalism, brawling, petty theft, vehicle theft, burglary, assault, incendiarism, gambling, procuring, homosexual activities, heavy hashish user. Long police record. One year in institution at age 14. On probation.

Family. Immigrated 1949 from Iraq. 5 children. Above average lower-class living conditions. Parents semiliterate. Frequent conflict. Father politically active and criminally involved.

Group status. Major delinquent influence. Well-liked.

Remarks. Good relationship with worker. Worker helped him sort out numerous Court cases, improve use of probation period, reduce hashish use. Move of family in summer 1965 to housing project did not reduce delinquency. Worker counteracted his influence on other boys, is now trying to get him to accept military service.

OFIR

Personal. Born 1948 in Yemen. Dropped out from elementary school. Fairly bright. Homosexual tendencies.

Delinquency. Vandalism, brawling, petty theft, vehicle theft, a few incidents of procuring. Police record. Rejected by probation department.

Family. Immigrated 1949 from Yemen. 6 children. Very poor living conditions. Some conflict. Parents semiliterate, religious.

Group status. Well-liked, admired for daring.

Remarks. Friendly but somewhat distant relationship with worker. Worker helped him improve work attitudes, resolve family conflict.

URI

Personal. Born 1948 in Morocco. Attended elementary school. Fairly bright.

Delinquency. Vandalism, brawling, petty theft, vehicle theft, police record.

Family. Immigrated 1950 from Morocco. 5 children. Very poor living conditions. Some conflict. Parents semiliterate.

Group status. Well-liked. positive influence in group.
Remarks. Very good relationship with worker. Worker prevented drift to more serious delinquency, helped him improve work attitudes.

ACHI

Personal. Born 1949 in Israel. Attended elementary school. Fairly bright
Delinquency. Vandalism, theft. No police record.

Family. Immigrated pre-1948 from Iraq. 4 children. Father died in 1964. Very poor living conditions. Parents semiliterate. Conflict with family.
Group status. Not fully accepted, exploited. Ribbed because he once dyed hair blond. Some respect because of success with girls.

Remarks. Very close relationship with worker. Worker succeeded in stopping his delinquency, improving his work attitudes, improving relations with family. Rejected for military service.

ELI

Personal. Born 1949 in Israel. Drop-out from elementary school. Low intelligence. Very strong.
Delinquency. Brawling, molesting women, vehicle theft. Police record. On probation.

Family. Immigrated 1949 from Yemen. 8 children. Very poor living conditions. Parents semiliterate, religious. Father chronically ill, some conflict with parents.
Group status. Not accepted in group until he participated in vehicle theft. Low status.

Remarks. Overdependent relationship with worker. Worker supported his interest in sports, stopped his delinquency, improved his work attitudes.

ELISHA

Personal. Born 1947 in Morocco. Attended elementary school. Fairly bright. Homosexual tendencies.
Delinquency. Vandalism, petty theft, vehicle theft, gambling, drinking, hashish. No police record.

Family. Immigrated in 1952 from Morocco. Poor living conditions. 10 children. Parents semiliterate, religious. Conflict with parents.
Group status. Low status. Sometimes exploited.

Remarks. Good relationship with worker. Worker helped him stop delinquency homosexual activities, improve work attitudes, improve relationships with family. Worker enabled him to make good adjustment in military service.

ELIEZER

Personal. Born 1948 in Morocco. Attended elementary school Fairly bright.
Delinquency. Petty theft, vehicle theft, forging of checks. Police record. Probation.

Family. Immigrated 1950 from Morocco. 5 children. Poor but bearable living conditions. Good relations. Parents semiliterate.

Group status. Well-liked but no influence.

Remarks. Very close relationship with worker. Worker prevented deeper involvement in delinquency, improved his work attitude, helped him use probation period constructively.

AMNON

Personal. Born 1947 in Israel. Drop-out from elementary school. Low intelligence.
Delinquency. Vandalism, brawling, petty theft, vehicle theft, burglary, hashish. Police record, probation.

Family. Immigrated pre-1949 from Iraq. 6 children. Very poor living conditions. Father drinks. Parents semiliterate. Conflict with parents.
Group status. Well-liked. Very active in delinquency activities.

Remarks. Tenuous relationship with worker. Stayed evasive and distrustful. Worker helped him in Court, co-operated with probation officer. Found unfit for military service.

AMITAI

Personal. Born 1949 in Tunisia. Drop-out from elementary school. Fairly bright.
Delinquency. Vandalism, brawling, petty theft, assault, vehicle theft, burglary, assault, gambling, drinking, hashish use. In institution summer 1962–summer 1964. Police record.

Family. Immigrated 1950 from Tunisia. 5 children. Poor living conditions. Parents semi-literate.
Group status. Well-liked. Active in delinquent activities.

Remarks. Very close relationship with worker. Worker returned him repeatedly to institution on runaways. Worker helped him improve work attitude, improve family relations, reduce frequency and severity of delinquent involvements.

ASSAF

Personal. Born 1950 in Israel. Drop-out from elementary school. Fairly bright.
Delinquency. Vandalism, petty theft, brawling, vehicle theft, burglary. In institution summer 1962–spring 1964. Police record.

Family. Israeli of Oriental descent. Father dead. Poor living conditions. Parents semi-literate. 10 children. Some conflict with family.
Group status. Well-liked but without influence, at times exploited.

Remarks. Friendly but tenuous relationship with worker. Worker helped him improve work attitudes, returned him repeatedly to institution on runaways, reduced his delinquency to some extent.

EPHRAIM

Personal. Born in 1949 in Iraq. Drop-out from elementary school. Weak, of low intelligence.

Family. Immigrated 1950 from Iraq. 4 children. Stepfather. Parents illiterate, reli-

Delinquency. Petty theft, burglary, police record, probation.

gious. Very poor living conditions. Severe conflict with parents.
Group status. Very low status scapegoat, exploited. Suspected of being police informer.

Remarks. Very few resources. Worker protected him against scapegoating, improved his work attitudes to some extent.

ARNON

Personal. Born 1948 in Israel. Attended elementary school. Fairly bright.
Delinquency. Brawling, vandalism, a few motorbike thefts. No police record.

Family. Israeli of Oriental descent. 5 children. Poor but bearable living conditions. Some conflict with parents.
Group status. Well-liked and respected, but somewhat detached.

Remarks. Very good relationship with worker. Worker encouraged his detachment from group, prevented his involvement in delinquency, helped him improve work attitudes, improve family relations.

ITAI

Personal. Born 1948 in Israel. Attended elementary school. Fairly intelligent. Strong.
Delinquency. Only mild mischief. No police record.

Family. Immigrated from Yemen in 1941. 9 children. Good relations. Parents semi-literate, religious. Poor living conditions.
Group status. Well-liked but not fully accepted, because he does not participate in delinquent activities.

Remarks. Very good relationship with worker. Worker supported his interest in sports, prevented his participation in delinquent activities, helped him improve work attitudes. Worker enabled him to get driver's licence and helped him make good adjustment in military service.

ETNAN

Personal. Born 1948 in Morocco. Drop-out from elementary school. Low intelligence, very talkative. Homosexual tendencies.
Delinquency. Petty theft, vandalism, brawling, gambling, hashish use. No police record.

Family. Immigrated 1952 from Morocco. 5 children. No parents, lives with relatives. Very poor living conditions.
Group status. Low status, liked but considered 'crazy' because of exaggerated stories. Branded a coward, exploited.

Remarks. Good relationship with worker. Worker helped him detach himself from group, stop delinquent behaviour, improve work attitudes. Found unfit for military service.

BINYAMIN

Personal. Born 1947 in Israel. Drop-out from elementary school. Fairly bright. Very strong.
Delinquency. Petty theft, brawling, a few motorbike thefts. No police record.

Family. Immigrated pre-1948 from Yemen. 6 children. Father drinks, gambles heavily. Poor but bearable living conditions. Some conflict with parents.
Group status. Well-liked and respected but not fully accepted because he does not participate in delinquent activities of Group.

Remarks. Very good relationship with worker. Worker stopped his delinquency, helped him improve work attitudes. Worker was instrumental in boy's volunteering for Parachutists, making good adjustment in military service.

BOAZ

Personal. Born 1948 in Israel. Attended elementary school. Above average intelligence.
Delinquency. A few motorbike thefts. No police record.

Family. Immigrated pre-1948 from Egypt. 4 children. Good relations. Poor but bearable living conditions.
Group status. Well-liked because of musical talent (plays guitar at parties), but not accepted because he does not participate in delinquent activities.

Remarks. Good relationship with worker. Worker helped him resist pressures to participate in delinquency, supported his interest in music. Worker helped him make good adjustment in military service.

BARUCH

Personal. Born 1947 in Egypt. Drop-out from elementary school. Low intelligence. Strong homosexual activities.
Delinquency. Homosexual involvements, hashish use and peddling, theft. No police record.

Family. Immigrated 1950 from Egypt. 7 children. Poor living conditions. Father involved in hashish peddling. Conflict with parents.
Group status. Accepted because of hashish connections but treated with contempt, exploited. Tends to carry out delinquent activities alone.

Remarks. Worker unable to form relationship, as boy is very evasive, distrustful. Worker has protected him at times from exploitation and helped him obtain jobs. Found unfit for military service.

Structure of Group I
This group tended to subdivide into two factions which we shall call the 'Mischief-makers' and the 'Thieves'. We chose these labels in order to distinguish between those youngsters in the group who were mainly engaged in brawling, vandalism and illicit adventurous ways of having fun, and those

youngsters who were involved in more serious delinquent behaviour, mainly concentrating on various forms of theft. There are several points which must be clearly understood, in order to avoid misconceptions: (*a*) When we distinguish between the delinquent involvements of the two factions we are speaking of *dominant trends*. We do *not* mean to imply that the Mischief-makers never steal, or that the Thieves do not, on occasion, brawl or exhibit vandalistic behaviour. (*b*) We are speaking of *one group*, the subdivisions we describe are significant, but they are not rigid and static. Many of the youngsters fluctuate back and forth between the two factions, and the two subgroupings have been known to draw close together or move apart according to the situation and the pressures of the moment. (*c*) Adherence to the *group norms* may show differences in emphasis in the two factions, but *all* members of the group share these norms to at least some degree.

Leadership of the group was centred on five of the Core Group boys: Abbi, Avner, Avshi, Aron and Adi. Of these Abbi was by far the outstanding personality of the group.

Abbi led the Mischief-makers, aided by Avner who acted as a sort of lieutenant and was his close friend. These two boys were among the more intelligent members of the group. Avner's interest in the group and his need to lead seemed much less pronounced than Abbi's. The latter sought to dominate the group and persistently, though not always successfully, asserted his leadership. His followers were on the whole, the less delinquent boys, but even among these there were many who resented his leadership, openly rejecting or evading his dominance, because of Abbi's tendency to bully and exploit others. Avner was well-liked and respected because he would readily fight, but had no need to push others around, and because his family was relatively well-to-do and he often prevailed upon his father (a building contractor) to provide members of the group with a few days' work.

The Avshi-Adi-Aron clique resented Abbi's leadership. This trio of youngsters led the more delinquent faction of the group, the ones we call the 'Thieves'. In contrast to Abbi's aggressive, active bid for leadership, Avshi, Adi and Aron made no special efforts to influence or sway the group. Their influence was based on the intensity of their involvement in delinquent activities, the key position they held in all matters regarding the more serious forms of delinquent behaviour.

Hashish smoking was a major factor in determining allegiance to one or the other faction of the group. Avshi, Adi and Aron, who were heavy users, formed the nucleus of those boys in the group who were involved in use, purchasing and peddling of hashish. The trio also took the lead in maintaining relationships focused upon hashish use with the 'seniors' of Group IV. The habitual use of hashish (*not* an occasional smoking session) constituted the one norm on which the group seemed clearly divided. Abbi and Avner's followers openly rejected the habitual use of hashish. The Avshi-Adi-Aron faction prided themselves in their skill and sophistication in the use of the weed. (However, even these boys admitted individually that hashish 'is bad for you', and explained the excessive smoking with being desperate, having lost all hope, or having been led to the habit by others.)

The personal friendship or patronage of the leaders, or their antagonism towards a particular youngster often determined the degree to which a boy was accepted in the group. Itai and Arnon were tied to the group mainly by their friendship to Abbi and Avner. However, they remained on the fringe and gradually drifted away during the second half of the eighteen months work period. Eli was feared and admired because of his great physical strength, but remained on the fringe for a long time, mainly because he avoided involvement in *any* kind of delinquent activities. Abbi was openly hostile to this boy, because he saw in Eli's physical strength a threat to his own status which was largely based upon his reputation as a fighter. Abbi's influence on the group was, at least partly, responsible for Eli's failure to establish friendship relationships with any of the other youngsters. (He was friendly with Assaf for a while, but eventually the latter acceded to group pressure and broke off relations with him.) However, Eli's situation changed markedly when he was caught stealing a motor-cycle. The theft gained him some recognition with the leaders of the Thieves, and even Abbi acknowledged that he had become 'one of the gang'.

Among the Regulars, Amnon held the highest status and was closest to the trio which led the Thieves. Amnon was something of a special case. He is a somewhat withdrawn boy and the fact that he was 'in' with the leadership clique of the Thieves seemed to have been mainly due to the fact that he was the group's main source-of-supply for hashish. His closest friendship ties were with two members of the 'Seniors' (Group IV), with whom he 'smoked' regularly. Elisha and Ephraim ranked lowest in status, often became the scapegoats of the group, were teased and exploited in various ways but can still be considered as regulars. Elisha, nicknamed 'the Moroccan', came in for some derisive remarks about his North African origin. He was known to have had homosexual contacts. Ephraim is a somewhat retarded boy who was also known as 'Nanousseh', the 'little runt'. While Elisha was generally liked, Ephraim was treated with contempt and tended to seek the company of the younger boys of Group II.

Despite the frequent tension and rivalry between the leaders of the Mischief-makers and the leaders of the Thieves, there was also much friendly interaction between these youngsters. They lent each other money, went on trips together and were often seen in each other's company. While the leaders of the Thieves held the record in delinquent activities, they did not necessarily carry out most of their thefts together, but often 'pulled a job' with other members of the group or with members of Group III. Of the three leaders of the Thieves, Avshi enjoyed the highest status in the group, but Adi and Aron interacted more frequently and intensively with other members of the group. These two boys had homosexual relations with each other. Aron also had homosexual relations with Ofir and with a Group II youngster (Guni).

Ofir, Assaf, Ephraim, Uri and Amitai vacillated between the two factions of the group. Amitai and Assaf were confined to a closed institution when the street club worker contacted the group. They were released about half a year after the start of the eighteen months work period, and although they had been members of the group before their commitment, found it difficult to establish relationships with the other youngsters. However, both youngsters finally found their place in the group. Amitai maintained his connections with the institution, and became a sort of a leader of the youngsters who were given home leave and came to the neighbourhood to visit him. Assaf formed a close friendship clique with Ofir and Uri.

Achi tried very hard to become accepted by the leaders of the Thieves and became the object of derision when he asked to be 'taught' the use of hashish.

Eliezer drew closer to Arnon when the latter's family moved out of the neighbourhood. Unlike Arnon, however, who began to drift away from the group, Eliezer returned to the neighbourhood regularly. He was one of Abbi's followers in the beginning, but gradually came under the influence of the leaders of the Thieves.

Etnan, Binyamin, Boaz and Baruch were fringe members of the group. Neither Etnan nor Binyamin were involved in serious delinquent activities, Although Etnan had some homosexual contacts with Elisha. Both boys remained outsiders, but while no one seemed to care particularly about Etnan, the group was more than willing to accept Binyamin because of his physical strength and his easy-going, likeable manners. However, this youngster resisted the attempts of the group to draw him in. He had his own friends outside the group and remained aloof, but was interested enough in the goings-on to hang around frequently.

Boaz came to play his guitar at parties given by the group, but it is doubtful whether he can even be considered a member. However, he had sufficient contact with the group and showed enough interest in their activities to be considered part of the fringe.

Baruch ranked lowest in status in the group. The low regard the group had for this boy may be partly due to the low status of his family, but it is more likely due to the fact that this is an evasive 'strange' boy who has difficulties in establishing relationships with his peers and exhibits behaviour which may indicate serious emotional disturbance. His father is known to sell hashish, and the youngester is a heavy user, but tends to smoke in isolation from others. His only tie to the group seemed to be superficial relationship with Assaf whom he met in the institution to which they were both committed. Baruch has been ribbed by the youngsters for having homosexual relations with adults.

In terms of the Cloward and Ohlin categories of delinquent subculture, Group I can be described as a Thieves Group with retreatist tendencies.

GROUP II

This is a small group of five fourteen- to sixteen-year-old boys. These youngsters hang around the periphery of Group I and can be regarded as a sort of 'satellite' group of the former. However, the youngsters of Group I do not, on the whole, interact closely with the boys of Group II as the latter are identified as a low status group by Group I boys.

This small group of youngsters appeared to be united primarily by their shared interest in, and rejection by Group I, rather than by group interests and goals of their own. The youngsters rate 'low' on delinquency in comparison with Group I, but showed a tendency to let themselves be exploited for a variety of services and delinquent activities by the latter. At times these youngsters were treated with considerable hostility and contempt by the Group I boys. One of the youngsters (Guni) was known to be easily accessible to homosexual advances, another boy (Gidon) was suspected of being a stool-pigeon (police informer).

Work adjustment in this group was very poor.

Membership List of KS-II
　　　　　　　　1.　Gavi g/1
　　　　　　　　2.　Gad g/1

3. Gidon g/1
4. Guni g/1
5. Gilad g/1

Personal profiles of members of KS-II

GAVI

Personal. Born 1950 in Israel. Drop-out from elementary school. Very low intelligence.
Delinquency. Petty theft, peddling without licence. Police record.

Family. Immigrated 1949 from Yemen. 8 children. Extreme poverty. Conflict. Parents illiterate, religious. Several siblings mentally retarded.
Group status. Very low status, bullied, severely exploited.

Remarks. Very close, over-dependent relationship with worker. Worker stopped his exploitation by Group I boys, got him a suitable job, improved his relationship with family.

GAD

Personal. Born 1950 in Israel. Attended elementary school. Fairly bright. Brother Dani in Group III.
Delinquency. Petty thefts, vehicle theft, police record. Rejected by probation service.

Family. Immigrated 1949 from Yemen. 7 children. Poor living conditions. Parents semi-literate, religious. Conflict with parents.
Group status. Well-liked, occasionally exploited by Group I boys.

Remarks. Good relationship with worker. Hero-worships brother Dani (Group III) who is motor-bike stunt champion of neighbourhood. Worker helped him improve work attitude, stop delinquency, improve relations with family, get away from influence of Group I.

GIDON

Personal. Born 1950 in Israel. Drop-out from elementary school. Fairly bright. Brother Chushi in Group III.
Delinquency. Petty theft, vandalism, vehicle theft, police record.

Family. Immigrated pre-1948 from Yemen. 7 children, poor but bearable living conditions. Notorious criminal family. Sisters are prostitutes. Conflict with parents.
Group status. Well-liked, occasionally exploited by Group I.

Remarks. Good relationship with worker. Worker co-operated with stable oldest brother in stopping boy's delinquency, improving his work attitudes. Worker got him away from influence of Group I.

GUNI

Personal. Born 1950 in Israel. Drop-out from elementary school. Strong homosexual tendencies. Low intelligence.

Family. Immigrated from Greece 1949. 4 children. Very poor living conditions. Severe

Delinquency. Petty theft, vehicle theft, bur- conflict with parents. Parents
glary, homosexual contacts. Institution in semiliterate.
1961. 9 months jail in 1965. Hashish user, **Group status.** Treated with
habitual gambler. contempt. Subject of severe
homosexual exploitation.

Remarks. Evasive, tenuous relationship with worker. Worker reduced homosexual exploitation by older boys, somewhat improved working attitude. Jail
sentence prevented further work. Boy attempted suicide in jail. Worker co-
operated with prison social worker in attempt at therapy.

GILAD

Personal. Born 1948 in Israel. Drop-out **Family.** Immigrated pre-1948
from elementary school. Some homosexual from Syria. 8 children. Parents
contacts. Brother Chasai in Group II. Fairly semiliterate. Poor living condi-
bright, strong. tions. Conflict with parents.
Delinquency. Vandalism, brawling, petty **Group status.** Well-liked, but
theft, vehicle theft, burglary, peddling with- keeps somewhat aloof from
out license. Police record. Probation. others.

Remarks. Very good relationship with worker. Worker instrumental in preventing second jail sentence in 1965. Worker helped him reduce delinquency,
improve work habits, improve literacy. In co-operation with probation officer,
worker sent him to Kibbutz in summer 1965.

Structure of Group II

As already stated, these five youngsters can hardly be called a group, but are
rather a small clique hanging around the fringe of Group I. They appeared
somewhat different from the rest of their peers in Group I, in that they were on
the whole less daring and weaker, some of them (especially Gavi, Guni and
Gidon) of lower-than-average intelligence. These boys seemed closest in 'type'
to Ephraim and Eli of Group I and, during the beginning phase of the eighteen
months work period, these two youngsters were indeed closely associated with
them.

The Group II boys essentially appeared to be 'loners', unable to establish
normal peer-relationships, but drawn to each other and to Group I. Gidon and
Gad formed a friendship pair and so did Guni and Gilad, while Gavi remained
something of an isolate. Even the relations between the friendship pairs were
tenuous. It is interesting to note that Guni, who was a willing passive partner in
homosexual relations with Group I youngsters, had no such relationship with
his closest friend Gilad. Almost all these boys were in contact with youngsters in
other areas and some of them had on occasions taken off to wander round the
country by themselves, a form of behaviour rarely encountered among the other
street corner youth of the neighbourhood.

GROUP III

This group is known as the 'G. Gang' throughout the city. According to the
story prevalent in the community the name is derived from a Detective-
Sergeant G. who gave these youngsters his special attention.

The group consists of seventeen youngsters in the sixteen to nineteen age
range. The group was already known as highly delinquent when we first contacted it. The boys engaged mainly in vehicle theft and burglary. Members of

the group carried out burglary sprees with stolen cars which led them to several towns and cities throughout the country. Several members had worked as procurers. A few delinquent girls were 'hanging out' with this group for some time, engaging in promiscuous sexual activities with members of the group and, on at least one occasion, participating in a burglary spree with a stolen car. Work adjustment in the group was extremely poor.

During April and May 1964, while the relationship with the street club worker was still in its beginning state, about two-thirds of the group's members were arrested and jailed for periods ranging from three to eighteen months. The girls disappeared at this time, and contact between them and the street club worker ceased.

The worker maintained contact with the jailed youngsters and with the scattered remnants of the group. We resumed work with the group when it reorganised on the release of most of the imprisoned boys. Some of the youngsters stopped their delinquent activities temporarily after their release from jail, others 'specialised' in procuring.

Toward the end of the eighteen months work period several of the group's members reorganised themselves into a tightly knit group of six. These youngsters (David, Gammi, Hillel, Chanock, Zachai and Chaz) returned to severely delinquent behaviour, mainly vehicle theft and burglary. They adopted a provokingly 'different' kind of dress, some of them carried knives and one was seen carrying a gun. Their behaviour has come to resemble the typical swagger and belligerence of the fighting gang, although theft remains the focus of their interest.

Membership of KS-III

'Core' Group :	1. Gami
	2. Gershon
	3. David
'Regulars' :	4. Dani g/4
	5. Hillel
	6. Zev
	7. Zavdi
	8. Zabul g/2/4
	9. Zachai
	10. Zera g/1/2/4
	11. Chagai g/1/4
	12. Chushi
	13. Chazai
	14. Chanoch
'Fringe' members :	15. Chanan g/4
	16. Kinan
	17. Chas g/1

Personal prolfies of members of Group III

GAMMI

Personal. Born 1948 in Israel. Drop-out from elementary school. Fairly bright, strong. Emotionally unstable.

Family. Immigrated pre-1948 from Egypt. 8 children. Father died 1965, unexpectedly left

Delinquency. Vandalism, petty theft, brawling, vehicle theft, burglary. Prison Apr. to Dec. 1965.

money. Very poor living conditions improved. Severe conflict with parents.

Group status. Leader. Well-liked, admired because of daring and skill in delinquency.

Remarks. Very good relationship with worker. Worker maintained contact with him in prison. Worker attempts to continue work with him after release from jail. Found unfit for military service.

GERSHON

Personal. Born 1947 in Israel. Attended elementary school, fairly bright, weak.

Delinquency. Brawling, petty theft, vehicle theft, burglary, hashish use, gambling. Prison Apr. to Dec. 1964.

Family. See brother Gilad of Group II.

Group status. Well-liked, member of leadership clique.

Remarks. Good relationship with worker. Worker co-operated closely with probation officer after release from jail, helped boy improve work adjustment, reduce delinquency. Steady girl friend caused him to leave group. Found unfit for military service.

DAVID

Personal. Born 1946 in Egypt. Drop-out from elementary school. Bright, strong, aggressive boy.

Delinquency. Brawling, assault, petty theft, vandalism, burglary, vehicle theft. Prison May 1964 to Sept. 1965. Carried gun.

Family. Immigrated 1953 from Egypt. 10 children. Bearable living conditions, but very neglected. Conflict with parents.

Group status. Leader. Not very popular, but admired and respected for daring, skill in delinquency and expert driving.

Remarks. Worker failed in attempts to establish relationship. Married after release from jail under pressure of family, marriage unsuccessful. Found unfit for military service.

DANI

Personal. Born 1947 in Yemen. Attended elementary school. Bright, strong.

Delinquency. Petty theft, vandalism, brawling, vehicle theft. Prison Dec. 1963 to Jan. 1966. Jailed again in autumn 1965.

Family. See brother Gad of Group II.

Group status. Very well-liked, admired as daring stunt rider on motor-bikes.

Remarks. Good relationship with worker after release from first prison sentence. Worker helped him obtain job, but could not counteract obsession with motor-bikes. Found unfit for military service.

HILLEL

Personal. Born 1946 in Israel. Drop-out from elementary school. Bright, handsome.

Delinquency. Brawling, vandalism, petty

Family. Immigrated pre-1948 from Egypt. 3 children. Bulgarian step-father. Real father theft, burglary, vehicle theft, gambling, hashish use, drinking, procuring. Prison Apr. 1964 to Apr. 1965.

killed in War of Independence. Extreme conflict with family. Poor but bearable living conditions.
Group status. Well-liked, influential. Provided girls for group.

Remarks. Friendly but tenuous relationship with worker. Worker failed in attempt to improve family relations. Boy became full-time procurer. Found unfit for military service.

ZEV

Personal. Born 1945 in Israel. Attended elementary school. Fairly bright.
Delinquency. Petty theft, vehicle theft, gambling. Probation in 1964.

Family. Israelis of Oriental descent. 3 children. Poor but bearable living conditions. Father gambles. Good relations with parents.
Group status. Well-liked but without influence. Easily followed lead of others.

Remarks. Very good relationship with worker. Worker prevented jail sentence, obtained probation for him. Worker helped him use probation period constructively, helped him improve work attitudes, stop delinquency. Married end of 1965, left neighbourhood. Found unfit for military service.

ZAVAI

Personal. Born 1945 in Israel. Drop-out from elementary school. Low intelligence. Very strong.
Delinquency. Brawling, vandalism, petty theft. Probation in 1964.

Family. Immigrated pre-1948 from Egypt. 6 children. Poor living conditions. Good relations with parents.
Group status. Very well-liked, admired because of physical strength, but no influence because of slowness.

Remarks. Very good relationship with worker. Worker was instrumental in obtaining probation instead of jail sentence. Worker helped him improve work attitudes, reduce delinquency, helped him make good adjustment in military service.

ZABUL

Personal. Born 1945 in Iraq. Drop-out from elementary school. Has disfigured face. Low intelligence. Some homosexual tendencies.
Relinqency. Petty theft, burglary, vehicle theft, hashish use. Prison Apr. 1964 to Sept. 1964.

Family. Immigrated 1950 from Iraq. 5 children. Father deserted. Poor living conditions.
Group status. Low status, but admired for skill with cars. Suspected of being informer in jail.

Remarks. Good relationship with worker. Worker helped him avoid delinquent involvements with group after release from jail, helped him make good work adjustment. Found unfit for military service.

ZACHAI

Personal. Born 1946 in Israel. Drop-out from elementary school, fairly bright.
Delinquency. Petty theft, burglary, hashish use, procuring. Prison Apr. 1964 to Dec. 1964.

Family. Immigrated pre-1948 from Yemen. 6 children. Very poor living conditions. Father drinks heavily. Conflict with parents.
Group status. Well-liked. Influential.

Remarks. Evasive, tenuous relationship with worker. Found unfit for military service. Continued heavy involvement in delinquency.

ZERA

Personal. Born 1948 in Israel. Attended elementary school, failed in vocational high school. Fairly bright, aggressive.
Delinquency. Brawling, vandalism, petty theft, vehicle theft, burglary, hashish.

Family. Immigrated in thirties from Turkey. 3 children. Better than average lower-class living conditions. Some conflict with parents.
Group status. Well-liked but without influence.

Remarks. Good relationship with worker. Worker helped him get suspended sentence instead of jail in Apr. 1964. Helped him reduce delinquency, hashish use, helped him improve work habits. Delinquency increased when most members of Group were released from jail in 1965. Worker helped him get probation instead of jail sentence in autumn 1965, has made fairly good adjustment since. Found unfit for military service.

CHAGAI

Personal. Born 1946 in Israel. Drop-out from elementary school. Bright, strong. Aggressive, bad-tempered. Some homosexual tendencies. Very manipulative. Sensitive about his dark skin and very verbal about ethnic discrimination. Brother of Yabal of Group IV.
Delinquency. Vandalism, brawling, petty theft, burglary, vehicle theft, assault, hashish use, rape, incendiarism. In prison 3 times between Jan. 1964 and Dec. 1965.

Family. Israelis of Oriental descent. Known for criminal reputation dating back to days of British Mandate. Poor but bearable living conditions. Leading family of deviant elements in neighbourhood. Fairly good relations with parents. 5 children.
Group status. Respected because of family connections but treated with derision because of frantic involvement in delinquency and bizarre eagerness to admit to police everything he did and did not do. Known as manipulator and liar.

Remarks. Tenuous relationship with worker because of boy's constant attempts to exploit and manipulate. Worker co-operated with brother in trying to prevent his greatest excesses, but without success. Found unfit for military service.

CHOSHI

Personal. Born 1945 in Egypt. Drop-out from elementary school. Weak, unstable, fairly bright.
Delinquency. Petty theft, hashish use. Prison Apr. 1964 to May 1965.

Family. Immigrated from Egypt in 1949. 4 children. Some conflict with parents. Above average lower class living conditions.
Group status. Unpopular, suspected of having informed on other boys.

Remarks. Friendly but tenuous relationship with worker. Worker co-operated with probation service after his release from prison, helped him to get job, keep away from group. Found unfit for military service. Worker counter-acted his influence on Boys of Groups I and II.

CHAZAI

Personal. Born 1947 in Israel. Drop-out from elementary school. Weak, extremely unstable. 9 months in mental hospital in 1964 (diagnosed acute schizophrenic).
Delinquency. Petty theft, burglary, procuring, selling stolen goods. 6 months jail sentence in summer 1965.

Family. Immigrated from Yemen pre-1948. 5 children. Boy does not live at home. Very poor living conditions. Parents illiterate.
Group status. Very low status because he is considered 'crazy', but liked and exploited. His room is used as group's hang-out.

Remarks. Friendly but very superficial relationship with worker. Worker most concerned with counteracting use of his room by younger boys. Found unfit for military service.

CHANOCH

Personal. Born 1947 in Turkey. Drop-out from elementary school. Low intelligence. Homosexual tendencies.
Delinquency. Petty theft, vandalism, burglary, vehicle theft, hashish use, homosexual activities. Prison Apr. 1964 to Apr. 1965. Procuring after release.

Family. Immigrated from Turkey 1950. 4 children. Extreme poverty. Both parents sick, father in his eighties. (Social Work Department helped older sister to become nurse.)
Group status. Very low status, laughed at because of sodomy with donkey.

Remarks. Worker did not succeed in establishing working relationship after his attempt to get probation for boy in Apr. 1964 failed. Found unfit for military service.

CHANAN

Personal. Born 1945 in Egypt. Drop-out from elementary school. Bright, strong. Some homosexual tendencies.
Delinquency. Brawling, assault, vehicle theft, some hashish use.

Family. Immigrated pre-1948 from Egypt. 10 children, very aged parents, semiliterate. Good relations with parents. Poor living conditions.

Group status. Well-liked, leader, respected because of reputation as fighter, great skill as delinquent in past, friendship with leaders of Group IV.

Remarks. Good relations with worker. Worker helped him with employment, enlisted his co-operation in counteracting delinquency of younger boys, help organise sports events. Found unfit for military service.

KINAN

Personal. Born 1946 in Israel. Attended elementary school. Fairly bright.
Delinquency. Petty theft, vandalism, gambling.

Family. Immigrated from Yemen pre-1948. Very poor living conditions. 8 children. Parents semiliterate. Conflict with parents.
Group status. Well-liked but not fully accepted because he does not participate in serious delinquent activities. Laughed at because he stole toys and games from youth centre.

Remarks. Good relationship with worker. No need for concern over delinquency, but this boy lives as a vagabond, absolutely refuses to work, gets handouts from all relatives and friends. Found unfit for military service.

CHAS

Personal. Born 1946 in Iran. Attended elementary school. Fairly bright, somewhat withdrawn.
Delinquency. Petty theft, burglary, vehicle theft. Arrested for burglary when on Army leave in 1964. Probation.

Family. No details known.
Group status. Remained outsider, of no influence.

Remarks. Good relationship with worker. Worker helped him obtain probation, kept him out of delinquency involvements and helped him make work adjustment. Discharged as undesirable by Army.

Structure of Group III

The leadership of this group consisted of a tight little clique of highly delinquent youngsters (Gammi, Gershon and David). Among these three, Gammi held the highest status for skill and daring as a thief, but was the least popular among the rank and file of the group, who found it easier to relate to Gershon and David, and admired the latter because his family was relatively well-to-do and cared enough for the boy to get him a lawyer whenever he was in trouble with the police. A fourth youngster, Chanan equalled the leadership trio in status in a curious way. This youngster remained on the fringe of the group. He did not participate in delinquent activities and remained somewhat detached from the social life of the group, but was highly respected, partly because of his physical strength, and partly because he could call upon the help of a large and feared family. (Two relatives of Channan, Chushi and Zavdi were members of KS-III). Chanan also had considerable influence in Group I and was liked and respected by the 'Seniors' of Group IV. It is interesting to note that Chanan never emphasised the fact that he did not participate in serious delinquent activities, but always asserted that he had, in the past, established his reputation as a daring and inventive thief.

Zev and Zavdi were popular, easygoing boys, well-liked in the group although not highly delinquent. Both boys went along with other group members on a 'job' from time to time 'to help out a friend', rather than because of their own need to steal.

Among the regulars, Hillel and Chushi ranked highest in status. Hillel especially impressed the group with his good looks and his success with girls. Chushi, Chagai, Zera and Zabul seemed to vie with the leadership clique in daring and frequent delinquent activities and made a determined bid to compete with the latter for the leadership of the group. Gershon failed in his attempts to prove himself as a rough and highly delinquent boy. He eventually drifted to the fringe of the group and sought acceptance with the youngsters of Group I. For a while he made frantic attempts to gain recognition and became known as being ready to 'pull a job' any time, anywhere, with anyone. He accumulated a record number of police charges, but this did not earn him the coveted status. On the contrary, the boys laughed at him because of his hectic and senseless activities. This boy also is a member of a large and powerful family (his older brother is Yabal, of the 'Seniors') and the youngsters of the Shkunah avoid conflict with him because of this.

Zera was mainly a 'follower', well-liked, but of relatively low status. Chushi turned informer when the police rounded up the gang in April 1964. The boys threatened to 'get even with him', but his relatives Chanan and Zavdi announced that, because of their kinship they felt obliged to protect him. As no one wanted to tangle with Chanan and his numerous brothers and cousins, Chushi remained unharmed, but was shunned by the others. His family moved to another area shortly after the arrests. He returned to the neighbourhood from time to time, but did not manage to regain acceptance. Zabul was considered unreliable, mainly because of his excessive use of hashish, but was respected for his remarkable skill in handling (and stealing) cars.

Chazai and Chanoch were the two youngsters in the group who showed the highest degree of pathology. Characteristically they were both exploited and held in low regard. Chazai had a history of mental disorder and was a quiet, withdrawn boy. The group tolerated him mainly because he had his own room which served as a hang-out for the group. Although the 'top-delinquents' of the group planned their exploits in Chazai's room and often met there to smoke hashish and sleep after a 'job', the boy was not often taken along. He sought acceptance among the youngsters of Group I who let him participate in their exploits from time to time.

Chanoch was the butt of the group's jokes and was ribbed severely and frequently because he had been observed committing sodomy with a donkey.

Kinan, another low-status boy, was tolerated, but derided because he had lost face by stooping to stealing toys from the local youth club. He was henceforth known as a 'stealer-of-toys'.

Group III was mainly a 'Thieves group with some retreatist tendencies before the arrests of April/May 1964. The situation at the end of the eighteen months work period is not clear, but the reorganised group has apparently added some 'conflict' (fighting gang) characteristics to their basic orientation.

GROUP IV

This group is the leading one among the street corner groups of the neighbourhood. Its members have the highest prestige and are the most feared and respected among the street corner youth. This group consists of nine members, ranging in age from eighteen to twenty-eight. The group may be regarded as the Senior group and consists actually of young adults rather than teenagers. The group had close ties to Group III before the arrests of April/May 1964. Some of the Group III boys who were not rounded up when most of the members of this group went to jail and some of the boys released from jail began to associate closely with Group IV.

This group is a loose one. The members' association is mainly based upon their nightly meetings in the 'Kicking Horse' cafe, their hashish smoking sessions and occasional group excursions to a night club in an adjacent lower class area.

The Project's street club worker encountered considerably greater difficulties in establishing relationships with this group than with the other three. At first the worker was under the impression that these young men, most of whom already had served jail sentences at the time of our first contact, had ceased or reduced their involvement in the more serious forms of delinquency. However, the worker soon began to suspect that the members of this group were continuing to commit criminal acts, but were more 'professional', more secretive and circumspect about it. The leaders of this group were found to use physical coercion and threats of violence to induce younger boys from other groups to co-operate in carrying out thefts.

Although some of the members of this group are skilled construction workers, work adjustment is generally poor.

The members of the group have girl friends of 'bad' reputation, some of them prostitutes, however these girls do not associate with the group openly in the neighbourhood and have no contact with the street club worker.

Membership of KS-IV

1. Yair
2. Yosh g/1/3
3. Yabal g/1

4. Yigal g/1
5. Yadon g/3
6. Didya g/3
7. Yuda g/1/3

8. Yoshua g/3
9. Yoav g/1/3

Personal profiles of members of KS-IV

YAIR

Personal. Born 1936 in Syria. Semiliterate. Big, quiet man.
Delinquency. Very active delinquent past, but now mainly smokes hashish.

Family. No details known. Lives by himself.
Group status. Well-liked and respected, still regarded as leader, but does not use influence.

Remarks. Keeps to himself. Friendly but very superficial relationship with worker. Found unfit for military service.

YOSH

Personal. Born 1942 in Israel. Fairly bright though illiterate. Very strong.
Delinquency. Vandalism, brawling, petty theft, assault, rape, procuring, burglary, vehicle theft, gambling, hashish use and peddling. Police record, jail and probation before 18 months work period.

Family. Immigrated from Kurdistan in the 'thirties. Large, powerful family. Much involved in criminal activities. Boy lives by himself.
Group status. Feared and respected leader, not liked. Reputation of best fighter in neighbourhood. Strong influence on all four groups.

Remarks. Worker encountered great distrust and hostility but established fairly good relationship. Yosh saw in worker threat to his leadership, avoided asking for his help, but co-operated at times with worker in reducing delinquency of younger boys. Found unfit for military service.

YABAL

Personal. Born 1940 in Israel. Fairly bright, semiliterate. Very strong. Brother of Chagai of Group III.
Delinquency. Vandalism, brawling, petty theft, assault, gambling, procuring, vehicle theft, burglary, use and peddling of hashish. Police record. Prison before 18 months work period. 18 months prison sentence summer 1965.

Family. See under Chagai, (Group III).
Group status. Leader of all groups. Feared and respected because of fighting reputation and powerful family. Well-liked.

Remarks. Very good relationship with worker. Often used his influence to help worker limit delinquency in younger groups. Frequently asked help with his own problems. Found unfit for military service.

YISAL

Personal. Born 1940 in Morocco. Bright, strong. Worked in England some years ago.
Delinquency. None in last 5 years, except hashish use.

Family. No details known. Lives by himself.
Group status. Well-liked but of no influence.

Remarks. Friendly but superficial relationship with worker. Often helpful in counteracting other Seniors' negative influence on younger boys. Helped worker organise soccer team. Found unfit for military service. Opened cafe in neighbourhood with Yosh's older brother.

YADON

Personal. Born 1945 in Israel. Attended elementary school. Fairly bright. Weak.
Delinquency. Vandalism, petty theft, burglary, hashish use. No police record.

Family. Immigrated pre-1948 from Turkey. 4 children. Poor living conditions.
Group status. Only boy in group who works. Low status, exploited.

Remarks. Friendly, but only superficial relationship with worker. Found unfit for military service.

DIDYA

Personal. Born 1944 in Egypt. Attended elementary school. Fairly bright. Strong. Brother of Abbi of Group I.
Delinquency. Vandalism, brawling, petty theft, procuring, use and peddling of hashish, gambling.

Family. See under Abbi, Group I.
Group status. Well-liked and respected.

Remarks. Fairly good relationship with worker. Co-operated with worker in attempt to reduce hashish involvement, delinquency of younger boys. Found unfit for military service.

YUDA

Personal. Born 1946 in Israel. Drop-out from elementary school. Low intelligence, strong. Somewhat withdrawn.
Delinquency. Petty theft, vehicle theft, hashish use. No police record.

Family. Immigrated pre-1948 from Iraq. 7 children. Very poor living conditions. Parents illiterate. Some conflict with parents.
Group status. Well-liked but without influence.

Remarks. Only superficial relationship with worker. Worker helped him to obtain employment. Found unfit for military service.

YOSHUA

Personal. Born 1945 in Israel. Drop-out from elementary school. Fairly bright. Weak.
Delinquency. Petty theft, vehicle theft, burglary, brawling, procuring, hashish use and peddling, gambling. 6 months in prison in 1965.

Family. Immigrated from Syria pre-1948. No other details known.
Group status. Fairly well-liked, but without influence. At times exploited by leaders.

Remarks. Only superficial relationship with worker. Found unfit for military service.

YOAV

Personal. Born 1939 in Syria. Illiterate. Low intelligence. Sickly and weak.
Delinquency. Theft, burglary. Hashish use and peddling.

Family. Immigrated pre-1948 from Syria. Father dead. Extreme poverty. Does not live at home.
Group status. Very low status, exploited and subjected to scapegoating.

Remarks. Only very superficial relationship with worker. Found unfit for military service.

Structure of Group IV
Yair, Yosh and Yabal are the undisputed leaders and authority figures not only of the seniors, but of the street corner youth of the entire neighbourhood. They

are close friends and habitually smoke hashish together. Yair, the oldest of the three, usually remains detached from the younger boys and restricts his association to Yosh and Yabal. He is good-natured, well-liked and as far as could be established, not involved in criminal activities. Yosh and Yabal assert their leadership over the neighbourhood youth openly and aggressively. Both are members of large and powerful families, both have legendary reputations as fighters and criminals. Of the two Yosh exploits and bullies the younger boys (especially the Group I youngsters) more persistently and aggressively, but also is more likely to come to their aid and fight their battles for them. Yabal is rather good-natured and less exploitative on the whole. He is well-liked and, on one occasion, all the younger boys worked for two days and two nights to build a one-room house for him (without building permit) and were rewarded with food, liquor and hashish. Of the two, Yosh was the more destructive influence. He frequently took younger boys along on thefts and burglaries, introduced them to hashish and provided prostitutes for his own group as well as for the members of Groups I and II. He has beaten the younger boys on several occasions and no one dares oppose his wishes. Yabal has been known to use force to get his way with the younger boys, but he also tends to be protective of them. Neither Yosh nor Yabal have had much success in trying to impose their will upon the high-status members of their own group, such as Didya and Yigal, nor have they proved a match for Chanan of Group III.

Yigal's main connection with the Seniors is hashish, which he smokes habitually. He runs a coffee house with Yosh's older brother and seems to refrain from delinquent activities. He and Chanan (under the street club worker's guidance) organised soccer games for the younger boys and Yigal assumed the leadership in this endeavour. Didya smokes hashish and participates in criminal activities with Yabal and Yosh. He is known as the group's 'hashish specialist' and has done some pimping. Yuda is accepted as one of the Regulars but he associates closely with youngsters of Groups I and III with whom he holds hashish-smoking sessions. He is the least intelligent of the group and is said to refrain from 'serious' stealing because he is afraid of the police. Yoshua has low status among the Regulars, but participates in criminal activities and asserts some influence upon the younger boys of the other groups.

Yadon and Yoav are the lowest status members of the group. Yadon is tolerated mainly because he is the only one who works regularly and can always be relied upon to help the others with money. On occasions he has subjected to being exploited and has been excluded from the group until he changed his mind. Yadon tried to stay away from delinquent activities, but finally succumbed to the pressure of the group, participated in car thefts and burglaries with Yasal and Yosh and was arrested. Yoav is the 'heaviest' hashish smoker of the group and his excessive use of the weed makes him an unreliable and barely tolerated hanger-on. He is said to 'do anything', no matter how degrading, for a 'fix', and he is often the butt of the group's practical jokers. On cold winter nights, however, Yoav comes into his own, because he is the 'specialist' for building bonfires around which the Seniors and some privileged younger boys gather to smoke and talk. Yoav is the only member of the Seniors whom the younger boys dare to tease and defy.

Theft and hashish are equally the focus of this group's interest, and this group can be described as a 'Thieves Group' with strong 'retreatist' tendencies.

2. Process and evaluation

The Project's street club worker had spent several months in casual contact with youngsters in the 'Lower' part of the neighbourhood when, in November 1963, he became aware of the fact that the more delinquent boys were drifting toward the 'Upper' area and becoming involved in the activities of a street corner group there. The worker began to visit this part of the neighbourhood in order to find out what was happening.

In December 1963 one of the most influential 'Lower' area street corner boys, Zev, was caught in a burglary with three members of a group known as the G. Gang (Group III). The worker's first contacts with this group of highly delinquent youngsters centred around Zev's arrest and trial.

The worker attended Zev's trial in an attempt to help the boy obtain probation, rather than be sent to prison. At the court he met a number of fourteen- to seventeen-year-old youngsters (later identified as members of Group I) and Yabal (Group IV), Zev's uncle, a young man who was pointed out to him as the leading 'strong-man' of the Upper Kfar. The worker's concern for Zev therefore provided him with an opportunity to gain the trust and co-operation of one of the leaders of the local street corner youth

Trying to contact the street corner groups and learn more about them, the worker began to frequent the Tnuva Cafe, halfway between the 'Lower' and the 'Upper' area, Izchak's Cafe and the Kicking Horse, both located in the centre of the 'Upper' area. He found that the Kicking Horse had the worst reputation of the three cafes and was frequented by the most delinquent youngsters. Generally regarded as a police detective (Balash) he was received with thinly veiled hostility and open distrust in the Kicking Horse. It took till the middle of 1964 before the worker felt that he had overcome this attitude and was welcome at the cafe. (Yabal later confessed that, though he had accepted the worker's help for Zev, he had warned all the other youngsters not to trust him.)

For a while the worker divided his attention between the 'Lower' and 'Upper' area youngsters. As it became increasingly obvious that the most severe delinquency problems were centred in the 'Upper' area groups, the project director decided (in January 1964) that the worker would gradually disengage himself in the 'Lower', and concentrate his service upon the 'Upper' area youngsters.

Although the worker's first contacts in the 'Upper' area had been with members of the G. Gang, he found it easier to further a relationship with the youngsters of Group I whom he had met at Zev's trial, and with Group II, a small satellite group on the fringes of Group I. He was greatly helped in this by Avshi, one of the core members of this group, who had many friends in the 'Lower' area and had known about the worker's activities there for some time.

It did not take long before the worker had gained a measure of acceptance in Group I. Within a few weeks of his first contact, the boys began to deluge him with a jumble of stories of their adventures, their thefts, burglaries, joy-rides in stolen vehicles, their family problems and their demands for help in obtaining employment and straightening out their pending court cases. This sometimes overwhelming and confusing onslaught of the demands for attention and help by approximately twenty problem-ridden youngsters continued at a steady pace for over a year and only began to slow down towards the end of the eighteen months work period, in the spring of 1965. At first the main function assigned to the worker by the youngsters of this group was that of 'sympathetic listener'. There was so much the boys had to tell and ask and discuss, that the worker was rarely able to extricate himself before midnight in order to go home and get some sleep.

Toward the end of the first six months period with Group I the worker made an attempt to refer the group to the local youth club, run jointly by Noar Oved (a labour-oriented youth organisation) and GADNA. This attempt failed. The youngsters told him that they had visited the club for a while in 1963 because they liked the Noar Oved youth leader. However, when this young man left, they could not get along with the new *Madrikh* (leader). There was open conflict between the group and the club, and the boys had disrupted the programme there, stolen equipment and smashed the furniture.

Beginning with the first day of his contact with Group I the worker began to extend concrete help to the youngsters. Hardly any of the boys were employed. The worker helped them cope with the procedures at the Youth Employment Service, helped them obtain suitable jobs, and often in direct contact with employers, tried to keep them on the job. Many of the youngsters were on probation and exhibited a negative attitude towards this highly beneficial service. The worker established contact with each boy's probation officer and helped the youngsters work through their relationship with the officer. A number of the boys had court cases pending. The worker helped them to understand the procedures, went to court with them and, in a great number of cases, was instrumental in preventing jail sentences which would have precluded all chances for rehabilitation. Many of the boys repeatedly ran away from home and lived in the streets, finding shelter with other youngsters and deviant adults. The worker, always in agreement with the youngsters, contacted families and tried to resolve conflicts with parents. A number of the boys who left home lived in the room of Chazai, a member of the G. Gang, whose shack served as a meeting place for this highly delinquent group, a hashish smoking centre and a storage place for stolen goods. The worker met with Chazai and other members of Group II and persuaded them to bar Group I youngsters from using the room.

With regard to delinquent behaviour, the worker restricted himself to listening and learning during the first few months. Gradually he initiated group discussions on the pros and cons of certain delinquent activities, supporting the more positive elements in the group, making the youngsters understand and face the realities and consequences of their behaviour, throwing doubt upon their irrational beliefs, attitudes and rationalisations. As his relationship to the group deepened and the youngsters learned to trust and respect him, the worker began to exert his influence to prevent outbreaks of delinquent behaviour, to restrain individual youngsters from participating in delinquent group activities and to counteract the influence of the 'top delinquents'. In order to reduce the emphasis upon delinquent behaviour as a source of satisfaction in the life of the group, the worker sought to provide alternative satisfactions by helping the group organise parties, trips, soccer games, etc. Many an evening was 'saved' because the worker had the youngsters engrossed in listening to stories, discussing the latest events, taking rides in his car[1] or going to a movie with him. Many of the

[1] Rides in the worker's car were a major source of satisfaction to the youngsters. We have records of boys stating that they were able to forego the temptation of a joy-ride in a stolen vehicle because of the offer of a ride in the worker's car. Unfortunately the project director could not obtain funds to compensate the worker for his expenses in the upkeep and use of his car, and he was forced to sell it. The worker also counteracted the epidemic car-stealing by initiating the *renting* of cars with money saved by the group.

weaker youngsters were enabled to resist the pressure to engage in daring delinquent acts in order to gain status in the group, because the worker provided them with opportunities to gain respect of the group in other, non-delinquent areas of activities.

During the beginning phase of his work with the Group I, the worker became aware of a small clique of low-status boys who were hanging around on the periphery of the group, barely tolerated, but frequently the objects of exploitation. These youngsters were involved in a series of thefts with Group I boys and, at first, the worker thought them to be part of the group. He soon felt, however, that there was something in the style and behaviour of this clique which set them apart from the others. In view of the fact that these five boys, whom we designated Group II, did not seem to adhere to deviant norms to the same degree as the other street corner groups, and as it became clear that their main function for Group I was to serve as the objects of exploitation, the worker made it his goal to separate these youngsters from the larger group. While the worker spent a considerable amount of time with Group II youngsters, he discouraged their participation in the delinquent as well as the non-delinquent group activities of Group I. The worker succeeded in this and the Group II youngsters gradually ceased their involvement in delinquent activities. The worker failed in his attempts to refer two emotionally disturbed boys for therapy, but helped all the boys make better work adjustments. He arranged for the most highly delinquent, but potentially most promising member of Group II to leave the neighbourhood and join a youth group in a kibbutz.

While work was proceeding in a promising manner with Group I, the worker made efforts to establish a relationship with Group III (G. Gang). From the outset the worker was faced with a dilemma. There was a large amount of interaction between members of Groups I and III, much of it centred round delinquent behaviour. On the one hand the worker found that this made his task of establishing and maintaining relations with the youngsters of both groups easier. On the other hand he became increasingly aware of the fact that contact with G. Gang was detrimental to the youngsters of Group I and led to an increase in the severity of delinquent adaptation in this group. A clear cut choice between the two groups was not possible, as it was highly doubtful whether the worker would be permitted to work with *any* group in the neighbourhood unless he had the backing of Group III *and* the Seniors of Group IV. The following decisions were reached in the spring of 1964:

1. The worker could work most intensively with Group I. Part of his service would be to reduce interaction between this group and the older more delinquent groups in the area. This would be attempted through such measures as supporting positive and cohesive forces in Group I in order to make it unnecessary for members to lean on other groups, as well as through enriching the positive satisfactions of group life through programming in order to reduce the need of the group to satisfy their cravings for fun and adventure with the help of other groups.

2. The worker would establish and maintain friendly and helpful contact with Groups III and IV in order to assert a measure of influence and controls upon the behaviour of these groups, and to gain their support in trying to reduce delinquency in Group I.

In practice this proved a tall order, enough to occupy two full-time workers. The worker experimented by initiating meetings with Group I at the Tnuva

Cafe, so as to draw the youngsters of this group away from the Kicking Horse, which was the headquarters of Groups III and IV. This proved unwise, as it aroused resentment among the older groups and caused conflict among the Group I boys who wanted to remain in the vicinity of their heroes. As a compromise solution the worker induced Group I to meet at Yizchak's Cafe. This was successful, as it left the youngsters within earshot of the older groups, but gave them a measure of independence. Group III boys did not object, because the Juniors were within easy reach, but 'out of their hair' when they preferred not to have them around. The atmosphere at Yizchak's was better than at the Kicking Horse, partly because the criminal adult elements of the neighbourhood, among them the habitual hashish smokers, drunkards and gamblers, preferred the Kicking Horse.

A few months after Group I's move to Yizchak's the Kicking Horse was raided by the police and a number of arrests for gambling and possession of hashish were made. After this the cafe was not considered 'safe' any more by the criminal adult element and the older street corner boys. When these moved out, the worker and Group I moved in and remained there to the end of the eighteen months work period. While the worker acknowledged the need for a meeting place which was acceptable to the youngsters, he made every effort to reduce the 'cafe-squatting', and to use alternate meeting places in healthier surroundings.

The worker strengthened his contacts with Group III by offering concrete assistance to individual members of this group much in the same manner as in Group I. This quickly bore fruit. However, before the worker could deepen and strengthen his relationship with this group, the police rounded up the majority of the members in April and May 1964. Some of the G. Gang served short prison sentences, but a considerable number remained in jail for as long as a year. The worker extended his help to those of the arrested boys for whom probation or suspended sentences seemed preferable. He maintained contact with the boys in jail and continued to make himself available to the scattered remnants of the group.

The Seniors of Group IV, many of them involved in serious criminal activities, remained suspicious of the worker and kept him at arm's length for quite a while. For about half a year contact between these young men and the worker remained restricted to discussions of his assistance to the Seniors younger brothers, cousins and nephews in Groups I and III and to casual greetings and exchanges of small-talk. The 'strong men' of the neighbourhood watched the worker's progress without interference, and it became clear later on that they were well informed about the worker's activities. Gradually members of the Seniors also began to come to the worker for help with a variety of problems.

Yabal of the Seniors was the first one of the 'strong men' to establish a close and friendly relationship with the worker. As Yabal was feared and respected by all the youngsters, his backing and openly declared friendship immediately raised the worker's standing among the street corner youth and greatly added to his authority. It became much easier for the worker to limit aggressive acting-out behaviour and to prevent delinquent activities through direct intervention, in fact by saying: 'Stop that, I won't let you go ahead with this.'

Yosh of Group IV, who was Yabal's equal as one of the 'top' men in the delinquent subculture of the neighbourhood, presented a more difficult problem. This young man seemed much more dependent upon his undisputed rule over the street corner groups, whose members lived in fear of him and rarely ever dared refuse his demands for their services. Yosh used and exploited the younger boys for his own criminal schemes and saw in the worker a threat to his way of life and a rival for leadership. While Yabal was Yosh's match in every respect, he remained carefully neutral in the situation. The worker had to move very cautiously, as any open conflict with Yosh could involve not only a loss of influence with all four groups, but might even have led to physical danger. The worker carefully avoided any direct challenge of Yosh's leadership, did not remonstrate with Yosh about certain aspects of his behaviour (as he could safely do with Yabal and other members of Group IV), and refrained from any derogatory remarks when the younger boys talked admiringly about his exploits. Yosh unbent a little when the worker sought his advice in organising parties, soccer games and trips with Group I on several occasions. By December 1964 the worker had made sufficient gains in his relationship to Yosh to permit him to ask him and Yabal to stop holding their habitual hashish-smoking sessions in close proximity to the Group I and II boys and to refrain from inviting the younger boys to participate. The Seniors complied with this request. Nevertheless, some tension between Yosh and the worker remained and the former sought to provoke the worker from time to time. The following abridged excerpt from one of the worker's reports provides a typical example of the problems this raised:

During one of the Questions-and-Answers periods which had become one of the worker's weekly program features with Groups I and II (members of Group III occasionally participating), Yosh walked up, listened for a while, then said provocatively: 'If you know so much, perhaps you can tell me if it's going to rain tomorrow.' The worker treated the question as a serious one and opened a discussion upon weather-forecasting, ranging from 'grandmother's rheumatism' to the known wisdom of certain Bedouin sages and the meteorological reports on the radio. Yosh continued to try to disrupt the discussion, but the youngsters were sufficiently interested to ignore these attempts. Yosh then 'ordered' the boys to go the movies with him. They complied, but asked the worker to come along. In the movie-house in the worker's presence, Yosh passed out 'P'gaseem' (specially twisted cigarettes containing a mixture of tobacco and hashish) and most of the youngsters smoked. The worker thought it wise not to oppose this activity at the time. He remained with the group to the end of the performance, as his demonstrative getting up and leaving (a procedure used on other such occasions), would have constituted a 'victory' for Yosh.

At the end of the eighteen months work period the following situation prevails:
Group I now consists of only twelve youngsters, the others drifted away from the group and made satisfactory adjustments in work and military service. Among this smaller group the distinction between Mischief-makers and Thieves has become less pronounced. The youngsters continue to be involved in delinquent activities, but delinquent behaviour is less severe and less frequent than it was during the first half of the eighteen months work period. The influence of Group IV upon these youngsters has been greatly reduced, however, the re-organisation of G. Gang (Group III) threatens to bring this group once more under the influence of a highly delinquent power group in the Shkunah. It was therefore decided that the worker continue his intensive service to these youngsters.

Group II has dispersed and its members are no longer regarded as a delinquency problem. The worker remains in contact with these boys, but there is no further need for intensive group work services.

As stated previously, six youngsters of Group III have banded together once more on their release from jail and are engaged in highly delinquent activities. There is a possibility that this group will take over as a power group in the neighbourhood from Group IV. The worker has been advised to 'stay close' to this group and deepen his relationship with these youngsters in order to help them break away from their deviant adaptation, and in order to counteract their influence upon the other youngsters of the area. The majority of the members of Group III have disbanded, some of them to pursue criminal careers as thieves and procurers in other areas of the city, some of them to make positive adjustment in work and military service. The worker remains in contact with some of these boys and continues to be available to them for help and counsel. One of these former Group III boys, Chanan, has become a positive influence among the delinquency-prone youngsters of the neighbourhood and an important source of support for the street club worker.

The young men of Group IV continue to meet and smoke hashish together. However, the split between the highly criminal element (represented by Yosh and Yabal) and the more positive 'strong men' (led by Yigal and Chanan, who has been accepted by this group) is more pronounced, and the influence of the 'criminals' upon the street corner youth of the neighbourhood has been reduced. Yigal has joined Chanan in helping the worker 'straighten out' the younger groups. The worker remains in contact with Group IV and maintains his good relationship with this group.

A *new* group of approximately twelve youngsters aged fourteen to fifteen who have recently finished elementary school seems to continue the traditions of the neighbourhood's delinquent subculture. These youngsters, already surrounded by small cliques of interested and admiring hangers-on aged eleven to thirteen, have engaged in petty thefts, vandalism and car stealing. The worker is a known and respected figure to them and they are receptive to his approaches. The worker has been advised to concentrate his efforts upon serving this group in order to try to prevent the crystallisation of rigid patterns of delinquent norms and behaviour among these youngsters.

References

ABRAHAMSON, A. C. (1959) *Group Methods in Supervision and Staff Development.* Harper, New York.

ACKELY and FLIEGEL (1960) 'A social work approach to street corner girls', *Social Work,* **5,** no. 4.

AICHHORN (1955) *Wayward Youth.* Meridian Books, New York; first published in Vienna, Internationaler Psychoanalytischer Verlag, 1925.

ALEXANDER, Franz (1932) 'Contribution to psychological factors in anti-social behaviour', *The Family,* **13.**

ALISSI, A. S. (1965) 'Social influences on group values', *Social Work,* **10,** no. 1.

ALLCORN, D. H. (1955) 'The social development of young men in an English industrial suburb', University of Manchester Ph.D. Thesis.

ALONI, Shulamith (1964) *The Rights of Children in Israel* (Hebrew). Tarbut V'Chinuch, Tel Aviv.

ANTONOVSKY, A. (1964) *Integration of Ethnic Groups* (Hebrew), Amot.

ASBURY, Herbert (1927) *The Gangs of New York.* Knopf, New York.

AUSTIN, D. M. (1957) 'Goals for gang workers', *Social Work,* **2,** no. 4.

AUSUBEL, D. P. (1958) *Drug Addiction: Physiological, Psychological and Sociological Aspects.* Random House, New York.

BALDWIN, James (1962) *Fifth Avenue, Uptown,* ed. E. and M. Josephson. Dell Publishing Co., New York.

BEARD, C. A. (1932) *A Charter for the Social Sciences.* Scribners, New York.

BELL, D. (1956) *Work and Its Discontents.* Beacon Press, Boston.

BENDIX and LIPSET, ed. (1953) *Class, Status and Power.* The Free Press, Glencoe, Ill.

BERELSON and STEINER (1964) *Human Behaviour.* Harcourt, Brace, New York.

BERNARD, J. (1957) *Social Problems at Midcentury.* Dryden, New York.

BERNSTEIN, Saul (1964) *Youth on the Streets.* Association Press, New York.

BIVEN, B. and HOLDEN, H. M. (1966) 'Informal youth work in a cafe setting', *The Howard Journal of Penology and Crime Prevention,* **12,** no. 1.

BLAU, P. M. and SCOTT, W. R. (1963) *Formal Organizations.* Routledge and Kegan Paul.

BLOCH and NIEDERHOFFER (1958) *The Gang.* Philosophical Library, New York.

BONNER, H. (1959) *Group Dynamics.* The Ronald Press, New York.

BRAGER, George (1962) 'Improving services for street corner youth', in *Social Work Practice.*

BROOM, L. and SELZNIK, P. (1957) *Sociology.* Harper and Row, New York (3rd edn. 1963).

CHERNS, Albert (1967) 'The use of the useful', *Social Science Research Council Newsletter*. London, November.

CHILDREN'S BUREAU OF THE U.S. DEPARTMENT OF HEALTH, EDUCATION AND WELFARE (1967), *Children*, **14,** no. 4.

CHOMSKY, N. (1967) 'On resistance', *The New York Review*, 7 December.

CLOWARD, R. A. (1960) *Agency Structure as a Variable in Service to Groups*. New York, Mimeogr.

CLOWARD, R. A. and OHLIN, L. E. (1960) *Delinquency and Opportunity*. The Free Press, Glencoe, Ill., 1960.

COHEN, A.K. (1955) *Delinquent Boys*. The Free Press, Glencoe, Ill.

COHEN, Albert K. (1959) 'The study of social disorganization and deviant behaviour', Merton, Broom and Cottrell (1959).

COHEN, R. S. (1955) 'On the Marxist philosophy of education', Henry (1955).

COHEN, Yona (1965) 'Prevention of delinquency in Israel', Drapkin *et al.* ed. (1965).

COHEN, Yona (1959) 'Criteria for the probation officer's recommendation', *Megamot*, **10,** no. 1. pp. 65–75 (in Hebrew; English abstract provided).

COLLORD, J. C. ed. (1930) *The Long View—Papers and Addresses by Mary E. Richmond*. Russell Sage Foundation, New York.

DOWNES, D. M. (1966) *The Delinquent Solution*. Routledge and Kegan Paul.

DRAPKIN *et al.*, ed. (1965) *The Prevention of Crime and the Treatment of Offenders in Israel*. Report to the Third United Nations Congress on the Prevention of Crime and the Treatment of Offenders, Stockholm.

DUNHAM and KNAUER (1954) 'The Juvenile Court and its relationship to adult criminality', *Social Forces*, March, pp. 290–6.

EAST HARLEM PROTESTANT PARISH NARCOTICS COMMITTEE (1959) 'A Statement on Narcotics Addiction and Some Suggestions for Treatment', New York Mimeogr.

EATON, J. W. (1964) *Prisons in Israel*. University of Pittsburgh Press.

EATON, J. W. (1965) *The Achievement Crisis*. Jerusalem, Mimeogr.

EATON, J. W. (1967) *The Immobile Poor*. Paper read at the National Conference of Social Welfare, Dallas, Texas, Mimeogr.

EISENSTADT, S. W. (1953) 'The process of absorption of immigrants in Israel', in C. Frankenstein (1953a).

FINESTONE, H. (1960) 'Cats, kicks and color', in Stein, Vidich and White (1960).

FRANKENSTEIN, Carl (1953b) 'The Problem of ethnic differences in the absorption of immigrants', Frankenstein (1953a).

FRANKENSTEIN, Carl (1953c) 'Youth aliyah and the education of immigrants', in Frankenstein (1953a) *Between Past and Future*.

FRANKENSTEIN, Carl, ed. (1953a) *Between Past and Future*. Szold Foundation, Jerusalem.

FRANKENSTEIN, Carl (1959) *Die Aeusserlichkeit des Lebensstils*. Meulenhoff, Amsterdam.

FYVEL, T. R. (1964) *Troublemakers*. Schocken Books, New York.

GEIS, G. (June, 1965) *Juvenile Gangs*. President's Committee on Juvenile Delinquency and Youth Crime Washington, D.C.

GLUECK, S. and GLUECK, E. (1959) *Predicting Delinquency and Crime*. Harvard University Press.

GLUCKSTEIN, Naomi (May 1961) 'Slum quarters in Jerusalem, Tel Aviv and Haifa', *Megamoth*, **11,** no, 3. p. 391 (Hebrew, English abstract provided).

GOETSCHIUS, G. W. and TASH, M. J. (1967) *Working with Unattached Youth.* Routledge & Kegan Paul.

GOODMAN, Paul (1960) *Growing Up Absurd.* Random House, New York.

GOODMAN, Paul (1963) *Making Do.* The New American Library, New York.

GROSSBARD, H. (1954) 'Methodology for Developing Self-Awareness', *Social Casework*, November.

HALLEK, S. L. (1963) 'The impact of professional dishonesty on behaviour of disturbed adolescents', *Social Work*, **8** (April), no. 2.

HAMILTON, Gordon (1954) 'Self-awareness in professional education', *Social Casework*, November.

HANDLIN, Oscar (1958) 'The family in Old World and New', in Stein and Cloward (1958).

HENRY, N. B., ed. (1955) *Modern Philosophies of Education.* University of Chicago Press.

HERMON, Z. (1965) 'The institutional treatment and after-care of adult offenders and juvenile delinquents in Israel', in Drapkin *et al.* (1965).

HOROVITZ, M. (1965) 'Probation in Israel', in Drapkin *et al.* (1965).

HOUWINK, Eda (July 1967) 'Supervision is teaching and enabling', *Case Conference and ASW News*, **14**, no. 3.

HOVAV, M. (1965) 'Police treatment of juvenile delinquents', in Drapkin *et al.* (1965).

HYMAN, WRIGHT, and HOPKINS (1962) *Applications of Methods of Evaluation.* University of California Press.

JAFFE, *et al.*, (1961) 'Legitimizing after care for institutionalized adults in Israel'. The Hebrew University, Jerusalem (mimeogr.)

JONES, David (1967) 'Social work and social action: Developments in American social welfare', *Social Service Quartlery*, Spring.

JOSEPHSON, Eric and JOSEPHSON, Mary, ed. (1962) *Man Alone.* Dell Publishing, New York.

JUDD, KOHN and SCHULMAN (1962) 'Group supervision: a vehicle for professional development', *Social Work*, **7** (Jan.) no. 1.

KAHN, A. J. (1959) 'The function of social work in the modern world', in A. J. Kahn, ed., *Issues in American Social Work.* Columbia University Press.

KAHN, Alfred J. (1966) *Neighborhood Information Centers.* Columbia University School of Social Work, New York.

KELLEY, Pat (1959) *Reaching the Teen-Age Addict—A Study of Street Club Work with a Group of Adolescent Users.* New York City Youth Board.

KILLINGTON, Gary (1964) 'The history and development of the streetwork project initiated by the Service to Youth Council, Incorporated', in *Streetwork in South Australia*, Papers delivered at the Seminar on 'Streetwork' held at the University of Adelaide, 30 May. Mimeogr.

KOBRIN, S. (1953) *Drug Addiction Among Young Persons in Chicago.* Illinois Institute for Juvenile Research.

KOBRIN, S. (1958). 'The conflict of values in delinquency areas', in Stein and Cloward (1958).

KONOPKA, Gisela (n.d.) *Group Work Concepts: Methods and Techniques as Applied to Correctional and Rehabilitation Settings.* University of Minnesota. Mimeogr.

KONOPKA, G. (1963) *Social Group Work.* Prentice-Hall, Englewood Cliffs, N.J.

KREITLER, H. and KREITLER, S. (August 1964) 'The Attitude of Israeli Youth Toward Social Ideas', *Megamoth*, **13**, no. 2 (Hebrew, English abstract provided).

KVARACEUS, W. C. (1965) *Prevention of Juvenile Delinquency: Evaluation of Different Types of Action: A review of reports from nine countries.* Eleventh Session of the International Union for Child Welfare Advisory Committee on Delinquent and Socially Maladjusted Children, Vaucresson, France (25 April–1 May) .

KVARACEUS, W. C. (1966) *Dynamics of Delinquency.* Merrill Books Inc., Columbus, Ohio.

LARNER, J. and TEFFERTELLER, R. (1966) *The Addict in the Street.* Penguin Books.

LEISSNER, A. (1962) 'Streetclub Work Supervision' unpublished paper, New York.

LEISSNER, A. (April 1965) *Introducing the streetclub work approach in Israel.* Collection of Papers submitted to the 11th Session of the International Union for Child Welfare Conference, Vaucresson, France.

LEISSNER, A. (1967) *Family Advice Services.* Longmans and The National Bureau for Co-operation in Child Care, London.

LEISSNER, A. with the assistance of N. RUBIN and S. BORS (1967) *Research Project on Forces Acting in Street Corner Gangs.* Jerusalem. A report on an action-research project carried out under the auspices of the Israel Ministry of Social Welfare and prepared under a grant from the Welfare Administration, Department of Health, Education and Welfare, U.S.A. 2 vols. Mimeogr.

LEONARD, P. (1966). *Sociology in Social Work,* Routledge and Kegan Paul.

LEVITAS, G. (July 1966) 'On the fringe', *Work* (Tel Aviv), **17**, no. 45.

LEWIS, Oscar (1967) *La Vida.* Secker and Warburg.

LINDSAY, Anne W. (1952) *Group Work Recording.* Woman's Press, New York.

LOS ANGELES COUNTY PROBATION DEPARTMENT AND YOUTH STUDIES CENTER (1963) *A Study of Delinquent Gangs.* 2nd Annual Progress Report, 1 July 1962–30 June 1963. Mimeogr.

LOS ANGELES COUNTY PROBATION DEPARTMENT AND YOUTH STUDIES CENTER (1964) *A Study of Delinquent Gangs.* 3rd Annual Progress Report, 1 July 1963–30 June 1964. Mimeogr.

MAAS and POLANSKY, N. A. (1960) 'Collecting original data', in Polansky (1960).

McCORD, W. *et al.* (1959) *Origins of Crime.* Columbia University Press.

MacIVER, R. M. and PAGE, C. H. (1962) *Society.* Macmillan, London.

MAKARENKO, A. S. (1955) *The Road to Life.* 2nd edn., 3 vols., Foreign Languages Publishing House, Moscow.

MATZA, D. (1964) *Delinquency and Drift.* Wiley, New York.

MATZA, D. and SYKES (1961) 'Delinquency and subterranean values', *American Sociological Revue,* **26**, no. 5, pp. 712–19.

MAYER, Clara W. (1964) *The Manmade Wilderness.* Atheneum, New York.

MAYS, J. B. (1965) 'The role of social work', in Kellmer Pringle (1965).

MERTON, R. (1958a) 'Continuities in the theory of social structure and Anomie', in Stein and Cloward (1958).

MERTON, R. K. (1958b) 'Social structure and anomie', in Stein and Cloward (1956).

MERTON, A. K., BROOM and COTTRELL, ed. (1959) *Sociology Today.* Basic Books, New York.

MILLER, Walter B. (1958) 'Lower-class culture as a generating milieu of gang delinquency', *Journal of Social Issues,* **14**, no. 3.

MILLS, C. Wright (1959) *The Sociological Imagination.* Oxford University Press, New York.

MOBILIZATION FOR YOUTH INC. (1961) 'A Proposal for the Prevention and Control of Delinquency by Expanding Opportunities'. New York, December.

MORSE, Mary (1965) *The Unattached*. Penguin Books, London.

MURRAY, C. E. *et al.* (1954) *Group Work in Community Life*. Association Press, New York.

NATIONAL ASSOCIATION OF SOCIAL WORKERS (1964) *News*, November.

NATIONAL CONFERENCE ON SOCIAL WELFARE (1962) *Social Work Practice*, 1962. Selected Papers, 89th Annual Forum (New York, 27 May–1 June 1962).

NATIONAL FEDERATION OF SETTLEMENTS AND NEIGHBORHOOD CENTERS (1967) *Neighborhood Gangs—A Case Book for Youth Workers*. New York.

NEW YORK CITY YOUTH BOARD (1960) *Reaching the Fighting Gang*. New York.

OSWALD, M. (May 1965) 'Detached work among two adolescent groups', *Australian Journal of Social Work*, **18**, no. 1.

OHLIN, PIVEN and PAPPENFORT (1958) 'Major dilemmas of the social worker in probation and parole', in Stein and Cloward (1958).

ONTELL and JONES (1963) *Discontinuities in the Social Treatment of Offenders*. Mobilization for Youth, New York. Mimeogr.

OTTAWA YOUTH SERVICES BUREAU (1963) *Identifying and Controlling Delinquent Groups of Boys*. Ottawa Welfare Council.

PARK, R. E. (1927) Preface to Thrasher (1927).

PARSONS, Talcott (1953) 'A revised analytical approach to the theory of social stratification', in Bendix and Lipset (1953).

PERRY and GAWEL, ed. (1953) *Harry Stack Sullivan M.D.—The Interpersonal Theory of Psychiatry*. Norton, New York.

POLANSKY, N. A. ed. (1960) *Social Work Research*. University of Chicago Press.

PRINGLE, M. L. Kellmer, ed. (1965) *Investment in Children*. Longmans.

RESEARCH SERVICES LIMITED (1967) *Racial Discrimination*. Political and Economic Planning, Sponsored by the Race Relations Board and the National Committee for Commonwealth Immigrants, London.

REIFEN, David (1965) 'Observations on the juvenile court in Israel, in Drapkin *et al.* (1965).

REINHOLD, Ch. (1953) 'Dynamics of Youth Aliyah groups', in Frankenstein (1953a).

RIESSMAN, Frank (1962) *The Culturally Deprived Child*. Harper, New York.

REISSMAN, L. (1958). 'A study of the role conceptions in bureaucracy', in Stein and Cloward (1958).

REYNOLDS, Bertha C. (1942) *Learning and Teaching in the Practice of Social Work*. Rinehart, New York.

RICHMOND, M. E. (1930) *The Long View: papers and addresses by Mary E. Richmond*, ed. J. C. Collord, Russell Sage Foundation, New York.

RITTWAGEN, M. (1959) *Sins of their Fathers*. Pyramid Books, New York.

ROBISON, Sophia M. (1960) *Juvenile Delinquency*. Holt, New York.

ROLPH, C. H., ed. (1961) *Women of the Streets*. The New English Library, Ace Books, London.

ROSENHEIM, M. (1962) *Justice for the Child*. The Free Press, Glencoe, Ill.

ROSS and VAN DEN HAAG (1957) *The Fabric Society*. Harcourt, Brace, New York.

SAXTON, R. H. (1967) 'Three years of the Neighbourhood Youth Corps', *Children*, U.S. Children's Bureau, July-August.

SAYRE, Nora (1967) 'A riot prevented', *New Statesman*, 22 September.

Schmelz, O. (1965) 'Statistical data on crime amongst Jews in Israel', in Drapkin *et al.* (1965).

Schorr, Alvin L. (1964) *Slums and Social Insecurity.* Nelson, London.

Schur, E. M. (1962). *Narcotic Addiction in Britain and America.* Indiana University Press.

Schwartz, M. (1965) *Community Work in Israel.* United Nations Programme of Technical Assistance. Mimeogr.

Scott, Peter (1956) 'Gangs and delinquent groups in London', *British Journal of Delinquency*, July.

Sellin, Th. (1962) 'A sociological approach to the study of crime causation', in Wolfgang, Savitz and Johnston (1962).

Selzer, M. (1965) *The Outcasts of Israel.* The Council of the Sephardi Community, Jerusalem.

Shaw and McKay (1962) 'Theoretical implications of the ecological analysis of Chicago', in Wolfgang, Savitz and Johnston (1962).

Shoham, S. (1962) 'The application of the "culture-conflict" hypothesis to the criminality of immigrants in Israel', *Journal of Criminal Law, Criminology and Police Science*, **53**, no. 2.

Shoham, S. and Hovav (1964) *Some Social Factors, Treatment Aspects and Criminal Careers of 'Bnei Tovim', Middle and Upper Class Juvenile Delinquency in Israel.* Tel Aviv. Mimeogr.

Shoham and Slonim (1963) 'The moral dilemma of penal treatment', *The Juridical Review, The Law Journal of the Scottish Universities*, pt 2.

Short, J. F. (1961) 'Address at the Annual Conference of the California Probation, Parole and Correctional Association' cited in Los Angeles County Probation Department 2nd Annual Progress Report.

Shumsky, A. (1955) *The Clash of Cultures in Israel.* New York.

Shuval, Judith (1961) 'Emerging patterns of ethnic strain in Israel', *Megamoth* (Hebrew, English extract provided) cited in Selzer (1965), p. 6.

Small, A. W. (1905) *General Sociology.* University of Chicago Press.

Smith, C. S. (1966) 'The Youth Service and delinquency prevention', *The Howard Journal of Penology and Crime Prevention*, **12**, no. 1.

Spencer, John (1964) *Stress and Release in an Urban Estate.* Tavistock Publications, London.

Spergel, I. (1961) 'An exploratory research in delinquent subcultures', *The Social Service Review*, **35** (March), no. 1.

Stein and Cloward, ed. (1958) *Social Perspectives on Behaviour.* The Free Press, Glencoe, Ill.

Stein, M. R., Vidich and White, ed. (1960) *Identity and Anxiety.* The Free Press, Glencoe, Ill.; Collier-Macmillan.

Stott, D. H. (1960) 'The prediction of delinquency from non-delinquent behaviour', *British Journal of Delinquency*, **10** (Jan.), no. 3.

Sykes and Matza 'Techniques of neutralization', *American Sociological Review*, **22**.

Taft, D. R. (1950) *Crimonology.* Macmillan, New York.

Tash, M. J. (1967) *Supervision in Youth Work.* The National Council of Social Service, London).

Thrasher, F. W. (1927), *The Gang*, 2nd edn., University of Chicago Press.

Time Magazine (1965) 'The poor amidst prosperity', 1 October.

Toby, Jackson (1962) 'The differential impact of family disorganization', in Wolfgang, Savitz and Johnston (1962).

Toby, Jackson (1961) 'Early identification and intensive treatment of predelinquents: a negative view', *Social Work*, **6** (July), no. 3.

Wakefield, Dan (1960) *Island in the City*. The Citadel Press, New York.

Waldorf, Dan (1967) 'New Town Youth Club,' *New Society*, 2 March.

Weber, Max (1946) *Essays in Sociology*. Trans. H. H. Garth and C. Wright Mills, Oxford University Press.

West, D. J. (1967) *The Young Offender*. Penguin Books, London.

White, William F. (1943) 'A slum sex code', *The American Journal of Sociology*, **49** (July), pp. 24–31.

Wilensky and Lebeaux (1958) *Industrial Society and Social Welfare*. Russell Sage Foundation, New York.

Wilfert, Otto (1962) *Gefaehrdete Jugend*. Springer Verlag, Wien.

Williamson, M. (1961) *Supervision—New Patterns and Processes*. Associated Press, New York.

Willmott, P. (1966) *Adolescent Boys of East London*. Routledge and Kegan Paul.

Witmer and Kotinsky, ed. (1955) *New Perspectives for Research on Juvenile Delinquency*. Children's Bureau, U.S. Department of Health, Education and Welfare, Washington, D.C.

Witmer and Tufts (1954) *The Effectiveness of Delinquency Prevention Programs*. Children's Bureau, U.S. Department of Health, Education and Welfare, Washington, D.C.

Wittels, F. (1955) 'The ego of the adolescent', in K. R. Eissler, ed., *Searchlights on Delinquency*. International Universities Press, New York, Second Edition.

Wittenberg, R. M. (1949) *So You Want to Help People*. Association Press, New York.

Wolfgang, Savitz and Johnston, ed., (1962) *The Sociology of Crime and Delinquency*. Wiley, New York.

Yablonsky, L. (1962a) *The Violent Gang*. Macmillan, New York.

Yablonsky, L. (1962b) 'The delinquent gang as a near group' in Wolfgang, Savitz and Johnston (1962).

Youth Service Development Council (1967) Report of Committee on *Immigrants and the Youth Service*. H.M.S.O., London.